YEAR
W

A WOMEN'S LECTIONARY FOR THE WHOLE CHURCH

A Multi-Gospel Single-Year Lectionary

WILDA C. GAFNEY

CHURCH
PUBLISHING
INCORPORATED

*For those who have searched for themselves in the scriptures
and did not find themselves in the masculine pronouns.*

Church Publishing
19 East 34th Street
New York, NY 10016

Cover art by Pauline Williamson
Cover design by Tiny Little Hammers
Typeset by Rose Design

Library of Congress Cataloging-in-Publication Data

Names: Gafney, Wilda, 1966- author.
Title: A women's lectionary for the whole church : Year W : a multi-gospel
   single-year lectionary / Wilda C. Gafney.
Description: New York, NY : Church Publishing, [2021]
Identifiers: LCCN 2021009257 (print) | LCCN 2021009258 (ebook) | ISBN
   9781640654747 (paperback) | ISBN 9781640654754 (epub)
Subjects: LCSH: Common lectionary (1992) | Bible--Feminist criticism. |
   Lectionaries.
Classification: LCC BV199.L42 G344 2021 (print) | LCC BV199.L42 (ebook) |
   DDC 264/.03034--dc23

LC record available at https://lccn.loc.gov/2021009257
LC ebook record available at https://lccn.loc.gov/2021009258

CONTENTS

Acknowledgments vii

About the Cover Images viii

Abbreviations x

Biblical Resources xi

Introduction xii

Text Selection xvi

Using *A Women's Lectionary* xviii

About the Translations xx

The Lessons with Commentary 1

Advent I / 1

Advent II / 4

Advent III / 7

Advent IV / 11

Christmas I / 15

Christmas II / 18

Christmas III / 21

First Sunday after Christmas / 23

Feast of the Holy Name, January 1 / 27

Second Sunday after Christmas / 30

Feast of the Epiphany / 33

Epiphany I / 37

Epiphany II / 40

Feast of the Presentation, February 2 / 45

Epiphany III / 48

Epiphany IV / 51

Epiphany V / 54

Epiphany VI / 57

Epiphany VII / 61

Epiphany VIII / 64

Last Sunday of Epiphany / 66

Lent—Ash Wednesday / 70

Lent 1 / 74

Lent II / 78

Lent III / 81

Lent IV / 85

Lent V / 89

Feast of the Annunciation, March 25 / 93
Palm Sunday—Liturgy of the Palms / 96
Palm Sunday—Liturgy of the Word / 98
Monday in Holy Week / 106
Tuesday in Holy Week / 110
Wednesday in Holy Week / 113
Maundy Thursday / 116
Good Friday / 120
Holy Saturday / 128
Easter—The Great Vigil / 133
Easter Day—Early Service / 145
Easter Day—Principal Service / 145
Easter Day—Evening Service / 151
Monday in Easter Week / 155
Tuesday in Easter Week / 157
Wednesday in Easter Week / 159
Thursday in Easter Week / 160
Friday in Easter Week / 163
Saturday in Easter Week / 165
Second Sunday of Easter / 167
Third Sunday of Easter / 172
Fourth Sunday of Easter / 175
Fifth Sunday of Easter / 178
Sixth Sunday of Easter / 181
Feast of the Ascension / 185
Seventh Sunday of Easter / 188
Pentecost Vigil (or Early Service) / 192
Pentecost Principal Service / 198
Trinity Sunday / 202
Season after Pentecost (29) / 205
Proper 1 (Closest to May 11) / 205
Proper 2 (Closest to May 18) / 208
Proper 3 (Closest to May 25) / 213
Proper 4 (Closest to June 1) / 216
Proper 5 (Closest to June 8) / 220
Proper 6 (Closest to June 15) / 223
Proper 7 (Closest to June 22) / 227
Proper 8 (Closest to June 29) / 231
Proper 9 (Closest to July 6) / 235

Proper 10 (Closest to July 13) / 238
Proper 11 (Closest to July 20) / 242
Feast of Mary Magdalene, July 22 / 246
Proper 12 (Closest to July 27) / 249
Proper 13 (Closest to August 3) / 253
Proper 14 (Closest to August 10) / 257
Feast of the Ever-Blessed Virgin Mary, August 15 / 261
Proper 15 (Closest to August 17) / 265
Proper 16 (Closest to August 24) / 269
Proper 17 (Closest to August 31) / 273
Proper 18 (Closest to September 7) / 278
Proper 19 (Closest to September 14) / 282
Proper 20 (Closest to September 21) / 286
Proper 21 (Closest to September 28) / 290
Proper 22 (Closest to October 5) / 294
Proper 23 (Closest to October 12) / 298
Proper 24 (Closest to October 19) / 302
Proper 25 (Closest to October 26) / 306
Feast of All Saints, November 1 / 310
Proper 26 (Closest to November 2) / 313
Proper 27 (Closest to November 9) / 317
Proper 28 (Closest to November 16) / 322
Majesty of Christ (Closest to November 23) / 325

Appendix: God Names and Divine Titles 329
Bibliography 331
Scripture Index 335

ACKNOWLEDGMENTS

I would like to thank the Louisville Institute for the 2019 Sabbatical Grant for Researchers; the trustees, administration, faculty, and staff of Brite Divinity School for a twelve-month sabbatical in 2019; and the rector, Mike Kinman, vestry, and members of the All Saints Episcopal Church in Pasadena for ongoing material, spiritual, and temporal support during this project and for committing to a year-long trial use of the lectionary in 2020–2021.

Special thanks to the RevGalBlogPal community and Martha Spong for an early hearing of the work and a collaborative digital space in which to try out lesson and translations choices. For valuable feedback, support, and inspiration, many thanks to the women, nonbinary persons, and men who attended collaborative consultation sessions across the country, including Martha Simmons of the African American Lectionary Project. Thanks to Alicia Hager for administrative support in the first year and to NaShieka Knight, my research assistant at Brite.

I remain grateful for translations and translators that have inspired me to take up the text: Marcia Falk, Everett Fox, Hugh Page, and Joel Rosenberg. I am appreciative for the *Wisdom Psalter* by Laura Grimes; it was an early resource and she an early collaborator. The psalms in these volumes are shaped by that interaction.

I am deeply grateful for all who have expressed support and encouragement and impatience for delivery in person, through correspondence, and on social media.

Lastly, I mourn those who will not see this project, especially those who died due to Covid 19 and its complications. They are legion.

ABOUT THE COVER IMAGES

I first saw Wil Gafney in chapel at Candler School of Theology in October of 2016, during a service where Leea Allen read an amazing poem "Heart Matters" and Dr. Gafney preached a sermon entitled "Love God Herself," drawn from Beyoncé's song "Don't Hurt Yourself." I was inspired. I didn't have anything that day other than a regular piece of paper and my colored pens—this was before I unapologetically carted my markers into services, because I do most of my work in situ—but I drew the image of a woman standing proud, brown face crowned with locks of dark hair, clothed in green, and holding up the world. She speaks to me of triumph.

This was not the last time that Dr. Gafney's words would inspire my art.

In a Queer and Feminist Theology course I took, we read Dr. Gafney's article "Don't Hate the Playa, Hate the Game." In it, she refocused our attention on the fullness of Delilah's story, teasing out details and possibilities of connection that reframed both Delilah's motivations and power. If you haven't read it, I suggest you do. It spoke to me of honey, and fire, and memory, and love, and retribution, and these things all shaped the piece I created in response: "Remembering the Fire."

Since then, I've been inspired many times over.

When I was beginning a Lenten series, I read Dr. Gafney's article "Ritualizing Bathsheba's Rape" and drew, in response, "In the Ashes." The piece depicts Bathsheba sitting by a fire in ashes, weeping and cradling her dead child while David laments outside. I also did a series of pieces of the women in Saul's life that were inspired by what Dr. Gafney wrote in her incredible *Womanist Midrash*. Time and time again, I know that if I want to be schooled in a text, brought closer to the nuances and truths contained therein, and inspired by those truths, I will find that wisdom in Dr. Gafney's works. Without a doubt, the volume you currently hold in your hands contains this wisdom, and I hope you are similarly inspired.

My pieces for the *Women's Lectionary* were created in the same theme and seek to center and lift up the power that Black Women have in these stories of salvation. I drew "Queen of Heaven" (the cover image for Volumes A, B, and C) in June of 2017 using Tombow Watercolor Markers on Bristol Vellum paper. It shows Mary, enthroned and crowned with all the planets of the solar system and the wonders of the Universe bearing witness, clothed in life and light and holding the Christ Child in her arms. She is the guardian, and the bearer of God—Theotokos; she is the creation honored by the Creator.

The next work, "No Longer Lost" (the cover image for Volume W), speaks of the parable where God is imaged as a woman, the woman who lost her coin and finds it. She celebrates with all of her neighbors as God celebrates with the host of heaven when the lost ones come home. Surrounding her in these coins are us, connecting, praying, studying, dancing. You can also see the dove, and the lost sheep, and the broom, because some things need cleaning up, not the least of which are our misconceptions and our preconceived notions, which have grown dusty as we have let them sit.

Let the words of the Rev. Dr. Wil Gafney clear up some of those misconceptions and open windows to shed light on truth in a way you have never before seen. Sit with these words. Let them sink in. Feel their power and be empowered by the story of the Good News told in ways you may have never experienced before. May the luminous wisdom of the Word find a home within you, and may it spark your inner fire.

Pauline Williamson, creating as *Seamire*

ABBREVIATIONS

Alter	*The Hebrew Bible: A New Translation with Commentary,* trans. Robert Alter
AYBD	*Anchor Yale Bible Dictionary*
BigS	*Bibel in gerechter Sprache*
BDAG	*A Greek-English Lexicon of the New Testament and Other Early Christian Literature,* revised and edited by Frederick William Danker
BDB	*Brown-Driver-Briggs Hebrew and English Lexicon*
CEB	*Common English Bible*
DCH	*Dictionary of Classical Hebrew*
DSS	Dead Sea Scrolls
Fox	*The Five Books of Moses,* trans. Everett Fox
GSJPS	*A Gender-Sensitive Adaptation of the JPS Translation*
HALOT	*Hebrew and Aramaic Lexicon of the Old Testament*
IB	*The Inclusive Bible*
JPS	Jewish Publication Society *TANAKH*
KJV	King James Version
LXX	Septuagint
MT	Masoretic Text
NRSV	New Revised Standard Version
RCL	Revised Common Lectionary
SP	Samaritan Pentateuch

BIBLICAL RESOURCES

Original Language Texts

Dead Sea Scrolls
Hebrew Masoretic Text
Nestle-Aland Greek New Testament, 28th ed.
Peshitta (both testaments)
Samaritan Pentateuch
Septuagint
Targums
Vulgate

Bibles in Translation

Bishops Bible, 1568
Common English Bible, 2011
Dead Sea Scrolls Bible, 1999
Douay-Rheims Bible, 1582 (NT), 1610 (HB)
The Early Prophets: Joshua, Judges Samuel, Kings, Everett Fox 2014
Five Books of Moses, Everett Fox, 1995
A Gender-Sensitive Adaptation of the JPS Tanakh, 2006
Geneva Bible, 1599
The Hebrew Bible: A Translation with Commentary, Robert Alter, 2018
Inclusive Bible, 2007
Jewish Publication Society Tanakh, 1985
King James Version, 1611
A New English Translation of the Septuagint, 2000
New Revised Standard Version, 1989
Revised Standard Version, 1971
Tyndale's (incomplete) translation, 1525
Wycliffe Bible, 1384

Commentaries

Hermeneia
Jewish Publication Society Torah Commentary
The Torah, A Women's Commentary
The Wisdom Commentary
Women's Bible Commentary
The Yale Anchor Bible Commentary

INTRODUCTION

What does it look like to tell the Good News through the stories of women who are often on the margins of scripture and often set up to represent bad news? How would a lectionary centering women's stories, chosen with womanist and feminist commitments in mind, frame the presentation of the scriptures for proclamation and teaching? How is the story of God told when stories of women's brutalization and marginalization are moved from the margins of canon and lectionary and held in the center in tension with stories of biblical heroines and heroes? More simply, what would it look like if women built a lectionary focusing on women's stories? These were my initial questions when I sat down to draft a proposal for a women's lectionary, a lectionary designed by women—or an individual woman—for the whole church. I do not imagine that my questions and perceptions are the questions and perceptions of all other women. But I do believe that my questions and perceptions invite women, men, and nonbinary readers and hearers to engage the scriptures in new ways and in that engagement, they might find themselves and their questions represented.

The lectionary is a catechetical tool. There are more than two billion Christians in the world according to the Pew Research Center's Forum on Religion and Public Life (Global Religious Landscape). As of 2015, there were nearly 2.3 billion Christians representing slightly more than 31 percent of the world's total population. With Roman Catholics making up an estimated 1.2 billion, and accounting for Orthodox Christians, Anglicans, Episcopalians, Methodists, Presbyterians, Lutherans, and other Reformed traditions along with some Baptist and congregational churches that use a lectionary, the overwhelming majority of Christians receive their scripture mediated through a lectionary; that would be nearly 1.4 billion persons whose customary exposure to the scriptures occurs through a lectionary. Based on the numbers in the Pew Research Center's May 12, 2015, report, "America's Changing Religious Landscape," as many as 60 percent of American Christians attend services in churches that use lectionaries.

The scriptures are androcentric, male-focused, as are the lectionaries dependent upon them. Those lectionaries are not simply *as* androcentric as are the scriptures, but in my experience as a congregant and priest, women are even less well represented in them than they are in the biblical text. For example, there are at a minimum one hundred and eleven named women in the Hebrew Scriptures—which is itself underrepresented in preaching lectionaries and not always preached upon or even read—and that reckoning does not account for the numbers of unnamed women and girls. Yet not many of my students or parishioners can name even ten women in the Hebrew Scriptures or even the entire biblical canon. The extant lectionaries do not introduce us to even a tithe of them. As a result, all many congregants know of the Bible is the texts they hear read from their respective lectionary.

As a biblical scholar, it is my hope to see congregants exposed to the Bible more broadly and deeply and see them equipped to engage the sacred texts of their tradition critically, with nuance. As a Hebrew biblical scholar, it is my hope to see congregations embrace the Hebrew Scriptures as a full and sufficient canon of scripture, revealing God and her word in conversation with, but not subjected to, the Christian scriptures that follow, honoring the ancient texts and *their* contexts. As a professor, priest, and preacher, I am keenly aware that it is the stories of women and girls, female characters and their names (when given), that are most likely to be unknown by congregants and seminarians and, all too often, clergy. A more expansive, more inclusive lectionary will remedy that by introducing readers and hearers of scripture to "woman story" in the scriptures. (Adapted from April D. Westbrook, *"And He Will Take Your Daughters . . .": Woman Story and the Ethical Evaluation of Monarchy in the David Narrative.*)

Biblical women are often generalized as a monolith of oppressed biblical womanhood. In my years teaching in theological classrooms and Jewish and Christian congregations, I find scripture readers unfamiliar with women prophets (the subject of my first book, *Daughters of Miriam: Women Prophets in Ancient Israel*), or the more than twenty named Israelite and Judean queens preserved in the text (addressed in my most recent monograph, *Womanist Midrash: A Reintroduction to the Women of the Torah and the Throne*), or the female assassins who execute their would-be rapists, or many other texts in which women have unexpected power and agency. A significant aim of this project is increased biblical literacy, beginning with scripture's most neglected population.

Recognizing that the scriptures are an androcentric collection of documents steeped in patriarchy, this lectionary grapples with the gender constructs of the text rather than romanticizing admirable heroines. Indeed, it questions "admirable" constructs of womanhood rooted in birthing and mothering. The extent to which women's narratives uphold the patriarchal agendas of the scriptures is held in tension with those passages in which women demonstrate agency, wielding power and authority. Sometimes those are the same texts. The degree to which the scriptures are (and are not) liberating for all of their characters and claimants will be, hopefully, more accessible to preacher and reader and other interpreters and exegetes.

Biblical values and norms around gender occupy a central place in biblical interpretation, providing opportunity for preachers to engage them and their impact on the construction of gender norms in the world in which these texts are interpreted.

I believe it is crucial to reframe the texts so that women and girls are at the center of the story, even though they are, to one degree or another, literary creations of pre-modern men. It is important that women who are often second-class citizens in the text and in the world in which the text is interpreted have a text selection and reading paradigm that centers the interests and voices of women in the text, no matter how constructed. The task of preachers is to proclaim a word—of good news, of liberation, of encouragement, of prophetic power, of God-story, and sometimes, of lament, brokenness, and righteous rage. These lectionaries will provide a framework to do that and attempt to offer some balance to the register in which the word has often been proclaimed.

A significant aspect of the work of shaping a lectionary and preaching from it is hermeneutical. I was (and remain) convinced it ought to be possible to tell the story of God and God's people through the most marginalized characters in the text. That is my practice as a preacher. This project, *A Women's Lectionary for the Whole Church*, intends to do that in a three-year lectionary accompanied by a stand-alone single-year lectionary. The three-year cycle, Years A, B, and C, will feature the Gospels of Matthew, Mark, and Luke respectively, with John interwoven, as is the case in the Revised Common Lectionary (RCL) and Episcopal Lectionary (similar to the RCL but with the inclusion of deuterocanonical texts not deemed canonical by churches outside of the Anglo-Catholic and Orthodox streams). Year W (for "Women") covers all four Gospels.

Specifically, the *Lectionary* includes:

1. companion texts in the traditional four-fold model, first lesson, generally Hebrew Bible, Psalm (or other Canticle), Christian Testament lesson, and Gospel appropriate to the liturgical season;

2. fresh translation of the lessons for each Sunday, the Principal Feasts, Holy Week, and the Feasts of the Ever-Blessed Virgin Mary and Mary Magdalene, using gender-expansive language and, in the case of the Psalms, explicitly feminine God-language (see "About the Translations");

3. brief text commentaries on each day's lections, and

4. brief preaching commentaries on each day's lections.

The lectionary *does not* include collects. The lack of collects—prayers that tie together the readings that open the Liturgy of the Word—is intentional, that clergy and lay liturgists might develop their own in conversation with the lectionary.

A final word about gendered language: as a women's lectionary, this project specifically and intentionally makes women visible in these lectionary texts. This will inevitably seem strange to some hearers and readers. Some will find it welcome and a signifier of inclusion. Some will find it discordant and I invite those to think deeply about what that discomfiture signifies. These responses may well be multiplied when reading and hearing the psalms using feminine pronouns. And some will find the language in these volumes insufficiently inclusive, particularly with regard to nonbinary and a-gender persons. While there is nonbinary language for human and divine subjects, the purpose of this project is to make women and girls more visible. Nonbinary and inclusive language can obscure women and girls. The commitment to the visibility of women and girls is not in conflict or competition with the commitment to visibility of nonbinary persons; this language, my language, like all language, is simply inadequate to express the fullness of God in and beyond the world or even in human creation.

Most simply, these translations seek to offer and extend the embrace of the scriptures to all who read and hear that they might see and hear themselves in them and spoken to by them. Similarly, taking seriously that we are all created in the image of God, these translations seek to display a God in whose Image we see ourselves reflected and reflecting.

TEXT SELECTION

I crafted lectionaries that centered the telling of the stories of scripture on the stories of women and girls in the text, without regard to whether they are named or voiced in the text or whether their experiences of and with God support the narrative and theological claims made by and on behalf of the text or not. Specifically, I prioritize passages in which women and girls are present whether named or not, whether speaking or not. In addition, I selected passages in which women and girls are present but obscured in plurals and other groupings, e.g., "children," "Israelites," "people," "believers," etc. As is the case with all lectionaries, some passages recur and others are omitted all together. None of the extant Christian lectionaries offers comprehensive reading of any of the canons of scripture. This lectionary is no exception.

My methodology was broadly as follows:

1. First, I established a female canon within the broader canons of scripture by using Accordance Bible Software to identify passages in which there is explicit language for female persons. I designed a Boolean search to capture as many terms as possible in singular and plural constructions and varied grammatical forms (mother* <or> daughter* <or> sister* <or> wom*n <or> wife <or> wives <or> widow* <or>*maid* <or> mistress* <or> lady <or> ladies <or> prostitute* <or> prophetess* <or> princess* <or> queen* <or> sorceress* <OR> womb <OR> pregnan* <or> midwi*e*.) My search terms were not necessarily exhaustive, but they were more than sufficient for the task. I used the *Dictionary of Women in Scripture,* edited by Carol Meyers et al., to supplement this list.

2. Then, beginning with the liturgical season and its themes, I identified Hebrew biblical or deuterocanonical texts from the female canon. (Year W does not use the deuterocanonical texts apart from select readings during one or more of the Principal Feasts, such as Judith during the Great Vigil of Easter).

3. Next, I looked for readings that shared thematic language or specific words that related to the liturgical season and first lesson. I saved my Boolean search results in text groups: Hebrew Bible, Psalms, books that make up the New Testament lesson—Acts, the Epistles, and Revelation—and the Gospels. That meant I did not have to search the entire canon each time I worked on a specific reading. One nontraditional aspect of these lectionaries is that I occasionally use the Acts of the Apostles as the New Testament lesson, expanding the options for readings with female characters.

4. Sometimes a specific passage in a Gospel, psalm, or Epistle would suggest itself. Other times, I would move through the lesson categories looking for connective language. Most often the selection sequence was Hebrew Bible followed by a psalm then the Gospel and the New Testament lesson last.

Text selection was one of the most time-consuming aspects of the project, second only to translating the text. I was greatly facilitated in this world by collaboration circles, in person in Atlanta, Chattanooga, Chicago, Dallas, Fort Worth, Pasadena, Richmond (VA), and in Kapaa, Kilauea, and Wailua, Kauai (HI) in addition to international trips to Managua (Nicaragua) and a continuing education event for clergy on a Central and South American cruise where the *Lectionary* was one of the teaching topics. There is also an ongoing digital collaboration through a closed Facebook working group.

My conversation partners included sixty-three participants from across the United States, United Kingdom, Scotland, Canada, and New Zealand in one setting, Episcopal parishes in Kauai and Pasadena during separate one-month residencies, and a series of individual and small group consultations, some seventeen collaborations, some of which were composed of multiple sessions. Denominations represented included: African Methodist Episcopal, Anglican, Baptist (of various sorts), Disciples of Christ, Episcopal, the Fellowship of Affirming Ministries, Lutheran, Presbyterian, Unitarian Universalist, United Church of Canada, United Church of Christ, United Church of Scotland, and United Methodist.

I deliberately engaged potential users of the *Lectionary,* including clergy, seminarians, and lay leaders, with a range of gender identities and expressions. I also held a specific session for queer-identifying and nonbinary readers and hearers of the text focusing on the use and implications of binary language, even in service to womanist/ feminist work, in an increasingly postbinary world.

I am beyond grateful for the contributions, questions, and suggestions of all of these conversation partners, including their assessment for wording and translation choices in addition to text pairings.

USING *A WOMEN'S* LECTIONARY

The *Women's Lectionary* is designed for congregational and devotional life. It will also serve well in theological classrooms in preaching, worship arts, liturgy, and spiritual formation. The *Lectionary* is also suitable for clergy lectionary study groups. Individuals and congregations will have a number of options for use. Each set of readings is accompanied by text and translation notes and a preaching commentary. In addition, the *Lectionary* comes with a list of the divine names and titles used for God in these translations that might be used in public liturgy and private prayer. There is also an index of all of the passages of scripture in the lectionary, making them available for individual study. Suggested practices for public reading follow in the "About the Translations" section.

CONGREGATIONAL USE

The gender-expansive translations throughout the *Women's Lectionary* and explicit feminine God language in the psalter provide an opportunity for Christian education and formation on matters of biblical authority and translation issues, oft neglected conversations in congregations (beyond creedal statements).

- Adopt the *Lectionary* fully, Years A, B, and C for three years using these lessons in this translation.
- Adopt the *Lectionary* for a single year, using Year W for representation from all four Gospels. This would be especially suitable for churches that do not use a multiyear lectionary.
- Adopt the *Lectionary* to replace a year in the three-year lectionary currently in use.
- Adopt the *Lectionary* readings using another translation of the scriptures for public proclamation. (This may be a useful option in a congregation that might balk at hearing feminine pronouns used for God in scripture proclamation.)
- Use the *Lectionary* for substitute readings for the same day and liturgical season in a particular year (for example, when the Episcopal or RCL lessons are unsatisfactory).
- Use the *Lectionary* for Bible study, whether preaching from the *Lectionary* or not. The preaching prompts may be used as conversation starters.
- Use the list of divine names and titles for God to enrich the theological language of the community in liturgy, corporate, and personal prayer.

DEVOTIONAL USE

The *Lectionary* is designed for oral reading; read it out loud. Use the *Lectionary* for devotional reading, daily or weekly, whether your congregation uses the *Lectionary* or not. The four lessons can be read together every day of the week in their liturgical setting or spread out over the course of the week. The index can be used to identify individual passages for study and the list of divine names in the appendix can be used to augment the vocabulary of prayer.

THEOLOGICAL EDUCATIONAL USE

As a resource in the theological classroom, the *Lectionary* offers a much-needed alternative to the long-standing Episcopal and Revised Common Lectionaries for the study of liturgy and worship planning, offering a relevant and expansive vocabulary at a time when many clergy, congregations, and denominations are looking for liturgical alternatives and some are considering revisions of prayer books and hymnals for this very purpose.

These translations make a specific contribution to the oft-neglected but necessary conversation about the nature, function, and scope of biblical translation beyond the standard rubric of formal literalism and dynamic flexibility.

ABOUT THE TRANSLATIONS

Gender matters. Gender matters in the text, in the world, in the world of the text, and in the world of the translator. Gender matters to me and to countless numbers of women hearers and readers of the biblical text for whom it is Scripture. Gender matters significantly to those who have been and are marginalized because of gender, especially when it is done in the name of God, appealing to the Scriptures. And gender matters to men. Gender matters to hearers and readers of the Scriptures who are privileged to share the gender of the dominant portrayal of God, the majority of biblical characters, the majority of biblical characters who have speaking parts, the majority of translators of biblical texts, and the majority of interpreters of biblical texts.

—Wilda Gafney, *Womanist Midrash: A Reintroduction to the Women of the Torah and the Throne*, 289

While prompted in part by my experience of hearing the scriptures read and proclaimed in nearly exclusively masculine language, multiplied in effect by equally, if not more, male liturgical language, this *Women's Lectionary* is a lectionary for the whole church. Androcentrism, sexism, and misogyny in the scriptures, in their translation and in their preaching and liturgical use, hurts men and boys and nonbinary children and adults as much as it does women and girls. Exclusively masculine language constructs and reinforces the notion that men are the proper image of God and women are secondary and distant. Further, the simple reality that men and boys have always heard their gender identified with God cannot be overlooked as a source of power and authority and security in terms of their place in the divine household and economy. Many, if not most, women and girls have not heard themselves identified by their gender as and with the divine and for those who have had that experience, it has been profoundly moving, rare, and even sometimes profoundly disturbing. The translation choices employed in the *Women's Lectionary* offer an opportunity to hear the scriptures in public and private settings in a different timbre, a feminine vocal register. Specific translation choices are annotated in the text notes that follow each set of readings.

The *Women's Lectionary* is a multilayered work. In addition to the compilation of entirely new lectionary readings for the three-year cycle and composite single year, the production of entirely new gender-expansive translations and in the Psalms, explicitly feminine translations distinguish this lectionary. Gender-expansive means expanding collections of people, e.g., Israelites, children, nations, and even "people" to reflect gendered subgroups such as "the women, children, and men of Israel." (These translations generally place women before men in translation.) In every place where it can be reasonably inferred a group is composed of persons of more than one gender, I reflect that in the translation. Where gender neutral or inclusive language is used, it is used for male subjects; for example, "child" is used preferably to "son."

In genealogies, gender expansiveness means that lineages are presented matrilineally. For example, rather than "the God of Jacob," the *Lectionary* uses "the God of Rebekah's line." When supplemental language is added to establish the maternal genealogy, it is placed in brackets, i.e., "[Rachel-born] Benjamin." In each case, the original reading and translation choices are clearly identified in the text notes. For this project, explicitly feminine language is preferable to inclusive and neuter language, which obscures and erases women and girls. In addition, singular neuter gender and inclusive plurals do not disrupt the learned gender patterns, as many readers and hearers interpret them through their previously learned gender pattern and experience them as male. There is also some nonbinary language for human beings and God throughout the *Lectionary*; erasure of any gendered minority is contrary to the aims of this project.

Because so many readers pray the psalms devotionally, I wanted to offer an opportunity to hear those compositions speaking to, by, and about women and girls primarily and to encounter God in explicitly feminine language so readers of all genders will have the experience of praying to God in the feminine gender. Therefore, these translations of the psalms use feminine pronouns for God primarily, supplemented by nonbinary pronouns.

Following the practice of translators before me, I have adopted the practice of choosing descriptive expressions for the name of God and other divine names and titles. Given the most commonly used title for God in the Hebrew Scriptures, LORD (with the large and small caps indicating it is a substitutionary word for God's unpronounceable Most Holy Name represented by the letters YHWH) is the common male human slave holding title; it is not used for God in the *Lectionary*. The *Lectionary* preserves the ancient biblical and rabbinical practice of substituting something that can be said for that which cannot. (In some places the Hebrew Masoretic text uses Elohim, "God," as a substitute). In rabbinic and subsequent practice, *HaShem*, "the Name," is a common substitution; there are others.

Dr. Joel Rosenberg of Tufts University translated selected psalms for the Kol Haneshamah Reconstructionist prayer book. He renders the divine name using choices such as "THE ETERNAL," "THE ONE," and in Psalm 29, "THE ONE WHO CALLS over many waters." I was deeply impacted by these translations during the time I spent as a member of the Dorshei Derekh Reconstructionist minyan of the Germantown Jewish

Centre in Philadelphia and adopted and expanded the practice in my own translations for teaching, preaching, and publication. The translations in *Lectionary* draw from a robust list of options for naming God listed in an appendix. Some examples include: ARK OF SAFETY, DREAD GOD, FIRE OF SINAI, ROCK WHO GAVE US BIRTH, SHE WHO IS HOLY, etc. The list numbers more than one hundred and twenty. I preserve "Lord" for human beings, as that is the origin of the title, respectful address, and functionally the title refers to a slaveholder or other hierarchical role.

Similarly, in the Second Testament, I also reserve "Lord" for human beings— apart from Jesus. There are two sets of divine names and titles for the Christian Testament in the appendix. For Jesus I use: Anointed, God-born, Messiah, Rabbi, Redeemer, Savior, Son of Woman, Teacher, and Woman-Born. Son of Woman and Woman-Born both derive from the expressions previously and commonly translated as "son of man" (in the KJV) and more recently as "Mortal" or "the Human One" in translations like the NRSV and CEB. The underlying Greek expression, *huios tou anthropou*, means "son [male offspring] of a human" ("person of either sex" according to the standard authoritative BDAG lexicon); it also means "humankind" collectively. Whether one speaks or writes from a human, biological perspective or a theological one, the humanity of Jesus stems from his mother. Grammatically, Son of Woman and Woman-Born are both correct. Inasmuch as generic "man" is no longer used to represent humanity in totality, an argument can be made that Son of Woman is more theologically correct. The expression *huios tou anthropou* is not *de novo* to the Second Testament; it occurs in the First Testament in both Hebrew as *ben adam* and the same Greek expression in the LXX. *Ben adam* means son (and generic child) of humanity. In the First Testament and deuterocanonical books, I use woman-born where it is a human title signifying mortality. In at least one occurrence, in a poetic text, I translate it as "children of earth and Eve," given that the root of *adam* is *adamah*, "earth" (soil).

There is a second list of divine titles for God (apart from Jesus) used in the Second Testament. Those names and titles are: Creator, Creator of All, Dread God, Faithful One, Father, Holy One, Living God, Majesty, (our) Maker, Most High, One Parent, Provider, Shepherd-Of-All, Sovereign, and Weaver (of lights). While I do preserve "Father" in some places, I employ it much less frequently than it occurs in the text. I reserve it for places where the parentage of Jesus is being addressed specifically. As it pertains to God's whereabouts and way of being in this world and the world beyond this one, I eschew "king" and "kingdom" in the *Lectionary*. As with all human attempts to describe God, monarchal language is inadequate; it is particularly unsuitable in that it stems from a rather brutal human system of governance that is unnecessary in the space where God is. Instead, I utilize "reign" and "realm" individually or in combination and "majesty." (The latter is feminine in Greek and functions as a divine title in Hebrews 1:3 and 8:1.) When translating from the Hebrew Bible and deuterocanonical texts, I use "ruler" preferentially.

I take special care with translation choices for the Christian Testament because of the long history of anti-Judaism and anti-Semitism in biblical translation and interpretation and, in some cases, in the texts themselves. This lectionary intentionally excludes texts that blame Jews for the death of Jesus. The expression "the Jews" in Christian literature, including scripture, and in broader Christian discourse is very often negative. In the Greek New Testament, *Ioudaioi* can mean Jews, Judeans (people from Judea), or Jewish Christians in distinction from Gentile Christians. I use Judeans preferentially. In addition, because "scribes" can be easily misunderstood as simple copyists, I translate them as "biblical scholars" to make their underlying expertise more readily apparent.

Because scripture is read and heard and understood contextually, I am mindful of the ways in which the Scriptures have been read and heard and understood in the broader Western and specifically American contexts. Across both testaments and the writings in between, slavery is ubiquitous, including on the lips of Jesus. While many translations use "servant" preferentially, I find that to be dishonest given that the persons so named were owned, controlled, raped, impregnated, bred, sold, maimed, and killed. Even when the bondage was of short *durée* or to pay off a debt, the lord and master had complete control of the subjugated person's body and sometimes retained their children after their liberation. So while it is certain to produce discomfort in the reader and hearer, I preserve "slave" and invite the reader and preacher to wrestle with that term and its influence on and in crafting and defending the American slavocracy. Minimizing the footprint of slavery in the scriptures weakens the link between them and subsequent slaveholding societies and the churches that unite them and us. Readers are welcome to replace the word "slave" with "servant" knowing that doing so writes over the degree to which the scriptures are slaveholding texts with no imagination of the possibility of abolition. I would encourage congregations to talk about that language and why they will or will not retain it.

Also bearing in mind the American context in which these translations were produced and the related contexts in which they will be read, I chose to disrupt the traditional biblical language of light and white to mean good and dark and black to mean something negative or even evil. While there is no concept of race in the Hebrew Bible or Christian Testament and people and nations are not assessed based on skin color and physical characteristics, that language has been mapped onto human bodies in the postbiblical world, justifying dehumanizing treatment, including slavery and legalized discrimination, including in the Church. Not all dark/black language in the biblical text is negative. Where it indicates something positive or holy, I retain it; for example, "God dwells in thick darkness" throughout the Scriptures.

In sum, the translations in the *Lectionary*:

- Identify original language and translation choices in accompanying text notes.
- Indicates quoted material from the First Testament in the Christian Testament using italics.
- Identify supplemental expansive translations with brackets.
- Expand people groups to make the presence of women and girls explicit.
- Use feminine and nonbinary pronouns for God in the Psalms.
- List genealogical information maternally.
- Use expansive descriptive language for the name of God instead of "Lord."
- Limit use of "Father" to texts addressing Jesus's parentage.
- Replace "kingdom" with "reign" and "realm" or with "majesty" (ruler is used preferentially in the Hebrew Bible).
- Use "Judeans" rather than "Jews" preferentially where appropriate.
- Maintain slave language rather than weaken or minimize with "servant."
- Modulate "dark/black" negative language as "shadow" and "bleak/ness."

It is my hope that this lectionary will enrich the experience of hearing and reading scripture and invite readers and hearers into deeper study of the scriptures, their translation, and interpretation. It is also my hope that liturgy, the work of the people in service to God, will be a place where all people can experience themselves as fully created in the image of God whose words they hear through the scriptures, and in prayer and preaching.

THE LESSONS WITH COMMENTARY
Year W

ADVENT I

Genesis 16:7–13; Psalm 71:4–11; Philippians 2:5–11; Luke 1:26–38

Genesis 16:7 Now the messenger of the ALL-SEEING GOD found Hagar by a spring of water in the wilderness, the spring on the way to Shur. [8] And the messenger said, "Hagar, slave-girl of Sarai, from where have you come and where are you going?" And she said, "From my mistress Sarai am I fleeing." [9] The messenger of the INSCRUTABLE GOD said to her, "Return to your mistress, and subject yourself to her."

[10] The messenger of the WELLSPRING OF LIFE said to Hagar, "Greatly will I multiply your seed, so they cannot be counted for multitude." [11] Then the messenger of the FOUNT OF LIFE said to her,

"Look! You are pregnant and shall give birth to a son,
and you shall call him Ishmael (meaning God hears),
for the FAITHFUL ONE has heard of your abuse.
[12] He shall be a wild ass of a man,
with his hand against everyone,
and everyone's hand against him;
and he shall live in the sight of all his kin."

[13] So Hagar named the LIVING GOD who spoke to her: "You are El-ro'i"; for she said, "Have I really seen God and remained alive after seeing God?"

Psalm 71:4–11

[4] My God, rescue me, from the hand of the wicked,
from the clutch of the cruel and the ruthless.
[5] For you are my hope, Sovereign, WORTHY ONE,
my trust, from my youth.
[6] Upon you I have leaned from birth;
from my mother's belly, you cut me.
You will I praise for all time.
[7] As a portent have I served to many,
yet you are my strong refuge.
[8] My mouth is filled with your praise,
all the day, with your glory.

⁹ Do not cast me off in the time of old age;

when my strength is spent, do not forsake me.

¹⁰ For my enemies speak about me,

and those who watch my life take counsel together.

¹¹ They say, "Pursue and seize them,

God has forsaken them,

for there is none to deliver."

Philippians 2:5 Let the same mind be in you all that was in Christ Jesus,

⁶ who, though he was in the form of God,

did not regard equality with God

as something to be seized,

⁷ but emptied himself,

taking the form of a slave,

being born in human likeness;

then being found in human form,

⁸ he humbled himself

and became obedient to the point of death,

even death on a cross.

⁹ Therefore God also highly exalted Jesus

and gave him the name

that is above every name,

¹⁰ so that at the name of Jesus

every heavenly and earthly knee should bend,

along with those under the earth,

¹¹ and every tongue should confess

that Jesus Christ is Savior,

to the glory of God the Sovereign.

Luke 1:26 In the sixth month the angel Gabriel was sent by God to a town of Galilee, Nazareth, ²⁷ to a virgin betrothed to a man whose name was Joseph, of the house of David. And the name of the virgin was Mary. ²⁸ And the angel came to Mary and said, "Rejoice, favored one! The Most High God is with you." ²⁹ Now, she was troubled by the angel's words and pondered what sort of greeting this was. ³⁰ Then the angel said to her, "Fear not Mary, for you have found favor with God. ³¹ And now, you will conceive in your womb and give birth to a son, and you will name him Jesus. ³² He will be great and will be called the Son of the Most High, and the Sovereign God will give him the throne of his ancestor David. ³³ He will reign over the house of Jacob forever, and of his sovereignty there will be no end." ³⁴ Then Mary said to the angel, "How can this be, since I have not known a man intimately?" ³⁵ The angel said to her, "The Holy Spirit, She will come upon you, and the power of the Most High will overshadow you; therefore the one born will be holy. He will be called Son of God. ³⁶ And now, Elizabeth your kinswoman has even conceived a son in her old age, and this is the sixth month for she who was called barren. ³⁷ For nothing will be impossible with God." ³⁸ Then Mary said, "Here am I, the woman-slave of God; let it be with me according to your word." Then the angel left her.

PROCLAMATION

Text Notes

The language of Hagar's annunciation parallels the promise to Abraham in Genesis 13:16 closely; each is promised that their "seed" (or offspring) will be numerous beyond counting. Hagar is the first woman in scripture granted an annunciation, the unnamed mother of Samson follows in Judges 13:3–7, followed in turn by Mary the mother of Jesus. Hagar and Rebekah (Genesis 24:60) are the only women in the canon credited with their own seed/offspring; the language is usually reserved for men. (Rebekah's seed is blessed by her matrilineal family; her father Bethuel ben Milcah bore his mother's name, not his father's.) Notably, God speaks to Abraham *about* Sarah in Genesis 17:15–16, as do the divine messengers in Genesis 18:9–10, even when she is within hearing; none speak to her.

Hagar's abuse or affliction, more rightly, Sarah's abuse of Hagar in verse 11, is articulated with a verb that encodes both physical and sexual violence; the verb is also used of the abuse the Israelites suffered at the hands of the Egyptians. The divine demand that Hagar "subject herself" to Sarah is communicated with a reflexive form of the same verb; she is told to subject herself to more potential violence. Some translate Ishmael's fate in verse 12 as living "in opposition," i.e., conflict, with his kin rather than "opposite," i.e., in their sight or presence; the verb has both senses.

In verse 4 of the psalm, God is named as "lord" (corresponding to lowercase use as is common when addressing men) in combination with God's unpronounceable Name, YHWH, usually rendered as "Lord GOD" (capitalized for deity). In verse 6 the "God-as-midwife" theme familiar from Psalm 22:9 takes a dramatic turn with God "cutting" rather than "drawing" the baby out. The difference is *gochi* versus *gozi*, a single letter, perhaps indicating recall of the former psalm without access to the text. The cutting itself could range from a cesarean delivery—practiced in ancient Egypt—to cutting the cord as in CEB.

In Mary's linguistic and cultural world, in Hebrew and Aramaic, the Spirit is feminine; the Syriac text uses a feminine verb for the Spirit in Luke 1:35. Also in her world, there was no distinction between servant and slave. Mary is not saying she will wait on God hand and foot in verse 38; she is giving God ownership of her body, ownership slaveholders claimed without consent. This volume uses "slave" normatively, reflecting the troubling language in the scriptures and their contexts.

Preaching Prompts

This first lesson in each Sunday of Advent in this volume is an annunciation story: Hagar, Sarah and Abraham, the mother of Samson, and Hannah. Annunciations communicate an understanding of God involved in history and deeply involved in the lineage—ancestral and descendent—of God's people. Mary's annunciation and the story of Jesus's first advent stand on that foundational understanding.

In traditional readings these women are all but reduced to biological functions, a function which not all women have or choose to perform. Yet there is space in that "all but" to see that even in a very reductionistic text these women are more than incubators. They are theologians and divine conversation partners and, in Hagar's case, a philologist. They are also evidence that God is concerned with those who are at the bottom of all the hierarchies: women, the enslaved, foreigners, and, as so often is the case, persons in more than one category (all for Hagar), whose overlapping identities result in intersectional oppressions.

Jesus, as the incarnation of God, continued to identify with those on the margins and those excluded by the margins, "taking the form of a slave" according to Philippians 2:7. He did so scandalously, between a woman's thighs and, as Cornel West says (paraphrasing Augustine), far too close to the orifices for urine and feces. The psalm makes clear this is not a new arena for the divine Midwife, who does not simply passively "catch" babies who largely birth themselves, but she actively intervenes to ensure a live birth, cutting what needs to be cut. Perhaps she will also deliver Mary when her time comes.

Mary takes on the language of enslavement, subjecting herself to God and God's will, where Hagar seems to have come into bondage as a child, if not from birth. Yet there is a question in the mind of some readers as to whether Mary actually had the option to consent given Gabriel tells her what *will* happen to her, to her body. It is unclear what would have happened had she demurred. Yielding herself to God, Mary joins the ranks of those deemed "servants," slaves of God: Moses, David, Paul, James. Through her yielding the first Advent comes to us, through her model and that of Hagar, we prepare for the second Advent.

ADVENT II

Genesis 17:15–22; Psalm 78:1–7; Romans 8:18–25; Luke 1:39–45

Genesis 17:15 Thus God said to Abraham, "Now as for Sarai your wife, you shall not call her name Sarai, for Sarah is [now] her name. 16 And I will bless her, and indeed of her will I give you a son. And I will bless her, and she will become nations; rulers of peoples shall come into being from her." 17 Then Abraham fell on his face and laughed, and said to himself, "Can a child be born to one a hundred years old? And can Sarah, ninety years old, give birth?" [18] Then Abraham said to God, "If only Ishmael could live in your sight!" [19] God said, "Nevertheless your wife Sarah shall give birth to a son for you, and you shall call his name Isaac. And I will establish my covenant with him, an everlasting covenant for his offspring after him. [20] Now as for Ishmael, I have heard you and I will bless him and make him fruitful and I will make him exceedingly, exceedingly numerous and he shall be the father of twelve chieftains, and I will make him a great nation. [21] But my covenant I will establish with Isaac, whom Sarah shall give birth to for you at this season next year." [22] And when God had finished speaking with him, God ascended from Abraham.

Psalm 78:1–7

[1] Give ear, my people, to my teaching;
   incline your ear to the utterances of my mouth.
[2] I will open my mouth in a proverb;
   I will utter riddles from of old.
[3] Which we have heard and known,
   and which our mothers and fathers have told us.
[4] We will not hide them from their daughters and sons;
   we will recount to generations to come
   the praiseworthy deeds of SHE WHO SPEAKS LIFE,
   and her might and the wonderful works she has done.
[5] She gave her decrees for Rebekah's descendants
   and placed teaching among Sarah's offspring,
   which she commanded their mothers and fathers
   to make known to their daughters and sons.
[6] In order that a coming generation, children yet to be, might know,
   and will rise up and tell their daughters and sons.
[7] Then they will put their confidence in God,
   and not forget the works of God, but will keep her commandments.

Romans 8:18 I consider that the sufferings of this present time are not worth comparing with the glory about to be revealed to us. [19] For the creation waits with eager longing for the revealing of the daughters and sons of God; [20] for the creation was subjected to futility, not of its own will but by the will of the one who subjected it, in hope [21] that the creation itself will be set free from its bondage to decay and will obtain the freedom of the glory of the daughters and sons of God. [22] We know that the whole creation has been groaning in labor pains until now; [23] and not only the creation, but we ourselves, who have the first fruits of the Spirit, groan inwardly while we wait for adoption, the redemption of our bodies. [24] For in hope we were saved. Now hope that is seen is not hope. For who hopes for what is seen? [25] But if we hope for what we do not see, we wait for it with patience.

Luke 1:39 Mary set out in those days and went to the hill country with haste, to a Judean town. [40] There she entered the house of Zechariah and greeted Elizabeth. [41] Now when Elizabeth heard Mary's greeting, the baby leaped in her womb and Elizabeth was filled with the Holy Spirit. [42] Elizabeth exclaimed with a loud cry, "Blessed are you among women, and blessed is the fruit of your womb. [43] From where does this [visit] come to me? That the mother of my Sovereign comes to me? [44] Look! As soon as I heard the sound of your greeting in my ear, the baby in my womb leaped for joy. [45] Now blessed is she who believed that there would be a fulfillment of those things spoken to her by the Holy One."

PROCLAMATION

Text Notes

Genesis 17:20 uses the word *nasi'* to describe the children of Ishmael; its semantic range includes "prince," "leader/ruler," and "chief." As princes they would be rulers of individual principalities, not the offspring of more senior monarchs (generally indicated by *sar*, the root of Sarah's name). I have adopted Robert Alter's "chieftain" to maintain the distinction for lexical fidelity.

Both Mary and Elizabeth have venerable names: Mary, Miriam, goes back to the prophet Miriam, who led the people through the sea. (Exodus 15:20 presents Miriam leading the women and calling for the men to follow them in verse 21—the "them" there is masculine/common plural.) Elizabeth is a form of Elisheba, mother of Israel's priestly line, wife of Aaron (Exodus 6:3) and Elizabeth's own foremother. Her question is nearly inarticulate, "and from where this to me," in keeping with the joyful shock of the passage.

Preaching Prompts

Underlying annunciation stories is a reading that valorizes women chiefly for fertility and treats them as little more than incubators. An updated reading might focus on the symbolism of children for a world that continues under God's care no matter the present circumstances—remembering that the scriptures are produced and collated under wave after wave of oppression. In a transgenerational reading, all who produce and nurture children participate in God's work in the world and are recipients of the promise of God's care and keeping.

While the texts and traditional interpretations privilege some children, characters, and lineages above others, God's promise to Hagar, her son, and their descendants is an act of fidelity that transcends deeply rooted regional and ethnic conflicts. No matter how fractured the relationship—and there would be bloodshed—Israelites and Ishmaelites (Edomites) remain bound together as kin.

Psalm 78 offers such a transgenerational reading; through these women and men and their children and descendants, God builds families, communities, and peoples, all the family of God. In this family, as in many on a much smaller scale, there are divisions and hostilities, enmities and ruptures that also cross generational lines and lineages and trouble the relationship between God and humanity. Romans 8 speaks to those divisions and the living hope of the world, itself very much alive, for healing and reconciliation.

To this world of fractured and unreconciled peoples, God sends a holy child as the embodiment of reconciliation. This singular extraordinary child is sent to a family (Mary and Joseph), an extended family (Elizabeth and Zechariah), a series of communities (Bethlehem, Nazareth, Capernaum, and more), a people (Israel), and all peoples (Gentile and Jew representing the fullness of humanity).

Elizabeth's greeting comes from scriptures she well could have known: Judges 5:24 and Judith 13:18. They invite speculation on her contact with them orally or in writing. Women's literacy was not unheard of in the ancient world. Like Jezebel, royal women were most likely to be literate. Elizabeth's proximity to the temple and its liturgies and her own priestly lineage may have increased the likelihood of literacy. Both forerunners of this greeting are associated with bloody violence: Deborah's war against the Canaanites and Jael's execution of Sisera, and an Assyrian siege and Judith's execution of Holofernes. Further, both Judith and Jael are in sexually scandalous situations: attempted rape and assignation and seduction. Mary's own pregnancy is scandalous, hinting at sexual infidelity. Elizabeth's words provide transgenerational support and comfort.

As Advent readings, these texts call us to attend to our place in this lineage, this family, this community, this people, and prepare for the return of this holy child who will complete the work of reconciliation and restoration.

ADVENT III

Judges 13:2–7; Psalm 115:9–15; 1 John 3:1–3; Luke 1:46–56

Judges 13:2 Now there was a certain man from Zorah, of the tribe of the Danites, and his name was Manoah. His wife was barren; she had never given birth. 3 And the messenger of the HOLY ONE appeared to the woman and said to her, "Look now, you are barren, having never given birth, you shall conceive and give birth to a son. 4 Now please be on guard not to drink wine or strong drink, and you shall not eat anything unclean. 5 For look! You shall yet conceive and give birth to a son. No razor shall be upon his head, for a nazirite to God shall the boy be from the womb. And he shall begin to deliver Israel from the hand of the Philistines." 6 Then the woman came and spoke to her husband saying, "Someone from God came to me, and their appearance was like that of a messenger of God, incredibly awesome; I did not ask the messenger from where they came, and their name they did not tell me. [7] Yet they said to me, 'You shall conceive and give birth to a son; do not drink wine or strong drink, and do not eat anything taboo, for a nazirite to God shall the boy shall be from the womb unto the day of his death.'"

Psalm 115:9–15

[9] Israel, trust in the HOLY ONE OF OLD!
Their help and their shield is she.
[10] House of Aaron, trust in the HOLY ONE OF SINAI!
Their help and their shield is she.
[11] You who revere the HOLY ONE, trust in the HOLY ONE!
Their help and their shield is she.
[12] The FAITHFUL ONE remembers us; she will bless;
she will bless the house of Israel;
she will bless the house of Aaron.
[13] She will bless those who revere GOD WHO IS HOLY,
both small and great.
[14] May the GENEROUS ONE add to, increase, you all,
both you and your children.
[15] *May you all be blessed by the AGELESS ONE,*
Maker of the heavens and the earth.

1 John 3:1 See what kind of love has our Maker given to us, that we should be called children of God; and we are. The reason the world does not know us is that it did not know God. [2] Beloved, now are we God's children and it has not yet been revealed what we will be. We do know that when God is revealed, we shall be like God, for we shall see God just as God is. [3] And everyone who has this hope in God purifies themselves, just as God is pure.

Luke 1:46–56

[46] "My soul magnifies the Holy One,
[47] and my spirit rejoices in God my Savior,
[48] for God has looked with favor on the lowliness of God's own womb-slave.
Surely, from now on all generations will call me blessed;
[49] for the Mighty One has done great things for me,
and holy is God's name.
[50] God's loving-kindness is for those who fear God
from generation to generation.
[51] God has shown the strength of God's own arm;
God has scattered the arrogant in the intent of their hearts.

52 God has brought down the powerful from their thrones,
   and lifted up the lowly;
53 God has filled the hungry with good things,
   and sent the rich away empty.
54 God has helped God's own child, Israel,
   a memorial to God's mercy,
55 just as God said to our mothers and fathers,
   to [Hagar and] and Sarah and Abraham, to their descendants forever."

56 And Mary remained with Elizabeth about three months and then she returned to her home.

PROCLAMATION

Text Notes

Though Hebrew does not have a distinct word for "wife," English and religious conventions generally find "his wife" preferable to "his woman." Therefore I use "wife" selectively and "woman" whenever possible. (The same holds true for "man" and "husband.")

The Hebrew "messenger," *mal'ak* in verse 3, can refer to humans or supernatural beings who deliver messages or speak on behalf of someone else; see Numbers 24:12; Deuteronomy 2:26; Joshua 6:17, etc. for human examples. The figure of the messenger of the Holy One often functions as God in disguise (or perhaps, in drag), evident as the character switches between speaking in third person on God's behalf and in first person as God (compare verses 3–4 with verses 22–23). I use the pronoun "they" for the messenger, though Hebrew does not have a neuter gender to signal the otherness of the being, beyond human categories like gender. The expression "man of God," here "someone from God," indicates prophets throughout the Hebrew Bible. The divine messenger in this passage in Judges seems to be the sole exception.

The pair of words traditionally translated "clean" and "unclean" are separate words and not an antithetical pair. *Tahor* is to be ritually acceptable and has to do with preparation, which might include a ritual bath. *Tamei* is better translated "taboo," not in an appropriate state for ritual, but not impure and not sinful (see Illona Rashkow, *Taboo or Not Taboo: Sexuality and Family in the Hebrew Bible*).

The alternating shifts in voice in Psalm 115:9–11 make sense when it is read antiphonally as marked, an initial line in the imperative (which is a second-person form) followed by a line in the third-person function as an aside. As the rest of the passage also works well responsively, for continuity I have marked it so as well. Verse 14 uses the same verb meaning both "to add" and "to do again" twice in a row. The duplication makes more sense as different words, hence, "add to, increase."

Preaching Prompts

The scriptures discuss women's fertility with language that equally applies to agriculture, reflecting limited understanding of human reproduction and profound ignorance of women's contribution to conception, imagining women's bodies as fertile or infertile fields. (The human ova was not discovered until 1876.) Curiously, Israelites never suspected male "seed" of being unviable, though they had surely seen diseased and other unviable plant seed.

The woman in Judges 13, rendered nameless, follows Hagar and Sarah in receiving a divine promise of progeny (Hannah, Mary, and Elizabeth will follow her). She joins a smaller list of (temporarily) barren women—Sarah, Hannah, and Elizabeth—whose barrenness God dramatically reverses. Curiously, only this woman has her name stripped from her. There is a robust rabbinic tradition supplying a variety of names for her, including other women's names in the scriptures with minimal or no narrative development, i.e., Zlelponi and Hazlel in *Bemidbar Rabbah* 10:5, Hazlelponi bat Yehudah from 1 Chronicles 4:3 in *b. Baba Bathra* 91*a*, where she has a daughter, Nashyan.

She will be a nazarite so that Samson will be a nazirite "from the womb." Women could and did take nazirite vows, Numbers 6:2ff, though subsequently, Numbers 30:1–13 permits husbands and fathers (when the daughter lives with them) to annul women's vows with no negative consequence for breaking the vow.

In the larger narrative, Samson's mother, like Hagar before her, knows with whom she has communed and is presented as sage and sensible while her husband is a buffoon. Yet her sensibility about the things of God is disclosed in a narrative dependent on her fertility and does not represent the experiences of the overwhelming majority of women living with infertility. That these stories employ a common ancient trope for introducing legendary heroes does not take the sting out of scripture proclaiming these miracles to only a very select few. In response, the psalm offers an opportunity to talk about the blessing and blessings of God in broader terms, and the Epistle calls us all, equally, into the family of God as children together where we are not valued on what we do, have done, or are capable of doing.

Mary's Magnificat is not thanksgiving for fertility in the place of barrenness. Her miraculous pregnancy relates her to women like Samson's mother, literarily, in introducing a significant child, but also distinguishes her as her conception will be unique in the Hebrew Scriptures (though not in its world). Her thanksgiving is about what this child will do with his life, not whether he will create life. As an Advent reading, this lesson calls us to that life and that work while we await his return.

ADVENT IV

1 Samuel 1:19–28; Canticle of Hannah: (1 Samuel 2:1–10);
Titus 3:4–7; Matthew 1:18–25

1 Samuel 1:19 Hannah and Elkanah rose early in the morning and bowed down and worshiped before the HOLY ONE OF OLD; then they turned back and went to their house at Ramah. Elkanah knew his wife Hannah, and the HOLY ONE remembered her. ²⁰ And it was with the turning of the days that Hannah conceived and gave birth to a son. She called his name Samuel (God hears), for she said, "From the GOD WHO HEARS have I asked him."

²¹ Now the man Elkanah went up along with his whole household to offer to the HOLY ONE the yearly sacrifice, on account of a vow. ²² Yet Hannah did not go up, for she said to her husband, "[Not] until the child is weaned, then will I bring him, that he may be seen in the presence of the MOST HIGH and remain there perpetually. I will present him as a nazirite in perpetuity, for all the days of his life." ²³ Her husband Elkanah said to her, "Do what is best in your eyes, stay until you have weaned him. May the FAITHFUL GOD establish the words of your mouth." So, the woman remained and nursed her son until she weaned him. ²⁴ And she took him up with her after she had weaned him along with a three-year-old bull, an ephah of flour, and a jug of wine. Hannah brought him to the house of the EVER-LIVING GOD at Shiloh and the boy was just a little boy. ²⁵ Then they slaughtered the bull, and they brought the boy to Eli. ²⁶ And Hannah said, "My lord! As you live, my lord, I am the woman, the one who was standing beside you in this [place] to pray to the GOD WHO HEARS. ²⁷ For this boy I prayed; and the FAITHFUL GOD gave me my asking, what I asked from God. ²⁸ Therefore have I bequeathed him to the GRACIOUS GOD; all his days will he be a bequest to the GOD WHOSE NAME IS HOLY."

So, she left him there and she bowed down and worshiped the FAITHFUL GOD.

Canticle of Hannah (1 Samuel 2:1–10)

¹ Hannah prayed and she said,
 "My heart exults in the HOLY ONE OF OLD;
 my horn is lifted up in my God.
 My mouth [opens] wide against my enemies,
 for I will rejoice in my victory.
² "There is none holy like the MOST HIGH,
 none besides you;
 there is no rock like our God.
³ Speak proudly no more, multiplying pride,
 nor let arrogance come from your mouth;
 for the AGELESS GOD is a God of knowledge,
 and by God deeds are accounted.

4 The bows of the mighty are broken,
   yet the feeble gird on warrior-strength.
5 Those who were full have hired themselves out for bread,
   yet those who were hungry are fat.
   She who was barren has birthed seven children,
   yet she who has many children languishes.
6 The CREATOR OF ALL kills and gives life;
   brings down to Sheol and raises up.
7 The GRACIOUS ONE makes poor and makes rich;
   brings low and also lifts up.
8 God raises the poor from the dust,
   and lifts the needy from heaps of human waste,
   to seat them with nobles and inherit a seat of honor.
   For to the CREATOR belong the pillars of the earth,
   and on them God has set the world.
9 God will guard the feet of the faithful who belong to God,
   while the wicked perish in shadow;
   for it is not by might that one prevails.
10 The HOLY ONE OF SINAI!
   Those who strive against God shall be shattered;
   God thunders against them from heaven.
   The FOUNT OF JUSTICE will judge the ends of the earth;
   God will give strength to God's ruler,
   and exalt the power of the anointed of God."

Titus 3:4 When the graciousness and loving kindness of God our Savior appeared, 5 God saved us through the water of rebirth and renewal by the Holy Spirit, not because of any works of righteousness that we had done, but according to God's mercy. 6 This Spirit God poured out on us abundantly through Jesus Christ our Savior, 7 so that, having been justified by God's grace, we might become heirs according to the hope of life eternal.

Matthew 1:18 Now this is how the birth of Jesus the Messiah happened: When his mother Mary had been betrothed to Joseph, but before they came together, she was found to have a child in her womb from the Holy Spirit. 19 Joseph her husband was a just man and unwilling to shame her, he wanted to divorce her secretly. 20 But when he deliberated this, suddenly an angel of the Most High God appeared to him in a dream and said, "Joseph, son of David, do not be afraid to take Mary as your wife, for in her is conceived a child from the Holy Spirit. 21 She will give birth to a son, and you are to name him Jesus, for he will save his people from their sins." 22 All this happened to fulfill what had been spoken by the Most High God through the prophet:

^{23} "Look now! The virgin shall conceive a child in her womb and give birth to a son,
   and they shall call him Emmanuel,"

which translated means, "God is with us." ^{24} When Joseph got up from sleep, he did as the angel of the Most High God commanded him. He took her as his wife, ^{25} yet did not know her sexually until her birthing of a son and named him Jesus.

PROCLAMATION

Text Notes

I chose "GOD WHO HEARS" to render the divine name in 1 Samuel 1:20 to reiterate the etymology of Samuel's name. Some scholars argue that the etymology belongs more properly to Saul, whose name stems from the verb for "to ask"; the "bequest" of verse 28 is the same spelling and pronunciation of Saul, *Shaul*. I preserve Hannah's use of "lord" for Samuel as a reminder it is a human male title.

According to Targum Onqelos, Hannah worships on her own in 1 Samuel 1:19, without her husband. She names her child in accordance with the broader practice in ancient Israel; the episodes where God or a father name a child should be viewed as exceptions. Hannah's participation in the slaughter of her offering is signaled by the "they" in verse 25; the exact nature of that participation is unclear.

Hannah's last line in verse 22, "I will present him . . ." comes from the Qumran scroll 4QSam^a and is not present elsewhere. According to the older reading supported by the LXX, in verse 23 Elkanah prays that God would establish the words of *Hannah's* mouth; the Masoretic Text has "the words of God's mouth." The same scroll corrects "three bulls" in verse 24 to "three-year-old bull." The end of verse 24 is simply the word for "boy" or "youth" repeated twice; the meaning must be reconstructed and construed form context. I use "bequeath/bequest" in verse 28 to mirror the continuing verb "ask," now in a causative form that indicates fulfilling a request. The very last line occurs in two forms: "They bowed down and worshipped God there" from the MT, and "she left him there and worshipped" from Qumran. The Dead Sea Scrolls are the oldest, most complete manuscripts of the Hebrew scriptures and generated nearly ninety corrections to the Hebrew Bible, the bulk in Samuel.

Verse 4 of the Canticle uses *chayil*, denoting warrior strength, a warrior's heart, or an army; it characterizes Boaz (Ruth 2:1) and Ruth (Ruth 3:11) and the desirable wife in Proverbs 31:10 (whose attributes are selected by another woman as well as for the man, 31:3), and Pharaoh's army (Exodus 14:4). I use "shadow" in verse 9 for "darkness" given the way "dark" has been conflated negatively with "black" and black people in interpretation for harm. "Shattered" in verse 10 also has the sense of being terrified.

Curiously, "child" is missing from verses 18 and 20 of the Gospel. *Apolusai* has the sense of legally ending a contract or marriage, hence "divorce" in verse 19. Often softened to "quietly," the literal meaning of *lathra* is "secretly"; see Herod calling the magi secretly in the next chapter.

Matthew 1:23 quotes the LXX version of Isaiah 7:14; in the two Greek texts the young woman is a virgin, *parthenos*, and contemporaneously pregnant having a child "in womb," *en gastri*, and "will give birth," future tense. This is at odds with the Hebrew text in which the young woman, *almah*, is not specified as virginal, cultural expectations notwithstanding. Further, in Isaiah in Hebrew the young woman is pregnant at the time of Isaiah's speech: he uses the adjective "pregnant," not a verbal form. Christian translations often change the text to support traditional teaching.

Preaching Prompts

The sum of these Advent lessons and those across the weeks might be expressed in rebranding the season as Annunciation (the proper Feast of the Annunciation on March 25 often receives short shrift and gets revisited in Advent). The coming birth of Jesus is framed in annunciations to Mary and Joseph and Elizabeth, and to Hagar and Sarah and Hannah and the mother of Samson. The birth of a great leader from a barren or virgin mother (including some God-spawned) is one the ancient world loved to tell in and beyond the Hebrew Scriptures. The final annunciation of Matthew is virtually without peer in the stories of the ancient Afro-Asiatic world, "God is with us," not a demi-god, but the fullness of God in the frailty of flesh, woman-flesh, infant-flesh.

The Gospel treads lightly around the consequences should the betrothed but not married Blessed Virgin be found to be pregnant, particularly when her intended denied paternity, tantamount to an accusation of adultery. In spite of the stoning provision in the Torah, there are no stories of women or men actually being stoned for adultery in spite of its fairly regular occurrence in the scriptures (not until Jesus breaks up an attempted stoning later). We cannot say with certainty that she would have been stoned, but it was a possibility. Her shame would have made it unlikely for her to marry and therefore be socially and economically vulnerable, relegated to the margins of society.

It is in this context that Jesus is born and named "The Holy One Saves." God's saving work did not begin with Jesus; we see it borne witness to throughout the scriptures as Hannah sings of it in her time and in days to come as would Mary, echoing her song. Jesus is the continuation and embodiment of that salvation, himself an annunciation, of good news.

CHRISTMAS I

Isaiah 26:16–19; Psalm 68:4–13; 1 Thessalonians 4:13–18;
Luke 2:1–14 or 2:1–20

Isaiah 26:16 HOLY ONE, in distress they sought you,
    they pressed out a whispered prayer
    when your chastening was on them.
17 Just as an expectant mother
    writhes-in-labor and cries out in her pangs
    when her birthing time is near;
    thus were we because of you, Holy One.
18 We too were expectant, we writhed-in-labor,
    but it was as though we birthed only wind.
    No victories have we won on earth,
    neither do the inhabitants of the world fall.
19 Your dead shall live; their corpses shall rise.
    Awake and sing for joy you who dwell in the dust!
    For your dew is a radiant dew,
    and the earth shall release those long dead.

Psalm 68:4–11

  4 Sing to God, sing praises to her Name;
    exalt her who rides upon the clouds;
    HOLY is her Name, rejoice before her!
  5 Mother of orphans and defender of widows,
    is God in her holy habitation!
  6 God settles the solitary in a home bringing prisoners into prosperity;
    while the rebellious shall live in a wasteland.
  7 God, when you marched before your people,
    when you moved out through the wilderness,
  8 the earth shook, even the heavens poured down,
    at the presence of God, the One of Sinai,
    at the presence of God, the God of Israel.
  9 Rain in abundance, God, you showered abroad;
    when your heritage grew weary you prepared rest.
  10 Your creatures found a dwelling in her;
    God, you provided in your goodness for the oppressed.
  11 The AUTHOR OF LIFE gave the word;
    the women who proclaim the good news are a great army.

1 Thessalonians 4:13 Now we do not want you to be ignorant, sisters and brothers, about those who have fallen asleep, so that you might not grieve as those do who have no hope. [14] For since we believe that Jesus died and rose, even so they who sleep, will God by Jesus, bring with him. [15] For this we declare to you by the word of the Most High God, that we who are alive, who remain until the coming of Jesus, will not precede those who have fallen asleep. [16] For Jesus himself, with a command, in the voice of the archangel and with the trumpet of God, will descend from heaven, and the dead in Christ will rise first. [17] Then we who are alive who are left, together with them, will be caught up in the clouds to meet Jesus in the air; and so we will be with Jesus forever. [18] Therefore comfort one another with these words.

Luke 2:1 Now it happened in those days that a decree went out from Caesar Augustus that all the world should be registered (for taxation). [2] This was the first registration and occurred while Quirinius was governor of Syria. [3] So all went to be registered; each to their own towns. [4] Joseph also went up from Galilee, out of the city of Nazareth in to Judea, to the city of David called Bethlehem, for he was from the house and heritage of David. [5] He went to be registered with Mary, to whom he was betrothed and who was pregnant. [6] So it was, that, while they were there, the time came for her to birth her child. [7] And she gave birth to her firstborn son and swaddled him, and laid him in a manger, because there was no place for them in the inn.

[8] Shepherds were in that region there staying in the fields, keeping watch over their flock by night. [9] Then an angel of the Most High God came upon them, and the glory of the Living God shone around them, and they were greatly terrified. [10] But the angel said to them, "Fear not. Look! For I proclaim to you good news of great joy for all the people: [11] For there is born to you this day a Savior who is the Messiah, the Sovereign God, in the city of David. [12] This will be a sign for you: you will find a baby swaddled and lying in a manger." [13] And immediately there was with the angel a multitude of the heavenly array, praising God and saying,

[14] "Glory to God in the highest heaven,
and on earth peace among peoples whom God favors!"

[15] And it happened when the angels had departed from them into heaven, the shepherds said to one another, "Let us go now to Bethlehem and see this thing that has come to be, which the Sovereign God has made known to us." [16] So they came hurrying and found Mary and Joseph, and the baby lying in the manger. [17] Now seeing this, they made known what had been spoken to them about this child. [18] And all who heard marveled at what was spoken by the shepherds to them. [19] But Mary preserved all these words and pondered them in her heart. [20] The shepherds returned, glorifying and praising God for all they had heard and seen; it was just as it had been told them.

PROCLAMATION

Text Notes

The psalm portion ends with women proclaiming the good news of deliverance using the verbs that will come to mean "proclaim the gospel" in Hebrew and Greek (the LXX uses *euaggelizo*). Unfortunately, NRSV, RSV, CEB, and KJV obscure that this "company of preachers" is exclusively female.

The Epistle uses "Lord" repeatedly in such a way that it is not clear whether the author means God or Jesus. The translation above seeks to clarify the referents; however, the reader should be aware of the likely intentional ambiguity.

Preaching Prompts

The Hebrew Scriptures offer a variety of positions on life after death, including "sleep" to which all succumb and none rise (see Job 14:10–12,14). This unit of Isaiah uses the language of pregnancy and birth to speak of life beyond death. This first reading for Christmas brings images of a heavily pregnant woman in conversation with the heavily pregnant and laboring Virgin in the Gospel—though the text and tradition gloss over or minimalize her travail. The pregnant woman is the people who have not been able to deliver themselves or have someone to deliver them—rather than a deliverer, they have only produced wind. God is perhaps midwife here. Because of God's response to her people's prayers across the ages, the equally heavily pregnant earth will one day give birth to the dead.

In both the first lesson and psalm, there is water that renews and refreshes dry places. In the regendered psalm, God is the mother of orphans (fatherless children in Hebrew idiom), protector of widows, and provides homes (families) for the lonely. She is also sovereign of the skies, source of rain, and shepherd of her people. The women who functioned as town criers, proclaiming good news of victory in times of war, proclaim the good news of God's providence.

The Epistle takes up the theme of the dead rising and makes it a promise guaranteed by Jesus's own resurrection. Each of these texts with its focus on birth, life, and life beyond frames the Gospel and its presentation of the good news of Mary's child and the portents of his birth which she pondered.

CHRISTMAS II

Isaiah 66:10–13; Psalm 103:1–17; 1 Peter 1:22–2:3; Luke 2:15–20 or 2:1–20

Isaiah 66:10 Rejoice with Jerusalem, and celebrate with her
  all you who love her;
  rejoice with her in joy,
  all who mourn deeply over her;
¹¹ in order that you all may nurse and be satisfied
  from her comforting breast;
  that you all may drink deeply and delight yourselves
  from the glory of her breast.
¹² For so says the HOLY ONE OF OLD:
  Watch! I will extend to her flourishing like a river,
  and the wealth of the nations like an overflowing stream;
  and you all shall nurse and be carried on her arm,
  and you all shall be bounced on her knees.
¹³ As a mother comforts her child,
  so will I comfort you all;
  you all shall be comforted in Jerusalem.

Psalm 103:1–17

¹ Bless the FOUNT OF WISDOM, O my soul,
  and all that is within me, bless her holy Name.
² Bless the FOUNT OF WISDOM, O my soul,
  and forget not all her benefits.
³ She forgives all your sins
  and heals all your infirmities;
⁴ She redeems your life from the grave
  and crowns you with mercy and lovingkindness;
⁵ She satisfies you with good things,
  and your youth is renewed like an eagle's.
⁶ SHE WHO IS WISDOM executes righteousness
  and judgment for all who are oppressed.
⁷ She made her ways known to Miriam and Moses
  and her works to the children of Israel.
⁸ WISDOM'S womb is full of love and faithfulness,
  slow to anger and overflowing with faithful love.
⁹ She will not always accuse us,
  nor will she keep her anger forever.

10 She has not dealt with us according to our sins,
    nor rewarded us according to our wickedness.

11 For as the heavens are high above the earth,
    so indomitable is her faithful love upon those who revere her.

12 As far as the east is from the west,
    so far has she removed our sins from us.

13 As a mother's love for her children flows from her womb,
    so too does Wisdom's love for those who revere her flow from her womb.

14 For she herself knows whereof we are made;
    She remembers that we are but dust.

15 Our days are like the grass;
    we flourish like a flower of the field;

16 When the wind goes over it, it is gone,
    and its place shall know it no more.

17 But the faithful love of She Who is Wisdom endures forever
    on those who revere her,
    and her righteousness on children's children.

1 Peter 1:22 Now that you have purified your souls by your obedience to the truth so that you have the love without pretense of children raised together; from a pure heart love one another persistently. ²³ You have been born again, not of corruptible seed but of incorruptible seed through the living and enduring word of God. ²⁴ For:

> *"All flesh is like grass*
> *and all its glory like the flower of grass.*
> *The grass withers,*
> *and the flower falls,*
> ²⁵ *but the word of the Living God abides forever."*

This is the word that was proclaimed to you as good news. ²:¹ Lay aside, therefore, all malice, and all deceit, pretense, envy, and all slander. ² Like newborn babies, long for the pure spiritual milk, so that by it you may grow into salvation—³ if you have tasted that the Sovereign God is good.

See Gospel Reading in Christmas I.

PROCLAMATION

Text Notes

The poet responsible for Isaiah 66 seems to have reached beyond the Hebrew language for the expression "glory of her breast" in verse 11. The underlying expression "teat" or "udder of glory" may well have come from Akkadian and has an Arabic cognate (see the corresponding entry in the *Dictionary of Classical Hebrew*). In verse 12, "flourishing" is a better, less-materialistic reading of *shalom* than "prosperity."

The one comforted by their mother in Isaiah 66:13 is a man; the grammar of his passive comforting relegates his mother to the end of the sentence and makes him the focus: "As a man is comforted by his mother . . ." Common convention (JPS, NRSV, CEB) inverts the sentence, "As a mother comforts . . ." Mother-love in Psalm 103:13 is attributed to a father: "As a father mother-loves his children" (using the verbal form of the noun "womb"). The verse could be translated: "As a father loves his children with a mother's love . . ." As with Isaiah 66, the maternal image, here womb-love, is also attributed to God.

First Peter 1:22 uses *philadelphia*, sibling-love, where I have translated "children raised together" rather than "sisters and brothers" to avoid excluding reader-hearers who do not identify with a binary understanding of gender. The divine mother's milk is described as "spiritual," a somewhat elliptical rendering of *logikos*, which has to do with "carefully thought through, thoughtful" deliberations, particularly in religious contexts. It also connotes "spiritual" in contrast with "literal." (See the corresponding entry in *A Greek-English Lexicon of the New Testament and Other Early Christian Literature* [known as BDAG for its authors]).

Preaching Prompts

These Christmas lessons center an image rarely proffered in liturgy or preaching but common in art and culture: the nursing mother as an icon of love. In Isaiah 66:11 Jerusalem is the nursing mother with abundant "comforting" breasts that are her "glory." (In the CEB she is full-breasted.) In Psalm 103, God's love is womb-love, suggesting but not articulating an accompanying abundance of breastmilk (verses 8, 13). In 1 Peter 2:2–3, God's children are to long for the gospel as babies long for milk and at the breast of God "taste and see that God is good"—offering a new way to hear that very common refrain. In Luke 2 the newly delivered Virgin Mother nurses her holy child through the visits of mortals and angels without notice in the text.

In Isaiah 66:13, the poet-prophet uses the image of a mother—clearly nursing in light of the earlier verses—as an image of God. This intersects in interesting ways with the parental image in the psalm; mother-love of human and divine parents in verses 8 and 13 provides the lexicon for divine imagery. Even with some masculine grammatical language in the texts, the dominant divine images are feminine, rooted in birthing, nursing, and mothering, a reversal of the more common dominant masculine and male imagery. Similarly, the Gospel presents a woman-born Sovereign God swaddled in human flesh, nourished at his mother's breast. Of all the changes that the Christmas miracle births into the world, the ability to experience and name God more richly can be easily neglected.

The imagery of pregnancy, birthing, nursing, and mothering is integral to the Christmas story. It is also the primary trope for women in the scriptures, often reducing them to one dimension. It is not, however, the universal experience of women, and biblical portrayals of women can be painful for those who cannot mother, were not mothered, or were poorly mothered. These images can also be frustrating for these who choose not to mother.

CHRISTMAS III

Wisdom 9:1–6, 9–11; Psalm 33:1–9; Colossians 1:15–20; John 1:1–14

Wisdom 9:1 "O God of my ancestors and Author of mercy,
    who have made all things by your word,
2 and by your wisdom have formed humankind
    to govern the creatures you have made,
3 and oversee the world in holiness and righteousness,
    and render judgment as the soul of righteousness:
4 Give me the wisdom that sits by your throne,
    and do not reject me from among your children.
5 For I am your slave, the child of your slave girl,
    one who is weak and short-lived,
    with little understanding of judgment and laws;
6 for even one who is perfect among human beings
    will be regarded as nothing without the wisdom that comes from you.
9 With you is Wisdom, she who knows your works
    and was present when you made the world;
    she knows what is pleasing in your sight
    and what is right according to your commandments.
10 Send her forth from the holy heavens,
    and from your throne of glory send her,
    that she may labor with me,
    and that I may learn what is pleasing to you.
11 For she knows and understands all things,
    and she will guide me wisely in my actions
    and guard me with her glory.

Psalm 33

1 Rejoice in the ALMIGHTY, you righteous;
    it is good for the just to sing praises.

² Praise She Who is Majesty with the harp;
  play to her upon the psaltery and lyre.
³ Sing for her a new song;
  sound a fanfare with all your skill upon the trumpet.
⁴ For the word of Wisdom is right,
  and all her works are sure.
⁵ She loves righteousness and justice;
  the faithful love of the Mother of All fills the whole earth.
⁶ By the word of Wisdom were the heavens made,
  by the breath of her mouth all the heavenly hosts.
⁷ She gathers up the waters of the ocean as in a waterskin
  and stores up the depths of the sea.
⁸ Let all the earth revere She Who is Wisdom;
  let all who dwell in the world stand in awe of her.
⁹ For she spoke, and it came to pass;
  She commanded, and it stood fast.

Colossians 1:15 Jesus is the image of the invisible God, the firstborn of all creation; [16] for in him all things in the heavens and on earth were created, things visible and invisible, whether thrones or dominions or rulers or powers—all things have been created through him and for him. [17] Jesus himself is before all things, and in him all things hold together. [18] Jesus is the head of the body, the church; he is the beginning, the firstborn from the dead, so that he might come to have preeminence in everything. [19] For in Jesus all the fullness of God was well pleased to dwell, [20] and through Jesus God was well pleased to reconcile to Godself all things, whether on earth or in heaven, by making peace through the blood of his cross.

John 1:1 In the beginning was the Word, and the Word was with God, and the Word was God. [2] The Word was with God in the beginning. [3] Everything came into being through the Word, and without the Word not one thing came into being that came into being. What has come into being [4] in the Word was life, and that life was the light of all people. [5] The light shines in the bleakness, and the bleakness did not overtake it.

[6] There was a man sent from God, whose name was John. [7] He came as a witness to testify to the light, so that all might believe through him. [8] He himself was not the light, but he came to testify to the light. [9] The true light, which enlightens everyone, was coming into the world.

[10] He was in the world, and the world was created through him; yet the world did not know him. [11] To his own he came and his own did not receive him. [12] But all who did accept him, who believed in his name, he empowered to become children of God—[13] that is, those who were born, not of blood or of the will of the flesh or of the will of a human person, but of God.

[14] And the Word became flesh and lived among us, and we have seen his glory, glory as of a parent's only child, full of grace and truth.

PROCLAMATION

Text notes

The Greek word *pais* used in Wisdom 9:4 means both child and enslaved person. I choose the easier reading here and preserve the slave language in the following verse where two different words for an enslaved person occur.

Colossians uses the masculine pronoun repeatedly and does not include the name of Jesus in the Greek text. I have substituted it for some of the pronouns for smoothness and clarity.

Preaching Prompts

Today's Christmas readings focus on Wisdom and the Word. Both are invoked in the creation of the world: Wisdom in Wisdom 9:2 and Psalm 33:6, and the Word in John 1:1–2. Jesus is the word incarnate, unnamed in the Gospel portion. The Colossians reading names Jesus explicitly and links him to the creation of the world. This Sunday has traditionally focused on the preexistent Christ of John's Gospel, a concept expressed in grammatical gender (masculine for the Word and feminine for Wisdom in a similar portrayal), but ontologically beyond gender. These lessons present an opportunity to think about why we and our spiritual ancestors, our languages and theirs, gender things the way we do and what that really means.

The Wisdom reading also offers an opportunity to discuss the ubiquity of slavery in the biblical world and text. The scriptures use the language of slavery as more than a metaphor. Its normalcy is something with which we must contend. Many translations soften slave language to "servant." That seems dishonest given the total control—physical, sexual, reproductive, financial—over the lives and bodies of the persons at stake. Yet, it is hard to use slave language in scripture, prayer, and liturgy; doubly so for Black folk.

FIRST SUNDAY AFTER CHRISTMAS

Genesis 2:7–9, 15–17, 21–25; Psalm 8; 2 Corinthians 5:16–21; Matthew 1:1–16

Genesis 2:7 The SOVEREIGN God crafted the human from the dust of the humus and breathed into its nostrils the breath of life, and the human became a living soul. ⁸ And the SOVEREIGN God planted a garden in Eden, in the east, and there placed the human whom God had formed. ⁹ Out of the ground the SOVEREIGN God made grow every tree pleasant to the sight and good for food, and the tree of life in the middle of the garden, along with the tree of the knowledge of good and evil.

¹⁵ The SOVEREIGN God took the human and settled it in the garden of Eden to till and tend it. ¹⁶ Then the SOVEREIGN God commanded the human, "From every tree of the garden you may eat freely, ¹⁷ but of the tree of the knowledge of good and evil you shall not eat, for in the day you eat from it you shall surely die."

²¹ The SOVEREIGN God caused a deep sleep to fall upon the human, and it slept; then took one of its sides and closed up its place with flesh in place of it. ²² And the SOVEREIGN God built the side that had been taken from the human into a woman and brought her to the human. ²³ Then the human said,

"This time, this one is bone of my bones
and flesh of my flesh;
this one shall be called a woman,
for out of a man this one was taken."

²⁴ Therefore a man leaves his mother and his father and clings to his woman, and they become one flesh. ²⁵ And they were, the two of them, naked, the man and his woman [or the woman and her man], and were not ashamed.

Psalm 8

¹ WOMB OF LIFE, our Sovereign,
   how exalted is your Name in all the earth!
² Out of the mouths of children and nursing babes
   your majesty is praised above the heavens.
³ You have founded a stronghold against your adversaries,
 . to put an end to the enemy and the avenger.
⁴ When I consider your heavens, the work of your fingers,
   the moon and the stars you have established,
⁵ What are we that you should be mindful of us?
   the woman-born that you attend to them?
⁶ You have made us a little lower than God;
   you adorn us with glory and honor;
⁷ You give us mastery over the works of your hands;
   you put all things under our feet:
⁸ All sheep and oxen,
   even the wild beasts of the field,
⁹ The birds of the air, the fish of the sea,
   and whatsoever walks in the paths of the sea.
¹⁰ WOMB OF LIFE, our Sovereign,
   how exalted is your Name in all the earth!

2 Corinthians 5:16 Now from this moment, we consider no one according to the flesh, even though we once knew Christ according to the flesh; we know him no longer thus. [17] Therefore if anyone is in Christ, there is a new creation; everything old has passed away. Look! Everything has become new! [18] All of this is from God, who reconciled us to God through Christ, and has given us the ministry of reconciliation. [19] That is, in Christ God was reconciling the world to God, not counting their trespasses against them and entrusting the message of reconciliation to us. [20] We are ambassadors for Christ while God appeals through us, we entreat you on behalf of Christ, be reconciled to God. [21] For our sake God made Christ to be sin who knew no sin, so that in Christ we might become the righteousness of God.

Matthew 1:1–16 (alternative)

A genealogy of Jesus Christ, the son of Miriam, the daughter of Anna:

Sarah was the mother of Isaac,

And Rebekah was the mother of Jacob,

Leah was the mother of Judah,

Tamar was the mother of Perez.

The names of the mothers of Hezron, Ram, Amminadab,
    Nahshon, and Salmon have been lost.

Rahab was the mother of Boaz,
    and Ruth was the mother of Obed.

Obed's wife, whose name is unknown, bore Jesse.

The wife of Jesse was the mother of David.

Bathsheba was the mother of Solomon,

Naamah, the Ammonite, was the mother of Rehoboam.

Maacah was the mother of Abijam and the grandmother of Asa.

Azubah was the mother of Jehoshaphat.

The name of Jehoram's mother is unknown.

Athaliah was the mother of Ahaziah,

Zibiah of Beersheba, the mother of Joash.

Jecoliah of Jerusalem bore Uzziah,

Jerusha bore Jotham; Ahaz's mother is unknown.

Abi was the mother of Hezekiah,

Hephzibah was the mother of Manasseh,

Meshullemeth was the mother of Amon,

Jedidah was the mother of Josiah.

Zebidah was the mother of Jehoiakim,

Nehushta was the mother of Jehoiachin,

Hamutal was the mother of Zedekiah.

Then the deportation of Babylon took place.

After the deportation to Babylon

the names of the mothers go unrecorded.

These are their sons:

Jechoniah, Shealtiel, Zerubbabel,

Abiud, Eliakim, Azor and Zadok,

Achim, Eliud, Eleazar,

Matthan, Jacob, and Joseph, the husband of Miriam.

Of her was born Jesus who is called Christ.

The sum of generations is there: fourteen from Sarah to David's mother;

   fourteen from Bathsheba to the Babylonian deportation;

   and fourteen from the Babylonian deportation to Miriam, the mother of Christ.

("A Genealogy of Jesus Christ" was compiled by Ann Patrick Ware of the Women's Liturgy Group of New York, who has graciously put this text in the public domain for all to use.)

PROCLAMATION

Text Notes

God's creation of the human in Genesis 2:7 uses a verb for crafting pottery. "The human," *ha'adam* is a specific distinct creation; later *adam* will refer to humanity as a whole and serve as the name of the first male human. The earth from which this first earthling was crafted is *ha'adamah*.

I use the pronoun "it," lacking in Hebrew, for the first human that has within it what will be called woman, *isshah*, and man, *ish*. The earth-creature will be divided in half to generate the woman and man. The word *tzela* in Genesis 2:22 means "side" and not "rib," used for the sides of the ark and tabernacle in Exodus, sides of the temple in 1 Kings and Ezekiel, and hillsides in 2 Samuel. It is never translated as rib outside of the creation of woman story. In the LXX, *pleuron* also means side, generally in reference to the human body. There are no distinct words for wife and husband in Hebrew. Woman and man are used throughout the text.

There is a pun between Genesis 2:25 and 3:1, between the words for naked, *arom*, and crafty, *arum*; the serpent also changes the "you shall not eat" to an inclusive plural from masculine singular.

In 2 Corinthians 5:16, the verb "to know" is used throughout and translated with slight variability, including "we consider." Its repetition does not work as well in English grammar as in Greek.

Preaching Prompts

The birth of a baby is more than a new life; it can be a renewal of the lives of those around her, a shifting in priorities and perspective. These lessons present the birth of the baby Jesus as a renewal of all human life and so revisit the birth of humanity. And as Christ came to redeem not only humanity but also all creation, the Epistle rejoices in that renewal as well. The rejoicing of the psalm reminds us the world awaiting redemption is already glorious, the good gift and creation of a good and praiseworthy God.

Women are fully half of the people of God in the binary reckoning of the text, though the Genesis lesson and Gospel reading present them essentially only in their capacity as mothers, from Eve the mother of all to the mothers of the Messiah in Anne Ware's reconfigured genealogy. Yet while it makes a certain kind of sense to tell the story of the people of God genealogically, people are more than their potential to reproduce and are more gender-full than the binary acknowledges. Indeed, while the binary pair matches the binary portrait of God in Genesis 1:1–2, "He, God, created," and "She, the Spirit, fluttered," God transcends those categories and the language that would constrain God to them.

Human language in or out of the canon is insufficient to capture God and we, like biblical authors and editors, use our best but ultimately inadequate language. In its, their, gender-full creation, the first human, a nonbinary person, is the very image of God, the work of God's fingers (Psalm 8:7), fully human, equally worthy of redemption as a part of God's creation and adorned with glory (Psalm 8:6).

The epistle's proclamation that we no longer know one another in or by the flesh need not be read as a call to erase (or pretend to erase) differences or render them insignificant. Our renewal and redemption happen in these bodies of flesh with all of their expressions, not from them. Rather, God sanctifies human flesh, making it her, their, holy habitation.

FEAST OF THE HOLY NAME, JANUARY 1

Isaiah 7:3–16; Psalm 89:1–8, 14; Philippians 2:5–11; Luke 2:15–21

Isaiah 7:3 The HOLY ONE said to Isaiah, "Go out now to meet Ahaz, you and She'arjashub your son, at the end of the conduit of the upper pool on the highway to the Fuller's Field, 4 and say to him, 'Watch, hush, and fear not, and let not your heart faint on account of these two smoldering stumps of firebrands, because of the rage of Rezin and Aram or the son of Remaliah. 5 For indeed, Aram has plotted evil against you—with Ephraim and the son of Remaliah—saying, 6 'Let us go up against Judah and cut off Jerusalem and conquer it for ourselves and make the son of Tabeel king in it;' 7 therefore thus says the Sovereign GOD:

'It shall not stand,
and it shall not come to pass.
8 For the head of Aram is Damascus,
and the head of Damascus is Rezin.'
(In about sixty-five years Ephraim will be shattered, no longer a people.)

⁹ The head of Ephraim is Samaria,

and the head of Samaria is the son of Remaliah.

If you do not stand firm in faith,

you shall not stand firm at all.'"

¹⁰ Again the HOLY ONE spoke to Ahaz, saying, ¹¹ "Ask a sign of the HOLY ONE your God; from the deep of Sheol or the height of what lies above." ¹² Yet Ahaz said, "I will not ask, and I will not test the HOLY ONE." ¹³ Then Isaiah said, "Hear now, House of David! Is it not enough that you exhaust mortals, that you must exhaust my God also? ¹⁴ Therefore the selfsame Creator will give you a sign. See, the young woman is pregnant and she shall give birth to a son, and she shall name him Immanu-El. ¹⁵ He shall eat curds and honey when he knows how to refuse the evil and choose the good. ¹⁶ For before the child knows how to refuse the evil and choose the good, the land before whose two kings you dread will be deserted."

Psalm 89:1–8, 14

¹ I will sing of the faithful love of the FOUNT OF LIFE forever;

with my mouth I will make known your faithfulness from across the generations.

² When I declare that your faithful love is established forever;

your faithfulness is established in the heavens,

³ [you responded,] "I have inscribed a covenant with my chosen one;

I have sworn an oath to the descendants of Bathsheba:

⁴ 'I will establish your line forever,

your throne that I will build, will be to all generations.'"

⁵ The heavens confess your wonders, O WOMB OF CREATION,

and to your faithfulness in the congregation of the holy ones;

⁶ For who in the skies can be compared to the WOMB OF LIFE?

who is like the MOTHER OF ALL among the children of the gods?

⁷ a dread God in the council of the holy ones,

great and terrible above all who surround her.

⁸ WARRIOR PROTECTRIX, who is mighty like you?

YOU WHO ARE, your faithfulness surrounds you.

¹⁴ Righteousness and justice are the foundations of your throne;

enduring love and faithfulness go before your face.

Philippians 2:5 Let the same mind be in you all that was in Christ Jesus,

⁶ who, though he was in the form of God,

did not regard equality with God

as something to be seized,

⁷ but emptied himself,

taking the form of a slave,

being born in human likeness;
    then being found in human form,
8 he humbled himself
    and became obedient to the point of death,
    even death on a cross.
9 Therefore God also highly exalted Jesus
    and gave him the name
    that is above every name,
10 so that at the name of Jesus
    every heavenly and earthly knee should bend,
    along with those under the earth,
11 and every tongue should confess
    that Jesus Christ is Savior,
    to the glory of God the Sovereign.

Luke 2:15 And it happened when the angels had departed from them into heaven, the shepherds said to one another, "Let us go now to Bethlehem and see this thing that has come to be, which the Sovereign God has made known to us." 16 So they came hurrying and found Mary and Joseph, and the baby lying in the manger. 17 Now seeing this, they made known what had been spoken to them about this child. 18 And all who heard marveled at what was spoken by the shepherds to them. 19 But Mary preserved all these words and pondered them in her heart. 20 The shepherds returned, glorifying and praising God for all they had heard and seen, it was just as it had been told them.

    21 After eight days had passed, it was time to circumcise the child; and he was called Jesus, his name was the name given by the angel before he was conceived in the womb.

PROCLAMATION

Text Notes

Isaiah's son's name means "a remnant will survive." He is a prophetic sign in the text. The stem that means "cut off" in Isaiah 7:6 also means "terrorize." Hebrew hearers would have recognized both meanings. "Faith" in verse 9 and throughout the Hebrew Bible is more "faithfulness" than "belief in." Here belief is a significant portion of the faithfulness called for. The young woman, an *almah*, in 7:14 is not identified as a virgin, *betulah*. The text does not even stipulate that this is her first child. Many scholars, myself included, consider it possible that she was also the mother of Isaiah's (other) children with equally portentous names, She'ar Yashuv in 7:4 and Maher Shalal Hash Baz in 8:3. The woman's pregnancy is contemporaneous with Isaiah; she *is* pregnant, a descriptive adjective. The word "virgin" and the use of a future tense come from the LXX, rather than the Hebrew text, effectively transforming the text to read more easily as a prediction of Jesus.

In the traditional language of Psalm 89:3 God swears an oath to "David, my servant." Note that Bathsheba indeed has her own throne, symbolically if not literally passed down to the Judean Queen Mothers, see 1 Kings 2:19. The children of the gods refer to any number of divine or semidivine beings from other gods to angels depending on the age and redaction of the text. Warrior Protectrix in verse 8 is God of "hosts" or warriors.

Preaching Prompts

While biblical prophecy can include prediction, it is also at its heart contemporaneous, interpreting the present and speaking to the people for God as well as speaking to God on behalf of the people. While the framers of the New Testament, and likely the followers of Jesus, interpreted Isaiah 7:14 with reference to Jesus, they did not negate its original meaning in its original context. They interpreted it in their contemporary context as we ought, affirming both interpretations.

Read in context, Isaiah 7:14 is not a prediction but a demonstration of God's reliable fidelity, available in each generation. The young woman in Isaiah is already pregnant. By the time her child is eating soft foods, the two nations threatening Judah will be gone. The presence of Isaiah's son "A Remnant Shall Survive" is a promise that Judah will not be destroyed while those two nations decline. The promise is faithful, as is the God who made it.

Psalm 89 celebrates the eternal faithfulness of God, in this translation, expressing that *through* Bathsheba rather than *to* David. Such a reading does not redeem her rape; it does keep her centered in the story in which she continues to play a part.

Philippians 2 and Luke 2 are each traditional readings for the Feast of the Holy Name of Jesus observed on January 1. They celebrate the majesty of the name given by angels and the humble majesty of its bearer.

SECOND SUNDAY AFTER CHRISTMAS

Micah 4:5–10, 13a; Psalm 9:1–2, 7–11, 13–14; Galatians 4:1–7; John 1:1–5

Micah 4:5 All the peoples walk,
  each one in the name of their god,
  yet we will walk in the name of the AGELESS ONE our God
  forever and ever.
6 In that day—(a prophetic) utterance of the COMPASSIONATE ONE—
  I will assemble the lame
  and I shall gather those who have been driven away,
  and those whom I have harmed.
7 I will transform the lame into a remnant,

and the outcast into a strong nation;

and the MAJESTIC ONE shall reign over them in Mount Zion

from now on and forever.

8 And you, Migdal Eder (Watchtower of the Flock),

Hill of Daughter Zion, to you it shall come,

the former dominion shall come,

the queenship of Daughter Jerusalem.

9 Now, why do you scream, shout?

Is there no sovereign in you?

Has your counselor perished,

that you have been seized by writhing-pain like a woman birthing?

10 Writhe and let loose, Daughter Zion,

like a woman in labor;

for now you shall go forth from the city

and dwell in the open country.

You shall go to Babylon;

there you shall be rescued.

There the SAVING GOD will redeem you

from the hand of your enemies.

13 Rise and thresh Daughter Zion!

For I will make your horn iron and your hoofs bronze.

Psalm 9:1–2, 7–11, 13–14

1 I will give thanks to the GOD WHO SAVES with my whole heart;

I will tell of all your wonderful deeds.

2 I will rejoice and exult in you;

I will sing praise to your name, Most High.

7 GOD WHO IS MAJESTY sits enthroned forever,

she has established her throne for judgment.

8 She judges the world in righteousness;

she judges the peoples with equity.

9 SHE WHO IS FAITHFUL is a stronghold for the oppressed,

a stronghold in times of trouble.

10 They trust you, they who know your name,

for you do not forsake those who seek you, REDEEMING GOD.

11 Sing praises to the HOLY ONE enthroned in Zion.

Declare her deeds among the peoples.

13 Be gracious to me, GRACIOUS ONE.

See what I suffer from those who hate me.

You lift me up from the gates of death,

¹⁴ so that I may recount all your praises,
and in the gates of Daughter Zion,
rejoice in your salvation.

Galatians 4:1 I say that as long as heirs are minors, they are no better than slaves, though they are the masters of all; ² but they remain under guardians and trustees until the time set by the sovereign. ³ So also for us; while we were minors, we were enslaved by the constitutive elements of the world. ⁴ But when the fullness of time had come, God sent God's own Son, born of a woman, born under the law, ⁵ to redeem those who were under the law, so that we might receive adoption like children. ⁶ And because you are children, God has sent the Spirit of God's own Son into our hearts, crying, "Abba! Father!" ⁷ So you are no longer a slave but a child, and if a child then also an heir, through God.

John 1:1 In the beginning was the Word, and the Word was with God, and the Word was God. ² The Word was with God in the beginning. ³ Everything came into being through the Word, and without the Word not one thing came into being that came into being. What has come into being ⁴ in the Word was life, and that life was the light of all people. ⁵ The light shines in the bleakness, and the bleakness did not overtake it.

PROCLAMATION

Text Notes

The expressions *bat Zion* and *bat Jerusalem* can be translated as either "Daughter" or "daughter of" Zion or Jerusalem. Most often as here in Micah 4, Jerusalem/Zion is personified as God's daughter. Translators differ significantly on the nature of monarchal renewal in Micah 4:8: the kingship of Jerusalem's Daughter (Alter); the kingship of Fair Jerusalem; the sovereignty of daughter Jerusalem (NRSV); the royal power belonging to Daughter Zion (CEB); the kingdom shall come to the daughter of Jerusalem (KJV). While the text may indicate a return to Israel's monarchy, it may also signify the restoration of Jerusalem as a royal daughter herself. The second is my reading, hence "queenship."

The second verb in Micah 4:10 is unclear, *gochi* appears to be a form of *g-y-ch*, "to burst out." Translations vary significantly: "groan" (NRSV, Alter), "scream" (JPS, CEB), "labor" (KJV). Alternative manuscript traditions are equally varied: "be courageous" (LXX), "tremble" (Targum), and "be strong" (Peshitta).

In general, this volume will preserve "Father" in the Gospel when Jesus says it with reference to paternity.

Likewise, this volume will not whitewash slavery in the text and its world by softening it to servitude. That the enslaved could be beaten, killed, raped, and forced to breed more enslaved persons makes clear that slavery and its vocabulary is the appropriate translation for the assorted terms across the canon. The implications of slave language as normative in the text is something with which readers and hearers must wrestle honestly, particularly in light of the transatlantic trafficking of human persons and legacy of the American slavocracy, including in churches and denominations.

Preaching Prompts

Micah offers a vision of fidelity to God in a world where other people worship their own God. Though often cast as exclusively monotheistic, the Hebrew Scriptures are henotheistic, acknowledging other gods and their worship while calling for fidelity to one, often couched in terms of the superiority of that one. Christianity has a long history of imperialization and forced conversion building on conquest narratives in the Hebrew Bible, yet Micah offers a vision of a diverse plurality where those who believe and practice differently are not conquered or converted by force as the Church has so often done to its shame.

That vision is in the context of long-awaited restoration symbolized by childbirth. God is birthing a redeemed people, though in the metaphor Zion, Jerusalem, is the woman in labor. Inasmuch as Daughter Zion is God's daughter, God might be likened to a grandparent, evoking the way God is named in some indigenous cultures, including here in the Americas, Grandmother and Grandfather God. Redemption, like birth, only comes through bloody pain. Jerusalem's pain is the Babylonian occupation and deportation. The Christmas story that we are still telling in this season is also a story of redemption in the context of oppression. And while some early church writers imagine a somewhat more-than-human Blessed Virgin who conceived without pleasure and birthed without pain—revealing more about their discomfort with women's sexual and reproductive lives than the Christmas story—redemption through Christ comes with blood and pain at the beginning and end of his earthly life.

The psalm celebrates the God who saves, who saves from death, who will save Zion, and the Epistle proclaims the God who saves all through a literal, not metaphorical, woman and birth. The Gospel tells the story of Christ in cosmic terms without the blood and birth; the Word who exists beyond time.

FEAST OF THE EPIPHANY

Isaiah 60:1–6, 11; Psalm 67; 2 Timothy 1:5–10; Matthew 2:1–12

Isaiah 60:1 Arise, daughter; shine, daughter; for your light has come, daughter,
and the glory of the Holy One has risen upon you, daughter.
2 For—watch now, daughter!—bleakness shall cover the earth,
and thick bleakness the peoples;
and upon you, daughter, the Holy One will arise,
and over you, daughter, God's glory will appear.

³ Nations shall come to your light, daughter,
and monarchs to the brightness of your dawn, daughter.
⁴ Lift your eyes round about, daughter, and see;
all of them gather, they come to you, daughter;
daughter, your sons shall come from far away,
and your daughters shall be carried on their nurses' hips.
⁵ Then, daughter, you shall see and be radiant;
your heart, daughter, shall tremble and swell,
because the abundance of the sea shall turn toward you, daughter,
the wealth of the nations shall come to you, daughter.
⁶ A multitude of camels shall cover you, daughter—
young camels of Midian and Ephah—
all those from Sheba shall come.
They shall bring gold and frankincense,
and shall proclaim the praises of the Holy One.
¹¹ Your gates shall always be open, daughter;
day and night they shall not be shut,
so that nations shall bring you their wealth, daughter,
being led by their monarchs.

Psalm 67

¹ May God be merciful to us and bless us,
show us the light of her countenance and come to us.
² Let your ways be known upon earth,
your saving health among all nations.
³ Let the peoples praise you, O God;
let all the peoples praise you.
⁴ Let the nations be glad and sing for joy,
for you judge the peoples with equity
and guide all the nations upon earth.
⁵ Let the peoples praise you, O God;
let all the peoples praise you.
⁶ The earth has brought forth her increase;
may God, our own God, give us her blessing.
⁷ May God give us her blessing,
and may all the ends of the earth stand in awe of her.

2 Timothy 1:5 Considering the recollection of your faith without pretense, a faith that lived first in your grandmother Lois and your mother Eunice, now I am persuaded that faith lives in you. ⁶ For this reason I remind you to reignite the gift of God that is within you through the laying on of my hands; [7] for God did not give us a spirit of cowardice, but one of power and of love and of self-control.

[8] Be not ashamed, then, of the testimony of our Savior or of me Christ's prisoner, rather share in suffering for the sake of the gospel, do so through the power of God, [9] who saved us and called us with a holy calling, not according to our works, rather according to God's own purpose and grace which was given to us in Christ Jesus before the ages began. [10] Now it has been revealed through the appearing of our Savior Christ Jesus, who negated death and brought life and immortality to light through the gospel.

Matthew 2:1 Now Jesus was born in Bethlehem of Judea in the days of King Herod. Suddenly sages from the East came to Jerusalem, [2] asking, "Where is the one born king of the Judeans? For we have seen his star at its ascent and have come to reverence him." [3] When King Herod heard this, he was shaken, and all Jerusalem with him; [4] then calling together all the chief priests and religious scholars of the people, he inquired of them where the Messiah would be born. [5] They said to him, "In Bethlehem of Judea; for it has been written by the prophet:

[6] *'And you, Bethlehem, in the land of Judah,*
by no means are least among the rulers of Judah;
for from you shall come a ruler
who is to shepherd my people Israel.'"

[7] Then Herod secretly called for the sages and learned from them the time when the star had appeared. [8] Then he sent them to Bethlehem, saying, "Go, search diligently for the child, and when you have found him bring me word so that I may also go and reverence him." [9] When they had heard the king they left, and there suddenly was the star that they had seen at its ascent going before them until it stopped over the place where the child was. [10] When they saw that the star had stopped, they rejoiced; their joy was exuberant. [11] On entering the house, they saw the child with Mary his mother; and they fell down and reverenced him. Then, opening their treasure, they offered him gifts of gold, frankincense, and myrrh. [12] And having been warned in a dream not to return to Herod, they left for their own country by another road.

PROCLAMATION
Text Notes
Isaiah 60 speaks to a feminine entity, Zion, Jerusalem, frequently styled as God's daughter; each "you" and "your" is explicitly feminine and singular, rhythmic and repetitive in Hebrew. I have added "daughter" each place this occurs for the English speaker-reader-hearer. The daughters in verse 4 were already delineated; "hips" here is actually "side."

Bleakness: The thick bleakness of Isaiah 60:2 is the same (word) as the thick darkness in which God is veiled in other texts, i.e., Exodus 20:21; Deuteronomy 4:11, 5:22; 2 Samuel 22:10; 1 Kings 8:12.

"Spirit of fear" is a familiar and common translation of 2 Timothy 1:7. *Deilia* is cowardice, an important distinction. Fear is not a failing. It is a natural and healthy response. It is harmful to tell folks not to feel what they feel. What matters is how folk respond to fear.

Grammatically speaking not all of the *magoi* need be male, only one; note: no number of sages is specified. "Religious scholars" is preferable to scribes, which can suggest copyists. The Gospel famously quotes Micah 5:2 that a ruler with ancient origins shall come from Bethlehem of Judah. There is a variant to that text which states that out of Bethlehem of Judah "one shall not come forth" to rule. It is worth considering that both traditions were known at the time of the setting and production of the Gospel. The line "least among the rulers" is specific to the Gospel; it is among the "thousands," i.e., clans in Hebrew and Aramaic (Targum and Peshitta). LXX employs a different word for ruler, *archon* vs. *hegemon*.

The word *Ioudaioi* is regularly translated "Jews" but also means "Judeans" in an age where an ethnic name referred to a people, their land, language, and religion(s). "Judean" is often a preferable reading to "Jew" or "the Jews," which in contemporary discourse have often become an epithet in the mouths of anti-Semites. Further, the distinction is a helpful reminder that the Gospels refer to the Judeans of its world and not the Jewish communities of ours.

Preaching Prompts

These lessons frame a number of epiphanies: God's self-revelation and that of Christ to the world beyond Israel in Isaiah 60 and Psalm 67, in the traditional Epiphany gospel, Matthew 2, and in 2 Timothy 1. These epiphanies are manifest in or accompanied by light, sometimes set in opposition to darkness, sometimes paired with it, requiring thoughtful exegesis in a world in which darkness and blackness are regularly equated with Black and Brown people set in opposition to whiteness and white people.

In the commentary on Isaiah 60 in the *Jewish Study Bible*, Benjamin Sommer observes a shift from the traditional pattern centering on a male monarch as a royal figure. Rather God's daughter-city Zion is the locus of liberation wrought by God without human delegation. This is a helpful alternative to the common veneration of monarchy and the fallible members of David's lineage. Similarly, it is God and not a human who judges women and men, "the peoples," with equity, in the psalm.

It is worth asking how the women in and behind these texts experienced and articulated their epiphanies. The promises of restoration and reunification to daughter Jerusalem can be heard as the promises to the daughters of Jerusalem: the mothers, wives, sisters, and daughters of those who are in exile and captivity. Lois and Eunice in 1 Timothy have their own stories of faith. What might they have told us in their own epistle if they had not been relegated to grandmother and mother? (Note the absence of Timothy's male lineage.) These texts offer an opportunity to proclaim the ways in which God is manifest in the world in and beyond the scriptures, in old ways and new.

EPIPHANY I

Isaiah 52:1–10; Psalm 36:5–10; 1 Corinthians 1:26–31; Luke 2:41–51

Isaiah 52:1 Awake daughter, awake!
 Don your strength, daughter Zion!
 Don your beautiful garments, daughter,
 Jerusalem, the holy city;
 for no more shall the uncircumcised
 and the unclean enter you, daughter.
2 Shake yourself from the dust, daughter, rise up,
 Jerusalem, sit on your throne.
 Loose the bonds from your neck,
 captive daughter Zion!
3 For so says the SAVING GOD:
 For nothing were you all sold, and for no cost shall you all be redeemed.
4 For so says the SOVEREIGN GOD:
 First my people went down to Egypt to sojourn there as aliens, then Assyria—without cause—oppressed them. 5 So now, what am I doing here
 —utters the GOD WHO SEES—
 seeing that my people are taken without cause? Their rulers howl
 —utters the GOD WHO HEARS—

and continually, all day long, my Name is despised. 6 Therefore my people shall know my Name; therefore in that day they shall know that it is I who speak; here am I.

7 How beautiful upon the mountains
 are the feet of one who brings good news,
 proclaiming peace,
 bringing good news,
 proclaiming salvation,
 who says to Zion, "Your God reigns, daughter."
8 Daughter, the sound of your sentinels, lifting their voice!
 As one they sing for joy;

for from one eye to another they see
the return of the HOLY ONE OF SINAI to Zion.
⁹ Revel! Raise a song together,
you ruins of Jerusalem.
For the HOLY ONE OF OLD has comforted God's people,
God has redeemed Jerusalem.
¹⁰ The MIGHTY GOD has bared a holy arm
before the eyes of all the nations;
and all the ends of the earth shall see
the salvation of our God.

Psalm 36:5–10

⁵ HOLY ONE, throughout the very heavens is your faithful love,
your faithfulness beyond the clouds.
⁶ Your righteousness is like the eternal mountains,
your judgments are like the mighty deep;
you save humankind and animalkind alike, FAITHFUL ONE.
⁷ How precious is your faithful love, O God!
All the woman-born take shelter in the shadow of your wings.
⁸ They feast on the abundance of your house,
and you give them drink from the river of your delights.
⁹ For with you is the fountain of life;
in your light we see light.
¹⁰ Extend your faithful love to those who know you,
and your justice to the upright of heart!

1 Corinthians 1:26 Now look to your own call, sisters and brothers: not many of you were wise by mortal standards, not many were powerful, not many were highborn. ²⁷ Rather, God chose what is foolish in the world to shame the wise and God chose what is weak in the world to shame the strong. ²⁸ And what is insignificant in the world and what is despised God chose, to eradicate what is, ²⁹ so that no mortal can boast in the presence of God. ³⁰ God is the source of your life in Christ Jesus, who became for us Wisdom from God, and righteousness and sanctification and redemption, ³¹ in order that, as it is written, "Let the she or he who boasts, boast in the Messiah."

Luke 2:41 Now, the parents of Jesus went yearly to Jerusalem for the festival of Passover. ⁴² And when he was twelve years old, they went up as customary for the festival. ⁴³ And when the days of the festival were completed, they returned while the boy Jesus stayed in Jerusalem, and his parents did not know it. ⁴⁴ Thinking he was in the group of travelers, they went a day's journey and then they started to look for him among their kin and those who knew him. ⁴⁵ And when they did not find him, they returned to Jerusalem to search for him. ⁴⁶ Then after three days passed they found him in the temple, sitting among the teachers, listening to them and asking them questions. [47] And all who heard him were amazed at his understanding and his answers. [48] Then when his parents saw him, they were shocked and his mother said to him, "Child, why have you treated us thus? Look! Your father and I have been tormented in searching for you." [49] Then Jesus said to them, "Why were you searching for me? Did you not know that I must be in the house of my Abba?" [50] And they did not understand the thing he said to them. [51] And then, he went down with them and came to Nazareth and was subject to them. And his mother treasured all these things in her heart.

PROCLAMATION

Text Notes

Addresses to Zion and Jerusalem are often in the feminine as they are here. I use "daughter" to make the occurrences visible to the English reader where it is not explicit, as in verse 2. In verse 2 a dot (like a period or over a lowercase "i") distinguishes the command "sit!" to a feminine subject (KJV, JPS, and Alter following the Targum and LXX) from "captive" (NRSV and CEB); the "jot" of "jots and tittles" (see Matthew 5:18 in KJV). Further, the Targum has "on your glorious throne" picked up by Alter, included in brackets in JPS, both without "glorious." My translation follows suit. Verses 3 and 4 address the people collectively, verses 7 and 8 return to the feminine singular daughter Zion, and in verse 9 it is the plural "ruins of Jerusalem" that are addressed. "No cost" in verse 3 is "no silver" or "no money." In verse 8 "sentinels" is a synonym for prophets.

"Mortal standards" in 1 Corinthians 1:26 is "according to the flesh," the term repeats in verse 28.

Preaching Prompts

Epiphany is a season of light and life. The poet-prophet continuing Isaiah's work proffers a vision of salvation that brings both light and life to Jerusalem configured as God's daughter. This redemption is for Jerusalem alone, yet it is performed in the sight of all the nations, with "eyes" and "seeing" prominent, setting the stage for a more expansive proclamation of salvation. The psalm provides it. Here, God's love extends to the heavens and salvation is for humankind with no ethnic or national limitations and for animalkind as well. In the Epistle, it is the life of the believer that is seen in the world and ultimately, in the presence of God where the believer will be truly seen (but not heard boasting of anything but Christ). In the Gospel reading, the mundane life of the child Christ is revealed to be something more than mundane.

The way of salvation is slowly being revealed and is in conversation and some degree of continuity with the teaching of the elders at whose feet Jesus sits and learns. While often described and portrayed as "Jesus teaching the elders," a not-so-subtle denigration of Jewish knowledge, Jesus sits among the elders of his people respectfully, learning with the audacity and precociousness of children.

Daughter Zion is an archetype rooted in patriarchal and paternalistic notions of parenthood and the value and vulnerability of daughters. While later elevated to a virtually unattainable archetype, here Mary is a worried mother and one who gives her child a surprising amount of room, a full day to wander among the travelling group out of her direct sight before she goes to find him. Their cotravelers are unidentified, but they are like her and Joseph and Jesus, fellow Jews, women and men and children who can make the trip. One might imagine that Jesus's sisters (Matthew 13:56; Mark 6:3), along with his brothers (Matthew 13:55)—depending on when they were born—and Mary's own sister (John 19:25) were among them.

Lastly, the identification of Jesus with the feminine Wisdom (in both Hebrew and Greek) creates a gender-full or gender-fluid portrait of the (more than) human Jesus and the preexistent Christ.

EPIPHANY II

Isaiah 62:1–7, 10–12; Psalm 18:2–11, 16–19;
2 Corinthians 6:2–10; Matthew 3:1–6, 11–17

Isaiah 62:1 For the sake of Zion I will not keep silent,
 and for the sake of Jerusalem I will not keep still,
 until her vindication shines out like blazing light,
 and her salvation like a flaming torch.
2 The nations shall see your vindication, daughter,
 and all the monarchs your glory;
 and you shall be called by a new name
 that the mouth of the LIVING GOD will grant.
3 You, daughter, shall be a crown of beauty in the hand of God Most High,
 and a royal diadem in the hand of your God.
4 Daughter, no more shall you be called Forsaken,
 and no more shall your land be called Devastated;
 but you shall be called My Delight Is in Her,
 and your land, Married;
 for the FAITHFUL GOD delights in you,
 and your land shall be married.
5 For as a young man marries a virgin girl,
 so shall your builder marry you daughter,
 and as the bridegroom rejoices over the bride,
 so shall your God rejoice over you.

⁶ Upon your walls, daughter Jerusalem,
   I have posted sentinels;
   all the day and all the night,
   they shall never be silent.
   You who remind the GOD WHO SEES,
   take no rest for yourselves,
⁷ and give God no rest
   until God establishes Jerusalem
   and makes it renowned throughout the earth.
¹⁰ Go through, go through the gates!
   Prepare the way for the people!
   Build up, build up the highway;
   throw away (the loose) stones,
   lift up a banner over the peoples.
¹¹ Look! The GOD WHO SAVES has made it heard
   to the end of the earth:
   Say to daughter Zion,
   "See, your salvation comes;
   bringing reward and recompense first."
¹² They shall call them, "The Holy People,
   The Redeemed of the GOD WHO SAVES";
   and you, daughter, shall be called, "Sought Out,
   A City Not Forsaken."

Psalm 18:2–11, 16–19

² The ROCK WHO GAVE US BIRTH is my rock,
   and my fortress, and my deliverer,
   my God, my rock in whom I take refuge,
   my shield, and the horn of my salvation, my stronghold.
³ I call upon the HOLY ONE, may she be praised,
   and from my enemies I shall be saved.
⁴ The snares of death encompassed me;
   the rivers of wickedness assailed me.
⁵ The snares of Sheol encircled me;
   the snares of death confronted me.
⁶ In my distress I called upon SHE WHO HEARS;
   to my God I cried for help.
   From her temple she heard my voice,
   and my cry came before her, to her ears.

7 Then the earth shuddered and quaked;
  the foundations also of the mountains trembled
  and were shaken because of her anger.
8 Smoke went up from her nostrils,
  and consuming fire from her mouth;
  burning coals blazed forth from her.
9 She spread out the heavens, and descended;
  thick darkness was under her feet.
10 She mounted up on a cherub, and flew;
  she soared upon the wings of the wind.
11 She made darkness her veil around her,
  her canopy dark waters and thick clouds.
16 She reached down from on high, she took me;
  she drew me out of the multitude of water.
17 She delivered me from my strong enemy,
  and from those who hate me;
  for they were too mighty for me.
18 They confronted me in the day of my calamity;
  yet the SHELTERING GOD was my support.
19 She brought me out into a broad place;
  she delivered me, because she delights in me.

2 Corinthians 6:2 God says,

> *"At an acceptable time have I hearkened to you,*
> *and on the day of salvation have I helped you."*

Look! Now is the acceptable time; see, now is the day of salvation! 3 In no way, none, are we giving cause for offense, so there will be no reproach against ministry. 4 Rather, in every way have we commended ourselves as servants of God: through much endurance, in tribulations, in distress, in calamities, 5 in beatings, in imprisonments, in tumults, in labors, in sleepless nights, in hunger; 6 in purity, in knowledge, in patience, in kindness, in holiness of spirit, in love without pretense, 7 in truthful speech, and in the power of God; with the weapons of righteousness for the right hand and for the left; 8 amid honor and dishonor, amid slander and renown; as deceitful and yet genuine; 9 as unknown, and yet well known; as dying, and look! We are alive; as punished, and yet not killed; 10 as sorrowful, yet always rejoicing; as poor, yet making many rich; as having nothing, and yet possessing everything.

Matthew 3:1 In those days John the Baptizer appeared preaching in the wilderness of Judea, 2 and saying, "Repent, for the realm of the heavens is near." 3 This is the one of whom the prophet Isaiah spoke when he said,

"The voice of one crying out in the wilderness:
'Prepare the way of the Most High,
make God's paths straight.'"

[4] Now John had for his clothing camel's hair with a leather belt around his waist, and his food was locusts and wild honey. [5] Then the women and men of Jerusalem and all Judea were going out to him, and the whole region of the Jordan, [6] and they were baptized in the river Jordan by him, confessing their sins.

[11] "Indeed, I baptize you with water for repentance, but after me is coming one more powerful than I; I am not worthy to carry his sandals. He will baptize you with the Holy Spirit and fire. [12] His winnowing fork is in his hand, and he will clear his threshing-floor and will gather his wheat into the granary; but the chaff he will burn with unquenchable fire."

[13] Then Jesus came from Galilee to John at the Jordan, to be baptized by him. [14] John forbade him, saying, "I need to be baptized by you, yet you come to me?" [15] But Jesus answered him, "Let it go now; for this way is proper for us to fulfill all righteousness." Then John let it go. [16] Now when Jesus had been baptized, just as he came up from the water, suddenly the heavens were opened to him and he saw the Spirit of God, she descended like a dove and came upon on him. [17] And a voice from the heavens said, "This is my Son, the Beloved, with whom I am well pleased."

PROCLAMATION

Text Notes

The use of "daughter" in Isaiah 62 makes the divine address to a feminine subject, Zion, in verses 1–6 accessible to English readers as it is to those who read in Hebrew. The end of verse 6 addresses the people, or some among them, as a collective.

The poetry of verse 4 is impossible to replicate in English; note the four assonant three-syllable words: *Azuvah, Shamamah, Hephzibah,* and *Be'ulah* (not Beu-lah) and the corresponding lack of rhyme or rhythm in their translations: "Forsaken," "Devastated," "My Delight is in Her," and "Married." The pattern recurs in verse 12 with *D'rushah* and *Ir Lo Ne'etzavah*: "Sought Out" and "A City Not Forsaken."

The verb "marry" in Isaiah 62:4–5 is *ba'al,* which also means lord/master as a noun. (It may be familiar as the divine title for the god Ba'al, whose proper name, Haddu, is not generally used.) While the verb suggests a very hierarchal understanding of marriage, it is rarely used in the canon (five times for humans and in eleven divine metaphors). Sentinels, as in Isaiah 62:6, are often synonymous with prophets. Verse 10 uses the verb for stoning people for clearing the road. In verse 11 it appears the ends of the earth speak to Daughter Zion as the command to speak to her is plural.

In Psalm 18:2 I draw the divine name from Deuteronomy 32:18, "You neglected the Rock that gave birth to you, you forgot the God who writhed in birth-labor for you." Verse 3 of the psalm has the passive "be praised" without supporting grammar.

Other translators have added "*worthy to* be praised." Some translations render verse 3 in the future, see NRSV and KJV; however, the introduction makes clear David is reflecting on his past deliverance. The imperfect here is more present, i.e., because of God's faithfulness, whenever I call on God as before, I shall be saved.

Second Corinthians 6:2 quotes Isaiah 49:8.

Matthew 3:3 is famously muddled. Hebrew says: A voice cries, "In the wilderness prepare . . ." LXX and NT have: A voice cries in the wilderness: "Prepare . . ." The "people" coming to be baptized in Matthew 3:5 were women and men. It may be a useful exercise to make all of the human plurals explicitly women and men in study and teaching to note how often women are present but buried in the text. "Let it go," in Matthew 3:15 is to release an obligation, including divorce, or here, an objection.

Preaching Prompts

These Epiphany readings focus on salvation, God's history of delivering her people and God's plan of salvation incarnate in Jesus. In Isaiah 62 postdestruction Jerusalem will be rejoiced over as though she were a virgin bride; she, her land, will be married. Remembering that these metaphors are drawn from the experiences of women, this text offers a way to talk about life after trauma, including rape and other dehumanizing acts. Jerusalem's vindication can be read as the vanquishing of shame given her capture and ravishment deliberately invoke the rhetoric of rape. Those addressing the historic context might take note of the reluctance to address the violations of Israel's/Jerusalem's women and contemporary reluctance to address sexual violence even with the recent advances of the #MeToo movement.

The occasion of Psalm 18 is David's escape from Saul; that introduction takes up the first verse in Hebrew. The psalm proper begins with "He said," often included with the introductory verse. David's "love" in what is now verse 1, as Christian translations number the psalms, is *racham*, mother-love, love that is rooted in the womb, *rechem*, and otherwise used only by God to express her love. From David we should perhaps read it as gesturing toward a reciprocal love that originates deep within.

The Epistle rests on the foundation of God's acts of deliverance. It is a chastened affirmation, held through times of tribulation as well as times of celebration. The (invisible) women and men for whom the writer speaks bear witness to the promise of God, even at the cost of their lives, as did John the Baptizer.

The children of Abraham in Matthew 3:9 include the children of Hagar, Sarah, Keturah, and perhaps other women. This family saga can be an opportunity to talk about the disparities between these matriarchs, the complexity of families, especially blended ones, favoritism and rejection, or the many peoples of the One God. The families of the patriarchs were built through forced impregnation of enslaved women. Against this background, the ability of women to choose baptism and discipleship matters.

FEAST OF THE PRESENTATION, FEBRUARY 2

(The Feast falls variably in early Epiphany. For simplicity and consistency, it is placed after the Second Sunday of Epiphany in these volumes).

Leviticus 12:1–8; Psalm 48:1–3, 9–14; 1 John 5:1–5; Luke 2:22–38

Leviticus 12:1 The HOLY ONE OF SINAI spoke to Moses, saying: [2] Speak to the women and men of Israel, saying:

When a woman conceives and gives birth to a male, she shall be taboo seven days; as during the days of her menstruation, she shall be taboo. [3] On the eighth day the flesh of his foreskin shall be circumcised. [4] Then, thirty and three days shall she sit in blood purification; she shall not touch any holy thing, or come into the sanctuary, until the days of her restoration are fulfilled. [5] Now, if she gives birth to a female, she shall be taboo two weeks, as in her menstruation; her time of blood purification shall be sixty-six days.

[6] On completing the days of her purification for a daughter or for a son she shall bring a yearling lamb for a burnt offering—and a pigeon or a turtledove for a sin offering—to the priest at the entrance of the tent of meeting. [7] Then he shall offer it before the FIRE OF SINAI and make atonement on her behalf and she shall be restored from her flow of blood. This is the teaching for the woman who gives birth to a female or male. [8] If she cannot afford a sheep, she shall take two turtledoves or two pigeons, one for a burnt offering and the second for a sin offering; and the priest shall make atonement on her behalf, and she shall be restored.

Psalm 48:1–3, 9–14

[1] Great is the AGELESS GOD and greatly praised,
 in the city of our God is God's holy mountain.
[2] Beautiful in elevation, the joy of all the earth,
 Mount Zion, in the far north,
 is the city of the great Sovereign.
[3] Within her citadels God
 has made herself known as a bulwark.
[9] We contemplate your faithful love, God,
 in the midst of your temple.
[10] Like your Name, God, your praise,
 reaches to the ends of the earth.
 Your right hand is filled with righteousness.
[11] Let Mount Zion be glad,
 let the towns of Judah rejoice
 because of your judgments.
[12] Go about Zion, go all around her;
 count her towers.

¹³ Set your hearts upon her ramparts;
    go through her citadels,
    that you may recount to the next generation:
¹⁴ For this God is our God, our God forever and ever.
    She will be our guide until we die.

1 John 5:1 Everyone who believes that Jesus is the Messiah is born of God, and everyone who loves the parent loves the child of the parent. ² By this we know that we love the children of God, when we love God and undertake God's commandments. ³ For the love of God is this, that we keep God's commandments. And God's commandments are not difficult, ⁴ for anything born of God conquers the world. And this is the victory that conquers the world, our faith. ⁵ Who is it that conquers the world but the one who believes that Jesus is the Son of God?

Luke 2:22 Now when the days of their purification were fulfilled according to the teaching of Moses, they brought Jesus up to Jerusalem to present him to the Holy One: ²³ As it is written in the teaching of the Sovereign God, *"Every male who opens the womb [as firstborn] shall be called holy to the Sovereign One."* ²⁴ So they offered a sacrifice according to what is stated in the teaching of the Holy One, *"a pair of turtledoves or two young pigeons."*

²⁵ Now, there was a man in Jerusalem whose name was Simeon; this man was righteous and devout, waiting to welcome the consolation of Israel, and the Holy Spirit, she rested on him. ²⁶ It had been revealed to him by the Holy Spirit that he would not see death before he had seen the Messiah of the Most High God. ²⁷ Led by the Spirit, Simeon came into the temple. When the parents brought in the child Jesus, to do for him what was customary under that which was taught, ²⁸ Simeon took him in his arms and praised God, saying,

²⁹ "You release now your slave in peace, Master,
    according to your word;
³⁰ for my eyes have seen your salvation,
³¹ which you have prepared in the presence of all peoples,
³² a light for revelation to the Gentiles
    and for glory to your people Israel."

³³ And the child's mother and father were amazed at what was being said about him. ³⁴ Then Simeon blessed them and said to his mother Mary, "This child is set for the falling and the rising of many in Israel, and to be a sign provoking contention; ³⁵ also, your own soul a sword will pierce so that the true hearts of many will be revealed."

³⁶ There was also a prophet, Anna the daughter of Phanuel, of the tribe of Asher. She was of a great age, having lived with her husband seven years after her marriage, ³⁷ then as a widow to the age of eighty-four. She never left the temple but worshiped there with fasting and prayer night and day. ³⁸ At that moment she came and began to praise God, and to speak about the child to all who were looking for the redemption of Jerusalem.

PROCLAMATION

Text Notes

The traditional language "clean" and "unclean" is deeply implicated in biased treatment of women and girls, particularly after the onset of menstruation. The language lends itself easily to a debased understanding of women and girls, as that is inconsistent with full humanity and the image of God. These two distinct words, which are not antonyms, have the sense of being temporarily taboo, not ready to rejoin community, and restoration to a communally appropriate state (see Ilona Rashkow's *Taboo or Not Taboo*). The "purification" requires time, ritual bathing, and an offering. The use of the word "atonement" in verse 8 has made it easier to construct women's bodies and reproductive acts as in some way tainted. However, even moderating the language does not ameliorate the ways in which women and their bodies and reproductive biology are treated as dangerous and in need of control.

In the world of the Hebrew Scriptures, women are impregnated; in verse 2 the Hiphil verb is causative, "she is seeded/caused to bear seed." Contemporary translations tend to use "conceive," reflecting subsequent understanding.

In Psalm 48 Zion's superlatives hail from other cultures identifying their God as God of all the earth using the specific vocabulary of surrounding nations: *nof* signals "elevation" but is also the Egyptian name of Memphis, the capital city (and may also mean "fair," see JPS); Zaphon is the home of the Canaanite gods and is in the farthest northern reach unlike Zion/Jerusalem. In verse 14, God will be our God "until death"; "until we die" makes clear that it is not God who will die.

Luke 2:22 makes Mary's obligation under the Torah "theirs," Joseph's as well; this is counter to the text and practice between Leviticus and Luke and subsequent rabbinic and contemporary Jewish practice.

Preaching Prompts

When overlaid with the androcentrism, patriarchy, and occasional misogyny of the text, the ritual and language for the restoration to the community sounds harsh and discriminatory to many contemporary and non-Jewish ears. It is helpful to remember that biblical Hebrew has a much smaller vocabulary than English and uses some words in ways that extend far beyond their literal meaning. In Leviticus 12, the "purify," "atone," and "sin offering" apply to cleansing the woman and her physical spaces, including the sanctuary, from blood taboo, which was not a matter of sin or transgression. Arguably this period afforded the new mother rest and bonding time; the additional time for the female infant may account for the occasional vaginal discharge (or appearance of such) observable in newborn girls.

The *Churching of Women* is a Christian rite likely derived from these Leviticus and Luke texts, previously practiced in Catholic and Anglican congregations where a new mother refrained from attending church for four to six weeks and upon her return prayed a prayer of thanksgiving and received a blessing. However, some women experienced isolation and stigma, treated as unclean until they were "churched." The ritual has fallen into disuse.

While all spilled blood requires purification with both ritual and hygienic components, women and girls were subject to blood taboo and purity regulations. Contemporarily, our society seems obsessed with which bodies bleed and bear which organs to categorize and gender and assign identities and restrooms. Without either passing judgment on another culture or co-opting the specific practice of another religion, we can make physical and ritual space for human bodies in all of their life-stage changes and welcome and rewelcome folk to and back to the community upon and after significant transitions. This text can provide an opportunity to think about how we reintegrate a transperson into the congregation.

EPIPHANY III

Zephaniah 3:14–20; Psalm 17:6–9, 13, 15;
1 Timothy 4:1–6, 9–10; Mark 1:29–31

Zephaniah 3:14 Sing aloud, daughter of Zion; shout, all ye Israel!
   Rejoice, daughter, and exult with all your heart, daughter of Jerusalem!
¹⁵ The Judge of all Flesh has taken away the judgments against you,
   and has turned away your enemies, daughter.
   The sovereign of Israel, Creator of the Heavens and Earth,
   is in your midst, daughter; no longer shall you fear evil.
¹⁶ On that day it shall be said to Jerusalem:
   Fear not, Zion; do not let your hands grow weak, daughter.
¹⁷ The Ageless One, your God, is in your midst, daughter,
   a warrior who will deliver salvation;
   who will rejoice over you with gladness, daughter,
   God will renew you in love, daughter;
   God will exult over you, daughter, with loud singing.
¹⁸ Those who are grieved on account of the festivals,
   I will remove from you, daughter,
   so, daughter, that you will not bear their reproach.
¹⁹ I will deal with all your oppressors, daughter, at that time.
   And I will save the lame and gather the outcast,

and I will change their shame into praise
and renown in all the earth.
20 At that time I will bring you all home, at the time when I gather all of you;
for I will make you all renowned and praised
among all the peoples of the earth,
when I restore your fortunes before all of your eyes,
says the GOD WHO IS SALVATION.

Psalm 17: 6–9, 13, 15

6 I call upon you, for you will answer me, God;
extend your ear to me, hear my words.
7 Make your wondrous faithful love known,
Savior of those who seek refuge at your right hand,
from those who raise themselves up [against them].
8 Keep me as the apple of the eye;
hide me in the shadow of your wings,
9 from the wicked who despoil me,
my mortal enemies who surround me.
13 Rise up, HOLY PROTECTOR, confront them, overthrow them!
deliver my soul from the sword of wicked.
15 As for me, in righteousness shall I behold your face;
I shall be satisfied when I wake, having seen your likeness.

1 Timothy 4:1 Now the Spirit expressly says that in latter times some will leave the faith by paying attention to deceitful spirits and teachings of demons, 2 through the hypocrisy of liars whose consciences are seared with a hot iron. 3 They forbid marriage and demand abstinence from foods, which God created for receiving with thanksgiving by those who believe and know the truth. 4 For everything created by God is good, and nothing for rejection, rather received with thanksgiving. 5 For it is sanctified by God's word and by prayer. 6 Lay these things out to the sisters and brothers; you will be a good servant of Christ Jesus, nourished on the words of the faith and of the good teaching that you have followed.

9 This is a faithful saying and worthy of acceptance. 10 Therefore for this we toil and struggle, because we hope in the living God, who is the Savior of all people, especially of those who believe.

Mark 1:29 Immediately after [Jesus and the disciples] left the synagogue, they entered the house of Simon and Andrew, with James and John. 30 Now the mother of Simon's wife was in bed with a fever, and immediately they told Jesus about her. 31 Jesus came and lifted her up, taking her by the hand. Then the fever left her and she ministered to them.

PROCLAMATION

Text Notes

Bat Zion (or Jerusalem) can mean both Daughter Zion, the city, *or* a daughter of Zion, a woman from the city. In Isaiah 40:9 reading "daughter of" reveals a female prophet crying out to Jerusalem (compare NRSV and JPS translations). Because the addressee is feminine, all of the verbs to her are also feminine. I reproduce "daughter" in places where English masks the frequency of feminine address. Verse 18 is notoriously difficult to translate; see the discussion in my commentary on Zephaniah in the *Wisdom* series.

Psalm 17 offers two words in the first phrase of verse 7: "be wondrous" and "your faithful love." The translator must make sense of it in the language being read. The familiar expression "the apple of the eye" is a composite of similar expressions. In Zechariah 2:8 it is the apple, *bavah*; in Deuteronomy 32:10 and Proverbs 7:10 it the pupil, *ishon*, of the eye. In Psalm 17:8 it is "the pupil, the daughter of your eye"; similarly, Lamentations 2:18 refers to "the daughter of your eye." The euphemistic daughter is generally not translated. The winged God of verse 8 is often understood as a maternal image, a mother bird protecting her young, most often an eagle. "Mortal enemies" in verse 9 are the enemies of one's life (lit. "soul"); see JPS, NRSV and CEB "deadly enemies" and Alter's "with deadly intent." The summoning song calling God to action was uttered by Moses in Numbers 10:35 and by Solomon in 2 Chronicles 6:41 calling God to rest on the ark (repeated in Psalm 132:8). It is used throughout the psalms (3:7; 7:6; 9:19; 10:12).

The healing of Peter's (invisible) wife's mother varies slightly among the synoptic gospels: in Mark 1:29–31 the disciples *tell* Jesus about her; he takes her by the hand and lifts her up. In Matthew 8:14–15 Jesus sees her and touches her and she gets up on her own. In Luke 4:38–39 the disciples *ask* Jesus about her; he rebukes the fever without touching her and she gets up on her own.

Preaching Prompts

Behind all of these things is God's love, God's love for Israel, for all people and in the mind of the Epistle's author, a particular love for believers. In these Epiphany readings God is manifested through a number of gifts: deliverance, faithful love, sound teaching, faith, hope, and healing.

Using diverse language, the Church has spoken about evil in different ways. Contemporarily, "demon" language does not have as much use as in the world of the text except perhaps as a metaphor. The Epistle is highlighting how very much opposite of the spirit and teaching of Christ are the false doctrines they are rebuking; doctrines that limit and exclude. For some contemporary readers, condemnation of those who forbid marriage is a faithful response to those who would deny the sacrament of marriage to same-gender couples or couples with a trans or nonbinary partner.

In these texts women and girls form the basis of the metaphor of Jerusalem as God's daughter: in the chorus of voices that find themselves in the psalm, in the women and men who make up the early church, and in the women Jesus ministered to and who ministered to him represented by the mother of Peter's mother. Peter's wife remains as a silent signpost bearing witness to all of the women whose names and narratives have been cut out of the scriptures. An imaginative preacher might preach through her perspective, perhaps in dialogue with Peter as he encounters, affirms, follows, and betrays Jesus and bears witness to Jesus's death and resurrection, leading to his restoration to the faith.

EPIPHANY IV

Isaiah 16:1–5; Psalm 33:11–22; Ephesians 3:1–6; Luke 3:21–23, 31–38

Isaiah 16:1 "Send a lamb to the ruler of the land,
   from Sela, from the wilderness,
   to the mount of Daughter Zion.
2 And it will be that like a wandering bird
   pushed from the nest,
   so shall the daughters of Moab be
   at the fords of the Arnon.
3 Receive counsel, daughter; grant justice;
   make your shade like night at the midpoint of noon, daughter.
   Daughter, shelter the outcasts, the fugitive, do not expose.
4 Let them settle among you, daughter, the outcasts of Moab;
   be a shelter to them from the destroyer."
   For when the violence is no more,
   and destruction has ceased,
   and those who trample have vanished from the land,
5 then in faithful love shall a throne be established
   and on it one shall sit in faithfulness in the tent of David,
   rendering judgment and seeking justice and swift to do right.

Psalm 33: 11–22

11 The counsel of the JUST ONE stands for all time,
   the thoughts of her heart to all generations.
12 Happy is the nation for whom the CREATOR OF ALL is their God,
   the people whom she has chosen as her heritage.
13 From the heavens the MOST HIGH looks down;
   she sees all the woman-born.

14 From her eternal throne she gazes upon
   all who dwell upon the earth.
15 She who fashions their hearts alike
   is the one who discerns all their doings.
16 A monarch is not saved by a great army;
   a warrior is not delivered by great strength.
17 False hope is a horse for salvation,
   and its great might cannot save.
18 Look, the eye of the FAITHFUL ONE is on those who revere her,
   on those who hope in her faithful love,
19 to deliver their souls from death,
   and to keep them alive in famine.
20 Our soul waits for SHE WHO SAVES;
   she is our help and shield.
21 In her is our heart glad,
   because we trust in her holy Name.
22 Let your faithful love, COMPASSIONATE GOD, be upon us,
   for it is you in whom we trust.

Ephesians 3:1 For this reason am I, Paul, a prisoner for Christ Jesus, for the sake of you Gentiles. 2 Surely you have heard of the commission [to disseminate] God's grace that was given to me for you all: 3 through revelation was the mystery made known to me as I wrote briefly. 4 Moreover, reading this, you all will be able to comprehend my understanding of the mystery of Christ. 5 In former generations this mystery was not made known to the woman-born, as it has now been revealed to the women and men who are God's holy apostles and prophets by the Spirit: 6 that is, the Gentiles have become coinheritors, are of the same body, and sharers in the promise in Christ Jesus through the gospel.

Luke 3:21 Now when all the people were baptized and Jesus also had been baptized and was praying, heaven was opened, 22 and the Holy Spirit descended upon him bodily in the shape of a dove. Then a voice came from heaven, "You are my Son, the Beloved; with you I am well pleased."

23 Now Jesus was about thirty years old when he began his work. He was the child of [Mary and,] as was thought, of Joseph the child of Heli, 31 . . . son of Nathan, the child of [Bathsheba and] David, 32 the child of Jesse, the child of Obed, the child of [Ruth and] Boaz, the child of [Rahab and] Sala, the child of Nahshon, 33 the child of Amminadab, the child of Admin, the child of Arni, the child of Hezron, the child of Perez, the child of [Tamar and] Judah, 34 the child of [Leah and] Jacob, the child of [Rebekah and] Isaac, the child of [Sarah and] Abraham, the child of Terah, the child of Nahor, 35 the child of Serug, the child of Reu, the child of Peleg, the child of Eber, the child of Shelah, 36 the child of Cainan, the child of

Arphaxad, the child of Shem, the child of Noah, the child of Lamech, [37] the child of Methuselah, the child of Enoch, the child of Jared, the child of Mahalaleel, the child of Cainan, [38] the child of Enos, the child of Seth, the child of [Eve and] Adam, the child of God.

PROCLAMATION

Text Notes

The addressees of Isaiah 16 vary. Verse 1 is addressed to a plurality; following verses are addressed to a single feminine subject, likely Daughter Zion. While many translations have "give counsel" in Isaiah 16:3, the verb "to come" is causative, *Hiphil*, meaning "bring" or "receive" counsel.

In Psalm 33:14 God's "eternal throne" is "the fixed place [where] God sits." In verse 15 human hearts are *yachad*, "together" or "as one"—the cardinal number is the root word.

In Ephesians 3:5 the prophets and apostles, both of which groups include women and men, are made explicitly inclusive.

Preaching Prompts

God's concern for all the woman-born is the epiphany in these Epiphany readings. God calls on her daughter, Zion, Jerusalem, to welcome her Moabite sisters in their time of need. Israel's relationship with her border state was perpetually tumultuous even with shared ties; David was famously descended from Ruth the Moabite and turned to Moab to shelter his mother and father when under assault (1 Samuel 22:3). Isaiah 16 charges Daughter Zion to offer hospitality and refuge to Moabite women after some unknown upheaval. Often in the Hebrew Scriptures foreign women are treated as prospective danger, irresistible to Israelite men through sexual wiles, leading to Israelite men straying from their God. But in Isaiah 16, God calls on Israel to care for these vulnerable women.

In the psalm, God extends the thoughts of her heart to all generations. While some texts focus exclusively on God's special relationship with the people of Israel, this text embraces that position and another biblical tradition: God's sovereignty over and concern for all the earth and all of her peoples.

The authorship of Ephesians is disputed, but the author writes as would Paul, assuring their readers that the love of God incarnate in Christ Jesus is for all persons, here particularly for Gentiles. The Gospel presents this Jesus as a child of earth, woman-born as were we all, while omitting the women of his lineage. It is one of the chief contradictions of the scriptures that their message of a God who loves beyond categories is bound up in categorical language that minimizes, silences, and often excludes women.

EPIPHANY V

Song of Songs 4:9–15; Psalm 45:6–10, 12–15;
1 Corinthians 9:1–10; John 2:1–12

Song 4:9–15

9 You have taken my heart, my sister, my bride,
    you have taken my heart with a glance of your eyes,
    with a single jewel of your necklace.
10 How beautiful is your love, my sister, my bride.
    How much better is your love than wine,
    and the fragrance of your oils than every spice.
11 Nectar drops from your lips, my bride;
    honey and milk are under your tongue;
    the fragrance of your garments is like the fragrance of Lebanon.
12 A garden locked is my sister, my bride,
    a garden locked, a fountain sealed.
13 Your limbs are an orchard of pomegranates
    with luscious fruits, henna with nard.
14 Nard and saffron, calamus and cinnamon,
    with all kinds of frankincense trees,
    myrrh and aloes, with all superior spices;
15 a garden fountain, a well of living water,
    and flowing streams from Lebanon.

Psalm 45:6–10

6 Your God-given throne is everlasting;
    a scepter of integrity is your royal scepter.
7 You love righteousness and hate wickedness;
    therefore God, your God, has anointed you
    with the oil of gladness more than your companions.
8 Myrrh and aloes and cassia scent all your garments;
    from ivory palaces stringed instruments bring you joy.
9 Royal daughters are your treasures;
    the consort stands at your right hand in gold of Ophir.
10 Hear daughter, consider and incline your ear;
    forget your people and the house of your [mother and] father.
12 Daughter of Tyre, with gifts shall they seek your favor,
    the wealthiest of the people.

13 With all kinds of wealth is the princess ensconced;
    her garments are woven with gold.
14 In embroidery is she led to the king;
    behind her the maidens, her companions, follow.
15 They are brought with joy and gladness
    into the palace of the king.

1 Corinthians 9:1 Am I not free? Am I not an apostle? Have I not seen Jesus our Redeemer? Are you not my work in the Savior? ² If I am not an apostle to others, surely I am to you, for you are the seal of my apostleship in the Messiah.

³ This is my defense to those who examine me. ⁴ Do we not have the right to our food and drink? ⁵ Do we not have the right to travel with a sister, a wife, as do the other apostles and the brothers of the Messiah and Cephas? ⁶ Or is it only I and Barnabas who have no right to not work? ⁷ Who soldiers and pays their own expenses? Who plants a vineyard and does not eat any of its fruit? Or who shepherds a flock and does not taste any of the milk of the flock?

⁸ Do I say this as a human person? Does not the law also say the same? ⁹ For it is written in the teaching of Moses, *"You shall not muzzle a threshing ox."* Is it for oxen that God cares? ¹⁰ Or does God not, by all means, speak for our sake? It was indeed written for our sake, for the one who must plow should plow in hope and whoever threshes should thresh in hope of partaking.

John 2:1 On the third day there was a wedding in Cana of Galilee, and the mother of Jesus was there. ² Jesus and his disciples had also been invited to the wedding. ³ When the wine gave out, the mother of Jesus said to him, "They have no wine." ⁴ And Jesus said to her, "Woman, what concern is that to you and to me? My hour has not yet come." ⁵ His mother said to the servants, "Do whatever he tells you." ⁶ Now standing there were six stone water jars for the Jewish rites of purification, each holding twenty or thirty gallons. ⁷ Jesus said to them, "Fill the jars with water." And they filled them up to the brim. ⁸ He said to them, "Now draw some out, and take it to the chief steward." So they took it. ⁹ When the steward tasted the water that had become wine, and did not know where it came from (though the servants who had drawn the water knew), the steward called the bridegroom ¹⁰ and said to him, "Everyone serves the good wine first, and then the inferior wine after the guests have become drunk. But you have kept the good wine until now." ¹¹ Jesus did this, the first of his signs, in Cana of Galilee, and revealed his glory; and his disciples believed in him.

PROCLAMATION

Text Notes

In the Song the male beloved addresses the female beloved as "sister" and "bride." The use of familial terms for an intimate partner is common in some cultures: brother, bruh, sis, mama, and daddy in African American usage, mami and papi in Latinx usage, and daddy in some homosexual contexts. Indeed, Paul refers to a prospective bride as "a sister, a wife" in 1 Corinthians 9:5. The woman who is the primary speaker in the Song is also called a bride, but no wedding has yet taken place, hence their need to sneak off to be together, see Songs 8:1–2. For further study and comparison, I highly recommend the translation of the Song of Songs by Rabbi Marcia Falk in a standalone volume of the same title.

In Songs 4:9, taking someone's heart is expressed with a verb, *levav*, whose root is the heart, *lev*, so a single word encompasses the action and the object. For parity I add a second "my" to bride as is common; alternatively, see Alter's "my sister, bride." In other cases, the object is entirely missing, the "glance" of her eyes and "jewel" of her necklace. Verse 13 makes reference to "shoots," hence the "limbs" of the present translation, JPS, RSV, CEB, Falk, and Alter, and KJV's "plants," or a secondary meaning, "watercourse," yielding "emissions" in LXX and "channel" in NRSV, which negates the plural. The Peshitta has "nakedness."

Psalm 45 is the rare hymn of praise for a human person rather than God: "you are the most handsome of men" in verse 2. Verse 6 looks like a turn to God: see NRSV, KJV, and NETS, "your throne, O God." However, "throne" and "God" are in a construct chain, the same structure as "house of God." Here, "throne of God" means "God-given"; see "divine throne" in JPS and CEB. The royal wife is called a "consort," *shegal*, not queen, *malkah*, in verse 9, which term was not used by Israel for its royal women. (*Gevirah*, queen-mother was exclusive to the mother of the Judean king, see my *Womanist Midrash: A Reintroduction to the Women of the Torah and of the Throne* for more on royal women is Israel and Judah.) As a verb, *shagal* indicates sexual violence (see Deuteronomy 28:30; Isaiah 13:16; and Zechariah 14:2); it may be that the consort was a royal hostage to secure a peace.

Psalm 45 is a royal wedding psalm; the human monarch in Psalm 45 is most likely Ahab given the reference to the Tyrian princess in verse 12, which would make her Jezebel. Inexplicably, NRSV substitutes "people" for "daughter"; CEB uses "city"—while "daughter" can indicate a suburb or "daughter city," the bride is clearly the subject, see JPS, Alter, LXX, and KJV (though the latter adds language to make the bride the supplicant).

In 1 Corinthians 9:5, the "right" to food and drink provided and to marry is expressed as "power" or "authority." Verse 9 quotes Deuteronomy 25:4.

Preaching Prompts

The marriage metaphor that so often symbolizes the relationship between God and Israel, and Christ and the Church, has its roots in real human relationships. Marriage becomes a sacrament to make manifest the love of God in and between two people within a communal context. Marriage is socially constructed in and out of the Bible: abduction and rape marriages, polygamous marriages, and hierarchal domineering marriages are all biblical, but few would call them epiphanies of God's love. The Song evokes marriage, with the male lover calling the female love "bride," yet they are not married when they explore and celebrate their physical and sexual love. Marriage is heteronormative in the text; our understanding of the human person and sexuality has also evolved since the text and marriage continues to be shaped to make known the wideness of God's love.

It is for this reason that the Blessed Virgin chose to reveal her Son's glory at the wedding in Cana. In John 2, Mary, the mother of Jesus, prompts him to reveal himself in the miracle that is understood as the formal inauguration of his public ministry, verse 3. In so doing she leaves us with profound instructions for our Christian faith in verse 5, "Do whatever he, Jesus, tells you."

Paul's desire for a companion, a wife, who shares his faith is frank and honest. It is also instructive; depriving people of love, companionship, and sexual fulfilment flies in the face of what it means to be the church of the God who is love and created sex. (His argument in 1 Corinthians 9:9 about whether God cares for oxen *or* humans is as short-sighted as is common with binary claims.)

The elaborate wedding in the psalm is a royal spectacle; royal weddings continue to draw spectators and admirers. The scope of the luxury reflects the class standing of the monarch and is a mark of inequity in the text. Not every union was celebrated in such splendor, then or now, though there is for some considerable social pressure to meet an impossible standard, often leading to significant indebtedness.

In the scriptures joy is widely associated with wine—a challenge for those living with addiction or living sober lives for other reasons. The abundance of wine at the Cana wedding represented an abundance of joy, a theme that connects these readings (and for which Paul hopes). That joy characterizes Epiphany well. We are constantly being reminded that God is here manifest with us and that is indeed joyous.

EPIPHANY VI

1 Kings 17:8–16; Psalm 146; James 1:22–27; Luke 4:16–27

1 Kings 17:8 The word of the HOLY ONE to Elijah was, [9] "Get up, go to Zarephath, which is part of Sidon, and settle there; watch now, I have commanded a widow woman there to provide for you." [10] And Elijah got up and went to Zarephath. Then he came to the gate of the town, and look! a widow woman was there gathering sticks; so he called to her and said, "Bring me, please, a little water in a vessel, that I may drink." [11] She went to bring it, and he called to her and said, "Bring me, please, a bit of bread in your hand." [12] Then she said, "As the HOLY ONE your God lives, if I had a cake. There is only a handful of flour in a jar, and a little oil in a jug. Now look, I am gathering two sticks, then I will go home and prepare the oil and flour for myself and for my child; we will eat it, and we will die." [13] Then Elijah said to her, "Fear not; go and do as you have said, only make me a little cake of it and bring it to me first, then make something for yourself and your child afterwards. [14] For thus says the HOLY ONE the God of Israel: The jar of flour will not empty and the jug of oil will not decrease until the day that the HOLY ONE grants rain upon the earth." [15] She went and she did as Elijah said, and she and he, and her household, ate for many days. [16] The jar of flour did not empty and the jug of oil did not decrease according to the word of the HOLY ONE that God spoke through Elijah.

Psalm 146

[1] Hallelujah! Praise the AGELESS ONE, O my soul!

[2] I will praise the EVER-LIVING GOD all my life;
   I will sing praises to my God throughout my living.

[3] Put not your trust in the great, nor in any child of earth,
   for there is no help in them.

[4] When they breathe their last, they return to earth,
   and in that day their thoughts perish.

[5] Happy are these for whom the God of Rebekah's line is their help,
   whose hope is in the CREATOR OF ALL, their God.

[6] Maker of heavens and earth, the seas, and all that is in them;
   keeping faith forever.

[7] Bringer of justice to the oppressed,
   bringer of bread to the hungry;
   the COMPASSIONATE GOD sets the prisoners free.

[8] The ALL-SEEING GOD opens the eyes of the blind,
   the JUST GOD lifts up those who are bowed down;
   The RIGHTEOUS GOD loves the righteous.

[9] The MOTHER OF ALL cares for the stranger,
   orphan and widow she bears up,
   but the way of the wicked she confounds.

[10] The MAJESTIC ONE shall reign forever,
   your God, O Zion, from generation to generation. Hallelujah!

James 1:22 Now be doers of the word, and not just hearers who deceive themselves. [23] For if any are hearers of the word and not doers, they are like a person who looks at their face in a mirror. [24] They recognize themselves and, departing, immediately forget what they were like. [25] But those who look deeply into the perfect law, the law of liberty, and who persevere, not being hearers who forget rather doers who act, they will be blessed in their doing.

[26] If any think they are religious, and do not bridle their tongues but deceive their hearts, their religion is worthless. [27] Religion that is pure and undefiled before God, the Provider, is this: to care for orphans and widows in their distress, and to keep oneself spotless from the world.

Luke 4:16 Now Jesus came to Nazareth, where he had been nurtured and went, according to his practice on the day of the sabbath, to the synagogue. And he stood up to read. [17] Then was given him the scroll of the prophet Isaiah. He unrolled the scroll and found the place where it was written:

> [18] "*The Spirit of the Most High is upon me,*
> *because God has anointed me*
> *to proclaim good news to those who are poor.*
> *God has sent me to preach liberation to those who are captives*
> *and recovery of sight to those who are blind,*
> *to liberate those who are oppressed,*
> [19] *to proclaim the year of the Most High's favor.*"[1]

[20] Then Jesus rolled up the scroll, gave it back to the attendant, and sat down and every eye of all in the synagogue looked intently at him. [21] Then he began to speak to them, saying, "Today this scripture has been fulfilled in your hearing." [22] And all bore witness to him and marveled at the gracious words that came from his mouth. They said, "Is not this Joseph's son?"

[23] Then Jesus said to them, "Of course you all will quote me this proverb, 'Doctor, cure yourself!' And you all will say, 'The things we have heard you did at Capernaum, do here in your hometown.'" [24] And Jesus said, "Truly I tell you, no prophet is accepted in their hometown. [25] But I speak truth to you all, there were many widows in Israel in the days of Elijah, when the heavens were closed three years and six months, and there was a severe famine over all the land. [26] Yet, Elijah was sent to none of them, rather to Zarephath in Sidon, to a widow woman. [27] And there were also many lepers in Israel in the time of the prophet Elisha, and none of them was cleansed except Naaman the Syrian."

PROCLAMATION

Text Notes

In Psalm 146:1, "throughout my living" is derived from "in my continuing," where "continue" is the adverb meaning "longer," *'od*, with the first possessive suffix, "my" attached, a very complex idiomatic saying. The "great" in verse 2 are "nobles," sometimes royal offspring, hence "princes" in other translations. In verse 4 "Rebekah's line" replaces "Jacob." The nature of God's support for widow and orphan in verse 9 is unclear; the verb there is only used there and its derivation is unclear. NRSV's "uphold" derives from the LXX and provides the basis for my "bear up." Similarly, the Peshitta has "nourish/support."

---

1. Italicized text indicates First Testament quotations in the Second Testament.

"Look deeply" in James 1:25 has the sense of stopping and bending over to examine something closely.

"Nurtured" in Luke 4:16 has the particular sense of having been nourished, specifically, fed. Jesus's literacy is noteworthy in an age where illiteracy was more common than not. In comparison, very few of Israel's prophets were recorded as writing their oracles; Jeremiah was famously illiterate, relying on Baruch to read and write his scrolls. Jesus quotes Isaiah 61:1–2 and 58:6 in inverse order. The evangelist has him citing the LXX version, "the acceptable year of the Holy One" where the MT has "year of the Holy One's favor." Translations like the NRSV, CEB, and the present one use "favor" given Jesus would have been reading the Hebrew text (though whether it corresponded to the MT or LXX cannot be ascertained). Notably, Jesus or the author attenuates the Isaiah reading, omitting "the day of vengeance." In verse 25 I expand the pronoun in Jesus's proverb to reflect the inclusivity of the prophetic tradition in each canon.

Preaching Prompts

God's epiphanies are not reserved for princes and potentates; God reveals her presence, power, and providence to whom she will. Often, she chooses the most vulnerable, the outcast, and the overlooked to bear witness to her mercy and majesty. In these lessons, widows and their children are the primary concern of God in each lesson, and in keeping with the theme of Epiphany, God communicates through Elijah and Jesus that neither nationality nor ethnicity disqualify anyone from concern and caretaking. God's love is for all the peoples of earth and Jesus is the embodiment of that love; the scriptures have borne witness to that love across time.

God provides for all of her children in 1 Kings 17: the prophet, the "foreign" widow, and her son. (Widow's children were considered orphans because the technical term translated "orphan" actually means fatherless.) The widow is desperate and vulnerable, and not an Israelite. The demand of the prophet of a God she does not claim that she give him all she has to feed her child could easily have been exploitative. Contemporarily that is often the case.

In Psalm 146, women receive the same care from the hand of God. Not just widowed women in verse 9, but also women who are oppressed, hungry, and imprisoned in verse 7, women who are, blind, bowed down, and righteous in verse 8, and women who are strangers, sojourners, or immigrants, as well as women who are themselves orphans in verse 9. Each category in the psalm represents women and men, adults and children, Israelites and foreigners. The psalm shares these themes with Isaiah 61, which Jesus reads and quotes in the Gospel and makes clear that this liberation and these transformations are ultimately the work of God as human beings are not always trustworthy. Yet the Epistle of James makes clear that we are not to just leave the plight of women and their children suffering lack in the hands of God; that is the measure of our religion.

In this Gospel Jesus claims the title of Liberator that the scriptures bestow on God. In his mouth these ancient words are heard as though they are new; in them the people find grace and simply marvel at them on his tongue. Yet he is a hometown boy who has gone off and made a name for himself and they are quick to put him in his place, naming Joseph as his father and likely invoking the scandal of his questionable parentage, perhaps in front of his mother or other relatives.

Jesus cuts through the subtle dig to name the issue: familiarity breeds contempt for prophets as much as for anyone else. He tells a hard truth: your gifts may not be accepted, welcome, or lauded by the folk who should be in your corner. In so doing, he teaches that God will go right on doing her good work no matter what anyone thinks of her messenger, including to folk who were not thought worthy. These texts leave us with the knowledge that women and their children are still vulnerable and where they are, God is.

EPIPHANY VII

1 Kings 17:17–24; Psalm 116:1–9; Acts 9:36–42; Luke 7:11–17

1 Kings 17:17 After [the miracle multiplying the meal and oil], the child of the woman—the owner of the house—became ill and his illness was so overwhelming that there was no breath left in the child. [18] And she said to Elijah, "What is between me and thee man of God? You have come to me to bring my sin to remembrance and to kill my child!" [19] Then he said to her, "Give me your child," and he took the child from her bosom and carried the child up into the room upstairs where he, Elijah, was staying and laid the child on his own bed. [20] Then he cried out to the HOLY ONE OF OLD, "HOLY ONE my God, have you actually wrought evil upon the widow with whom I sojourn by killing her child?" [21] And Elijah stretched himself upon the child three times, and cried out to the MOST HIGH, "HOLY ONE my God, let this child's soul come into him again." [22] And the MOST HIGH GOD listened to the voice of Elijah and the soul of the child came into him again, and he revived. [23] Then Elijah took and brought the child down from the house's upstairs room, and gave the child to the mother and said, "Look! Your child lives." [24] So the woman said to Elijah, "Now this I know, you are a man of God and that the word of the HOLY ONE OF OLD in your mouth is truth."

Psalm 116: 1–9

[1] I love the GOD WHO SAVES, because she has heard
   my cry and my supplications.
[2] Because she inclined her ear to me,
   I will continue to call all my days.

³ The snares of death encompassed me,
    the pangs of Sheol found me,
    I found distress and anguish.
⁴ Then I called on the name of SHE WHO IS LIFE:
    "FOUNT OF LIFE, pray, save my life!"
⁵ Gracious is the SAVING GOD, and righteous;
    our God mother-loves deeply.
⁶ SHE WHO IS WISDOM protects those without guile;
    I was brought low and she saved me.
⁷ Return, my soul, to your rest,
    for SHE WHO IS FAITHFUL has rewarded you abundantly.
⁸ For you have delivered my soul from death,
    my eyes from tears, my feet from stumbling.
⁹ I will walk before the LIVING GOD
    in the land of the living.

Acts 9:36 Now in Joppa there was a disciple whose name was Tabitha—which translated into Greek is Dorcas; she was abundant in good works and benevolent giving. ³⁷ And it happened at that time she became ill and died and they washed her and laid her in a room upstairs. ³⁸ Now Lydda was near Joppa so the disciples who heard that Peter was there, sent two people to him urging, "Without delay, come to us." ³⁹ Then Peter got up and went with them; when he arrived, they took him to the room upstairs. And standing beside him were all the widows, weeping and displaying the tunics and other clothing that Dorcas made while she was with them. ⁴⁰ Then Peter put all of them outside, and got on his knees and prayed, and he turned to the body and said, "Tabitha, arise." And she opened her eyes, and seeing Peter, she sat up. ⁴¹ Then he gave her his hand and raised her up and calling the saints and widows, he presented her alive. ⁴² Now this became known throughout Joppa, and many believed in the Messiah.

Luke 7:11 The day after [healing a centurion's slave] Jesus went to a town called Nain, and his disciples and a large crowd went with him. ¹² He had just approached the gate of the town and suddenly, being carried out was a man who had died, his mother's only son and she was a widow; with her was a large crowd from the town. ¹³ When the Messiah saw her, he had compassion on her and said to her, "Do not weep." ¹⁴ Then Jesus came forward and touched the coffin, and the bearers stood still. And he said, "Young man, I say to you, rise!" ¹⁵ The dead man sat up and began to speak and Jesus gave him to his mother. ¹⁶ Fear seized all of them; and they glorified God, saying, "A great prophet has risen among us!" and "God visited God's people!" ¹⁷ This word about Jesus spread throughout Judea and all the surrounding country.

PROCLAMATION

Text Notes

"Lord/master" language indicates home ownership (Exodus 22:8; Judges 19:22–23); unfortunately, "mistress" reads as subordinate in English and does not convey the same sense of mastery or ownership, therefore I use "owner" in 1 Kings 17:17.

For syntactical reasons, the first line of the psalm can be: "*I love that* the FOUNT OF LIFE *has heard my cry and my supplications.*" The fluidity of tense in biblical Hebrew means that "incline" in verse 2 can correspond to either the present or past; missing words require supplementing the original "I will call my days" yielding "I will *continue to* call all my days." In verse 5 God's love is expressed by the verb *racham* whose root is *rechem*, the womb. Similarly, Jesus's deep compassion for the bereaved widow emanates from deep within him.

At the heart of the verb *splagchnizomai*, "to have compassion," is its root *splagchnon*, innards or guts, the locus of emotion.

Preaching Prompts

Each of Jesus's miracles is an epiphany. Each time he reveals himself, people struggle with where to put him in the lineage of Israel's prophets: he teaches like Moses, giving and revising Torah; and he has the power of the miraculous like Elijah and Elisha, including raising the dead to life. His audience would know that Nain is just on the other side of Moreh Hill from Shunem where Elisha would raise another woman's son from the dead (2 Kings 4:17, 32–37). In Acts, Peter also performs a resurrection closely patterned after Jesus raising a little girl in Mark 5:35–43. (Jesus says, "*Talitha qumi*," very similar to *Tabitha qumi* in his native Aramaic and as it is found in the Peshitta and contemporary Hebrew translations. Some manuscripts drop the "i," marking the feminine imperative; for the child he uses a word that also means lamb, here an endearment, "lambkin arise.") An upper room characterizes the site of Elijah's and Peter's miracles and holds resonances for those who look ahead in the story of Jesus to his own resurrection.

The miraculous power that Jesus embodies and manifests is the power of God made known through her prophets and in her own acts of deliverance. The psalm celebrates the God who cheats death, saves life, and delivers her people, individually and collectively. When Jesus rises from the dead without the help of a prophet or any other intermediary, he will demonstrate that he is more than heir to the legacy of the prophets, but one with the God who is the author of life and sovereign over death.

As the only woman identified as a disciple, Tabitha is noteworthy but should not be considered the only female disciple. It is worth asking why the descriptor is not used more commonly for the women who followed Jesus and the Jesus movement. Margaret Aymer observes in the *Women's Commentary* that Tabitha's dual names mark her as a Greek-speaking Jew and her charitable giving mark her as a woman of means; to that I would add having sufficient time to devote oneself to the needs of others can be a perk of wealth, privilege, and status as well. Among the female characters in these readings Tabitha stands out as neither wife nor widow nor mother. She is a disciple of Jesus Christ and named without regard to patriarchy or patrimony.

EPIPHANY VIII

Isaiah 2:1–5; Psalm 9:1–2, 7–11, 13–14; 1 Corinthians 1:25–31; John 1:1–5

Isaiah 2:1 The word that Isaiah son of Amoz envisioned about Judah and Jerusalem:
2 And it will be in coming days,
 the mountain of God's home
 shall the highest of the mountains,
 and shall be elevated beyond the hills,
 all the nations shall stream to it.
3 Many peoples shall come and say,
 "Let us go and ascend the mountain of the HOLY ONE OF SINAI,
 to the home of the God of Jacob [of the line of Rebekah];
 that God may teach us God's ways
 and that we may walk in God's paths."
 For out of Zion shall go forth instruction,
 and the word of the HOLY ONE from Jerusalem.
4 God shall judge between the nations,
 and shall decide justly for many peoples;
 they shall beat their swords into plowshares,
 and their spears into pruning hooks;
 nation shall not lift up sword against nation,
 neither shall they learn war any more.
5 O house of Jacob [line of Rebekah]
 come, let us walk
 in the light of the HOLY ONE OF OLD!

Psalm 9:1–2, 7–11, 13–14

1 I will give thanks to the GOD WHO SAVES with my whole heart;
 I will tell of all your wonderful deeds.
2 I will rejoice and exult in you;
 I will sing praise to your name, Most High.
7 GOD WHO IS MAJESTY sits enthroned forever,
 she has established her throne for judgment.

8 She judges the world in righteousness;
   she judges the peoples with equity.
9 SHE WHO IS FAITHFUL is a stronghold for the oppressed,
   a stronghold in times of trouble.
10 They trust you, they who know your name,
   for you do not forsake those who seek you REDEEMING GOD.
11 Sing praises to the HOLY ONE enthroned in Zion.
   Declare her deeds among the peoples.
13 Be gracious to me, GRACIOUS ONE.
   See what I suffer from those who hate me.
   You lift me up from the gates of death,
14 so that I may recount all your praises,
   and in the gates of Daughter Zion,
   rejoice in your salvation.

1 Corinthians 1:25 Now God's foolishness is wiser than mortal wisdom, and God's weakness is stronger than human strength. [26] Consider your own call, sisters and brothers, since not many of you were wise according to mortal flesh, not many powerful, not many highborn. [27] Rather, what is foolish in the world is what God chose to shame the wise, and what is weak in the world God chose to shame the strong. [28] Also, what is of low status in the world God chose along with that which is despised, that which is nothing, in order to bring to naught that which already is, [29] so that no mortal flesh might boast in the presence of God [30] who is the source of your life in Christ Jesus, who became for us wisdom from God, righteousness and sanctification and redemption, [31] in order that, as it is written, *"Let the one who boasts, boast in the Holy One."*

John 1:1 In the beginning was the Word, and the Word was with God, and the Word was God. [2] The Word was with God in the beginning. [3] Everything came into being through the Word, and without the Word not one thing came into being that came into being. What has come into being [4] in the Word was life, and that life was the light of all people. [5] The light shines in the bleakness, and the bleakness did not overtake it.

PROCLAMATION

Text Notes

In 1 Corinthians 1:25 Paul uses *anthroupou*, "human," to emphasize the limitations of mortal human wisdom and strength; verses 26 and 29 use *sarx*, "flesh" in the same manner. In each case "mortal" conveys the sense. In verse 31 he refers to, but does not directly quote, Jeremiah 9:24: "Let those who boast boast in this, that they understand and know me, that I am the HOLY ONE."

Preaching Prompts

This Sunday in Epiphany is optional pending the fall of Easter. It envisions God's self-disclosure to all of the peoples of earth through *torah*, the "instruction" of Isaiah 2:3 and in verb form, "teach" in the same verse. The root means revelation and instruction as well as law in addition to the specific books of the Torah. Here God is revealed in her words, wisdom, works, and worlds, everything through which she instructs creation.

The first lesson bids us walk in the light of God with peoples from all the nations of earth. The psalmist responds to this faithful and trustworthy God as an individual acknowledging God's goodness and justice to all peoples.

Paul's discourse on wisdom rejects human wisdom as insufficient and points to God's wisdom as transcending human wisdom and its categories; God will not be boxed in. Paul's notion of wisdom is heavily influenced by Greek philosophy, yet his own Israelite tradition has a vibrant stream in which Wisdom herself is divine, an extension of God (see Proverbs 8–9, expanded upon in the deuterocanonical books Wisdom and Sirach).

John 1 makes the fundamental Christian claim that this great, majestic, awe-inspiring One comes to dwell in this Word, embodied and incarnate. The Gospel builds to a dramatic revelation of the identity of the Word. Absent from the Gospel is the woman and the womb in which the Word was prepared.

God's self-disclosure in Epiphany is to all people, but all people are hard to tease out in these lessons. Naming the Israelites as the lineage of Rebekah and not just the house of Jacob offers an opportunity to remember that she was among the ancestral figures to whom God speaks and promises a lineage (Genesis 25:22–23). The wisdom tradition that Paul critiques is a male tradition. One could read his exhortation as elevating discounted wisdom, folk wisdom, women's wisdom, the wisdom of folk deemed uncivilized as the wisdom held in low regard that God elevates.

LAST SUNDAY OF EPIPHANY

Zechariah 8:1–8; Psalm 95:1–7; 1 Corinthians 2:1–13; Luke 7:24–35

Zechariah 8:1 The word of the Sovereign of heaven's legions came to me, saying: [2] Thus says the Commander of heaven's vanguard: I am jealous for Zion with great jealousy, and with great wrath am I jealous for her. [3] Thus says the Ruler of the multitudes of heaven: I will return to Zion and will dwell in the midst of Jerusalem, and Jerusalem shall be called "The Faithful City" and the mountain of the Sovereign of the vanguard of heaven shall be called "The Holy Mountain." [4] Thus says the Holy One of heaven's armies: Elder women and elder men shall again sit in the streets of Jerusalem, each with staff in hand because of their great age. ⁵ And the streets of the city shall be full of girls and boys playing in its streets. ⁶ Thus says the Majesty of the Heavens: Though it seem miraculous in the eyes of the remnant of this people in these days, should it also seem miraculous to me, says the Commander of winged warriors? ⁷ Thus says the Sovereign of heaven's legions: It is I who will save my people from the east land and from the west land. ⁸ Then I will bring them to dwell within Jerusalem; they shall be my people and I will be their God, in faithfulness and in righteousness.

Psalm 95:1–7

¹ Come, let us sing joyfully to the Rock Who Birthed Us;
   let us shout to the rock of our salvation!
² Let us come into her presence with thanksgiving;
   with songs of praise let us shout to her!
³ For the Ever-Living God is a great God,
   and a great Majesty above all gods.
⁴ For in her hand are the depths of the earth;
   the heights of the mountains are hers also.
⁵ For hers is the sea, for she made it,
   and the dry land, which her hands have crafted.
⁶ Come, let us worship and bow down,
   let us kneel before the Ageless God, our Maker!
⁷ For she is our God,
   and we are the people of her pasture,
   and the sheep of her hand.
   If only you would listen to her voice today!

1 Corinthians 2:1 Now when I came to you sisters and brothers, I did not come with lofty words or wisdom proclaiming the mystery of God to you. ² For I determined to know nothing among you all except Jesus Christ, and him crucified. ³ And so in weakness and in fear and in much trembling I came to you. ⁴ My message and my proclamation were not in persuasive wise words, rather with a demonstration of the Spirit and of power, ⁵ so that your faith might rest not on human wisdom but on the power of God.

⁶ Wisdom is what we speak to the mature, wisdom that is not of this age or of the rulers of this age who are doomed to perish. ⁷ But we speak God's wisdom through a mystery that has been hidden, which God decreed before the ages for our glory. ⁸ This, none of the rulers of this age comprehended, for if they had comprehended, they would not have crucified the Sovereign of glory. ⁹ Yet, as it is written,

"*What no eye has seen, nor ear has heard,*
   Nor come upon a human heart,
   what God has prepared for those who love God."

[10] To us God has revealed these things through the Spirit, for the Spirit searches all things, even the depths of God. [11] For what human person knows what is human except by the human spirit within that person? Also, in the same way, no one comprehends what is truly God except by the Spirit of God. [12] Now then, we have not received the spirit of the world, rather the Spirit that is from God, in order that we may understand the gifts bestowed on us by God. [13] And these things we speak of not in words of human-taught wisdom but rather Spirit-taught, interpreting spiritual things to those who are spiritual.

Luke 7:24 When John's messengers had gone, Jesus began to speak to the crowds about John: "What did you all go out into the wilderness to see? A reed shaken by the wind? [25] What then did you go out to see? A person dressed in luxurious robes? Look, those whose clothing is lavish and who live in self-indulgence are in royal palaces. [26] What then did you all go out to see? A prophet? Yes, I tell you, and more than a prophet. [27] This is the one about whom it is written,

> '*Look, I am sending my messenger ahead of you,*
> *who will prepare your way before you.*'

[28] I tell you, among those born of women no one is greater than John; yet the least in the reign of God is greater than he." [29] Now all the people who heard this, including the tax collectors, professed the righteousness of God, being baptized with the baptism of John. [30] But by refusing to be baptized by him, the Pharisees and the legal scholars rejected God's counsel for themselves.

[31] "To what then will I compare the people of this generation, and what are they like? [32] They are like children in the marketplace sitting and calling to one another,

> 'We played the flute for you all, and you did not dance;
> we wailed, and you all did not weep.'

[33] For John the Baptizer has come eating no bread and drinking no wine, and you all say, 'He has a demon.' [34] The Son of Woman has come eating and drinking, and you all say, 'Look, a glutton and a drunkard, a friend of tax collectors and sinners!' [35] Yet Wisdom is vindicated by all her children."

PROCLAMATION

Text Notes

The title "Lord of Hosts" may be familiar, particularly from hymnody—"Lord Sabaoth" in *A Mighty Fortress*—but is not always understood. "Hosts," *tzavaoth*, is a measure of armed forces like a legion or battalion; God's celestial army is often portrayed as stars and other heavenly bodies. See Deuteronomy 4:19; 1 Kings 22:19; Nehemiah 9:6. The title is repeated in nearly every verse of the first lesson. As with "Lord," I translate the title in a variety of ways to limit repetition and facilitate theological imagination.

The language for God in Psalm 95:1 comes from Deuteronomy 32:18, where God is: "The Rock who gave birth to you . . . the God who gave you birth."

There is some variation among manuscripts for 1 Corinthians 2:4, whether "words of" modifying "plausible" is included. Verse 9 quotes Isaiah 64:4 and adds the line about the human heart, not present in the primary Hebrew text, the MT, or in the LXX, Targum, or Dead Sea Scrolls.

Jesus uses the expression "woman-born" as shorthand for humanity, while he is presented as the Son of Woman, son of humanity, human child, mortal one. The old "Son of Man" translation misses that *anthropos* means human, not male, and "man" is not generic. Where KJV and RSV use "son of man" throughout both testaments, NRSV has dropped it from the First Testament altogether; CEB follows suit. Instead, they use versions of "mortal (one)," "human one," and "human being." This has the effect of limiting the expression to Jesus, misrepresenting its widespread use in the Hebrew Scriptures. As the title emphasizes humanity, I use Son of Woman to emphasize Jesus's woman-born humanity, which is its primary use in the New Testament (see its use throughout Ezekiel, where it is often translated "mortal"). In contrast, in Daniel 7:13 the term has a more supernatural connotation, which can also be found in regard to Jesus (see Matthew 19:28 and 24:30).

John's messengers in Luke 7:24 are *aggelōn*, but not "angels," which is an anglicized transliteration of the same Greek word. In Greek as well as in Hebrew, the terms for messenger refers to human as well as supernatural envoys; as a result, this project uses "messenger" nearly exclusively. God's divine messenger in verse 27, quoting Malachi 3:1, is articulated with the same term. In Luke 7:25 (and Matthew 11:8) John's robe is described with a word that can mean "soft," "fancy," or with regard to men, one who is sexually penetrated. (I avoid "homosexual" contra to the dominant Greek lexicon, BDAG; that is a contemporary understanding of sexual orientation not applicable to the ancient world.)

Preaching Prompts

Epiphany closes with God's promise to gather her dispersed people in Zechariah. For the prophet and his audience, God's power was made manifest in the return of the diasporized Jews to Israel under the Persian regime. Contemporary readers may find in this reading a promise to sustain us through the Lenten wilderness when read in light of God's fidelity. The psalm can be read as focusing primarily on Israel, yet its description of God as sovereign above all other gods (and mountains for good measure) is universalist.

The Epistle and Gospel engage wisdom as a locus for divine revelation. Paul rejects sophistry, the human wisdom of the elite as the locus of God's disclosure, rather finding her in divine wisdom revealed by the Spirit. Jesus is the Word enfleshed and the embodiment of Wisdom personified, a feminine construct in his scriptural tradition.

It is this tradition in which Jesus positions himself as the child of Wisdom; her deeds are his deeds. In so doing, Jesus offers expansive language for the Divine, Mother. His words also remind me of a practice from my own culture: some Black parents will say to a partner when a child is being particularly precocious, "That's *your* child." What behaviors does Jesus associate with his divine Mother? A life full of joy and celebration, including those who, in the words of Paul, are low status and despised. Yet he does not disdain the ascetic's path John follows; indeed he commends John with unparalleled praise. There is no single way to follow Jesus.

Finally, in Luke 7:30 there is a layer of the anti-Pharisee tradition that has yielded, and in some cases still does yield, anti-Semitic interpretation. It is critical to remember and reject the harm supercessionist rhetoric in and out of the text does, especially as anti-Semitic attacks are recently resurgent.

LENT—ASH WEDNESDAY

Joel 2:1, 12–17, 21–22; Psalm 90:1–10, 12; 1 Corinthians 15:45–49; Matthew 6:1–12

Joel 2:1 Blow the trumpet in Zion!
 Cry the alarm on my holy mountain!
 Let all the inhabitants of the land quake,
 for the day of the Holy God is coming, it is near.
 ¹² Yet even now, says the HOLY ONE,
 return to me with all your hearts,
 with fasting, with weeping, and with lamenting.
 ¹³ Tear your hearts and not your clothing.
 Return to the HOLY ONE, your God,
 for God is gracious and loves as a mother,
 slow to anger, and abounds in faithful love,
 and reluctant to impose harm.
 ¹⁴ Who knows whether God will not turn and relent,
 and leave a blessing behind,
 for a grain offering and a drink offering
 to the HOLY ONE, your God?
 ¹⁵ Blow the trumpet in Zion;
 sanctify a fast;
 call a solemn assembly.
 ¹⁶ Gather the people:
 Sanctify the congregation;
 assemble the aged;
 gather the children,
 even breastfeeding babies.

Let the bridegroom leave his room,
and the bride her canopy.

17 Between the portico and the altar
let the priests, the ministers of the HOLY ONE, weep.
Let them say, "Spare your people, HOLY ONE,
and do not offer your heritage as a mockery,
a byword among the nations.
Why should it be said among the peoples,
'Where is their God?'"

21 Fear not, O land!
Be glad and rejoice,
for the HOLY ONE has done great things!

22 Fear not, O animals of the field!
For the pastures of the wilderness are green;
the tree lifts up its fruit,
the fig tree and vine give their riches.

Psalm 90:1–10, 12

1 MOTHER OF THE MOUNTAINS, you have been our refuge
from one generation to another.

2 Before the mountains were born,
or you writhed the land and the earth into birth,
from age to age you are God.

3 You turn mortal flesh back to the dust and say,
"Turn back, you who are woman-born."

4 For a thousand years in your sight are like yesterday when it is past
and like a watch in the night.

5 You sweep them aside; they are an illusion;
In the morning flourishing and in the evening wilting and withering.

6 In the morning it is green and flourishes;
in the evening it is dried up and withered.

7 For we are consumed in your displeasure;
we are afraid because of your wrathful indignation.

8 Our iniquities you have set before you,
and our hidden sins in the light of your countenance.

9 When you are angry, all our days are gone;
we bring our years to an end like a sigh.

10 The span of our life is seventy years, perhaps in strength even eighty;
yet the sum of them is but labor and sorrow,
for they pass away quickly and we are gone.

¹² So teach us to number our days
   that we may apply our hearts to Wisdom.

1 Corinthians 15:45 Thus it is written, "The first human, Adam, became a living soul"; the last Adam became a spirit that gives life. ⁴⁶ But it is not the spiritual that is first, but the physical, and then the spiritual. ⁴⁷ The first human was from the earth, dust; the second human is from heaven. ⁴⁸ As was the one of dust, so are those who are of dust; and as is the one of heaven, so are those who are of heaven. ⁴⁹ Just as we have borne the image of the one of dust, we will also bear the image of the one of heaven.

Matthew 6:1 [Jesus said,] "Now, beware of practicing your justness before other people in order to be seen by them; surely, lest you have no reward from your Creator in heaven.

² "So when you give alms, do not trumpet before yourself, as the hypocrites do in the synagogues and in the streets, in order that they may be praised by other people. Truly I tell you, they have received their reward. ³ But when you give alms, do not let your left hand know what your right hand is doing, ⁴ in order that your alms may be secret; and your Creator who sees in secret will reward you.

⁵ "And when you pray, do not be like the hypocrites; for they love to stand and pray in the synagogues and on the street corners, in order that they may be seen by other people. Truly I tell you, they have received their recompense. ⁶ But whenever you pray, go into your room and shut the door and pray to your Creator who is in secret; and your Creator who sees in secret will reward you.

¹⁶ "And when you fast, do not be sullen like the hypocrites, for they disfigure their faces in order to show other people that they are fasting. Truly I tell you, they have received their reward. ¹⁷ But when you fast, put oil on your head and wash your face, ¹⁸ in order that your fasting may be seen, not by others, but by your Creator who is in secret, and your Creator who sees in secret will reward you.

Matthew 6:9 "Pray then in this way:

   Our Father in heaven,
   hallowed be your name.
¹⁰ Your kingdom come.
   Your will be done,
      on earth as it is in heaven.
¹¹ Give us this day our daily bread.
¹² And forgive us our debts,
      as we also have forgiven our debtors.
¹³ And do not bring us to the time of trial,
      but rescue us from the evil one.

PROCLAMATION

Text Notes

"Land" in verses 1 and 21 is soil, not the nation. The hearts of the people in Joel 2:12–13 form a collective one, "the heart of you all."

In Psalm 90:2 God's grammatical gender is masculine, and the imagery used for God is feminine, birthing imagery (in the cisgender ancient Israelite world), yielding the name for God in verse 1. "Turn" in verse 3 means both "turn around" and "repent." Also in verse 3, "mortal flesh" renders "man," and "woman-born" renders "children/descendants of humanity/humankind" or "mortals."

First Corinthians 15:47 quotes Genesis 2:7; throughout the passage Paul uses *anthropos*, "human," rather than *aner*, "man," following Genesis where the first earthling is "human," not "man."

In Matthew 6:1, "justness/justice," "uprightness," and "righteousness" are all translations of *dikaiosynēn*. Those righteous acts include far more than the almsgiving, prayer, and fasting in the following verses. The prayer room in verse 6 is an inner one, making one's prayer less likely to be seen.

Preaching Prompts

Joel 2 is a call to solemn assembly in fasting and repentance in response to a locust infestation and resulting economic loss and famine seen as divine punishment. It will be important to unravel the blame language. The text is explicitly inclusive across gender and age categories. The image of God as the mother of the mountains in Psalm 90:2 builds nicely on the maternal imagery present in God's mother-love in Joel 2:13.

The people of the land are to quake at God's power and presence (Joel 2:1), but the land itself (herself) should not fear (verse 21). Notably, God addresses the earth and her creatures in verses 21–22 (excluded from the designated verses in the BCP). God cares for them and whether humanity repents or not, God will care for them.

God's essential characteristics delineated in Joel 2:13, graciousness, loving from her womb (the noun and verb share a root), slow to anger, abounding in faithful love, and being slow to inflict retribution, recur in Exodus 34:6, Deuteronomy 4:31, and Jonah 4:2, and throughout the psalms.

The Epistle makes clear that we are all both earthly dust and the stuff of heaven. We are all equally bearers of the divine image now, and even more so in the age to come. Paul's use of a paradigm distinguishing the spiritual from the physical in 1 Corinthians 15:46 lends itself easily to body/soul dichotomies and hierarchies; it also seems to unhelpfully deemphasize the Incarnation.

As with the Epistle, the implicit gender claims in the Gospel will need to be made explicit. Oiling the head, actually hair, is a common grooming practice for those of African descent like the Afro-Asiatic Israelites and their descendants; it is common in some Asian and other cultures as well. It is less comprehensible in the European culture that has colonized the text and its iconography.

In Matthew 6:6–7, omitted, Jesus tells his disciples not to pray like Gentiles who essentially babble repeatedly, and in that context introduces the Lord's Prayer. It is worth remembering that Jesus initially understood his ministry to be only to "the lost sheep of the house of Israel" (see Matthew 10:4, 15:6). After his encounter with the Syro-Phoenician woman, his ministry extended to the Gentiles.

A final note, when reciting Psalm 51 in the liturgy of the day, consider recentering Bathsheba's abduction, rape, and forced impregnation along with the murder of her husband.

LENT I

Genesis 2:7–9, 15–25; Psalm 104:1–4, 10–15, 27–30;
Colossians 3:1–11; Mark 16:9–15

Genesis 2:7 The SOVEREIGN God crafted the human from the dust of the humus and breathed into its nostrils the breath of life, and the human became a living soul. [8] And the SOVEREIGN God planted a garden in Eden, in the east, and there placed the human whom God had formed. [9] Out of the ground the SOVEREIGN God made grow every tree pleasant to the sight and good for food, and the tree of life in the middle of the garden, along with the tree of the knowledge of good and evil.

[15] The SOVEREIGN God took the human and settled it in the garden of Eden to till and tend it. [16] Then the SOVEREIGN God commanded the human, "From every tree of the garden you may eat freely, [17] but of the tree of the knowledge of good and evil you shall not eat, for in the day you eat from it you shall surely die."

[18] Then the SOVEREIGN God said, "It is not good that the human should be alone; I will make it someone to rely on as its partner." [19] Then the SOVEREIGN God crafted from the humus every creature of the field and every bird of the skies and brought them to the human to see what it would call them; and whatever the human called every living soul, that was its name. [20] The human gave names to all cattle, and to the birds of the air, and to every animal of the field; but for the human there was not found one to rely on as its partner.

[21] The SOVEREIGN God caused a deep sleep to fall upon the human, and it slept; then took one of its sides and closed up its place with flesh in place of it. [22] And the SOVEREIGN God built the side that had been taken from the human into a woman and brought her to the human. [23] Then the human said,

> "This time, this one is bone of my bones
> and flesh of my flesh;
> this one shall be called a woman,
> for out of a man this one was taken."

²⁴ Therefore a man leaves his mother and his father and clings to his woman, and they become one flesh. ²⁵ And they were, the two of them, naked, the man and his woman [or the woman and her man], and were not ashamed.

Psalm 104:1–4, 10–15, 27–30

¹ Bless the FOUNT OF LIFE, O my soul.
MOTHER OF ALL, my God, you are very great.
You don honor and majesty,

² Wrapped in light as a garment,
you stretch out the heavens like a tent-curtain.

³ She who lays on the waters the beams of her upper chambers,
she who makes the clouds her chariot,
she is the one who rides on the wings of the wind.

⁴ She is the one who makes the winds her celestial messengers,
fire and flame her ministers.

¹⁰ She is the one who makes springs gush forth in the torrents;
they flow between the hills.

¹¹ They give drink to every wild animal;
the wild donkeys slake their thirst.

¹² By the torrents the birds of the heavens dwell;
among the branches they give voice.

¹³ She is the one who waters the mountains from her high chambers;
the earth is satisfied with the fruit of your work.

¹⁴ She is the one who makes grass to grow for the cattle,
and vegetation for human labor,
to bring forth food from the earth,

¹⁵ and wine to make the human heart rejoice,
with oil to make the face shine,
and bread to sustain the human heart.

²⁷ All of these hope in you
to provide their food in due season.

²⁸ You give it to them, they glean it;
you open your hand, they are well satisfied.

²⁹ You hide your face, they are dismayed;
when you collect their breath, they die
and to their dust they return.

³⁰ You send forth your spirit, they are created;
and you renew the face of the earth.

Colossians 3:1 If indeed you have been raised with Christ, seek the things that are above, where Christ is seated at the right hand of God. ² Reflect upon things that are above, not on things that are on earth. ³ For you all have died, and your life hidden with Christ in God. ⁴ When Christ is revealed, the one who is your life, then you all will also be revealed with him in glory.

⁵ Put to death, therefore, whatever part of you that is of the earth: sexual immorality, impurity, passion, evil desire, and greediness, which is idolatry. ⁶ Because of these [things] the wrath of God is coming on the spawn of disobedience. ⁷ In these things you all also once followed, when you were living in that way. ⁸ But now you all must put away all anger, wrath, wickedness, slander, and bad language from your mouth. ⁹ Do not lie to one another, seeing that you have stripped off the old self with its deeds. ¹⁰ And you all have clothed yourselves with the new self, which is being made new in knowledge according to the image of its creator. ¹¹ There is no longer Greek and Jew, circumcised and uncircumcised, barbarian, Scythian, slave and free, rather Christ is all and in all.

Mark 16:9 Now after he rose early on the first day of the week, Jesus appeared first to Mary Magdalene from whom he had cast out seven demons. ¹⁰ She went out and she told the ones mourning and weeping who had been with him. ¹¹ But when they heard that he lives and was seen by her, they did not believe. ¹² After this Jesus was made known in another form to two of [the disciples] as they were walking into the countryside. ¹³ And they went back and told the rest, but they did not believe them. ¹⁴ Now later on, while they were sitting at table, Jesus appeared to the eleven themselves and he rebuked their lack of faith and stubbornness, because they did not believe those [the women] who saw Jesus after he had risen. ¹⁵ Then Jesus said to them, "Go into all the world and proclaim the good news to all creation."

PROCLAMATION

Text Notes

The divine Name in this passage is composed of two elements: the word *adonai,* which means "lord," and the Tetragrammaton, the four letters YHWH that represent God's unpronounceable Name. The latter is traditionally pointed with the vowels for *adonai,* its substitute pronunciation. To avoid the repetitive *adonai adonai,* the doubled divine Name is pointed with the vowels for *elohim,* God, customarily yielding "LORD God."

God's creation of the human in Genesis 2:7 uses a verb for crafting pottery. "The human," *ha'adam* is a specific distinct creation; later *adam* will refer to humanity as a whole and serve as the name of the first male human. The earth from which this first earthling was crafted is *ha'adamah.* To preserve the word play I have used human/ humus (earthling/earth works as well): humus, pronounced "HUE-muss," is dark, richly fertile, life-giving soil, the matrix of human creation.

To quote Robert Alter, "The Hebrew *'ezer kenegdo* (King James Version "help meet") is notoriously difficult to translate. . . . "Help" is too weak because it suggests a merely auxiliary function, whereas *'ezer* elsewhere connotes active intervention on behalf of someone, especially in military contexts, as often in the Psalms" (*The Hebrew Bible: A Translation with Commentary*, p. 14). The partner or companion God provides is someone who will have your back, your "ride or die" (roll or ride—originally biker vernacular), the person whom you will accompany, even in the face of certain or inevitable death.

I use the pronoun "it," lacking in Hebrew, for the first human that has within it what will be called woman, *isshah*, and man, *ish*. The earth-creature will be divided in half to generate the woman and man. The word *tzela* in Genesis 2:22 means "side" and not "rib," used for the sides of the ark and tabernacle in Exodus, sides of the temple in 1 Kings and Ezekiel, and hillsides in 2 Samuel. It is never translated as rib outside of the creation of woman story. In the LXX, *pleuron* also means "side," generally in reference to the human body. There are no distinct words for "wife" and "husband" in Hebrew. The language for woman and man has not changed in the text.

Psalm 104 switches between second and third person as is common in the genre. Verses 14–15 use the word that means both bread and food in general in both senses.

"Sexual immorality," *porne* in Colossians 3:5, is a broad brush that generally refers to sex outside of (an appropriate) marriage, including adultery, prostitution, and use of prostitutes. The term is also used more broadly; the author of Hebrews calls Esau *pornos*, "sexually immoral" in 12:6. However, no biblical or postbiblical texts attribute inappropriate sexual behavior to him beyond marrying Hittite women against his mother's wishes (Genesis 26:34–35; 27:46). "Evil desire" is not (simply) lust, sexual or otherwise; it is wrong or inappropriate desire for that which is not acceptable. It is not a condemnation of sexual desire. In verse 8 the root for "slander" is "blaspheme"; at one level blasphemy is slander against God. "Bad language" is broad, including obscenity and talk considered in "poor taste" according to BDAG, where it is bound up with class in Aristotle, the way a slave speaks but not a free "gentleman." (See the entry on *aischrologia* in *A Greek-English Lexicon of the New Testament and Other Early Christian Literature* [known as BDAG].)

Preaching Prompts

Lent often begins with a return to our most ancestral story, to remind us that we are all earthlings, creatures of earth, of the soil we till, the soil to which we shall return. There is both dignity and humility in our creation at the hands of God, breathed into living by the Spirit of God.

Lenten reflection on our own failings and finitude is cast back to these ancestral figures now shrouded in postbiblical notions of "fall" and "original sin." The aftermath of those theologies and doctrines is regularly patriarchal, often misogynistic, demonizing—and in some cases, quite literally damning—God's treasured, hand-made creation. The story of the first woman and the fruit from the tree of knowledge has been translated and interpreted and taught in ways that subordinate and demean women in ways not warranted by the text. (See the classic treatment by Phyllis Trible, *God and the Rhetoric of Sexuality*.)

The primordial human is a pluripotent entity that will be divided into equal halves to form two human persons, yielding different theological implications than turning a man's rib into a woman. Inserting "wife" and "husband" in Genesis 2:23–24 also has theological and interpretive ramifications: Why would marriage be necessary in paradise with only two people? The text does not mention marriage; the assumption suggests specific understandings of sex and shame not (yet) present in the text. There is a chasm between Genesis and Colossians.

Reading these texts together invites us to hold onto the glories of creation and her Creator voiced in the psalm while acknowledging those created in her image do real harm to each other on this good earth that is no longer paradise. We read in the company of the One who is of earth as much as heaven, for whom earth is womb and tomb and heaven's majesty is at hand, incarnate on this very earth.

LENT II

Genesis 3:1–7; Psalm 92:1–5, 12–15; Ephesians 2:4–10; Matthew 7:15–20

Genesis 3:1 Now the serpent had more naked intelligence than any other animal of the field that the SOVEREIGN God had made. And it said to the woman, "Indeed, did God say, 'You two shall not eat from any tree in the garden'?" [2] The woman said to the serpent, "From the fruit of any tree in the garden we may eat, [3] though of the fruit of the tree that is in the middle of the garden God said, 'You two shall not eat and shall not touch it lest you two die.'" [4] Then the serpent said to the woman, "You two will certainly not die, [5] for God knows that when you eat of it your eyes will be opened, and you two will be like God, knowing good and evil." [6] So when the woman saw that the tree was good for food, and that it was a delight to the eyes, and that the tree was to be desired to make one wise, she took of its fruit and ate; and she also gave some to her man, who was with her, and he ate. [7] Then the eyes of both of them were opened, and they knew that they were naked, and they sewed fig leaves together and made loincloths for themselves.

Psalm 92:1–5, 12–15

[1] It is good to give thanks to the AGELESS GOD,
   to sing praises to your name Most High;

[2] to declare your faithful love in the morning,
   and your trustworthiness by night,

[3] upon the ten strings and the harp,
   upon the murmurings of the lyre.

4 For you have made me glad,
   WELLSPRING OF LIFE, by your work;
   at the works of your hands I sing for joy.

5 How great are your works, WOMB OF CREATION!
   Your designs are so very profound.

12 A righteous woman or man flourishes like a palm tree,
    and grows like a cedar in Lebanon.

13 They are planted in the house of SHE WHO IS HOLY;
    in the courts of our God, they flourish.

14 Still producing fruit in their elder years;
    fat with sap and ever green.

15 They declare that the MIGHTY GOD is upright;
    she is my rock, and there is no unrighteousness in her.

Ephesians 2:4 Now God, who is rich in mercy, loving us with a great love [5] when we were dead through our trespasses, brought us to life together with Christ—by grace have you all been saved. [6] And God raised us up together with Christ and seated us all together in the heavenly realms in Christ Jesus. [7] This, that God might show in the ages to come, the abundant riches of God's grace in kindness toward us in Christ Jesus. [8] For by grace have you all been saved through faith, and this is not from yourselves; it is the gift of God. [9] It is not the result of works, so that no one may boast. [10] For we are what God has crafted, created in Christ Jesus for good works, which God prepared beforehand to be our path.

Matthew 7:15 "Beware of false prophets, who will come to you all in sheep's clothing but inside are rapacious wolves. [16] By their fruits you will know them. Are grapes gathered from thorns, or from thistles, figs? [17] Thus, every good tree bears beautiful fruit, but the rotten tree bears wicked fruit. [18] A good tree cannot bear wicked fruit, nor can a corrupt tree bear beautiful fruit. [19] Every tree that does not bear beautiful fruit is cut down and thrown into the fire. [20] Thus you will know them by their fruits.

PROCLAMATION

Text Notes

There is a pun between Genesis 2:25 and 3:1: "And the man and his woman were both *arom*, naked, and were not ashamed. . . . Now the serpent had more *arum*, naked intelligence . . ." The serpent also changes the "you shall not eat" to an inclusive plural from masculine singular in 2:16.

I use "murmuring" in Psalm 92:3 to render *higgion*; the wider semantic range includes melodic speech, song, the sound of instruments, and murmuring (Psalms 9:16 [v. 17 in Hebrew]; 19:14; 92:3; Lamentations 3:62). "Elder years" in verse 15 is *sevah*, "gray hair."

This passage of Ephesians includes a long sentence that extends from verses 4 to 9. I have broken it into more manageable pieces. The plural adjective "heavenly" in verse 6 has no noun to describe; I supply "realms" in keeping with God's majesty.

In Matthew 7:17–18 the writer (or speaker) uses a variety of adjectives: good and a separate superlative that also means good/beautiful, along with corrupt/rotten and wicked/evil. Many translations reduce the vivid imagery to "good" and "bad" fruit and trees.

Preaching Prompts

Lent offers an opportunity to reflect on the nature and limitations of humanity, including the consequences of our actions and inactions and our responsibility in and for this world. In the garden God offers life, provision, knowledge (conditionally), and boundaries. In the serpent God creates a creature who will stir human curiosity to potentially dangerous limits. It is useful to consider the serpent apart from the crutch of postbiblical misidentification with Satan. In the text, the God-crafted serpent is agent provocateur and fall guy, an external place for humans to place blame. Perhaps rather than "tempter," the serpent is "tester." What will humanity do in response to boundaries? Test them, bend them, break them. The serpent also tests something else—how humans hear, remember, tell, question, and interpret God's words: "Did God say . . . ?" And "in the day that you eat of it you shall surely die . . ." except they didn't, not "in the day you eat from it." And "neither shall you touch it . . ." was not in God's recorded speech. These two chapters somewhat surprisingly model the study of scripture, its genres, transmission, and interpretive possibilities, well in keeping with the Lenten disciplines. The woman and the serpent have been long demonized for their exegetical work, but perhaps we should take their example more seriously.

The unfettered praise of the psalm celebrates all of creation on the other side of the garden. Our curiosity has neither doomed nor damned us. We inhabit the good world of a good God, a God whose abundant love manifests as saving grace in and through Christ Jesus according to the Epistle. Unlike in the garden where humanity helped itself to proscribed knowledge, we are helpless to save ourselves. Those who say otherwise may well be among the false prophets of the gospel.

The Gospel offers words to govern our lives—and arguably theology and biblical interpretation. Know a tree—a person, a love, a theology, a biblical interpreter, and their interpretation—by its fruits. Rather than focus on the outward appearance—serpent, woman, out and queer, trans, Black, Brown, bilingual, disabled—examine the fruit of their lives and their interpretation of the scriptures. Is it good? Beautiful? Nutritious? Corrupt? Rotten?

LENT III

Genesis 3:8–21; Psalm 96; Romans 8:31–39; Mark 13:14–22

Genesis 3:8 The woman and man heard the sound of the Sovereign God walking about in the garden in the breezy part of the day, and the woman and her man hid themselves from the presence of the Sovereign God among the trees of the garden. ⁹ Then the Sovereign God called to the man, and said to him, "Where are you?" ¹⁰ And the man said, "I heard the sound of you in the garden, and I was afraid because I was naked and I hid myself." ¹¹ Then God said, "Who told you that you were naked? Did you eat from the tree which I commanded you not to eat?" ¹² And the man said, "The woman whom you gave to stand with me, she gave me fruit from the tree, and I ate." ¹³ Then the Sovereign God said to the woman, "What is this that you have done?" The woman said, "The serpent deceived me, and I ate." ¹⁴ The Sovereign God said to the serpent,

> "Because you have done this,
> cursed are you among all herd animals
> and among all wild creatures;
> upon your belly you shall go,
> and dust you shall eat, all the days of your life.
> ¹⁵ I will put enmity between you and the woman,
> and between your offspring and hers;
> her offspring will strike your head,
> and you will strike the heel of her offspring."

¹⁶ To the woman God said,

> "I will greatly increase your painful toil and your pregnancies;
> in pain shall you birth children,
> and your desire shall be for your man, yet he shall rule with you."

¹⁷ And to the man God said,

> "Because you have listened to the voice of your woman,
> and have eaten of the tree which I commanded you,
> 'You shall not eat from it,'
> cursed is the ground because of you;
> in painful toil you shall eat of it all the days of your life.
> ¹⁸ Thorn and thistle shall it grow for you;
> and you shall eat the plants of the field.
> ¹⁹ By the sweat of your brow
> shall you eat bread
> until you return to the ground;

for out of it you were taken,
you are dust, and to dust you shall return."

20 The man named his wife Eve, because she was the mother of all living. 21 And the SOVER-
EIGN God made garments of skins for the woman and her man, and clothed them.

Psalm 96

1 Sing to the EXALTED a new song;
sing to the CREATOR, all the earth.
2 Sing to the MOST HIGH, bless her name;
proclaim from day to day her salvation.
3 Declare among the nations her glory,
among all the peoples, her marvelous works.
4 For great is the AGELESS GOD, and greatly to be praised;
revered is she above all gods.
5 For all the gods of the peoples are idols,
yet the WOMB OF LIFE made the heavens.
6 Splendor and majesty are before her;
strength and beauty are in her sanctuary.
7 Give to the MAJESTIC ONE, you families of the peoples,
give to the MIGHTY ONE glory and strength.
8 Give to the FIRE OF SINAI the glory due her name;
bring an offering and come into her courts.
9 Bow down and worship the SOVEREIGN ONE in majestic holiness;
tremble in her presence, all the earth.
10 Say among the nations, "The EVER-LIVING GOD reigns!
Indeed, the world is firmly established; it shall never be moved.
God will judge the peoples with equity."
11 Let the heavens rejoice, and let the earth be glad;
let the sea roar, along with what fills it.
12 Let the field exult, and all that is in it.
Then shall all the trees of the forest sing for joy
13 before the WISDOM OF THE AGES; for she is coming,
for she is coming to judge the earth.
She will judge the world with righteousness,
and the peoples with her truth.

Romans 8:31 What then shall we say about these things? If God is for us, who is against us?
32 God is the one who did not spare the very Child of God, but rather for all of us, handed the
Messiah over. Will not God—with Christ—also give us everything else? 33 Who then will bring
any charge against the elect of God? God is the one who justifies. 34 Who will condemn? It is

Christ Jesus, the one who died, moreover the one who was raised and who is at the right hand of God, who intercedes for us. ³⁵ Who will separate us from the love of Christ? Will affliction, or distress, or persecution, or famine, or nakedness, or peril, or sword? ³⁶ As it is written,

> "For your sake we are being killed all day long;
> we are accounted as sheep to be slaughtered."

³⁷ No, in all these things we are completely victorious through the one who loved us. ³⁸ For I am convinced that neither death, nor life, nor angels, nor powers-that-be, nor things that are, nor things that will be, nor powers, ³⁹ nor height, nor depth, nor anything else in all creation, will be able to separate us from the love of God in Christ Jesus our Redeemer.

Mark 13:14 "Now when you all see the *desolating sacrilege* set up where it ought not to be—let the reader understand—then those in Judea must flee to the mountains. ¹⁵ The woman or man on the housetop should not go down or enter the house to take anything out. ¹⁶ And the one in the field should not turn back to grab a garment. ¹⁷ Woe to those who have a child in womb and to those who are nursing infants in those days! ¹⁸ Pray that it be not winter. ¹⁹ For in those days there will be affliction, of such a kind as has not been from the beginning of the creation that God created until now, no, and never will be. ²⁰ And if the Living One had not cut short those days, no flesh would be saved; rather for the sake of the elect, whom God chose, God has cut short those days. ²¹ And if anyone says to you all at that time, 'Look! Here is the Messiah!' or 'Look! There is the Christ!'—do not believe it. ²² False messiahs and false prophets will appear and produce signs and omens, to lead astray, if possible, the elect."

PROCLAMATION

Text Notes

The verb that articulates God's ambulation in Genesis 3:8, *halakh*, is in a self-reflective conjugation, *Hitpael*, and can be humorously understood as God taking Godself for a walk just as the human pair hid themselves. "The breezy part of the day" lacks a specific temporal indicator in the MT. In the LXX, NRSV, and CEB it is in the evening; in the Targum, the "decline" of the day and in the Peshitta, in the "turning" of the day. In verse 12, "stand with me" is "with me," lacking a verb; NETS, NRSV, and KJV supply "*to be* with me" while the Targum and CEB render the woman the man's property: "*provided for* me" and "*gave* me" respectively. My choice of "stand" is a pun of the sort that populate the text where "with me" here is *'imadi* and "stand" shares the same consonants, taking into account the JPS translation, "the woman you put at my side." The offspring of the woman in verse 15 is collective, her "seed"; "he" of RSV and NRSV contribute to readings that thrust Christian messianism upon the text. Rather see the use of "they," "seed," "offspring," etc. in JPS, NETS, CEB, and KJV. Significantly, verse 16 describes the man as ruling *with* rather than over the woman, using the preposition *b*, meaning "with," "in," or "through." I choose the least hierarchical option. The same word encompasses "pain" and "toil/hard work" and describes childbirth and the agricultural labor of Noah and these first humans (Genesis 3:16–17; 5:29; see Everett Fox's "pain-staking labor" in Genesis 3:17). Verse 17 marks the first place the man is called Adam. In verse 19, by the sweat of your "nose" becomes "brow."

Romans 8:36 quotes Psalm 44:22. The familiar martial language "more than conquerors" found in NRSV and KJV is not required by the text of verse 37; the primary meaning is victorious to the point of a rout. Given the harm of militarized Christianity, I follow the Peshitta and CEB in preserving "victorious" for *hupernikomen*. Rulers and their domains, *archai*, the latter the "principalities" of the Peshitta and KJV, are encompassed in the "powers-that-be" of verse 38. Romans 8:35 and Mark 13:19 share the specific language of "affliction," *thlipsis*.

The original "desolating sacrilege" refers to the idol of Zeus in the temple which provoked the Maccabean wars beginning in 167 BCE (see Daniel 11:31, 12:11). According to Lawrence M. Wills in the *Jewish Annotated New Testament* (Oxford), the Markan reference may pertain to an image of Caligula intended for the temple forestalled by his assassination in 40 CE. It is not clear if the Divine in verse 20 is Jesus, the risen Christ, or God herself; the "Living One" encompasses both options. Similarly, in the same verse, "no flesh,"—a more literal translation—encompasses humankind and animalkind (and perhaps by extension, all creation).

Preaching Prompts

God's response to the first human pair helping themselves to proscribed knowledge is harsh; there are curses involved. Yet counter to common misapprehension, God does not curse womankind; God does not curse humans at all. God curses the ground and God curses the serpent. The story leaves the reader with a view of women constrained by hormones, love, sexual desire, and childbirth, and the man doomed to subsistence labor. Yet the story is not prophetic; it is an etiology, an origin story to explain why the essentials of human survival—reproduction and food production—are so hard and provides a vision of an Edenic world in which people did not have to struggle. Humanity lives with and within those parameters, occasionally transcending them.

Humanity offers transcendent praise in Psalm 96 to the God who enables them to flourish in the hostile world that gave rise to the stories of Genesis. The world, though difficult, is not actively hostile and joins with humanity in praise in verses 11–12. The Epistle speaks a word of comfort: we are the beloved of God and nothing can separate us from her love—not even the harsh language of Genesis or hegemonic patriarchal structures built in its name.

Yet there is trouble in the world and more on the way. The danger to humanity is not the biological imperatives of women, real or imagined. In the larger chapter Jesus prepares his disciples for the danger they will face for refusing to bow to the empire or its idols. The danger is such that believers would be better off dropping everything and fleeing. Jesus expresses concern for the women who are pregnant and nursing. It is more than concern over their slower pace; it is also a reminder that women and children are often most vulnerable to systems that wield power.

These readings present women as the mothers of creation, possessors of forbidden knowledge, bound by reproductive cycles, part of a creation that gives praise, inseparable from the love of God, and disciples of Jesus endangered by their faith yet among the elect who will ultimately be saved. This micro-canon tells the story of salvation that will be retold in its longer form at the conclusion of Lent in the Easter Vigil.

LENT IV

Song of Songs 4:7–16; Psalm 136:1–16; 1 John 4:7–12; John 3:11–17

Song 4

To a woman . . .

7 All of you is beautiful, my beloved companion;
   there is no flaw in you.
8 With me! From Lebanon, my bride, come with me;
   come with me from Lebanon.
   Depart from the peak of Amana,
   from the peak of Senir and Hermon,
   from the dens of lions,
   from the mountains of leopards.
9 My heart is yours, my sister, my bride,
   my heart is yours with just one of your eyes,
   with one jewel of your necklace.
10 How beautiful is your love, my sister, my bride!
   How much better is your love than wine,
   and the fragrance of your oils more than every spice!
11 Honied sweetness drips from your lips, my bride;
   honey and milk are under your tongue;
   the scent of your garments is like the scent of Lebanon.
12 A garden locked is my sister, my bride,
   a garden locked, a fountain sealed.
13 Your limbs are an orchard of pomegranates
   with all choicest fruits: henna with nard,

¹⁴ nard and saffron, sweet cane and cinnamon,
with every kind of frankincense tree,
myrrh and aloes, with all the best spices:
¹⁵ A garden spring, a well of living water,
streaming from Lebanon.

To a woman's beloved . . .

¹⁶ Awake, Zaphon, northern wind,
and come, Teman, southern wind!
Blow upon my garden
that its spice-scent might flow.
Let my beloved come to their garden,
and partake of its choicest fruits.

Psalm 136:1–16

¹ Give thanks to the FOUNT OF LIFE, who is good,
for her faithful love is everlasting.
² Give thanks to the God of gods,
for her faithful love is everlasting.
³ Give thanks to the Majesty of Majesties,
for her faithful love is everlasting;
⁴ who alone does great wonders,
for her faithful love is everlasting;
⁵ who through insight made the heavens,
for her faithful love is everlasting;
⁶ to the one who spread out the land upon the waters,
for her faithful love is everlasting;
⁷ to the one who made the great lights,
for her faithful love is everlasting;
⁸ the sun to govern the day,
for her faithful love is everlasting;
⁹ the moon and stars to govern the night,
for her faithful love is everlasting;
¹⁰ who struck Egypt through their firstborn daughters and sons,
for her faithful love is everlasting;
¹¹ and brought Israel out from among them,
for her faithful love is everlasting;
¹² with a strong hand and an outstretched arm,
for her faithful love is everlasting;
¹³ who cut the Red Sea in two,
for her faithful love is everlasting;

¹⁴ and made Israel pass over through the midst of it,
    for her faithful love is everlasting;
¹⁵ but churned Pharaoh and his army in the Red Sea,
    for her faithful love is everlasting;
¹⁶ who walked her people through the wilderness,
    for her faithful love is everlasting.

1 John 4:7 Beloved, let us love one another, because love is from God and everyone who loves is born of God and knows God. [8] Whoever does not love does not know God, for God is love. [9] In this way God's love was revealed among us: God sent God's only Son into the world so that we might live through him. [10] In this is love, not that we loved God but that God loved us and sent God's own Son to be the means of forgiveness for our sins. [11] Beloved, if God loves us thus, we ought also love one another. [12] God no one has ever seen. Yet if we love one another, God lives in us, and God's love is made complete in us.

John 3:11 "Very truly, I tell you, we speak of what we know and we testify to what we have seen; yet you all do not receive our testimony. [12] If I have told you all about earthly things and you do not believe, how can you all believe if I tell you about heavenly things? [13] Now then, no one has ascended into the heavens except the one who descended from the heavens, the Son of Woman. [14] And just as Moses lifted up the serpent in the wilderness, so must the Son of Woman be lifted up, [15] that whoever believes in him may have eternal life.

[16] "For God so loved the world that God gave God's only Son, so that everyone who believes in him may not perish but may have eternal life. [17] Indeed, God did not send the Son into the world to condemn the world, but in order that the world might be saved through him."

PROCLAMATION

Text Notes

In the Song the gender of the addressee is indicated by the binary Hebrew grammar. Rather than identify speaking voice (deductively) and reinforce the heteronormativity of the text, I identify the hearer leaving room for anyone to address her, in this case, as "beloved." Similarly in verse 16, I use the pronoun "their" for the woman's beloved. In Song 4:7, the endearment *ra'yat* is translated variably: "my love" (NRSV, KJV), "my darling" (JPS), "my dearest" (CEB), "my closest [one]" (Peshitta and LXX); its root meaning is "companion," with the sense of nearest/dearest and here, "beloved." "Bride from Lebanon" is missing the possessive "my" in verse 8 as is "bride" in verses 9 and following. "Depart" in verse 8 is one of a set of homophonic verbs that can mean "look" as in KJV, form II, but fits better in its form I, meaning "travel." Verse 9 lacks a proper verb. The noun "heart" is conjugated like a verb, "you hearted me"; there is no basis for the problematic "ravish" of KJV and NRSV. The plural "branches" in verse 13 are here "limbs," human and arboreal. The orchard of verse 13, *pardes*, derives from Zoroastrian scripture in the Avestan language, *pairidaēza*, and the source of our word "paradise."

In 1 John 4:10, Jesus is the "means of forgiveness" for our sins. The method of that facilitation has been traditionally narrowed to "sacrifice," "expiation," "propitiation," etc. in an atonement theory framework. "Means of forgiveness" offers a full range of salvific possibility not limited to the death of Jesus but intentionally including his life, his love, his teaching, his very incarnational existence. In spite of the absolute certainty in the author's rhetoric that no one has seen God "at any time" in verse 12, the scriptures insist that God spoke to Moses "face to face," literally "mouth to mouth"—Jacob makes a similar claim—and records Moses seeing God's "back parts" and Isaiah testifies he has indeed seen the Holy One as does Ezekiel (see Genesis 32:30; Exodus 33:11, 23; Isaiah 6:1, Ezekiel 1:1). In verse 12 God's love is "made complete" in us, "made whole" in the sense of "finished." The older translation "perfection" does not readily convey that sense of wholeness.

Jesus as the Son of Woman is more than biologically true; it is grammatically true in that *anthroupou* is fundamentally human, not specifically male.

Preaching Prompts

The weightiness of Lent is lightened a bit on Laetare Sunday, named from the historic introit meaning "rejoice." These weeks of penitent contemplation can leave one with a nearly unredeemable portrait of humanity. These lessons offer reason for rejoicing in contemplating God's good world of which we are a part and God's love manifest in creation and ultimately through Jesus.

The garden image that dominates biblical imagination is often Eden, the site of brokenness. Yet scripture also offers the garden paradise of lovers in which the ruptures of the first garden appear healed: The desire of the lovers is mutual and the ground is abundantly fruitful with no evidence of human labor; Phyllis Trible compares these two gardens in *God and the Rhetoric of Sexuality*. The poet's emphatic speech in the Song defies grammar as poets are wont to do. (For a more poetic translation of the Song, see Marcia Falk, *The Song of Songs: Love Lyrics from the Bible*.)

Indeed, God as poet of creation creates her own grammar. The psalm celebrates the poetry of creation as evidence of God's faithful love. The theological idiom of the Iron Age further characterizes God's actions that harm others as evidence of God's love for Israel, the fate of Pharaoh and the Egyptians in the psalm (verses 10, 15). Yet the inclusion of wider creation—the heavens and sun, moon and stars, and land and sea—in verses 5–9 point to an even wider love not limited by nation, tribe, clan, or kin.

The love the Epistle writer celebrates is similarly articulated in insider, communal terms, "beloved" addresses fellow believers, yet that great love of God is not limited to followers of the Way. The Epistle supplies the image of a God who gives birth to her beloved: "Everyone who loves is born of God" (1 John 4:7). The Epistle also leaves the image of God's love as not yet, not quite, completed, and extraordinarily, dependent upon us in verse 12: Our love is part of God's love; God's love is not complete without our love for one another.

The evangelist articulates God's love in singular incarnational woman-born terms. We rejoice on this rejoicing Sunday because God's love is made manifest in and through creation, in and through humanity, and in and through Jesus. We return to our Lenten devotions and disciplines secure in this love and convicted of our call to complete God's love in loving all who, all that, she loves.

LENT V

Isaiah 51:1–8; Psalm 148; Romans 11:13–24; Luke 13:18–21

Isaiah 51:1 Listen to me, all you that pursue righteousness,
    all you that seek the AUTHOR OF LIFE.
    Look to the rock from which you were hewn,
    and to the quarry from which you were dug.
2 Look to Abraham your father,
    and to Sarah who writhed-in-labor for you all;
    he was just one when I called him,
    but I blessed him and made him many.
3 For the GOD WHO SAVES has comforted Zion;
    she has comforted all her waste places.
    And she shall make her wilderness like Eden,
    her desert like the garden of the CREATOR OF ALL;
    joy and gladness will be found in her,
    thanksgiving and the sound of song.
    [Sorrow and mourning will flee away.]
4 Listen to me, my people,
    and my nation, to me give heed;
    for a teaching shall from me go forth,
    and my justice for a light to the peoples.
    I will do so suddenly.
5 My deliverance is near,
    my salvation has gone forth
    and my arms will govern the peoples;
    for me the coastlands wait,
    and upon my arm they await.

6 Lift up your eyes to the heavens,
   and look to the earth below.
   For the heavens like smoke will vanish,
   the earth like a garment will wear out,
   and those who live on it will die like gnats;
   yet my salvation will be forever,
   and my deliverance will never be broken.
7 Listen to me, you who know righteousness,
   you people who have my teaching in your hearts;
   fear not the reproach of others,
   and when they revile you, do not be dismayed.
8 For like a garment a moth will devour them,
   and like wool a worm will consume them;
   yet my deliverance will be forever,
   and my salvation to all generations.

Psalm 148

1 Praise the ALMIGHTY!
   Praise the EXALTED from the heavens;
   praise her on the heights!
2 Praise her, all her angels;
   praise her, all her starry warriors!
3 Praise her, sun and moon;
   praise her, all you stars of light!
4 Praise her, you highest heavens,
   and you waters above the heavens!
5 Let them praise the Name of the MIGHTY GOD,
   for she commanded and they were created.
6 She established them forever and ever;
   she set boundaries that cannot be crossed.
7 Praise the CREATOR OF ALL from the earth,
   sea monsters and all watery deeps,
8 Fire and hail, snow and frost,
   swirling wind fulfilling her word!
9 Mountains and all hills,
   fruit trees and all cedars!
10 Animals wild and tame,
   creeping things and winged birds!
11 Queens and kings of the earth and all peoples,
   royal seed and all rulers of the earth!

¹² Young women and men alike,
 aged and young together!
¹³ Let them praise the Name of the ETERNAL,
 for her name alone is exalted;
 her glory is above the earth and the heavens.
¹⁴ She has raised up a horn for her people,
 praise for all her faithful,
 for the daughters and sons of Israel who are close to her.
 Praise the ALMIGHTY!

Romans 11:13 Now to you Gentiles am I speaking. Since I am, on the one hand, an apostle to the Gentiles, I glorify my ministry ¹⁴ in order to make my own in the flesh jealous, and thus save some of them. ¹⁵ For if their rejection is the reconciliation of the world, what is their acceptance but life from the dead? ¹⁶ If the first fruits are holy, then the whole batch is holy, and if the root is holy, thus are the branches also.

¹⁷ Now, if some of the branches were broken off and you, a wild olive shoot, were grafted among them to share the oil-rich root of the olive tree, ¹⁸ do not boast against the branches. If you should boast: It is not you that bears up the root, rather the root bears you up. ¹⁹ You may say, "Branches were broken off so that I might be grafted in." ²⁰ Well then, through unbelief were they broken off while you stand only through faithfulness. So be not proud, rather be in awe. ²¹ For if God did not spare the natural branches, God may not spare you. ²² Behold the graciousness and the sternness of God: toward those who have fallen, sternness, while toward you, graciousness, provided you continue in that graciousness; otherwise you also will be cut off. ²³ And yet, if they do not remain in unbelief, they will be grafted in, for God has the power to graft them in again. ²⁴ For if you out of what is by nature a wild olive tree have been cut and, contrary to nature, grafted into a cultivated olive tree, how much more will these natural branches be grafted back into their own olive tree?

Luke 13:18 Jesus asked, "What is the realm of God like? And to what should I compare it? ¹⁹ It is like a mustard seed that someone took and tossed in the garden and it grew and became a tree, and the birds of the air made nests in its branches."

²⁰ Speaking again Jesus said, "To what should I compare the realm of God? ²¹ It is like yeast that a woman took and mixed in with three measures of flour until all of it was leavened."

PROCLAMATION

Text Notes

Sarah's labor in Isaiah 51:2 is described with a verb that means "writhe" and "twist" in birthing and, in some cases, dancing, as in Psalm 150:4. In verse 3 God has already begun to comfort Zion (see JPS); the future tense translation of NRSV and KJV neglects the immediate nature of God's response. The tense changes in the third verse, emphasizing the ongoing work of God (JPS keeps the passage in the past tense). The last line of verse 3 comes from the Great Isaiah Scroll of the Dead Sea collection, 1QIsaᵃ; the reader may choose to omit it. While some unnecessarily move the last verb constituting the final line of verse 4 to verse 5 (NRSV, CEB, Alter), it is entirely comprehensible in its place.

As a psalm of praise, Psalm 148 has opening and closing hallelujahs typically not said in Lent, and verbs from the *Hallel* root throughout the first five verses. The "hallelujahs" are translated as "Praise [the divine Name]" so the psalm might be more easily used in Lent.

In Romans 11:20, *apotomia* serves as the opposite or inverse of *chrēstotēs*, goodness, kindness, beneficence; it is only used there in the Scriptures. Related, *apotomos* occurs in the Wisdom of Solomon (Ecclesiasticus 5:20; 6:5; 11:10; 12:9; 18:15), translated as "stern" more often than "severe." Here the pair are rendered "graciousness" and "sternness."

The "tossed" seed, literally "thrown," is described as scattered rather than planted. The same word, "heaven/s," includes the realm of the "birds of the [air]" and the realm of God.

Preaching Prompts

The metaphor of the Lenten wilderness draws its imagery from the many wilderness sojourns of Israel and individual figures across the canon as well as use of that imagery to describe the state of Israel under and after occupation. Salvation and restoration imagery often draw upon garden imagery: well-watered trees and plants flourishing as markers of restoration. Here at the end of Lent these readings move through garden scenes—remembering that the Hebrew garden is often an orchard—to texts with flourishing trees representing God's people as God's planting. The flora anticipate the flowers of Easter as the joyful praise of the psalm has unpronounced (but translated) hallelujahs.

The poet writing in Isaiah's name envisions God's restoration of Israel, and for those who struggled to see the vision, she reminds them of who God is—the one who waters the wilderness—and what God has done—built a new people through Sarah and Abraham. God promises a salvation that will endure when even the earth crumbles away. That salvation is national, corporate, not individual, generally meaning deliverance from the physical threats of individuals and nations. The psalm's riot of praise is a further reminder of who God is and what she has done.

In Romans, the garden imagery represents Paul's Israelite kin and Christian kin; some, like him, were both. At one level Romans 11 is a caution against anti-Judaism in the early church: we are all branches on the same tree and we who are Christians are grafted into the ancient Israelite tree with deep roots. At another level the text is firmly in the supercessionist tradition, rejecting Judaism and those who do not put their faith in Christ. While it can be a narrow line to walk, one can proclaim Jesus in the broad tradition of Paul without perpetuating anti-Judaism.

In the Gospel reading, tree imagery provides one vision of God's realm. The mustard seed grows with very little cultivation while the baker is hands-on, tending, kneading her creation. In these paired parables, as with the shepherd of lost sheep (Luke 15:3–7) and woman with coins (Luke 15:8–10), Jesus uses a mix of gendered language back to back, answering the same question. The response is not a description of heaven that one could draw or blueprint, but rather a description of God as a Creator who sparks creation and allows it to flourish on its own *and* as a Creator who carefully tends her creation.

FEAST OF THE ANNUNCIATION, MARCH 25

Zephaniah 3:14–20; Canticle 15, the Magnificat (Luke 1:46–55);
2 Corinthians 6:16b–18; Luke 1:26–38

Zephaniah 3:14 Sing aloud, daughter of Zion; shout, all ye Israel!
Rejoice, daughter, and exult with all your heart, daughter of Jerusalem!
15 The JUDGE OF ALL FLESH has taken away the judgments against you,
and has turned away your enemies, daughter.
The sovereign of Israel, CREATOR OF THE HEAVENS AND EARTH,
is in your midst, daughter; no longer shall you fear evil.
16 On that day it shall be said to Jerusalem:
Fear not, Zion; do not let your hands grow weak, daughter.
17 The AGELESS ONE, your God, is in your midst, daughter,
a warrior who will deliver salvation;
who will rejoice over you with gladness, daughter,
God will renew you in love, daughter;
God will exult over you, daughter, with loud singing.
18 Those who are grieved on account of the festivals,
I will remove from you, daughter,
so, daughter, that you will not bear their reproach.
19 I will deal with all your oppressors, daughter, at that time.
And I will save the lame and gather the outcast,
and I will change their shame into praise
and renown in all the earth.
20 At that time I will bring you all home, at the time when I gather all of you;
for I will make you all renowned and praised

among all the peoples of the earth,

when I restore your fortunes before all of your eyes,

says the GOD WHO IS SALVATION.

Canticle 15, the Magnificat, Luke 1:46–55

46 "My soul magnifies the Holy One,

47 and my spirit rejoices in God my Savior, *

48 for God has looked with favor on the lowliness of God's own servant.

Surely from now on all generations will call me blessed; *

49 for the Mighty One has done great things for me,

and holy is God's name.

50 God's loving-kindness is for those who fear God *

from generation to generation.

51 God has shown the strength of God's own arm; *

God has scattered the arrogant in the intent of their hearts.

52 God has brought down the powerful from their thrones, *

and lifted up the lowly;

53 God has filled the hungry with good things, *

and sent the rich away empty.

54 God has helped God's own child, Israel, *

a memorial to God's mercy,

55 just as God said to our mothers and fathers,

to Abraham and Hagar and Sarah, to their descendants forever."

2 Corinthians 6:16 For we are the temple of the living God; as God said:

"I will dwell in them and walk among them,

and I will be their God,

and they shall be my people."

17 Therefore, *"Come out from them,*

and be separate from them," says the Holy One,

and *"Touch nothing unclean,"*

then *"I will take you all in."*

18 and *"I will be your parent,*

and you shall be my daughters and sons,"

says the Almighty Everlasting God.

Luke 1:26 In the sixth month the angel Gabriel was sent by God to a town of Galilee, Nazareth, 27 to a virgin betrothed to a man whose name was Joseph, of the house of David. And the name of the virgin was Mary. 28 And the angel came to Mary and said, "Rejoice, favored one! The Most High God is with you." 29 Now, she was troubled by the angel's words and pondered what sort of greeting this was. 30 Then the angel said to her, "Fear not Mary, for you have found favor with God. [31] And now, you will conceive in your womb and give birth to a son, and you will name him Jesus. [32] He will be great and will be called the Son of the Most High, and the Sovereign God will give him the throne of his ancestor David. [33] He will reign over the house of Jacob forever, and of his sovereignty there will be no end." [34] Then Mary said to the angel, "How can this be, since I have not known a man intimately?" [35] The angel said to her, "The Holy Spirit, She will come upon you, and the power of the Most High will overshadow you; therefore the one born will be holy. He will be called Son of God. [36] And now, Elizabeth your kinswoman has even conceived a son in her old age, and this is the sixth month for she who was called barren. [37] For nothing will be impossible with God." [38] Then Mary said, "Here am I, the woman-slave of God; let it be with me according to your word." Then the angel left her.

PROCLAMATION

Text Notes

Bat Zion (or Jerusalem) can mean both Daughter Zion, the city, *or* a daughter of Zion, a woman from the city. In Isaiah 40:9 reading "daughter of" reveals a female prophet crying out to Jerusalem (compare NRSV and JPS translations). Because the addressee is feminine, all of the verbs to her are also feminine; I reproduce "daughter" in places where English masks the frequency of feminine address. Verse 18 is notoriously difficult to translate, see the discussion in my commentary on Zephaniah in the *Wisdom* series.

In Luke 1:55, the inclusive plural *pateras* can mean ancestors, parents or fathers. Since God's promises were not just to Abraham and God also made promises to Hagar (Genesis 16:10–13; 21:17–18) and for Sarah (through Abraham in Genesis 17:15–16), I have expanded "Abraham and his descendants" to reflect that. Abraham also had children with Keturah; their offspring would also be beneficiaries of the promises made to Abraham. However, God does not make a promise directly to her in the scriptures.

In Mary's linguistic and cultural world, in Hebrew and Aramaic, the spirit is feminine; the Syriac text uses a feminine verb for the spirit in Luke 1:35. Also in her world, there was no distinction between servant and slave. Mary is not saying she will wait on God hand and foot in verse 38; she is giving God ownership of her body, ownership slaveholders claimed without consent.

Preaching Prompts

In its original context daughter Zion was most likely the city. Here I suggest hearing it through the experience of the pregnant Virgin reflecting on her scriptures in light of her experience.

The appointed Epistle is a collection of verse fragments strung together, many out of context. The phrases are inexact quotes, whether looking at Hebrew or Greek antecedents, shaped for deployment here. Leviticus 26:11–12 has the same sense as in 2 Corinthians 6:16. Verse 17 of the Epistle links a fragment found in both Ezekiel 20:34 and 20:41 to a line from Isaiah 52:11 calling for a second Exodus from Egypt. Verse 18 takes God's promise to David for Solomon to be his father in 2 Samuel 7:14 and makes it second person plural, "your all" instead of "his," and adds "daughters" to the altered text in Greek.

Angelic lore is largely pseudepigraphal beginning in 2 Esdras. While Gabriel and Michael appear in the Hebrew Bible (Daniel 8:16; 9:21; 10:13, 21; 12:1), they are not identified as angels. However, Raphael is called an angel in Tobit 5:4.

There is some irony in the pains the Gospel takes to connect Jesus to David and the Hebrew Scriptures, and in the choice of translators to anglicize the names of the holy family and disciples, undermining their Jewish identity. A further irony is that Jesus's Davidic heritage rests on Joseph's genealogy and the supposition that Mary is from the same tribe, as was common but not required. Mary's only relative in the text, Elizabeth, is the wife of a priest. Priests married within the priestly line nearly exclusively, making her likely a *bat cohen*, priest's daughter as well. What this means for Mary's heritage and that of Jesus is unclear.

PALM SUNDAY—LITURGY OF THE PALMS

Matthew 21:1–11; Psalm 118:19–29

Matthew 21:1 Now they had come near Jerusalem and reached Bethphage on the Mount of Olives, then Jesus sent two disciples, ² saying to them, "Go into the village before you, and immediately you will find a donkey tied, and a colt with her; release them and bring them to me. ³ If anyone says anything to you, just say this, 'The Son of Woman needs them.' And they will send them immediately." ⁴ This took place to fulfill what had been spoken through the prophet, saying,

⁵ "Tell the daughter of Zion,
'*Look, your sovereign is coming to you,*
humble, and mounted on a donkey,
and on a colt, the foal of a donkey.'"

⁶ The disciples went and did just as Jesus had instructed them; ⁷ they brought the donkey and the colt, and put their cloaks on them, and he sat on them. ⁸ A very large crowd spread their cloaks on the road, and others cut branches from the trees and spread them on the road. ⁹ The crowds that were going before him and the one following were shouting, saying:

"*Hosanna to the Son of David!*
Blessed is the one who comes in the name of the Holy One!
Hosanna in the highest!"

¹⁰ When Jesus entered Jerusalem, the whole city was shook, asking, "Who is this?" ¹¹ The crowds were saying, "This is the prophet Jesus from Nazareth in Galilee."

Psalm 118:19–29

¹⁹ Open for me the gates of righteousness,
that I may enter them
and give thanks to the LIVING GOD.

²⁰ This is the gate to the HOLY PRESENCE;
the righteous shall enter through it.

²¹ I thank you that you have answered me
and you have become my salvation.

²² The stone that the builders rejected
has become the chief cornerstone.

²³ This is OUR GOD's doing;
it is marvelous in our eyes.

²⁴ This is the day that the FONT OF CREATION has made;
let us rejoice and be glad in it.

²⁵ Ah! HOLY ONE, help, save us!
Ah! HOLY ONE, haste, deliver us!

²⁶ Blessed is the one who comes in the name of the MOST HIGH GOD.
We bless you from the house of the HOLY ONE.

²⁷ The FAITHFUL ONE is God,
and she has given us light.
Bind the festal offering with ropes of branches,
up to the horns of the altar.

²⁸ You are my God, and I will give thanks to you;
you are my God; I will exalt you.

²⁹ Give thanks to the HOLY ONE, for she is good,
for her faithful love endures forever.

PROCLAMATION

Text Notes

The text has Jesus use the title "Lord" of himself in Matthew 21:3. In keeping with the aims of this volume, expansive and explicitly feminine language for God and humanity, I employ a translation of the messianic title Jesus often uses for himself here. (See commentary on Advent 1, Year A.) In verse 5 the Gospel quotes Zechariah 9:9, seeming not to understand the poetic parallelism that describes the same animal in two ways; he appears to sit on both in verse 7. The Gospel adds an introduction to *"the* daughter of Zion," adding the definite article not common in this expression in Greek, begging the question to whom it is addressed. In verse 9, the crowd chants Psalm 118:26, a procession psalm for entering the temple also recited during Passover.

The assonant and alliterative poetry of Psalm 118:25 (the "Hosanna") verse, is difficult to reproduce: *Ana Ya hoshia na; Ana Ya chatzlicha na.* The "hosanna" pronunciation comes from the Greek transliteration of the Hebrew. Verse 27 is unclear in a number of places: "bind the feast with clouds." Since portions of sacrificial animals were eaten, "festal offering" is likely; and "ropes" and "branches" are each one letter away from "clouds." "God's faithful love endures forever" is one of the oldest liturgical refrains in the Hebrew Bible, see the opening and closing of this psalm and Psalm 118.

Preaching Prompts

While this is not traditionally a preaching occasion, one may choose to frame the liturgy with a brief preface or blurb in the leaflet, or alternatively address it in the subsequent sermon (if the liturgy precedes another service).

The ubiquity of monarchy in the scriptures and the worlds from which they emerge reflect more about the humans who received and recorded, and translate and interpret them, than it does about God who inspired and speaks through them. Monarchs were the most powerful persons in those worlds and they and their power, reigns, and regalia provided a vocabulary for talking about God. Jesus subverts that to some degree by reinterpreting that title in such a way as to perplex even those who knew him best.

These lessons provide an opportunity to talk about our language and imagery for God in and out of the Bible (and this lectionary) and its impact on persons in terms of class, gender, the performance of gender, and sexual orientation.

PALM SUNDAY—LITURGY OF THE WORD

Isaiah 49:5–16; Psalm 22:1–11; Galatians 3:23–4:7;
Mark 14:32–15:47 (or Mark 14:32–52)

Those who prefer to continue the Gospel through the Passion will find the successive verses in the Good Friday readings.

Isaiah 49:5 And now says the AUTHOR OF LIFE,
   who formed me in the womb to be God's slave
   to return Jacob back to God,
   and that Israel might be gathered to God;
   I am honored in the sight of the HOLY ONE OF OLD,
   and my God is my strength.

6 God says,

"It is too light a thing that you should be my slave
to raise up the tribes of Jacob [the line of Rebekah],
and to restore the survivors of Israel [born of Rachel and Leah, and Bilhah and Zilpah].
I will give you as a light to the nations,
for it will be that my salvation reaches to the end of the earth."

7 Thus says the FAITHFUL ONE,
the Redeemer of Israel, God's holy one,
to one despised, abhorred by the nations,
the slave of rulers,
"Queens and kings shall see and arise,
princes and princesses, and they too shall prostrate themselves,
on account of the FIRE OF SINAI, who is faithful,
the Holy One of Israel, who has chosen you."

8 Thus says the MIGHTY GOD:
In a favorable time have I answered you,
on a day of salvation have I helped you;
I have kept you and given you
as a covenant to the people,
to establish the land,
to apportion the desolate portions;

9 saying to the prisoners, "Go free!"
to those who are in darkness, "Let yourselves be seen."
Along the paths they shall pasture,
and on all the bare heights shall be their pasture.

10 They shall not hunger nor shall they thirst,
neither shall heat nor sun strike them down,
for the one who mother-loves them shall lead them,
and by springs of water shall guide them.

11 And I will turn all my mountains into a pathway,
and my highways shall be raised up.

12 Look! These shall come from far away,
and see! These from the north and from the sea to the west,
and these from the southland of Syene.

13 Sing for joy, you heavens, and exult O earth;
let mountains break forth into singing!
For the TENDER LOVING ONE has comforted God's people,
and will mother-love God's suffering ones.

14 But Zion said, "The EVERLASTING GOD has forsaken me,
my Sovereign has forgotten me."

¹⁵ Can a woman forget her nursing child,

or mother-love for the child of her womb?

Even these may forget,

yet I, no, I will not forget you.

¹⁶ See, I have engraved you on the palms of my hands;

your walls are continually before me.

Psalm 22:1–11

¹ My God, my God, why have you forsaken me?

Why are you so far from my deliverance, from the words of my groaning?

² My God, I cry by day, and you do not answer;

and by night, and there is found no rest for me.

³ Yet you are holy,

enthroned on the praises of Israel.

⁴ In you our mothers and fathers trusted;

they trusted, and you rescued them.

⁵ To you they cried, and were freed;

in you they trusted, and they were not put to shame.

⁶ But I am a worm, and not human;

scorned by humankind, and despised by people.

⁷ All who see me mock me;

they flap their lips at me, they shake their heads:

⁸ "Commit yourself to the SAVING ONE; let God rescue

and deliver the one in whom God delights!"

⁹ Yet it was you who drew me from the womb;

keeping me safe on my mother's breast.

¹⁰ On you was I cast from birth,

and since my mother's womb you have been my God.

¹¹ Be not far from me,

for trouble is near

and there is none to help.

Galatians 3:23 Now before faith came, we were garrisoned and guarded under the law until the faith that was coming should be revealed. ²⁴ Therefore the law was our instructor until Christ came, so that we might be justified by faith. ²⁵ But now that faith has come, we are no longer subject to an instructor, ²⁶ for in Christ Jesus you are all daughters and sons of God through faith. ²⁷ So, as many of you as were baptized into Christ are clothed in Christ. ²⁸ There is no Jew or Greek, there is no slave or free, there is no male and female; for all of you are one in Christ Jesus. ²⁹ And if you belong to Christ, then you are Abraham's [and Sarah's] offspring, heirs according to the promise.

[4:1] I say that as long as heirs are minors, they are no better than slaves, though they are the masters of all; [2] but they remain under guardians and trustees until the time set by the father. [3] So also for us; while we were minors, we were enslaved by the constitutive elements of the world. [4] But when the fullness of time had come, God sent God's own Son, born of a woman, born under the law, [5] to redeem those who were under the law, so that we might receive adoption like children. [6] And because you are children, God has sent the Spirit of God's own Son into our hearts, crying, "Abba! Father!" [7] So you are no longer a slave but a child, and if a child then also an heir, through God.

[**Mark 14:32** Jesus and his disciples went to a place called Gethsemane and he said to his disciples, "You all sit here while I pray." [33] He took with him Peter and James and John and began to be deeply moved and distressed. [34] And said to them, "My soul is deeply grieved, to the point of death; you all stay here, and stay awake." [35] And going a little farther, he threw himself on the ground and prayed that, if possible, the hour might pass from him. [36] He said, "Abba, Father, all things are possible for you; remove this cup from me; yet, not what I want, but what you do." [37] Jesus came and found them sleeping; and he said to Peter, "Simon, are you sleeping? Could you not stay awake one hour? [38] Stay awake and pray that you all may not come into the time of trial; the spirit indeed is willing, but the flesh is weak." [39] And again he went away and prayed, saying the same thing. [40] And once more he came and found them sleeping, for their eyes were very heavy; and they did not know what to say to him. [41] Jesus came a third time and said to them, "Are you all sleeping, still, and taking your rest? Enough! The hour has come. Look! The Son of Woman is betrayed into the hands of sinners. [42] Get up, let us go. See, my betrayer is at hand."

[43] And instantly, while he was still speaking, Judas, one of the twelve, arrived; with him there was a crowd with swords and clubs from the chief priests, the religious scholars, and the elders. [44] Now the betrayer had given them a sign, saying, "The one I kiss is he; seize him and lead him away safely." [45] Then when Judas came, he went up to Jesus immediately and said, "Rabbi!" and kissed him. [46] Then they laid hands on him and took him. [47] But one of the bystanders drew his sword and struck the slave of the high priest and cut off his ear. [48] Then Jesus said to them, "Is it as for a bandit you all have come out with swords and clubs to seize me? [49] Daily I was with you all in the temple teaching, and you did not seize me. But let the scriptures be fulfilled." [50] All of them deserted him and fled. [51] A certain young man was following Jesus, with just a fine cloth on his naked flesh. They caught hold of him, [52] but he forsook the fine cloth and ran off naked.]

[53] They took Jesus to the high priest; and they assembled all the chief priests, the elders, and the religious scholars. [54] Now Peter followed him from afar into the courtyard of the high priest and was sitting with the attendants, warming himself at the fire. [55] Now the chief priests and the whole council sought testimony against Jesus to put him to death but found none. [56] For many gave false testimony against him, yet their testimony did not agree. [57] Some rose and gave false testimony against him, saying, [58] "Well, we heard him say, 'I will destroy this

hand-made temple, and in three days I will build another, that is not hand-made.'" [59] But even on this point their testimony did not agree. [60] Then the high priest stood up before them and said to Jesus, "No response? What are they testifying against you?" [61] But he was silent and answered nothing. Again, the high priest spoke to him, "Are you the Messiah, the Son of the Blessed One?" [62] Jesus said, "I am; and

> 'you will see the Son of Woman
> seated at the right hand of the Power,'
> and 'coming with the clouds of heaven.'"

[63] Then the high priest tore his clothes and said, "Why do we still need witnesses? [64] You all have heard his blasphemy! How does it appear to you?" All of them condemned him, "Guilty! This is death!" [65] Some began to spit on him, to blindfold him, and to strike him, saying to him, "Prophesy!" Then the attendants took him and beat him.

[66] While Peter was below in the courtyard, one of the high priest's enslaved girls came by. [67] When she saw Peter warming himself, she stared at him and said, "You were also with the Nazarene, Jesus." [68] But Peter denied it, saying, "I do not know or even understand what you are saying." Then he went out into the front courtyard. Then the cock crowed. [69] And the enslaved girl, on seeing him, began to say to the bystanders again that this man was one of them. [70] But again he denied it. Then after a little while the bystanders said to Peter again, "Certainly you are one of them, for you are a Galilean." [71] But he began to curse and swore, "I do not know this person you are talking about." [72] And suddenly the cock crowed for the second time. Then Peter remembered the thing Jesus had said to him, "Before the cock crows twice, you will deny me three times." And he threw himself down and sobbed.

[15:1] As soon as it was morning, the chief priests took a counsel with the elders and religious scholars and the whole council. They bound Jesus, led him away, and handed him over to Pilate. [2] Pilate asked him, "Are you the King of the Judeans?" He answered him saying, "You say so." [3] Then the chief priests accused him of many things. [4] But Pilate asked him again, "Have you no reply? See how many charges they bring against you." [5] But Jesus made no further reply, thus Pilate was amazed.

[6] Now at the festival Pilate used to release one prisoner to them, whoever they asked. [7] Now there was a man called Barabbas in prison with the rebels who in the rebellion had committed murder. [8] So the crowd came and began to ask Pilate to do for them according to his custom. [9] Then he responded to them saying, "Do you all want me to release the King of the Judeans to you?" [10] For he recognized that it was out of jealousy that the chief priests had handed him over. [11] Then the chief priests stirred up the crowd that instead Barabbas might be released for them. [12] Pilate again responded to them, "What then do you wish me to do with the one you call the King of the Judeans?" [13] They shouted more [than before], "Crucify him!" [14] Pilate asked them, "Why, for doing what evil?" But they shouted all the more, "Crucify him!" [15] So Pilate, wanting to satiate the crowd, released Barabbas to them; then he handed Jesus over for flogging and to be crucified.

[16] Then the soldiers led him into the courtyard of the property, which is the military headquarters, and they called together the entire cohort. [17] And they clothed him in purple, and they put on him thorns woven into a crown. [18] And they began saluting him, "Hail, King of the Judeans!" [19] They struck his head with a reed, spat upon him, and knelt in homage to him. [20] After mocking him, they stripped him of the purple and put his clothes on him. Then they led him away to crucify him.

[21] They compelled a passerby, a certain Simon of Cyrene who was coming from the countryside, to carry his cross; he was the father of Alexander and Rufus. [22] Then they brought Jesus to the Golgotha place (which means Skull Place). [23] And they offered him myrrh wine, but he did not take it. [24] And they crucified him, and divided his clothes casting lots among themselves for what each would take.

[25] It was the third hour [past dawn] when they crucified him. [26] The writing above of the accusation against him read, "The King of the Judeans." [27] And with him they crucified two revolutionaries, one on his right and one on his left.

[29] The passersby reviled him, shaking their heads and saying, "Ha! You would destroy the temple and build it in three days—[30] save yourself, and come down from the cross!" [31] In the same way the chief priests, with the religious scholars, mocked him among themselves and said, "He saved others; himself he is unable to save. [32] The Messiah, the King of Israel! Come down from the cross now that we may see and believe." Those who were crucified with him also demeaned him.

[33] Now when it was the sixth hour [of the day, or noon], darkness came over the whole land until the ninth hour [of the day, about three in the afternoon]. [34] At the ninth hour Jesus cried out with a loud voice, "*Eloi, Eloi, lema sabachthani?*" which means, "My God, my God, why have you forsaken me?" [35] When some of the bystanders heard it, they said, "Listen, he is calling Elijah." [36] And someone ran and filled a sponge with vinegary wine, put it on a stick, and gave it to him to drink, saying, "Wait, let us see whether Elijah will come to take him down." [37] Then Jesus gave a great cry and breathed out a final time. [38] And the curtain of the temple was torn in two, from top to bottom. [39] Now when the centurion, stationed facing him, saw that in this way Jesus breathed out at the end, he said, "Truly this man was God's Son!"

[40] There were also women watching from a distance; among them were Mary the Magdalene, and Mary the mother of James the younger and of Joses, and Salome. [41] These women followed him and ministered to him when he was in Galilee, and there were many other women who had come up with him to Jerusalem.

[42] When evening had come, since it was the day of Preparation—the day before the sabbath—[43] Joseph of Arimathea, a respected member of the council, who himself was also waiting for the reign of God, went boldly to Pilate and requested for the body of Jesus. [44] Then Pilate wondered that Jesus was now dead, and summoning the centurion asked him whether he had been dead for some time. [45] When he learned it from the centurion, he gave the corpse to Joseph. [46] Then Joseph bought a fine cloth, and taking him down, wrapped him in the fine cloth, and put him in a tomb that had been hewn out of rock. He then

rolled a stone against the door of the tomb. [47] Mary the Magdalene and Mary the mother of Joses saw where he was put.

PROCLAMATION

Owing to the length of the Palm Sunday Gospel, the commentary section will be longer than for other readings.

Text Notes

The same word is used in Isaiah 49:5 and verse 7, yet NRSV, JPS, and CEB all translate Israel as God's "servant" but the nation as the "slave of rulers." "Servant" occludes the expectation of complete domination/submission, including ability to maim, kill, breed, rape, impregnate, and sell the person without consequence.

Hebrew plurals like "monarchs/kings" and "princes" in Isaiah 49:7 are inclusive. I have expanded both to reflect the presence of female royals in and at the head of some nations. "Go free" in verse 9 uses the primary verb of the exodus. Syene, or Sinim, in verse 12 is an Egyptian town with a record of some Israelite settlement.

In Isaiah 49:5 and 15, "womb" is the more generic "belly" used broadly for women and men; it is also found in Psalm 22:9–10 (verse 10 also uses the more common specific "womb"). In Isaiah 49:13–15 it is paired with "mother-love" (the verb whose root is that same word) and children, including one at the breast, in verse 15. Translating this as "compassion" (NRSV), "pity" (CEB), or just "love" (JPS) eviscerates the intentionally crafted portrait of God as a mother, accomplished despite use of masculine forms.

The second phrase in Psalm 22:3 can also be translated as "you are holy, enthroned, the Praise of Israel." In verse 9 the Divine Midwife "extracts" the baby; she does not just "catch" him, perhaps suggesting a difficult birth.

In Galatians 3:23ff translation choices can present the law in an antagonistic and ultimately anti-Jewish manner as "prison" and "disciplinarian" (see NRSV). However, *ephrouroumetha* in verse 23 means to set a guard or garrison; that is a protective action. And in verse 24, a *paidagōgos* is a teacher; *torah* itself means "teaching" and "revelation" more than "law."

One of the verbs that describes Jesus's emotions in Mark 14:33 is only used in that place, making it difficult to define; suggestions range from "amazed" to "gloomy" to "distressed" to "troubled." In verse 34, Jesus expresses his sorrow using the language of Psalms 42:11 and 43:5 in Greek: "my soul is cast down." Similarly, the description of soldiers gambling for Jesus's clothes matches the wording of Psalm 22:18 in Greek. Judas is concerned that Jesus's arrest be done "safely" in verse 44; he is a complex character with mixed motives. The "attendants" in verse 54 can provide a number of services; the word is more "assistant" than "guard," as is commonly translated.

The enslaved "girls" in Mark 14:66–69 could be young women. "Girl" is often used to denote their minor legal status. The criminals crucified with Jesus in Mark 15:27 could have been thieves or highway bandits; the root of *lēstēs* is stolen goods. However, the semantic range includes revolutionaries and insurrectionists. This latter understanding may be what is meant given mention of imprisoned rebels (using a different word, *stasiastēs*) in verse 7. The vinegar wine in verse 36 draws on Psalm 69:21. The nature of the women's ministry to Jesus in 15:41 should be understood as wholistic: spiritual and material. Many Greek manuscripts use the more explicit *ptōma*, "corpse," rather than *soma*, "body," for Jesus's remains in Mark 15:44.

Preaching Prompts

As Holy Week begins, one may wish to explore God's sorrow over a world that crucifies as well as over a crucified beloved child, a mother's sorrow as well as a father's. In Isaiah 49, God is the divine mother whose love emanates from her womb, most specifically in verses 13 and 14.

Contemporary discomfort with slave language should not overshadow the degree to which it was normative in the biblical text and its theologies. For the biblical ear, "slave of God" and "slave of Sarah" were equally acceptable and nonremarkable. The linguistic distinction between being a "servant" of God and being held in slavery is entirely artificial to the text and permits slave-holding societies to embrace servitude of God as pertaining to them while holding others in bondage in a fictive distinct category.

In Psalm 22 the most obvious divine feminine image is God as midwife and lactation guide in verse 9. There is also the birthing mother who has no voice and makes no cry. In verse 10 God seems to have become a foster parent for a perhaps abandoned child; the child is thrown (away?) on to God. God can be both midwife and foster mother here. We do not know if the birth mother cannot or will not keep her child. She can be preached in conversation with the reminder that women do abandon children in Isaiah 49, yet without demonization. In keeping with Palm Sunday, she can be read as giving her child over to God, whatever his fate.

Galatians 3:23–24 describes the law as a protective, not punitive, garrison and guard. Though addressing a Gentile Church on whom the Torah (or *torah* broadly) was never binding, Paul uses "we" with regard to the law. In a rhetorical flourish, Paul argues that the particularities that characterize individuals and communities no longer exist "in Christ," yet he continues to operate as though those categories continue and are normative. Yet our adoption and kinship does not require us to leave ourselves, our identities behind.

There are very few women and girls in the Passion narratives. Here in Luke there are girls or women held in slavery by the chief priest. There is missing the wife of

Simon of Cyrene, the Cross-Bearer; he is named with reference to his sons, but no mention is made of their mother.

The Passion narratives on Palm Sunday and Good Friday have been used to incite lethal physical violence against Jewish communities by the Church and its ministers. They have also been used to craft violent, anti-Semitic theologies that blame Jews for the death of Jesus, demean and defame Judaism, and deem it failed and its covenants replaced. It is important to acknowledge that history while repudiating it and repenting of it and affirming God's fidelity to all her covenants and all her peoples. It is essential to be in conversation with our Jewish neighbors and to listen more than speak. I strongly recommend reading the scriptures in conversation with Jewish scholars, for example with the *Jewish Study Bible* and *Jewish Annotated New Testament*.

MONDAY IN HOLY WEEK

Jeremiah 31:8–13; Psalm 22:19–31; Hebrews 1:1–9; John 12:1–7

Jeremiah 31:8 Look! I am going to bring them from the land of the north,
   and I will gather them from the farthest parts of the earth,
   among them blind and lame, pregnant and birthing, together,
   a great assembly, they shall return here.
9   With weeping they shall come,
   and with consolations I will lead them back,
   I will have them walk by streams of water,
   on a straight path, they shall not stumble on it;
   for I am a parent to Israel,
   and Ephraim is my firstborn.
10   Hear the word of the HOLY ONE, you nations,
   and declare it in the islands far off;
   say, "The One who scattered Israel will gather him,
   and will keep him as a shepherd a flock."
11   For the FAITHFUL ONE has ransomed Jacob [of Rebekah's line]
   and has redeemed him from hands too strong for him.
12   They shall come and they shall sing on the heights of Zion,
   and they shall be radiant over the goodness of the GRACIOUS GOD,
   over the grain, and over the new wine, and over the oil,
   and over the young of flock and herd;
   their souls shall become like a watered garden,
   and they shall never languish again.
13   Then shall young women rejoice in dance,
   and young men and elders together.

I will turn their mourning to joy;
I will comfort them, and give them joy for sorrow.

Psalm 22:19–31

19 SAVING GOD, be not far away!
My strength, hasten to help me!

20 Deliver my soul from the sword,
my life from the clutch of the dog!

21 Save me from the mouth of the lion!
For on the horns of the wild oxen you have responded to me.

22 I will tell of your name to my sisters and brothers;
in the midst of the congregation, I will praise you:

23 You who revere the FOUNT OF LIFE, praise her!
all the offspring of Leah and Rachel, Bilhah and Zilpah glorify her.
Stand in awe of her all you of Rebekah's line.

24 For she did not despise or abhor
the affliction of the afflicted;
she did not hide her face from me,
and when I cried to her, she heard.

25 On your account is my praise in the great congregation;
my vows I will pay before those who revere her.

26 The poor shall eat and be satisfied;
those who seek her shall praise the MOTHER OF ALL.
May your hearts live forever!

27 All the ends of the earth shall remember
and turn to the WELLSPRING OF LIFE;
and all the families of the nations
shall worship before her.

28 For sovereignty belongs to the SHE WHO IS HOLY,
and she rules over the nations.

29 They consume and they bow down,
all the fat ones of the earth before her,
they bend their knees,
all who go down to the dust,
and cannot save their soul.

30 Later descendants will serve her;
future generations will be told about our God,

31 they will go and proclaim her deliverance
to a people yet unborn,
saying that she has done it.

Hebrews 1:1 Many times and in many ways God spoke to our mothers and fathers through the prophets, female and male. ² In these last days God has spoken to us by a Son, whom God appointed heir of all there is, and through whom God created the worlds. ³ The Son is the brilliance of God's glory and reproduction of God's very being, and the Son undergirds all there is by his word of power. When the Son had made purification for sins, he sat down at the right hand of the Majesty on high, ⁴ having become as much greater than the angels as the name he inherited is more excellent than theirs.

⁵ For to which of the angels did God ever say,

"You are my Child; today I have begotten you"?

Or this,

"I will be their Parent, and they will be my Child"?

⁶ Then again, when God brings the firstborn into the world, God says,

"Let all the angels of God worship him."

⁷ On the one hand of the angels God says,

"God makes winds into celestial messengers,
and flames of fire into God's ministers."

⁸ But of the Son God says,

"Your throne, O God, is forever and ever,
and the righteous scepter is the scepter of your realm.
⁹ *You have loved righteousness and hated lawlessness;*
therefore God, your God, has anointed you
with the oil of gladness beyond your companions."

John 12:1 Now Jesus, six days before the Passover, came to Bethany where Lazarus was who he raised from the dead. ² There they gave a dinner for him and Martha served while Lazarus was one of those at the table with him. ³ Mary took a pound of a balm made of expensive pure nard, anointed the feet of Jesus, and wiped them with her hair. The house was filled with the scent of the perfume. ⁴ But Judas Iscariot, one of his disciples, the one who was about to betray him, said, ⁵ "Why was this balm not sold for three hundred denarii and the money given to the poor?" ⁶ Now he said this not because he cared about the poor, but because he was a thief; he kept the moneybag and whatever was put into it, he stole. ⁷ Jesus said, "Leave her alone. It was for the day of my burial that she kept it."

PROCLAMATION

Text Notes

In Jeremiah 31:9, arguably "consolations" became "supplications," the literal reading, when a letter was dropped.

In Psalm 22:23, "the offspring of Jacob" are identified by their mothers/ matriarchs, enslaved and free; similarly "Rebekah's line" stands in for "the offspring of Israel."

In keeping with the aims of this work, foremothers and female prophets are made explicit in Hebrews 1:1. *Megalōsynēs*, "Majesty," in Hebrews 1:3, as a feminine noun, marks a rare use of feminine language to describe God or her attributes in the New Testament.

The following verses quote the earlier scriptures widely and often out of context: Hebrews 1:5 quotes Psalm 2:7 where the anonymous psalmist says God told them they were God's begotten child, probably initially heard with regard to David. The next quote is from 2 Samuel 7:14 (and its duplicate, 1 Chronicles 17:13), where the promise of God to be a parent to a future monarch is to one of David's descendants. Given the difficulty of asserting biological gender for heavenly beings, I use the neuter "child" and "parent" in verse 5. Verse 6 quotes Deuteronomy 32:43 and Psalm 97:7 from Greek where the original "gods" were replaced by "angels" to correct toward a pure monotheism. Verse 7 quotes Psalm 104:4, playing on the primary meaning of angel, "messenger." Verses 8–9 quote Psalm 45:6–7 where the first verse refers to God but the second refers to the king whose wedding psalm it is (Ahab since Jezebel is the only princess of Tyre to marry into Israel).

Preaching Prompts

A second iteration of the woman who anoints Jesus is traditional on Monday of Holy Week, an earlier version having been read on the last Sunday of Lent. Today the woman is Mary, sister of Martha and the resurrected Lazarus in John. The Jeremiah 31 reading offers the hope of consolation for those who mourn, just as Lazarus's resurrected body at the table with Jesus does.

The context of Jeremiah 31 is God's promise to restore Israel after the Babylonian devastation; our reading affirms the faithfulness of God to her people in each generation, building on, not replacing the earliest reading. In some ways Jeremiah 31 is an answer to the plea for salvation in Psalm 22. It is important to remember that "salvation" in the Hebrew Scriptures is physical salvation from death or other danger, and normally national or corporate. Paraphrased by Jesus (his recitation does not quite match Hebrew or Greek versions in either Matthew 27:46 or Mark 15:34), Psalm 22 became the Psalm of the Cross, a principal text of Holy Week.

Hebrews 1 calls us back to the fidelity of God who spoke through prophecy but now speaks through her Holy Child. (Some have concluded from this that prophecy came to an end; however, prophets appear scattered throughout the New Testament.) The amount of prooftexting in this short section raises the eyebrows of a biblical scholar, yet reminds us how flexible ancient interpreters found the scriptures. That flexibility enabled them to reinterpret them in light of Jesus while still holding their previous understandings. Christians have all too often abandoned contextual readings, seizing upon this type of exegesis and neglecting other biblical models.

The last line of the Gospel points us to the tomb, where we needs must linger.

TUESDAY IN HOLY WEEK[2]

Isaiah 49:1–6; Psalm 123; Philippians 3:17–21; Matthew 21:12–17

Isaiah 49:1 Listen to me, you coastlands,
   give heed, you peoples from far away!
   The LIFE-BREATH OF CREATION called me from the womb,
   from the innermost parts of my mother God made my name known.
2 God made my mouth like a sharp sword,
   in the shadow of God's own hand did God hide me;
   God made me a polished arrow,
   in God's own quiver did God hide me away.
3 And God said to me, "You are my slave,
   Israel, the one in whom I will be glorified."
4 But I said, "In vain have I labored,
   I have spent my strength in futility and vanity;
   yet surely my judgment is with the RIGHTEOUS JUDGE,
   and my recompense with my God."
5 And now says the AUTHOR OF LIFE,
   who formed me in the womb to be God's slave
   to return Jacob back to God,
   and that Israel might be gathered to God:
   I am honored in the sight of the HOLY ONE OF OLD,
   and my God is my strength.
6 God says,
   "It is too light a thing that you should be my slave

---

2. Careful observers may have noticed that both the principal Easter service and Tuesday in Holy Week use the same Isaiah 49 reading. I translated the reading twice, forgetting that I had previously translated it. The two different versions offer a window into the craft and flexibility of translation and the range of choices in some instances.

to raise up the tribes of Jacob [the line of Rebekah]
and to restore the survivors of Israel [born of Rachel and Leah, and Bilhah and Zilpah].
I will give you as a light to the nations,
for it will be that my salvation reaches to the end of the earth."

Psalm 123

1 To you I lift up my eyes,
the one who is enthroned in the heavens!
2 See! It is just as the eyes of the enslaved
are toward the hand of their lord,
as the eyes of an enslaved girl
toward the hand of her mistress,
just so our eyes look to the MIGHTY ONE our God,
until God shows us favor.
3 Have mercy upon us, MERCIFUL ONE, have mercy upon us,
for we have had more than our fill of contempt.
4 Our soul has had more than its fill
of the scorn of those who are at ease,
of the contempt of the proud.

Philippians 3:17 Become imitators of me together sisters and brothers, and observe those who walk according to our example. 18 For many of them—as I have often told you all, and now I tell you even with tears—walk as enemies of the cross of Christ. 19 Their end is destruction; their god is the belly; and their glory is in their shame; their minds are set on earthly things. 20 But our citizenship is in heaven, and it is from there that we are expecting a Savior, Jesus Christ, our Sovereign, 21 who will transform the body of our humiliation that it may bear the likeness of the body of his glory, through the force that also enables him to make all things subject to himself.

Matthew 21:12 Then Jesus entered the temple and drove out all who were selling and buying in the temple, and the tables of the moneychangers he overturned, as well as the station of those who sold doves. 13 He said to them, "It is written,

'My house shall be called a house of prayer';
but you all are making it a den of robbers.'

14 And they came to him in the temple, those who were blind and disabled, and he cured them. 15 Now when the chief priests and the religious scholars saw the amazing things that he did, and heard the girls and boys crying out in the temple, "Hosanna to the Son of David," they became angry. 16 They said to him, "Do you hear what these are saying?" Jesus said to them, "Yes; have you never read,

> 'Out of the mouths of infants and nursing babies
> you have prepared praise for yourself'?"

¹⁷ He left them, went out of the city to Bethany, and spent the night there.

PROCLAMATION

Text Notes

In Isaiah 49:4, the poet-prophet speaking in the first person emphasizes redundantly, "I, I said" what she or the unidentified servant about whom she is prophesying said to God upon being commissioned in God's service. Writing long past the time of Isaiah proper, the gender and identity of the prophet is unknown. (I discuss the possibility of the author being a woman in *Daughters of Miriam: Women Prophets in Ancient Israel*.)

Psalm 123 makes explicit the psalmist's understanding that God is a slave-master, and we, women and men alike, are God's slaves. This understanding pervades the scriptures. Linguistically, the human slave-master, "lord," in verse 2 is the same word as "Lord," most often used to represent God's unpronounceable name formed of the letters YHWH; this volume eschews that language while wrestling with its lingering theology. Philippians 3:20 uses the Greek equivalent for lord, *kyrion*, for Jesus.

In Philippians 3:19, the belly, *koilia*, the mark of one of the carnal obsessions of the "earthly" believer, can refer to innards broadly or to the womb, thereby perhaps to gluttony or lust.

Where the Greek text has "children" in Matthew 21:14, I have specified "girls and boys"; girls have extremely low visibility in the scriptures but would have been present in the temple. There is no reason to presume that only boys acclaimed him given the plural form allows for the presence of girls.

Preaching Prompts

These texts emphasize the sovereignty of God and of Christ, calling attention to the great gulf between God and humanity in troubling and troublesome language. At the same time, they frame the story of the One who crossed and closed that gulf, looking more human than divine this week. We may be helped by remembering the Church writes from a position of vulnerability, believing in faith that it won't always be that way. Paul in particular is imprisoned. One might wish to think of the crucified Church looking to its own resurrection.

The various servants in later Isaiah are sometimes the nation, sometimes a coming monarch, sometimes a messiah, sometimes indeterminate. This passage speaks in messianic terms and was so understood by Christian readers.

As is often the case, the Epistle distinguishes physical, bodily, and earthly from what is spiritual and heavenly. It is worth remembering that there was a widespread belief that Christ's return was imminent and we would soon have little use for this world. It is our task to interpret this text in light of our continuing reality and the season, Holy Week, in which the physicality of salvation is made manifest.

Matthew 21:13 fuses Isaiah 56:7 and Jeremiah 7:11 into a single citation. Dr. Amy-Jill Levine helpfully reminds that a "den of robbers" is not a place where there is criminal activity, just as a lion's den is not where lions do their hunting and killing. It is the refuge, or abode, meaning that the moneychangers who were essential to proper functioning of the temple were not robbing people. She suggests that Jesus's rebuke like Jeremiah's before him was that the unrepentant had made the temple a social club rather than a place of prayer; she also notes that the table turning would have been a rather small demonstration given the scale of the complex (*Entering the Passion of Jesus: A Beginner's Guide to Holy Week*, Chapter 2, "The Temple: Risking Righteous Anger").

Individual women are hard to locate in the Gospel reading but would have been among the worshippers, praying and making their own offering; some likely would have been among those Jesus healed. Jesus evokes but does not mention women when citing Psalm 8:2/3 in Greek (verse numbers vary by language): women birthed and nurse the infants who offer praise to God.

WEDNESDAY IN HOLY WEEK

Ezekiel 17:22–24; Psalm 36:5–10; 1 John 2:7–14; Matthew 23:37–39

Ezekiel 17:22 Thus says the Sovereign GOD:
    I myself will take a sprig of cedar
    from its very top;
    and I will place it;
    from the topmost of its most tender branch
    I will pluck it and I myself will plant it
    on a high and lofty mountain.
23 On the mountain height of Israel
    I will plant it,
    that it may lift up its boughs and bear fruit,
    and become a noble cedar.
    Under it every kind of bird shall live;
    every kind of winged creature shall nest
    in the shade of its branches.
24 All the trees of the field shall know
    that I am the CREATOR OF ALL.

I bring low the high tree,

I make high the low tree;

I dry up the green tree

and I make the dry tree sprout buds.

I the AGELESS GOD have spoken;

I will make it so.

Psalm 36:5–10

5 HOLY ONE, throughout the very heavens is your faithful love,
    your faithfulness beyond the clouds.
6 Your righteousness is like the eternal mountains,
    your judgments are like the mighty deep;
    you save humankind and animalkind alike, FAITHFUL ONE.
7 How precious is your faithful love, O God!
    All the woman-born take shelter in the shadow of your wings.
8 They feast on the abundance of your house,
    and you give them drink from the river of your delights.
9 For with you is the fountain of life;
    in your light we see light.
10 Extend your faithful love to those who know you,
    and your justice to the upright of heart!

1 John 2:7 Beloved, no new commandment do I write you all, but an old commandment that you have had from the beginning; that commandment is the word that you have heard. 8 Yet, I am writing you all a new commandment that is true in Christ and in you, because the shadow is passing away and the true light already shines. 9 Whoever says, "I am in the light," while hating a sister or brother, is in shadow still. 10 Whoever loves a sister or brother lives in the light, and in such a person there is no occasion for stumbling. 11 But whoever hates another sister or brother is in shadow, walks in shadow, and does not know where to go, because shadow dims the eyes.

12 I am writing to you, little children,
    because your sins are forgiven on account of Christ's name.
13 I am writing to you, mothers and fathers,
    because you know the one who is from the beginning.
    I am writing to you, young women and men,
    because you have conquered the evil one.
14 I write to you, children,
    because you know the Creator.
    I write to you, mothers and fathers,
    because you know the one who is from the beginning.

I write to you, young people,
because you are strong
and the word of God abides in you,
and you have overcome the evil one.

Matthew 23:37 "Jerusalem, Jerusalem, that kills the prophets and stones those who are sent to it! How often have I desired to gather your children together as a hen gathers her chicks under her wings, and you were not willing! [38] See, your house is left to you, desolate. [39] For I tell you all, you will not see me again until you say, 'Blessed is the one who comes in the name of the Holy One.'"

PROCLAMATION

Text Notes

In the psalm the noun *el*, God, is used as an adjective describing the mountains in verse 5.

Preaching Prompts

Today's lessons revolve around Jesus's journey to Jerusalem, where even on the way to his death, he expressed his longing to mother Jerusalem through its violent inclinations. In these lessons birds function as both images for a sheltering God and images for a huddled humanity and are themselves creatures of the natural world for whom God also cares.

Ezekiel 17:22–24 is a highly allegorical text that can be read as a description of a messianic figure who has noble (lofty) origins but is tender rather than hardened. The community founded around and beneath sheltering branches of this "tree" is diverse and flourishing. As in other prophetic texts, God brings low what is high and exalts what is low.

The psalm echoes the theme of God's faithfulness to bird and tree, extending it to all animals and all humanity. Here God is winged, sheltering all life within her wings.

The Epistle exhorts us to replicate the love God has for creation in our love for each other. It also offers a hint that the heaviness and shadow of Holy Week will give way to light.

Jesus's embrace of Jerusalem, its history and hopes, ugly realities, looming threats, sacred space, and all of its people, citizens, immigrants, pilgrims, and occupiers was all inclusive. There is room for all in his embrace.

MAUNDY THURSDAY

Exodus 15:11–21; Psalm 136:1–16; Hebrews 11:23–28; Matthew 26:17–56

Exodus 15:11 "Who is like you, MIGHTY ONE, among the gods?
Who is like you, resplendent in holiness,
revered praiseworthy, working wonders?
¹² You stretched out your right hand,
the earth swallowed them.
¹³ You led, in your faithful love, the people whom you redeemed;
you guided them by your strength to your holy abode.
¹⁴ The peoples heard, they quaked;
pangs like labor seized the inhabitants of Philistia.
¹⁵ Then the chiefs of Edom were dismayed;
the rulers of Moab, trembling seized them;
all the inhabitants of Canaan melted away.
¹⁶ Terror and dread fell upon them
by the might of your arm;
they became still as a stone
until your people, REDEEMING GOD, passed by,
until the people whom you acquired passed by.
¹⁷ You brought them and planted them on the mountain of your own possession,
the place, SHELTERING GOD, you made for your dwelling,
the sanctuary, Most High God, that your hands have established.
¹⁸ The EVERLASTING GOD will reign forever and ever."

¹⁹ The horse of Pharaoh and his chariots and charioteers went into the sea, and the MIGHTY GOD turned the waters of the sea back upon them; but the daughters and sons of Israel walked through the sea on dry ground.

²⁰ Then the prophet Miriam, Aaron's sister, took a hand-drum in her hand, and all the women went out after her with hand-drums and with dancing. ²¹ And Miriam sang to them, women and men:

"Sing to the INDOMITABLE GOD who has triumphed triumphantly;
horse and rider God has thrown into the sea."

Psalm 136:1–16

¹ Give thanks to the FOUNT OF LIFE, who is good,
for her faithful love is everlasting.
² Give thanks to the God of gods,
for her faithful love is everlasting.

³ Give thanks to the Majesty of Majesties,
  for her faithful love is everlasting;
⁴ who alone does great wonders,
  for her faithful love is everlasting;
⁵ who through insight made the heavens,
  for her faithful love is everlasting;
⁶ to the one who spread out the land upon the waters,
  for her faithful love is everlasting;
⁷ to the one who made the great lights,
  for her faithful love is everlasting;
⁸ the sun to govern the day,
  for her faithful love is everlasting;
⁹ the moon and stars to govern the night,
  for her faithful love is everlasting;
¹⁰ who struck Egypt through their firstborn daughters and sons,
  for her faithful love is everlasting;
¹¹ and brought Israel out from among them,
  for her faithful love is everlasting;
¹² with a strong hand and an outstretched arm,
  for her faithful love is everlasting;
¹³ who cut the Red Sea in two,
  for her faithful love is everlasting;
¹⁴ and made Israel pass over through the midst of it,
  for her faithful love is everlasting;
¹⁵ but churned Pharaoh and his army in the Red Sea,
  for her faithful love is everlasting;
¹⁶ who walked her people through the wilderness,
  for her faithful love is everlasting.

Hebrews 11:23 By faith Moses was hidden after his birth by his mother and father for three months, because they saw that the child was beautiful; and they were not afraid of the king's commandment. ²⁴ By faith Moses, after he had grown up, refused to be called a son of Pharaoh's daughter, ²⁵ rather choosing ill-treatment with the people of God than enjoyment of the transitory pleasures of sin. ²⁶ He considered abuse for the sake of the Messiah to be greater wealth than the treasures of Egypt, for he was looking ahead to the reward. ²⁷ By faith he left Egypt, unafraid of the anger of the king; for he persisted as though he saw the unseen. ²⁸ By faith he kept the Passover and the sprinkling of blood, in order that the destroyer of the first-born would not touch the firstborn daughters and sons of Israel.

Matthew 26:17 On the first day of Unleavened Bread the disciples came to Jesus, saying, "Where do you want us to prepare for you to eat the Passover?" ¹⁸ He said, "Go into the city to a certain person, and say, 'The Teacher says, My time is near; I will keep the Passover at your house with my disciples.'" [19] So the disciples did just as Jesus instructed them, and they prepared the Passover meal.

[20] When it was evening, he reclined at table with the twelve, [21] and while they ate, he said, "Truly I tell you, one of you will betray me." [22] And they became deeply grieved and each one began to say to him, "Not me, is it Rabbi?" [23] He responded and said, "The one who dipped his hand into the bowl with me will betray me. [24] Indeed, the Son of Woman goes away as it is written of him, but woe to the person by whom the Son of Woman is betrayed! It would have been better for that person not to have been born." [25] Judas, who betrayed him, responded and said, "It wasn't me was it, Rabbi?" He replied, "You said it."

[26] While they were eating, Jesus took a loaf of bread, and blessing it, he broke it, and gave it to the disciples, saying, "Take, eat; this is my body." [27] Then he took a cup, and giving thanks he gave it to them, saying, "Drink from it, all of you; [28] for this is my blood of the covenant, which is poured out for many for forgiveness of sins. [29] I tell you all, I will not drink again of this fruit of the vine until that day when I drink it new with you all in the realm of my Abba." [30] And when they had sung the hymn, they went out to the Mount of Olives.

[31] Then Jesus said to them, "You will all become scandalized to the point of desertion because of me this night; for it is written,

'For I will strike the shepherd,
and the sheep of the flock will be scattered.'

[32] But after I am raised, I will go ahead of you all to Galilee." [33] Peter said to him, "Though all become scandalized and desert because of you, I will never desert you." [34] Jesus said to him, "Truly I tell you, this very night, before the cock crows, you will deny me three times." [35] Peter said to him, "Should it be necessary I die with you, I will not deny you." Then likewise said all the disciples.

[36] Then Jesus came with his disciples to a place called Gethsemane, and he said to them, "You all sit here while I go pray there." [37] He took Peter and the two sons of Zebedee and began to be grieved and distressed. [38] Then he said to them, "My soul is deeply grieved, to the point of death; you all stay here, and stay awake with me." [39] And going on a little, he fell on the ground and prayed saying, "My Father, if it is possible, let this cup pass from me; nevertheless not what I want but what you do." [40] Then he came to the disciples and found them sleeping; and he said to Peter, "So, you all were not strong enough to stay awake with me one hour? [41] Stay awake and pray that you all may not come into the test; indeed, the spirit is willing, but the flesh is weak." [42] Again, for the second time, Jesus went away and prayed, saying, "My Father, if it is not possible for this to pass lest I drink it, let your will be done." [43] And again he came and found them sleeping, for their eyes were heavy. [44] So leaving them again, he went away and prayed for the third time, saying those words again. [45] Then he came to the disciples and said to them, "Sleep now and take your rest. See, the hour is at hand, and the Son of Woman is betrayed into the hands of sinners. [46] Get up, let us go. Look, my betrayer is at hand."

⁴⁷ While Jesus was still speaking, Judas, one of the twelve, came and with him was a large crowd with swords and clubs from the chief priests and the elders of the people. ⁴⁸ Now the betrayer had given them a sign, saying, "The one I kiss is he; take him." ⁴⁹ At once he came up to Jesus and said, "Shalom, Rabbi!" and kissed him. ⁵⁰ Jesus said to him, "Friend, this is why you have come." Then they came and laid hands on Jesus and took him. ⁵¹ Suddenly, someone with Jesus reached out with his hand, drew his sword, and struck the slave of the high priest, cutting off his ear. ⁵² Then Jesus said to him, "Return your sword to its place; for all who choose the sword will perish by the sword. ⁵³ Do you think I am not able to ask my Abba, who will at once send me more than twelve legions of angels? ⁵⁴ How then would the scriptures be fulfilled, which say it must be thus?" ⁵⁵ At that hour Jesus said to the crowds, "Is it as for a bandit you all have come out with swords and clubs to seize me? Daily in the temple I sat teaching, and you did not arrest me. ⁵⁶ But all this has happened, so that the scriptures of the prophets may be fulfilled." Then all the disciples deserted him and fled.

PROCLAMATION

Text Notes

In Exodus 15:13, God's holy "abode" can also be understood as a pasture. The instrument Miriam and the other women play in verse 20 is a hand-drum, traditionally played by women across the ancient Afro-Asiatic world. "Tambourine" is anachronistic; they did not yet exist. In verse 21, Miriam exhorts the entire community or just the men—either can be indicated by the plural verb; however, the women are already following her according to the previous verse.

In Matthew 26:18, the grammar used for the person who hosts Jesus is masculine; it may be generic for "person" as translated above. In verse 22 and elsewhere "Rabbi" replaces "Lord" for direct address. In verse 29 I use "shalom" as the greeting, reflecting the culture of Jesus rather than the literary world of the Greek text.

Preaching Prompts

Passover and Holy Week and Easter are linked seasonally, thematically, and theologically. In some languages the word for Easter is "Pascha," making the connection more explicit. The two seasons are also connected by violence. In the Exodus and Passover stories, Israel, God's beloved, is saved, and God sends their oppressors to their deaths. Painfully, those deaths are celebrated in psalms and songs. In Holy Week, Jesus, God's beloved, is executed by his—still God's beloved—people's oppressors. His death will also be commemorated in songs of praise. Each offers an opportunity to reflect on who we say God is in conversation with the scriptures.

The necessity for Jesus to observe Passover is just one of many reminders that Jesus was a religiously observant Jew who never broke with Judaism. The singular host in Matthew 26:18 seemingly obscures women from the household who would have done or helped with the actual work: cleaning, shopping, meal preparation, cooking, serving, and hosting. Since the more inclusive "disciples" is used rather than presumptively exclusively male "apostles," it is reasonable to expect the presence of women, particularly since these disciples prepared and served the meal (verse 19). Should female and male disciples have been present, it would be likely that children would be present given that the Passover is a family and community meal. (It should be noted that the form of the Passover meal at the time of Jesus, and even in the literary construction of the evangelists, was not a seder, a form which developed later.) The mention of "the twelve" in verse 20 does not foreclose the possibility of a larger group at more than one table.

GOOD FRIDAY

Judges 11:29–40; Psalm 22; Hebrews 12:1–4; Luke 22:14–23:56

Owing to the length of the Passion Gospel, the commentary section will be longer than for other readings.

Judges 11:29 The Spirit of the HOLY ONE, she was upon Jephthah, and he passed through Gilead and Manasseh. He passed on to Mizpah of Gilead, and from Mizpah of Gilead he passed on to the Ammonites. [30] And Jephthah vowed a vow to the HOLY ONE OF OLD, and said, "If you will give the Ammonites into my hand, [31] then it shall be that the one who comes out—whoever comes out—of the doors of my house to meet me, when I return having finished with the Ammonites, shall be the HOLY ONE's, I will offer them up as a burnt offering." [32] Then Jephthah crossed over to the Ammonites to fight against them and the HOLY ONE gave them into his hand. [33] He smote a mighty smiting on them from Aroer until you come to Minnith, twenty towns, and as far as Abel-keramim. So, the Ammonites were subdued before the people of Israel.

[34] Then Jephthah came to his home at Mizpah, and there was his daughter coming out to meet him with drums and with dancing. Only she, an only child; he had no son or daughter apart from her. [35] When he saw her, he tore his clothes, and said, "Ah! My daughter, you have knocked me down; you have become my trouble! I—I opened my mouth to the HOLY ONE, and I cannot take back my vow." [36] She said to him, "My father, you have opened your mouth to the HOLY ONE, do to me according to what has gone out of your mouth, after that the HOLY ONE has taken vengeance through you against your enemies, against the Ammonites." [37] And she said to her father, "Let be done for me this thing: Release me for two months, and I will go and go down among the hills, and weep for my virginity, I and my women-friends." [38] Then he said, "Go," and sent her away for two months. So, she left, she and her women-friends, and wept over her virginity among

the hills. ³⁹ And it was at the end of two months, she returned to her father, who did to her what he vowed in his vow. She had never known a man and she became an observance in Israel. ⁴⁰ Year by year the daughters of Israel would go out to tell the story of the daughter of Jephthah the Gileadite for four days.

Psalm 22

¹ My God, my God, why have you forsaken me?
   Why are you so far from my deliverance, from the words of my groaning?

² My God, I cry by day, and you do not answer;
   and by night, and there is found no rest for me.

³ Yet you are holy,
   enthroned on the praises of Israel.

⁴ In you our mothers and fathers trusted;
   they trusted, and you rescued them.

⁵ To you they cried, and were freed;
   in you they trusted, and they were not put to shame.

⁶ But I am a worm, and not human;
   scorned by humankind, and despised by people.

⁷ All who see me mock me;
   they flap their lips at me, they shake their heads:

⁸ "Commit yourself to the SAVING ONE; let God rescue
   and deliver the one in whom God delights!"

⁹ Yet it was you who drew me from the womb;
   keeping me safe on my mother's breast.

¹⁰ On you was I cast from birth,
   and since my mother's womb you have been my God.

¹¹ Be not far from me,
   for trouble is near
   and there is none to help.

¹² Many bulls surround me,
   mighty bulls of Bashan encompass me;

¹³ they open wide their mouths at me,
   like a lion, ravaging and roaring.

¹⁴ I am poured out like water,
   and all my bones are disjointed.
   My heart is like wax;
   it is melted within my being.

¹⁵ My mouth is dried up like a potsherd,
   and my tongue cleaves to my jaws;
   in the dust of death you lay me down.

16 For dogs are all around me;
   a conclave of evildoers encircles me.
   Like a lion they ravage my hands and feet.
17 I can count all my bones.
   They gloat and stare at me.
18 They divide my clothes among themselves,
   and for my clothing they cast lots.
19 SAVING GOD, be not far away!
   My strength, hasten to help me!
20 Deliver my soul from the sword,
   my life from the clutch of the dog!
21 Save me from the mouth of the lion!
   For on the horns of the wild oxen you have responded to me.
22 I will tell of your name to my sisters and brothers;
   in the midst of the congregation I will praise you:
23 You who revere the FOUNT OF LIFE, praise her!
   all the offspring of Leah and Rachel, Bilhah and Zilpah glorify her.
   Stand in awe of her all you of Rebekah's line.
24 For she did not despise or abhor
   the affliction of the afflicted;
   she did not hide her face from me,
   and when I cried to her, she heard.
25 On your account is my praise in the great congregation;
   my vows I will pay before those who revere her.
26 The poor shall eat and be satisfied;
   those who seek her shall praise the MOTHER OF ALL.
   May your hearts live forever!
27 All the ends of the earth shall remember
   and turn to the WELLSPRING OF LIFE;
   and all the families of the nations
   shall worship before her.
28 For sovereignty belongs to the SHE WHO IS HOLY,
   and she rules over the nations.
29 They consume and they bow down, all the fat ones of the earth before her,
   they bend their knees, all who go down to the dust,
   and cannot save their soul.
30 Later descendants will serve her;
   future generations will be told about our God,
31 they will go and proclaim her deliverance to a people yet unborn,
   saying that she has done it.

Hebrews 12:1 Therefore, since we are surrounded by so great a cloud of witnesses, let us also put aside every weight and entangling sin, and with endurance let us run the race that is set before us, [2] looking to Jesus the originator and perfecter of our faith, who for the sake of the joy that was set before him endured the cross, its shame disregarding, and at the right hand of the throne of God has taken his seat.

[3] Consider the one who endured such hostility against himself from sinners, so that you all may not grow weary or your souls grow faint. [4] Not to this point have you all in your struggles against sin resisted to the point of shedding blood.

Luke 22:14 Now when the hour came, he took his place at the table, and the apostles with him. [15] Then Jesus said to them, "I have greatly desired to eat this Passover with you all before I suffer. [16] For I tell you all, I will not eat it until it is fulfilled in the realm of God." [17] Then Jesus took a cup, giving thanks. He said, "Receive this and divide it among yourselves; [18] for I tell you all that from now on I will not drink of the fruit of the vine until the reign of God comes." [19] Then Jesus took a loaf of bread, giving thanks, he broke it and gave it to them, saying, "This is my body, which is given for you all. Do this in remembrance of me." [20] And he did the same with the cup after supper, saying, "This cup that is poured out for you is the new covenant in my blood. [21] Look, the hand of the one who betrays me is with me, on the table. [22] For indeed the Son of Woman is going as it has been determined, but woe to the one by whom he is betrayed!" [23] Then they began to ask among themselves, which one of them was about to do this.

[24] There was also an argument among them as to which one of them should be considered the greatest. [25] But Jesus said to them, "The royals of the Gentiles lord it over them, and those who have power over them are called benefactors. [26] But not so with you all, rather the greatest among you must become like the youngest, and the leader like one who serves. [27] For who is greater, the one who is at the table or the one who serves? Is it not the one at the table? Yet I am among you all as one who serves.

[28] "You are the ones who have remained with me in my trials, [29] so then I covenant with you all, just as my Abba has covenanted with me, a royal inheritance, [30] so that you all may eat and drink at my table in my realm, and you all will sit on thrones governing the twelve tribes of Israel.

[31] "Simon, Simon, listen! The Adversary has demanded to sift all of you like wheat, [32] but I have prayed for you in order that your faith not fail, and you, when you have turned back, strengthen your brothers." [33] Then he said to Jesus, "Rabbi, I am ready to go with you to prison and to death!" [34] But Jesus said, "I tell you, Peter, this day the cock will not have crowed three times, before you deny knowing me."

[35] Then Jesus said to them, "When I sent you out without a purse, bag, or sandals, did you lack anything?" They said, "Not a thing." [36] He said to them, "But now, the one who has a purse must take it, and likewise a bag. And the one who does not have one must sell his cloak and buy a sword. [37] For I tell you, this scripture must be fulfilled in me, '*And he was counted among the lawless*,' and indeed that which pertains to me is coming to its completion." [38] So they said, "Rabbi, see, here are two swords." He replied to them, "It is it is sufficient."

³⁹ Then Jesus came out and went, as was his custom, to the Mount of Olives and the disciples followed him. ⁴⁰ When he was at the place, he said to them, "Pray that you not enter into testing." ⁴¹ Then he withdrew from them about a stone's throw on bended knee and prayed, ⁴² "Father, if you are willing, take this cup away from me; yet not my will but yours be done." ⁴³ [Then an angel from heaven appeared to him and strengthened him. ⁴⁴ In agony he prayed more earnestly, and his sweat became like drops of blood falling down upon the ground.] ⁴⁵ When he rose from prayer, he came to the disciples and found them sleeping from grief. ⁴⁶ And he said to them, "Why are you sleeping? Get up and pray that you not enter into testing."

⁴⁷ While he was speaking, suddenly there was a crowd, and the one called Judas, one of the twelve, was leading them. He approached Jesus to kiss him. ⁴⁸ But Jesus said to him, "Judas, is it with a kiss that you betray the Son of Woman?" ⁴⁹ When those around him saw what was happening, they asked, "Rabbi, should we strike with the sword?" ⁵⁰ Then one of them struck a person enslaved by the high priest and cut off his right ear. ⁵¹ But Jesus responded, saying, "Enough of this!" And he grasped his ear and healed him. ⁵² Then Jesus said to the ones who had come for him, the chief priests, the officers assigned to the temple, and the elders, "Have you all come out with swords and clubs as if I were a bandit? ⁵³ When I was with you daily in the temple, you did not lay hands on me. But this is your hour, and the power of darkness!"

⁵⁴ Then they seized him and led him away, bringing him into the house of the high priest. But Peter was following from afar. ⁵⁵ They kindled a fire in the middle of the courtyard and sat down together; Peter sat among them. ⁵⁶ Then a slave-girl, seeing him near the fire, looked intently at him and said, "This one also was with him." ⁵⁷ But he denied it, saying, "Woman, I do not know him." ⁵⁸ After a time someone else, on seeing him, said, "You are one of them too." But Peter said, "Man, I am not!" ⁵⁹ Then about an hour later another one insisted, "On the truth, this one was with him too, for he is a Galilean." ⁶⁰ But Peter said, "Man, I do not know what you are talking about!" Immediately, while he was speaking, the cock crowed. ⁶¹ The Savior turned and looked at Peter. Then Peter remembered the word of the Messiah, how he had said to him, "Before the cock crows today, you will deny me three times." ⁶² And Peter went out and wept bitterly.

⁶³ Now the men who were holding Jesus mocked him and beat him; ⁶⁴ they also blindfolded him and asked him, "Prophesy! Who is it that struck you?" ⁶⁵ They yelled much other abuse at him.

⁶⁶ Then when day came, the elders of the people, both chief priests and religious scholars, gathered together and brought him to their council. ⁶⁷ They said, "If you are the Messiah, tell us." Jesus replied to them, "If I tell you, you will not believe, ⁶⁸ and if I ask a question, you will not answer. ⁶⁹ But from now on the Son of Woman will be seated at the right hand of the power of God." ⁷⁰ They all asked, "Are you, then, the Son of God?" He said to them, "You say that I am." ⁷¹ Then they said, "What further testimony do we need; we have heard it ourselves from his own lips!"

^{23:1} Then the assembly rose as a body and brought Jesus before Pilate. ² They began to accuse him, saying, "We found this man leading our nation astray, forbidding paying taxes to the emperor, and saying that he is a messiah, a king." ³ Then Pilate questioned him saying, "Are you the king of the Judeans?" He answered, "You say so." ⁴ Then Pilate said to the chief priests

and the crowds, "I find no cause for legal action against this person." ⁵ But they insisted saying, "Because he stirs up the people by teaching throughout all Judea, from Galilee to this very place."

⁶ Upon hearing this, Pilate asked if the person was a Galilean. ⁷ Now when he learned that he was under Herod's authority, he sent him to Herod, who himself was in Jerusalem at that time. ⁸ When Herod saw Jesus, he was extremely glad, for he had wanted to see him for a long time, because he had heard about him and hoped to see him perform some sign. ⁹ Herod questioned him to his satisfaction, but Jesus answered him nothing. ¹⁰ The chief priests and the religious scholars stood by, vehemently accusing him. ¹¹ Herod and his soldiers also treated him with contempt and mocked him, and he put a majestic robe on him, and sent him back to Pilate. ¹² That very moment Herod and Pilate became friends with each other; previously they had been each other's enemy.

¹³ Pilate then called together the chief priests, the leaders, and the people, ¹⁴ and said to them, "You brought me this person for leading the people astray. Look now, I have examined him in your presence and have not found this person guilty of your charges against him. ¹⁵ Nor has Herod, for he sent him back to us. Look here, there is nothing deserving death in his case. ¹⁶ Therefore whip and release him."

¹⁸ Then they shouted together, saying, "Away with him! Release for us Barabbas!" ¹⁹ (Who for a rebellion that had taken place in the city, and for murder, had been put in prison.) ²⁰ Again Pilate addressed them, wanting to release Jesus, ²¹ but they kept shouting, saying, "Crucify, crucify him!" ²² A third time he said to them, "Why, what evil has he done? I have found nothing deserving death in him; I will, therefore, have him whipped and release him." ²³ But they insisted with loud shouts that he should be crucified, and their voices prevailed. ²⁴ So Pilate passed sentence to grant their demand. ²⁵ So he released the one in prison for rebellion and murder who they asked for, and he handed Jesus over as they wished.

²⁶ As they led Jesus away, they seized Simon of Cyrene who was coming from the country, and they laid on him the cross to carry behind Jesus. ²⁷ A great number of people followed him, and a group of women who were beating their breasts and wailing for him. ²⁸ But Jesus turned to them and said, "Daughters of Jerusalem, do not weep for me, weep only for yourselves and for your children. ²⁹ Look, the days are surely coming when they will say, 'Blessed are barren women, and wombs that have never given birth, and breasts that have never nourished.' ³⁰ *Then they will begin to say to the mountains, 'Fall on us'; and to the hills, 'Cover us.'* ³¹ For if when the wood is green they do this, when it is dry what will happen?"

³² Now two criminals were also led away to be put to death with him. ³³ And when they came to the place called Skull, they crucified Jesus there with the criminals, one on his right and one on his left. ³⁴ [And then Jesus said, "Father, forgive them; for they know not what they do."] *They divided his clothing by casting lots.* ³⁵ And the people stood there, watching; but the leaders ridiculed him, saying, "Others he saved; let him save himself if he is the Messiah of God, God's chosen one!" ³⁶ The soldiers also mocked him, coming and offering him vinegar wine, ³⁷ and saying, "If you are the King of the Judeans, save yourself!" ³⁸ There was also an inscription above him, "This is the King of the Judeans."

³⁹ One of the criminals who was hanging there derided him, saying, "Are you not the Messiah? Save yourself and us!" ⁴⁰ But the other rebuked him, saying, "Do you not fear God, since you are under the same death sentence? ⁴¹ And we indeed justly, for what we have done merits what we are receiving, but this one has done nothing wrong." ⁴² Then he said, "Jesus, remember me when you come into your realm." ⁴³ Jesus replied to him, "Truly I tell you, today you will be with me in Paradise."

⁴⁴ And it was now about the sixth hour [of the day, or noon], and darkness came over the whole land until the ninth hour [of the day, about three in the afternoon]. ⁴⁵ The sun's light ceased, and the curtain of the temple was torn in the middle. ⁴⁶ Then Jesus, crying with a loud voice, said, "Father, into your hands I commend my spirit." Saying this then, he breathed out a final time. ⁴⁷ Now when the centurion saw what had happened, he praised God saying, "This man was indeed innocent." ⁴⁸ And all the crowds that had gathered for this spectacle saw what had happened, beating their breasts, they turned back. ⁴⁹ All those who knew him stood far off; the women who had followed him from Galilee were watching these things.

⁵⁰ Now, take note, there was a man named Joseph, a member of the council, a good man and a righteous one. ⁵¹ He had not agreed with the council and their action. He was from the Judean town of Arimathea, and he was waiting for the reign of God. ⁵² This man went to Pilate and requested the body of Jesus. ⁵³ Then he took it down, wrapped it in a linen cloth, and laid it in a tomb hewn from rock where no one had yet lain. ⁵⁴ It was the day of Preparation, and the sabbath was dawning. ⁵⁵ The women followed, the ones who had come with him from Galilee, and they saw the tomb and how his body was placed. ⁵⁶ Then the women returned, and prepared spices and balms.

On the sabbath they rested according to the commandment.

PROCLAMATION

Text Notes

In Judges 11:31, the word *shalom* is used to indicate completion; the verb is used similarly in Modern Hebrew, for example, to complete a purchase or pay the check. In verse 37 and following, virginity symbolizes a stage of life; the grief is about not reaching the full measure of womanhood in her culture, marrying and mothering. In verse 40, the women gather to memorialize the woman sacrificed by her father; the verb is "recount," not as usually translated, "lament."

The psalmist locates her heart in her "belly" in verse 14. The verb for the violence done to the psalmist's hands and feet is missing. The LXX and traditional Jewish exegesis (Rashi) supply it.

Throughout this passion account "Rabbi" replaces "Lord," so as not to further divinize slave language. For third-person references, Messiah, Christ, and Savior will be used. Also, "enslaved person" rather than "slave" distinguishes between a person and their circumstances. The eucharistic instruction in Luke 22:16 can be translated as "take" or "receive" (this cup). In the Hebrew Scriptures, to judge is to govern, administer, oversee, rule, and render justice. That full sense is intended in Luke 22:30, rather than passing judgment on Israel. The Adversary, the Satan, occurs in verse 31 with the definite article as in Hebrew where the term is a title or description; further contemporary notions of Satan are often postbiblical. Verses 43–44 in chapter 22 and verse 34 in chapter 23 are not present in all manuscripts as indicated by brackets.

In Luke 23:2 and 14, the more common translation "perverting" (rather "leading astray" here) has an unnecessary sexual connotation in English. Jesus's accusers testify that he says he is *a messiah*; there is no direct object. The term was not unique to Jesus. Hebrew *meshiach* is translated by Greek *christos*; David and Cyrus are each God's messiah, God's christ in the Hebrew and Greek versions of 2 Samuel 23:1 and Isaiah 45:1, which parallel Luke 23:35 where Jesus is disbelieved as the Christ/Messiah of God. The term, otherwise translated "anointed," also applies to monarchs and priests.

The robe with which Jesus was mocked in Luke 23:11 was "bright," or "shiny," suggesting rich embroidery or embellishment. Some less reliable manuscripts include a verse 17 that is generally removed from critical translations: "He had to release one prisoner for them because of the festival."

Jesus quotes Hosea 10:8 where people ask for the mountains and hills to cover them in Luke 23:30. Verse 34, "Father, forgive them . . ." is missing in many manuscripts. "Into your hands I commend my spirit" in verse 46 from Psalm 31:5 can also be translated "Into your hands I place my life." In verse 49, "those who stood" are a mixed gender as indicated by the text (grammatically, an all-male group is also possible); those who were watching were the women according to the feminine plural verb which excludes males. In contrast, the "they" who rested on the sabbath in verse 56 is inclusive.

A final note, the NRSV translation that Joseph of Arimathea, "who, *though* a member of the council" was "good and righteous" in Luke 23:50 excludes the whole of the Sanhedrin from the possibility of being good and righteous normatively. It is more than an uncharitable reading; it is anti-Judaistic and contributes to the anti-Semitic legacy and practices of the Church.

Preaching Prompts

This lectionary pairs the brutal deaths of Jephthah's daughter and Jesus. Each of their deaths is horrific; at one level, unnecessary slaughter, and each death is believed by someone in their respective story to serve a greater good. The disparate portraits and motives of the two fathers in relation to the death of their sole child offer fruitful space to address the crucifixion beyond the limits of atonement theology. Each of these texts requires us to ask who it is we think God is.

Jephthah, taken from his mother, a sex-worker, by his father Gilead, was rejected by his brothers and his father's wife. The troubled boy is not unrelated to the troubled man. He is desperate for affirmation. Note that God had already given Jephthah victory over the Ammonites in Judges 11:32 before he makes a vow to "ensure" his win. Jephthah's god is familiar to many: rigid and unyielding, apparently incapable of forgiving a rash vow, making human sacrifice the only acceptable appeasement. Jephthah doesn't test his theology; he doesn't bargain with God like Abraham. He doesn't offer himself as recipient of divine rage; he does not fight for the life of his child. His parenthood, like his theology, leaves much to be desired. As is the case in rigid, fundamentalist, patriarchal systems, women's lives hold little value and are expendable. Is spite of the lethal limits of the system in which she finds herself constrained, Jephthah's daughter carves out space for herself and other women, illuminating and memorializing the deficiencies of a god like Jephthah's.

The psalmist's God is lightyears away from the tyrant Jephthah worships, savior rather than destroyer. The psalmist's God is part nurse, part midwife, trustworthy and praiseworthy. In Matthew and Mark on the cross Jesus turns to this God and this psalm, making it virtually inseparable from Good Friday. In Luke's Passion, Jesus quotes Psalm 31, which shares the theme of trusting a trustworthy God for salvation.

Hebrews calls us to look to Jesus in the company of the faithful. Luke presents a roster of the faithful where women are more fully present than in other accounts. The spaces where women are missing are also instructive, such as a conversation about who is greater and injunction for the greatest to serve the least with apparently no women in the room. How different would the church have looked if that teaching were applied to systemic structural inequities between genders and cultures as a start?

Women are rendered invisible in the crowds that characterize the narrative, visible as enslaved girls, weeping women who accompany Jesus on his death march, and the women who were family, friends, followers, and disciples—some in more than one category—standing watch until the end. In spite of the gruesome horror, Jesus's female companions and followers, family and friends, watched and did not turn away according to Luke 23:49; the text cannot make the same claim of the male apostles and disciples. These women were faithful in and beyond the horror that seemed to mark the end of their shared journey.

HOLY SATURDAY

Job 14:1–14; Psalm 31; Philippians 2:1–8; Matthew 27:57–66

Job 14:1 "Woman-born,
  humankind is short of days and full of turmoil.
² They sprout like a flower and wither,
  flee like a shadow and do not endure.

3 Are your eyes, then, open to such a one as this?
  Do you bring me into judgment with you?
4 Who can make a clean thing out of an unclean thing?
  No one.
5 If their days are fixed,
  the number of their months is in your keeping,
  it is because you have set their boundaries that they cannot pass.
6 Look away from them, and they sit at ease,
  until they complete, like laborers, their days.
7 For there is hope for a tree,
  if it is cut down, that it will be renewed,
  and that its branches will not fail.
8 Its root grows old in the earth,
  and its trunk dies in the dust.
9 At the scent of water it will bud
  and put forth branches like a sapling.
10 Mortals die, and are carried away;
  the woman-born perish, and where are they?
11 As waters dissipate from a sea,
  and a river dries up and is depleted,
12 so a person lies down and does not rise again;
  until the heavens are no more,
  they will not awake or be stirred from their sleep.
13 Grant that you would hide me in Sheol,
  that you would cover me until your wrath is past,
  that you would set for me a boundary, and remember me.
14 If a person dies, will they live again?
  All the days of my service I would wait
  until my change come.

Psalm 31

1 In you, WOMB OF LIFE, I take refuge;
  let me not ever be put to shame;
  in your righteousness rescue me.
2 Incline your ear to me;
  quickly deliver me.
  Be for me a rock of refuge,
  a stronghold to save me.
3 For you are my rock and my stronghold;
  for your Name's sake lead me and guide me.

⁴ Free me from the net that is hidden for me,
for you are my refuge.

⁵ Into your hand I commit my spirit;
you have redeemed me, ARK OF SAFETY, God of truth.

⁶ I hate those who attend to worthless vanity,
but in the MOTHER OF ALL I place my trust.

⁷ I will exult and I will rejoice in your faithful love,
because you have seen my affliction;
you have studied my soul's sorrows.

⁸ Yet you have not handed me over to the hand of the enemy;
you have set my feet in a broad place.

⁹ Be gracious to me, MOTHER OF MERCY, for I am in distress;
my eyes waste away with angry tears,
my soul and body too.

¹⁰ For my life is spent in sorrow,
and my years in sighing;
because of my iniquity my strength fails,
and my bones waste away.

¹¹ Because of my enemies I am a disgrace to all,
and to my neighbors, more,
an object of dread to those who know me;
those who see me in the street flee from me.

¹² I have been forgotten from the heart like one who is dead;
I have become like a ruined vessel.

¹³ Because I hear the whispering of many,
terror surrounds in their scheming together against me,
as they plot to take my life.

¹⁴ Yet I, in you I trust, FAITHFUL GOD;
I declare, "You are my God."

¹⁵ My times are in your hand;
deliver me from the hand of my enemies and those who hound me.

¹⁶ Let your face shine upon your slave;
save me in your faithful love.

¹⁷ GRACIOUS GOD, let me not be put to shame,
for I call upon you;
let the wicked be put to shame;
let them go silent to Sheol.

¹⁸ Let lying lips be stilled,
the ones that speak against the righteous,
arrogant with pride and contempt.

¹⁹ How great is your goodness
that you have secured for those who fear you,
and that you do for those who take refuge in you,
before all the woman-born.
²⁰ In the shelter of your presence you shelter them
from human plots;
you hide them safe under your shelter
from contentious tongues.
²¹ Blessed be the MOTHER OF CREATION,
who is marvelous in her faithful love to me,
a city under siege.
²² Now I, I had said in my alarm,
"I am cut off from your sight."
However, you heard my supplications
when I cried to you for help.
²³ Love GOD WHOSE NAME IS HOLY, all you her godly ones.
The FAITHFUL GOD preserves the faithful,
and repays with interest the one who acts out of pride.
²⁴ Take courage, and she shall strengthen your hearts,
all you who wait for the MOTHER OF ALL.

Philippians 2:1 If then there is any encouragement in Christ, any consolation from love, any communion in the Spirit, any tenderness and compassion, ² make my joy complete. Be wise in the same way, having the same love, united and sharing the same wisdom. ³ Do nothing from self-interest, but in humility regard others as better than yourselves. ⁴ Each of you, look not to your own interests, but rather to the interests of others. ⁵ Let the same wisdom be in you all that was in Christ Jesus,

⁶ *who, though he was in the form of God,*
did not regard equality with God
as something to be seized,
⁷ *but emptied himself,*
taking the form of a slave,
being born in human likeness;
then being found in human form,
⁸ *he humbled himself*
and became obedient to the point of death,
even death on a cross.

Matthew 27:57 When it was evening, a rich person came from Arimathea, Joseph, who was also a disciple of Jesus. ⁵⁸ He went to Pilate and requested the body of Jesus; then Pilate commanded it to be given to him. [59] So Joseph took the body and wrapped it in clean linen, [60] and laid it in his new tomb, which he had hewn in rock. Then he rolled a great stone to the door of the tomb and departed. [61] Mary Magdalene and the other Mary were there, sitting before the tomb.

[62] Now, the next day, which was after the day of Preparation, the chief priests and the Pharisees gathered before Pilate. [63] They said, "Lord, we remember what that deceiver said while he was still alive, 'After three days I will rise.' [64] Command, therefore, the tomb be secured until the third day; otherwise his disciples may go and steal him, and tell the people, 'He has been raised from the dead,' and the last deception would be worse than the first." [65] Pilate said to them, "You may have a squad; go, as secure it as you can." [66] So they went with the guard and secured the tomb, sealing the stone.

PROCLAMATION

Text Notes

Job 14 begins its reflection on mortality using inclusive language, "those born of women," and "humanity in verse 1, then shifts to masculine language, "(male) warrior" in verses 10 and 14 and "man" in verse 12. I apply inclusive language to the other human references in the passage. Job's address shifts from second to third person in verses 6 and 13. Verse 13 could also begin, "Who will grant . . ." In his book-length legal complaint, Job looks (rhetorically at least) for someone to compel God to do justly by him. That is part of the theological scandal of the book.

In verse 4 of the psalm, "free me" is the "let my people go" verb of the exodus. In verse 9 there is only one "eye" and tears are lacking; "body" is "belly/womb." Somewhat contradictorily, "to go silently to Sheol" can also be "to go weeping to Sheol." "Godly ones" in verse 23 are often translated anachronistically as "saints," importing Christian language and theology into the Hebrew Scriptures.

There is considerable disagreement over the meaning of *eritheian* in Philippians 2:3, translated here as "self-interest"; some other possibilities are: strife, contentiousness, selfishness, or selfish ambition. According to its earlier usage in Aristotle, it may mean "a self-seeking pursuit" for political office in that case. (See the corresponding entry in the *A Greek-English Lexicon of the New Testament and Other Early Christian Literature [BDAG]*).

The use of "Lord" for Pilate serves as a reminder the title was not unique to Jesus, nor a particularly religious one, but one of hierarchy, signifying Pilate's authority as the face of the Roman occupation. Translations like NRSV that preserve it for Jesus but change it for other characters are intentionally misleading.

Preaching Prompts

Holy Saturday may be the most liminal space in the Christian liturgical cycle. Passion has become pathos. The death of Jesus stupefies, but the breaking dawn has not dispelled the waking dream. Yet the liturgical remembrance is part of a thousands-year-old cycle, and we know what the next dawn brings. We struggle not to anticipate that dawn. These lessons underscore our finitude, our mortality and that of all living things, and the mortality of Jesus, Son of Woman, Son of God, Child of Earth.

Job's reflection on his own mortality comes in the midst of his address to God in chapters 12–14, responding to Zophar's chapter 11 rebuke, blaming Job for the evil that has befallen him. In this lesson Job's rumination on his inevitable death is accompanied by the reminder that death is part of the cycle of life in nature. Without knowing the hope that Christians hold dear, Job expects a "no" to the question of whether a person who has died will live again. He and the psalmist expect all the dead to go to Sheol (Job 14:13; Psalm 31:17). The psalmist commits her fragile life (verse 5) and finite times (verses 14–15) into God's hands, fully aware of her own mortality. The psalm also includes the remembrance of God's fidelity (verses 7, 19–21, 23) and assurance that God hears the cry of her faithful, verse 22.

As a Holy Saturday text, Philippians 2 presents a Jesus as empty of divinity as his body in the tomb was empty of life. Here Jesus humbles himself to experience the finitude of the human experience, mortality, and one of its most common and most horrific occurrences, a violent death at human hands.

We hold all of these things in our hearts as we wrestle with implications, sitting, watching, and waiting with Miriam, Mary of Magdala, and another woman who also bears the name of Israel's first prophet. They knew not for what they waited. Though we know, we keep vigil with them.

EASTER—THE GREAT VIGIL

At least two of the following lessons are read, of which one is always the lesson from Exodus. After each lesson, the psalm or canticle listed, or some other suitable psalm, canticle, or hymn, is sung.

A God-Crafted Creation: Genesis 1:1–2, 26–27; 2:1–4

Genesis 1:1 When beginning he, God, created the heavens and the earth, ² the earth was shapeless and formless and bleakness covered the face of the deep, while the Spirit of God, she, fluttered over the face of the waters.

²⁶ And God said, "Let us make humankind in our image, according to our likeness; and let them rule the fish of the sea, and the birds of the heavens, and the animals, and the whole earth, and over every creeping creature that creeps upon the earth."

²⁷ So God created humankind in God's own image,

in God's own image, God created them;

female and male, God created them.

^{2:1} And the heavens and the earth were complete, along with all their multitude. ² Then God finished on the seventh day the work that God had done, and rested on the seventh day from all the work that they had done. ³ So God blessed the seventh day and sanctified it, because on it God rested from all the work that God had done in creation.

⁴ These are the generations of the heavens and the earth when they were created.

Canticle of the Three Young Men: Daniel (LXX) 3:52–60

⁵² "Let the earth bless the Creator of All;

let her sing hymns to God and highly exalt God forever.

⁵³ Bless the Creator of All, mountains and hills;

sing hymns to God and highly exalt God forever.

⁵⁴ Bless the Creator of All, all that grows in the ground;

sing hymns to God and highly exalt God forever.

⁵⁵ Bless the Creator of All, seas and rivers;

sing hymns to God and highly exalt God forever.

⁵⁶ Bless the Creator of All, you springs;

sing hymns to God and highly exalt God forever.

⁵⁷ Bless the Creator of All, you sea-monsters and all that swim in the waters;

sing hymns to God and highly exalt God forever.

⁵⁸ Bless the Creator of All, all birds of the air;

sing hymns to God and highly exalt God forever.

⁵⁹ Bless the Creator of All, all wild animals and cattle;

sing hymns to God and highly exalt God forever.

⁶⁰ "Bless the Creator of All, all people on earth;

sing hymns to God and highly exalt God forever.

The Salvation of Hagar and Ishmael: Genesis 21:2, 8–21

Genesis 21:2 Sarah conceived and gave birth to a son for Abraham in his old age, at the set time of which God had spoken to him.

⁸ The child grew, and was weaned, and Abraham made a great feast on the day of Isaac's weaning. ⁹ Then Sarah saw the son of Hagar the Egyptian woman, whom she had given birth to for Abraham, playing. ¹⁰ So she said to Abraham, "Drive out this slave woman with her son; for the son of this slave woman shall not inherit with my son, with Isaac." ¹¹ The situation was evil in Abraham's eyes on account of his son. ¹² And God said to Abraham, "See it not as evil in your eyes on account of the boy and on account of your slave woman. In all that Sarah says to you, obey her voice, for it is through Isaac that offspring shall be named for you. ¹³ Yet even the son of the slave woman I will make a nation also, because he is your offspring." ¹⁴ So

Abraham rose early in the morning, and took bread and a skin of water, and gave it to Hagar. He placed it on her shoulder, along with the child, and sent her away. Then she walked away and wandered in the wilderness of Beer-Sheba.

¹⁵ When the water in the skin was gone, she thrust the child under one of the bushes. ¹⁶ Then she went and sat herself down before him some way off, about the distance of a bowshot; for she said, "Let me not see the death of the child." So, she sat before him and she lifted up her voice and she wept. ¹⁷ And God heard the voice of the boy, and the messenger of God called to Hagar from the heavens, and said to her, "What troubles you, Hagar? Fear not; for God has heard the voice of the boy where he is. ¹⁸ Rise, lift the boy and hold him with your hand, for a great nation of him I will make." ¹⁹ Then God opened her eyes and she saw a well of water. She went, and filled the skin with water, and let the boy drink.

²⁰ God was with the boy, and he grew up; he settled in the wilderness, and became an archer. ²¹ He settled in the wilderness of Paran, and his mother acquired a wife for him from the land of Egypt.

Psalm 27:5–7, 10–14

⁵ She will shield me in her shelter
  when the day is evil;
  she will cover me under the cover of her tent;
  she will raise me high on a rock.
⁶ Now my head is raised up
  above my enemies surrounding me,
  and I will offer in her tent
  sacrifices with shouts of joy;
  I will sing and make melody to the GOD WHO SAVES.
⁷ Hear my cry, FAITHFUL ONE, when I cry aloud,
  be gracious to me and answer me!
¹⁰ If my mother and father forsake me,
  the COMPASSIONATE GOD will gather me in.
¹¹ Teach me, RIGHTEOUS ONE, your way,
  and lead me on a smooth path
  because of my enemies.
¹² Do not give me over to the throats of my foes,
  for lying witnesses rise against me,
  and they breathe violence.
¹³ If I but believe, I shall see the goodness of SHE WHO IS FAITHFUL
  in the land of the living.
¹⁴ Wait for the LIVING GOD;
  be strong, and let your heart take courage;
  wait for GOD WHOSE NAME IS HOLY!

From Slavery to Freedom: Exodus 14:26–29; 15:20–21

Exodus 14:26 Now the HOLY ONE said to Moses, "Stretch out your hand over the sea, so that the water may come back upon the Egyptians, upon their chariots and charioteers." ²⁷ So Moses stretched out his hand over the sea and the sea turned back; by the break of dawn it was back to its strength, and the Egyptians fled at its approach. Then the LIVING GOD shook the Egyptians in the midst of the sea. ²⁸ The waters returned and covered the chariots and the charioteers, the whole army of Pharaoh that came after them into the sea; not a single one of them remained. ²⁹ And the women, children, and men of Israel walked on dry ground through the sea, the waters a wall for them on their right and on their left.

^{15:20} Then the prophet Miriam, Aaron's sister, took a drum in her hand; and all the women went out after her with drums and with dancing. ²¹ And Miriam sang to them:

> "Sing to the GOD WHO SAVES, for God has triumphed triumphantly;
> horse and rider God has thrown into the sea."

Song of Miriam and Moses: Exodus 15:1–3, 11, 13, 17–18

Exodus 15:1 Moses and the women and men of Israel sang this song to the HOLY ONE OF OLD:

> "I will sing to the GOD WHO SAVES, for God has triumphed triumphantly;
> horse and rider God has thrown into the sea.
> ² The MIGHTY GOD is my strength and my might,
> God has become my salvation.
> This is my God, whom I will praise,
> my mother's God and my father's God, whom I will exalt.
> ³ The DREAD GOD is a warrior;
> TOO HOLY TO BE PRONOUNCED is God's name.
> ¹¹ "Who is like you, MOST HIGH, among the gods?
> Who is like you, majestic in holiness,
> awesome in splendor, working wonders?
> ¹³ "In your faithful love you led the people whom you redeemed;
> you guided them by your strength to your holy habitation.
> ¹⁷ You brought them in and planted them on the mountain that is your own possession,
> the place, FAITHFUL GOD, that you made your dwelling place,
> the sanctuary, SOVEREIGN ONE, that your hands have established.
> ¹⁸ GOD WHO IS MAJESTY will reign forever and ever."

Rahab's Salvation: Joshua 2:1–14; 6:15–17, 22–23

Joshua 2:1 And Joshua son of Nun sent two men, spies, secretly from Shittim, saying, "Go, surveil the land, surveil Jericho." So, they went, and entered the house of a prostitute—her name was Rahab—and they lay down there. ² Now the king of Jericho was told, "Look now, men have come here tonight from the Israelites to search out the land." ³ Then the king of

Jericho sent to Rahab, "Bring out the men, the ones who came to you, who came to your house, for they have come to search out the whole of the land." ⁴ Now the woman had taken the two men and hid them. Then she said, "True, the men came to me, but I did not know from where they came. ⁵ And it was when the gate was to close at dark that the men went out. I do not know where the men went. Hurry, chase after them, for you can reach them." ⁶ However, she had brought them up to the roof and hidden them in the stalks of flax that she had laid out for herself on the roof. ⁷ So the men chased after them along the path of the Jordan up to the fords. The gate was shut as soon as the pursuers had gone out.

¹² [Rahab said,] "Now I bid you all swear to me by the FAITHFUL GOD–for I have done faithfully by you all—that you also will do faithfully by my father's household. Give me a trustworthy sign. ¹³ Now, spare my mother and my father, my sisters and my brothers, and all who belong to them, and deliver our lives from death." ¹⁴ The men said to her, "Our life for yours, even unto death! If you do not tell this our business, then when the FAITHFUL GOD gives to us the land we will deal faithfully and honestly with you."

6:15 And it happened on the seventh day that they rose early, at the break of dawn, and circled the city in the same way seven times. Only on that day that they circled the city seven times. ¹⁶ And it was the seventh time, when the priests blew the ram's horns, Joshua said to the people, "Shout! For the FAITHFUL ONE has given you the city. ¹⁷ The city and all that is in it shall be devoted to the HOLY ONE. Only Rahab the prostitute, she shall live and all who are with her in her house because she hid the messengers we sent."

²³ So the youths who were the spies went in and brought Rahab out, along with her mother, her father, her sisters and brothers, and all who belonged to her—all her kinfolk they brought out—and set them outside the camp of Israel.

Canticle: Wisdom 5:1–5; 6:6–7

Wisdom 5:1 The righteous will stand with great confidence
 in the presence of those who have oppressed them
 and those who make light of their labors.
² When the unrighteous see, they will be shaken with a terrible fear,
 and they will be amazed at the unexpected salvation.
³ They will speak amongst themselves repenting,
 and out of distress of spirit they will groan, and say,
⁴ "These are persons whom we once held in derision
 and made the meaning of insult—we were foolish.
 We reckoned their lives as madness
 and their end without honor.
⁵ Why have they been numbered among the daughters and sons of God?
 And why is their lot among the holy ones?"
6:6 For the least may be pardoned in mercy,
 but the mighty will be mightily tested.

⁷ For the Sovereign of all will not draw back from anyone,
or show respect to greatness;
because small and great alike God made,
and God takes thought for all alike.

Deborah Saves the People: Judges 4:1–10, 23

Judges 4:1 And again the men and women of Israel did what was evil in the sight of the HOLY ONE OF SINAI, for Ehud [the Judge] was dead. ² So the HOLY ONE sold them into the hand of King Jabin of Canaan, who reigned in Hazor; the commander of his army was Sisera, who lived in Harosheth-ha-goiim. ³ Then the women and men of Israel cried out to GOD WHO HEARS; for Jabin had nine hundred chariots of iron, and had oppressed the Israelites with ruthlessness twenty years.

⁴ Deborah, a woman, a female prophet, a fiery woman, she was judging Israel at that time. ⁵ She used to sit under the palm of Deborah between Ramah and Bethel in the hill country of Ephraim; and the women and men of Israel came up to her for judgment. ⁶ She sent and called for Barak ben Abinoam from Kedesh in Naphtali, and said to him, "Did not the MOST HIGH, the God of Israel, command you? Go! March on Mount Tabor, and take ten thousand men from the tribe of Naphtali and the tribe of Zebulun. ⁷ I will march toward you to draw to you by the Wadi Kishon Sisera the commander of Jabin's army, with his chariots and his troops; and I will give him into your hand." ⁸ Then Barak said to her, "If you will go with me, then I will go; but if you will not go with me, I will not go." ⁹ And she said, "I will surely go with you; however, there will be no glory for you on the path you are taking, for the MIGHTY GOD will sell Sisera into the hand of a woman." Then Deborah got up and went with Barak to Kedesh. ¹⁰ Barak summoned Zebulun and Naphtali to Kedesh; and ten thousand men went up with him; and Deborah went up with him.

²³ And on that day, God subdued King Jabin of Canaan before the women and men of Israel.

Canticle of Deborah: Judges 5:1, 4–7, 12, 24, 31

Judges 5:1 Then Deborah and Barak ben Abinoam sang on that day, saying:

⁴ "MIGHTY ONE, when you went out from Seir,
when you marched from the field of Edom,
the earth and the heavens dripped,
even the clouds dripped water.
⁵ The mountains melted before the MOST HIGH, the One of Sinai,
before the ONE GOD, the God of Israel.
⁶ "In the days of Shamgar son of Anath,
in the days of Jael, caravans ceased
and travelers traversed the byways.
⁷ The mighty grew fat in Israel,
they grew fat on plunder,

until you arose, Deborah,
you arose as a mother in Israel.

12 "Awake, awake, Deborah!
Awake, awake, utter a song!
Arise, Barak, capture your captives,
ben Abinoam.

24 "Most blessed of women be Jael,
the wife of Heber the Kenite,
of tent-women most blessed.

31 "So perish all your enemies, Holy One of Old!
But those who love God will be like the sun rising in its might."

And the land was pacified for forty years.

Jehosheba Saves the King of Judah: 2 Kings 11:1–4, 10–12

2 Kings 11:1 Now Athaliah, Ahaziah's mother, saw that her son was dead, she stood up and destroyed all the royal offspring. [2] Then Jehosheba, daughter of King Joram, sister of Ahaziah, took Joash, Ahaziah's son, and she stole him away from among the daughters and sons of the king who were being killed; she put him and his nurse in a bedroom. Thus, she hid him from Athaliah, and he was not put to death. [3] [The prince] remained with Ahaziah's sister six years, hidden in the house of the Ever-Living God, while Athaliah reigned over the land.

[4] But in the seventh year Jehoiada [the High Priest and Josheba's husband] sent for the captains of the Carites and of the bodyguards and had them come to him in the house of the Holy One. He made a covenant with them and had them swear it in the house of the Holy One of Old; then he showed them the son of the king.

[10] The priest [Jehoiada] gave to the captains of the hundreds the spears and shields that had been King David's, which were in the house of the Living God. [11] Then the guards stood, each with his weapons in his hand, from the south of the temple to the north of the temple, next to the altar and the temple, around the king on every side. [12] Then he brought out the son of the king, put the crown on him, and gave Joash the testimony [of royalty]. They made him king and anointed him; they clapped their hands and shouted, "Long live the king!"

Psalm 9:1–2, 7–11, 13–14

1 I will give thanks to the God Who Saves with my whole heart;
I will tell of all your wonderful deeds.

2 I will rejoice and exult in you;
I will sing praise to your name, Most High.

7 God who is Majesty sits enthroned forever,
she has established her throne for judgment.

8 She judges the world in righteousness;
she judges the peoples with equity.

⁹ SHE WHO IS FAITHFUL is a stronghold for the oppressed,
a stronghold in times of trouble.

¹⁰ They trust you, they who know your name,
for you do not forsake those who seek you REDEEMING GOD.

¹¹ Sing praises to the HOLY ONE enthroned in Zion.
Declare her deeds among the peoples.

¹³ Be gracious to me, GRACIOUS ONE.
See what I suffer from those who hate me.
You lift me up from the gates of death,

¹⁴ so that I may recount all your praises,
and in the gates of Daughter Zion,
rejoice in your salvation.

Judith Saves Her People: Judith 8:9–10, 32–34; 13:3–14, 17–18

Judith 8:9 Now Judith heard the wicked words of the people against the ruler because they were disheartened from lack of water, and when she heard all the words that Uzziah said to them, and how he swore to them to surrender the town to the Assyrians after five days. ¹⁰ So she sent her slave-girl, who was set over all she possessed, to summon Uzziah and Chabris and Charmis, the elders of her town.

³² Then Judith said to them, "Hear me and I will do a thing that will go down from generation to generation of our daughters and sons. ³³ You all shall stand at the gate this night and I shall go out, I along with my slave-girl, and within the days which you have promised to handover the town to our enemies, the Holy One will visit Israel through my hand. ³⁴ None of you should investigate my task; for I will not tell you all until I have completed my work."

^{13:3} Now Judith had told her slave-girl to stand outside the bedchamber and to wait for her to come out, as she did other days; for she said she would go out for her prayer. She spoke to Bagoas these same words. ⁴ So everyone went out beyond sight, and no one was left in the bedchamber, either small or great. Then Judith, standing beside his bed, said in her heart, "Holy God of all power, look with care in this hour on the work of my hands for the exaltation of Jerusalem. ⁵ Now is the time to help your heritage and to carry out my intention to destroy the enemies who have risen up against us."

⁶ She came to the bedpost at Holofernes' head, and took down his sword from there. ⁷ Then she came towards his bed, caught the hair of his head, and said, "Give me strength today, Holy God of Israel!" ⁸ And she struck his neck twice with all her might, and cut off his head. ⁹ Then she rolled his body off the bed and snatched the canopy from the post. A little later she went out and gave Holofernes' head to her slave-girl, ¹⁰ who placed it in her food bag.

Then the two women went out together, according to their custom at the time for prayer. They passed through the encampment, circled the valley, and went up the mountain to Bethulia, and came to its gates. ¹¹ From a distance Judith called out to the guards at the gates, "Open! Open the gate! God, our God, is with us, working deeds of power in Israel and might against our enemies, as God has done today!"

¹² And it happened when the men of her town heard her voice, they rushed to come down to the gate of the city and summoned the elders of the city. ¹³ They all ran together, from small to great, for it was extraordinary to them that she returned. They opened the gate and welcomed the women. Then they lit a fire to provide light, and gathered around the women. ¹⁴ Then Judith said to them with a loud voice, "Hallelujah! Hallelujah! Praise God, who did not withdraw mercy from the house of Israel, but has broken our enemies by my hand this night!"

¹⁷ All the people were completely astounded. They bowed down and worshiped God, and said with one accord, "Blessed are you our God, who has this day humiliated the enemies of your people." ¹⁸ Then Uzziah said to Judith, "O daughter, you are blessed by the Most High God above all other women on earth, and blessed be the Holy God, who created the heavens and the earth, who has guided you to cut off the head of the leader of our enemies."

The Song of Judith: Judith 16:1–6, 13

Judith 16:1 Judith said:

> Begin praise for my God with drums,
>   sing to my Sovereign with cymbals.
> Craft a psalm and a praise for God;
>   exalt God and call upon God's name.
> ² For the Holy One is a God who crushes wars,
>   whose encampments are in the midst of the people,
>   who delivered me from the hands of my pursuers.
> ³ Assyria came down from the mountains of the north;
>   it came with multitudes of its warriors,
>   the same multitude blocked up the waterway,
>   and their cavalry covered the hills.
> ⁴ Assyria boasted that it would burn up my territory,
>   and kill my young men with the sword,
>   and throw my infants to the ground,
>   and give my children away as spoils of war,
>   and despoil my virgins.
> ⁵ But the Almighty God dismissed them
>   with a feminine hand.
> ⁶ For their mighty one did not fall by the hands of the young men,
>   nor did the sons of the Titans strike him down,
>   nor did tall giants lay him out;

but Judith daughter of Merari
with the beauty of her person undid him.

¹³ I will sing to my God a new song:
Holy One, you are great and glorious,
wonderful in strength, invincible.

Epistle: Acts 16:13–15

Acts 16:13 On the day of the sabbath we went out the gate by the river, where we thought there was a place of prayer; and we sat down and spoke to the women who gathered there. ¹⁴ Now a certain woman named Lydia, a merchant of purple cloth from the city of Thyatira, a worshiper of God, was listening to us. The Messiah opened her heart to listen eagerly to what was said by Paul. ¹⁵ As she was baptized along with her household, she urged us, saying, "If you have judged me to be faithful to Christ, come and stay at my home." And she persuaded us.

Gospel: Matthew 28:1–10

Matthew 28:1 After the sabbath, as the first day of the week was dawning, Mary Magdalene and the other Mary went to see the tomb. ² And look! There was a great earthquake, for a messenger of God, descending from heaven, came and rolled away the stone and sat upon it. ³ Its appearance was like lightning, and its clothing white as snow. ⁴ For fear of the messenger the guards shook and were as though dead. ⁵ But the messenger responded to the women and said, "Fear not; I know that you all are looking for Jesus who was crucified. ⁶ He is not here; for he has been raised, just as he said. Come, see the place where he lay. ⁷ Then go quickly and tell his disciples, 'He has been raised from the dead, and see, he is on to Galilee ahead of you; there you all will see him.' This is my message for you." ⁸ So the women left the tomb quickly with fear and great joy and ran to tell his disciples the news. ⁹ Then all of a sudden Jesus met them and said, "Shalom!" And they came to him, took hold of his feet, and bowed down worshipping him. ¹⁰ Then Jesus said to them, "Fear not; go and tell my sisters and brothers to go to Galilee; there they will see me."

PROCLAMATION

Text Notes

In the very first lines of Genesis, and therefore of the Bible, Jewish or Christian, both masculine and feminine verbs are used for God, masculine for God, feminine for the Spirit. Ultimately God's human creation will reflect their creator as female and male. The translation follows that early pattern and uses pronouns of both genders throughout the passage. In Genesis 2:2 I also use "they" for God, a reminder that God transcends the binary language in which God is disclosed and that some of those created in the image of God are nonbinary.

In Genesis 21:9, the nature of Ishmael's play (or mocking) is not explained. The NRSV and RSV add "with Isaac," which is not in the text, leading to demonization of Ishmael as a child. Some commentators go so far as to accuse him of sexually abusing Isaac based on this fiction. In verse 11, Abraham finds the situation "extremely evil," though the word encodes a range of negativity. Hagar's motion in putting her child under the tree is explosive: "throw," or "cast." The idiomatic expression in verse 17, "What is with you?" sounds harsher to English-speaking ears than the traditional "What troubles you?"

In Psalm 27:11, "teach" is the verbal form of *torah,* which is more properly "teaching" or "revelation" than law. In verse 12, "throats" translates *nephesh,* "soul." The usage is rare but occurs in Job 24:12, Jeremiah 4:10, and Habakkuk 2:5. In verse 14, the number of grammatically masculine subjects leave open another possible translation, familiar from the King James Version: "Be of good courage and God will strengthen your heart."

The Canticle of the Three Young Men comes from the Greek version of Daniel in the Septuagint. A larger selection of verses occurs in the Song of the Three Young Men used as a canticle in the Book of Common Prayer. In many Protestant Bibles like the NRSV, translations of Greek portions of Daniel and Esther are published in a separate section with the Deuterocanonical/Apocryphal books. In Catholic Bibles like the *Inclusive Bible,* the Greek-based portions are woven in, resulting in an alternate set of verse numbers. This passage is verses 74–82 in the *New English Translation of the Septuagint* (NETS). The NETS translation was influential in my own here.

In Exodus 15:2 I add "my mother's God." While Moses will have to ask who God is and what is the divine Name, Moses's mother Yocheved, Jochebed, bears the Name in the first syllable of her name and may be the oldest name in the Hebrew Bible including a portion of the Name. In verse 3 God is thoroughly anthropomorphized as "a man of war."

Like Miriam's Song, Judges 5 is one of the oldest works in the Hebrew Bible, replete with translation challenges. In Judges 4:4, Deborah is a woman of *lappidoth.* While many have contrived a husband, the word is the adjective "fiery" or "flaming" with a feminine ending. Further, unlike every male character in the book, *lappidoth* does not have any family information line for Barak son of Abinoam. The feminine singular verb in 5:1 indicates Deborah led the song and Barak followed her lead. An earlier version of the translation of Judges 4–5 and detailed translation notes can be found in *Daughters of Miriam: Women Prophets in Ancient Israel.*

Some details of 2 Kings 11 are filled in with the more detailed account in 2 Chronicles 23.

The sense of the story in Judith is that she dined with the enemy general, maintaining her virtue, got him drunk and assassinated him. In the critical scene the tent where Holofernes sleeps is confusingly described as hers in 13:3. Previously 12:1 and following indicate she is staying in his dining tent. In 13:14 I use the traditional "Hallelujah" for the Jewish woman (whose name means just that, a Jewish woman).

In Matthew 28 I have translated the divine messenger in neuter terms, since grammatical gender may not be biologically significant—if the category even applies—to a divine messenger.

Preaching Prompts

While these texts may not be preached on Easter, commentary is offered for those who will choose one for the early service on Easter day. Those preparing for nonlectionary sermons may find the lesson/canticle pairings fruitful. For example, Psalm 27 takes on new meaning when heard from the perspective of Hagar and Ishmael.

In the Exodus account, the God who saves Israelite lives takes Egyptian lives. The scriptures celebrate the liberation and often the deaths of the Egyptians, though later texts will acknowledge that the peoples of Egypt and Israel's other adversaries are also God's. The Exodus Canticle is understood by some scholars to have been Miriam's initially, perhaps just the contents of Exodus 15:21. The longer song in Exodus 15:1–18, then, derives from the shorter.

Note that in Joshua 2 the spies do not surveil the land or Jericho. They head straight for a brothel, and "lay down." That expression is used for sex and for sleeping. "Spend the night" unnecessarily shifts the reader away from the plain understanding of why men go to a brothel. Joshua 6:23 calls them "youth," or "boys," which may contribute to their decision. This text provides an opportunity to talk about sexwork and its criminalization and the (often upstanding) men who buy sex. Tying in Jesus's friendships with sex workers may help frame this text in an Easter sermon.

Note that Rahab's father's household in 2:12 is different from her household in 2:1. She seeks the salvation of her entire family, whether they live with her or not, perhaps, no matter what they think about her line of work. In verse 13, "spare" is less than a command and more than a request. She saves all who are in the house with her in verse 17; the ark of safety she offers may well encompass people who are not related to her. Rahab and her family are delivered using the primary verb of the exodus in Joshua 6:17–18.

Selections from Wisdom chapters 5 and 6 pair with the Rahab story, reminding the reader and hearer that God saves and redeems who God wills, including and particularly those who are thought to be sinful and beyond God's reach and care.

Athaliah is the only woman in the Bible to rule Israel or Judah on her own; functionally she was a king, as neither Israel nor Judah had queens, a title not used by royal wives. Separately, the queen-mothers of Judah were the mothers of the ruling king in Judah and did serve in an official capacity.

While some number of the women who followed Jesus were present at his resurrection in Matthew 28:10, there were certainly more who, like all of his male followers, were not.

EASTER DAY—EARLY SERVICE

The early Easter service traditionally uses lessons from the Great Vigil of Easter. Choose a first lesson from the Vigil and use the psalm, Epistle, and Gospel readings from the Vigil.

EASTER DAY—PRINCIPAL SERVICE

Isaiah 49:1–13; Psalm 18:2–11, 16–19; Hebrews 11:1–2, 23–24, 28–39;
Matthew 28:1–10 or John 20:1–10 (11–18)

Isaiah 49:1 Listen you coastlands, to me,
> And pay heed, you peoples from afar!
> The CREATOR OF ALL called me from the womb,
> from my mother's belly God made my name known.

2 God made my mouth like a sharpened sword,
> and in the shadow of God's own hand, hid me;
> God made me like a polished arrow,
> in God's own quiver, hid me.

3 And God said to me, "You are my slave,
> Israel, in you I am glorified."

4 But I, I said, "In vain have I labored,
> I have spent my strength for nothingness and vanity;
> surely my judgment is with the FAITHFUL ONE,
> and my wages with my God."

5 And now says the AUTHOR OF LIFE,
> who formed me in the womb to be God's slave,
> to return Jacob back to God,
> and that Israel might be gathered to God;
> I am honored in the sight of the HOLY ONE OF OLD,
> and my God is my strength.

6 God says,
> "It is too light a thing that you should be my slave
> to raise up the tribes of Jacob [the line of Rebekah],
> and to restore the survivors of Israel [born of Rachel and Leah, and Bilhah and Zilpah].
> I will give you as a light to the nations,
> for it will be that my salvation reaches to the end of the earth."

7 Thus says the FAITHFUL ONE,
> the Redeemer of Israel, God's holy one,
> to one despised, abhorred by the nations,

the slave of rulers,
"Queens and kings shall see and arise,
princes and princesses, and they too shall prostrate themselves,
on account of the FIRE OF SINAI, who is faithful,
the Holy One of Israel, who has chosen you."

8 Thus says the MIGHTY GOD:
In a favorable time I have answered you,
on a day of salvation I have helped you;
I have kept you and given you
as a covenant to the people,
to establish the land,
to apportion the desolate portions;

9 saying to the prisoners, "Go free!"
to those who are in darkness, "Let yourselves be seen."
Along the paths they shall pasture,
and on all the bare heights shall be their pasture.

10 They shall not hunger nor shall they thirst,
neither shall heat nor sun strike them down,
for the one who mother-loves them shall lead them,
and by springs of water shall guide them.

11 And I will turn all my mountains into a pathway,
and my highways shall be raised up.

12 Look! These shall come from far away,
and see! These from the north and from the sea to the west,
and these from the southland of Syene.

13 Sing for joy, you heavens, and exult, O earth;
let mountains break forth into singing!
For the TENDER LOVING ONE has comforted God's people,
and will mother-love God's suffering ones.

Psalm 18:2–11, 16–19

2 The ROCK WHO GAVE US BIRTH is my rock,
and my fortress, and my deliverer,
my God, my rock in whom I take refuge,
my shield, and the horn of my salvation, my stronghold.

3 I call upon the HOLY ONE, may she be praised,
and from my enemies I shall be saved.

4 The snares of death encompassed me;
the rivers of wickedness assailed me.

⁵ The snares of Sheol encircled me;
   the snares of death confronted me.
⁶ In my distress I called upon SHE WHO HEARS;
   to my God I cried for help.
   From her temple she heard my voice,
   and my cry came before her, to her ears.
⁷ Then the earth shuddered and quaked;
   the foundations also of the mountains trembled
   and were shaken because of her anger.
⁸ Smoke went up from her nostrils,
   and consuming fire from her mouth;
   burning coals blazed forth from her.
⁹ She spread out the heavens, and descended;
   thick darkness was under her feet.
¹⁰ She mounted up on a cherub, and flew;
   she soared upon the wings of the wind.
¹¹ She made darkness her veil around her,
   her canopy dark waters and thick clouds.
¹⁶ She reached down from on high, she took me;
   she drew me out of the multitude of water.
¹⁷ She delivered me from my strong enemy,
   and from those who hate me;
   for they were too mighty for me.
¹⁸ They confronted me in the day of my calamity;
   yet the SHELTERING GOD was my support.
¹⁹ She brought me out into a broad place;
   she delivered me, because she delights in me.

Hebrews 11:1 Now faith is the essence of things hoped for, the conviction of that which is not seen. ² By faith, indeed, were our ancestors approved.

²³ By faith Moses was hidden after his birth by his mother and father for three months, because they saw that the child was beautiful; and they were not afraid of the king's commandment. ²⁴ By faith Moses, after he had grown up, refused to be called a son of Pharaoh's daughter.

²⁸ By faith he kept the Passover and the sprinkling of blood, in order that the destroyer of the firstborn would not touch the firstborn daughters and sons of Israel.

²⁹ By faith they passed through the Red Sea as though on dry land, but when the Egyptians chose to try, they were drowned. ³⁰ By faith the walls of Jericho fell when encircled for seven days. ³¹ By faith Rahab the prostitute did not perish with those who did not believe, because she had received the spies in peace.

32 And what more should I say? For time would fail me to tell of Gideon, Barak, Samson, Jephthah, of David and Samuel and the prophets, female and male, 33 who through faith conquered realms, administered justice, obtained promises, stopped the mouths of lions, 34 quenched raging fire, escaped the edge of the sword, were made strong out of weakness, became mighty in war, felled foreign armies. 35 Women through resurrection received their dead. Other women and men were tortured, refusing to receive a release, in order to obtain a better resurrection. 36 Yet other women and men received a trial of mocking and whipping, and even chains and imprisonment. 37 They were stoned, they were sawed in two, they were slaughtered by sword; they went about in animal-skins, in sheepskin and goatskin, impoverished, oppressed, tormented. 38 The world was not worthy of them. They wandered in deserts and mountains, and in caves and holes in the ground.

39 And all these, commended for their faith, did not receive what was promised.

Matthew 28:1–10 is available with commentary in the readings for the Great Vigil of Easter. John 20 is the customary alternative. The reading from the Gospel of John may be read in longer or shorter form.

John 20:1 Now it was the first day of the week, Mary Magdalene came, early on while it was still dark, to the tomb and saw the stone removed from the tomb. 2 So she ran and went to Simon Peter and to the other disciple, the one whom Jesus loved, and said to them, "They have taken the Messiah out of the tomb, and we do not know where they have laid him." 3 Then Peter and the other disciple came and went to the tomb. 4 The two were running together, but the other disciple ran ahead of Peter and reached the tomb first. 5 And bending down to see, saw the linen wrappings lying there, but he did not enter. 6 Then Simon Peter came, following him, and went into the tomb, and he saw the linen wrappings lying there. 7 And the facecloth that had been on Jesus's head, not lying with the linen wrappings but rolled up separately in another place. 8 Then the other disciple, who reached the tomb first, went in and saw and believed. 9 Indeed they did not understand the scripture, that it was necessary for Jesus to rise from the dead. 10 Then the disciples returned once more to their homes. [11 Now Mary stood outside, facing the tomb, weeping. As she wept, she bent down to see in the tomb. 12 Then she saw two angels in white sitting, one at the head and the other at the feet, where the body of Jesus had been lying. 13 They said to her, "Woman, why do you weep?" She said to them, "Because they have taken my Savior, and I do not know where they have laid him." 14 Having said this, she turned around and saw Jesus standing, but she did not know that it was Jesus. 15 Jesus said to her, "Woman, why do you weep? For whom do you look?" Thinking that he was the gardener, she said to him, "Sir, if you have carried him away, tell me where you have laid him, and I will take him away." 16 Jesus said to her, "Mary." She turned and said to him in Aramaic, "Rabbouni!" (which means Teacher). 17 Jesus said to her, "Do not hold me, because I have not yet ascended to the Father. Rather, go to my brothers and say to them, 'I am ascending to my Abba and your Abba, to my God and your

God.'" [18] Mary Magdalene went and announced to the disciples, "I have seen the Savior"; and she told them that he had said these things to her.]

PROCLAMATION

Text Notes

Given there is no concrete present tense in biblical Hebrew, it can be difficult to determine whether an imperfect verb should be translated in present or future tense. In Isaiah 49:3 the question of whether God *is* glorified in Israel or *will be* is open. I have chosen the present to suggest that even in their brokenness, or perhaps because of it, God is glorified for her faithful relationship with an often unfaithful partner. A portion of Isaiah 49 read today overlaps with the one read on Psalm Sunday. See textual and preaching commentary there for further notes.

In Psalm 18:2 I draw the divine name from Deuteronomy 32:18, "You neglected the Rock that gave birth to you, you forgot the God who writhed in birth-labor for you."

The Greek word *hypostasis* means the essence of a thing, as in the relationship between Jesus and God articulated with this same word earlier in Hebrews 1:2–3. In Hebrews 11:1 faith is the essence of that which is hoped for. In 11:2, "to be approved" is the sense of the verb to "be martyred" or "bear witness" when it is the passive voice. The citizens of Jericho in Hebrews 11:31 can be translated as either they who "were disobedient" or "did not believe." Each is problematic in the context of the earlier story. If disobedient, when? To what message? If unbelieving, then to what?

Note that the celestial messengers speak with one voice in John 20:13. In verse 15 Mary addresses Jesus with the honorific given any man of status or used to show respect, "master" or "lord," also used of those who held slaves. It also signifies Jesus's own authority and sovereignty. Her demand that this unknown person tell her where Jesus has been taken is expressed in the imperative, as a command. Exclamation point or period? Does Jesus exclaim her name or call it softly or plainly in verse 16? I imagine the latter.

Hebrew and Aramaic are recognized as distinct languages now. They were not always so understood; the terms are used interchangeably in the scriptures.

Preaching Prompts

The anonymity of the Servant Songs in Isaiah has led to them being easily interpreted through the story of Jesus. As an Easter reading the text reminds of the import of the life Jesus lived, not just the death he died, a life that was shaped and molded by scriptures like Isaiah 49.

The psalmist is delivered from certain death in her time by being saved from her enemies and their traps. Yet that is not the limit of the power of the God who harnesses the clouds as her chariot. Psalm 18 also serves as a response to Psalm 22 in the earlier plaintive liturgies of Holy Week and Good Friday, the pleas for deliverance and trust in God are answered by the fact of deliverance. God is able to deliver. God is faithful to deliver. Even to and through death.

The Epistle to the Hebrews forms a bridge to the gospel. In this Epistle penned to Jewish, and therefore Hebrew, people, the author links that faith to the faith of their people (and collaborators) across time. Yet the list of heroes in Hebrews 11 that recounts that faith reads like a patriarchal revisionist history. For example, Barak replaces Deborah and Jephthah who murdered his own daughter is included in 11:32. (However, since Deborah ruled and delivered in the period mentioned, and other women prophets followed her, and the plural "prophets" includes both genders, I have specified "prophets, female and male.") Ironically, it will be women's faithfulness to Jesus at the cross and tomb that will lead to the first proclamations of his resurrection. As a second lesson, the last line of this reading points forward to a promise realized in that resurrection and its proclamation.

With all of the alleluias, it is hard to remember that Easter morning begins in sorrow. Grieving and dumbfounded, women make their way to the tomb where their friend, teacher, and savior lies. They are not singing alleluia. In John's Gospel their motivation has been erased; they have been reduced to Mary Magdalene and one "we" in verse 2. They do not enter the tomb, counter to other accounts. They fetch men who go first, then Mary follows them. The male disciples leave and once again Jesus is attended only by women, now just Mary. He reveals himself to her and sends her as his messenger, bearing his word.

She announces, *aggellousa*, the good news that Jesus has appeared to her and has a message for the men who were not present. That "announcement" is related to the words for messengers, human or divine ones sometimes called angels, and their message; they share a common root. Interpreters have struggled with what to make of Jesus telling Mary not to touch or hold or hold on to him in John 20:17. Some wince at what they hear as harsh language, as when he asks his mother, "Woman, what concern is that to you and to me?" in John 2:4. I wonder if it is that we do not hear "woman" charitably as a form of address. What may be missed are the parallels to Thomas: Mary sees, hears, speaks with, and touches her savior. Having seen his death, what other than the word of the risen Christ could compel her to let go?

EASTER DAY—EVENING SERVICE

Isaiah 25:6–9; Psalm 118:14–26; 2 Timothy 2:8–13;
Luke 24:13–35 (or 24:13–27)

Isaiah 25:6 The COMMANDER of heaven's legions will make for all peoples on this mountain,
a feast of rich food, a feast of well-aged wines,
of rich food prepared with marrow, of refined well-aged wines.

⁷ And God will destroy on this mountain
the shroud that shrouds all peoples,
the veil that veils all nations.

⁸ God will swallow up death forever.
Then the SOVEREIGN GOD will wipe away tears from every face,
and will sweep aside the shame of God's people from the whole earth,
for GOD WHOSE NAME IS HOLY has spoken.

⁹ It will be said on that day,
Look! This is our God; in whom we hope, and who saved us.
This is the CREATOR OF ALL in whom we hope;
let us be glad and rejoice in God's salvation.

Psalm 118:14–26

¹⁴ The MIGHTY GOD is my strength and my might
and has become my salvation.

¹⁵ The sound of song and of salvation is in the tents of the righteous:
"The right hand of the MOST HIGH is mighty;

¹⁶ the right hand of the MIGHTY GOD is exalted;
the right hand of the MOST HIGH is mighty."

¹⁷ I shall not die, but I shall live,
and recount the deeds of the ANCIENT OF DAYS.

¹⁸ The MERCIFUL GOD has punished me severely,
but to death did not hand me over.

¹⁹ Open to me the gates of righteousness,
that I may enter through them
and give thanks to the FOUNT OF JUSTICE.

²⁰ This is the gate of the LIVING GOD;
the righteous shall enter through it.

²¹ I thank you for you have answered me
and have become my salvation.

²² The stone the builders rejected
has become the chief cornerstone.

23 This is the MIGHTY GOD's doing;
  it is marvelous in our eyes.
24 This is the day that the CREATOR OF ALL has made;
  let us rejoice and be glad in it.
25 Save us, we pray, SAVING ONE!
  GENEROUS ONE, we pray, grant us prosperity!
26 Blessed is the one who comes in the name of GOD WHO IS HOLY.
  We bless you from the house of the EVER-LIVING GOD.

2 Timothy 2:8 Remember Jesus Christ, raised from the dead, from the line of David [and Bathsheba]; that is my gospel, 9 for which I suffer hardship, even to chains, like a criminal. But the word of God is not chained. 10 Because of this, therefore I endure everything for the sake of the elect, in order that they may also obtain salvation in Christ Jesus with eternal glory. 11 This is a trustworthy saying:

  For if we die together, we will also live together;
12 if we endure, we will also reign together;
  if we deny [Christ], he will also deny us;
13 if we are faithless, faithful he remains,
  for he cannot deny himself.

Luke 24:13 Now see, two of them on that very day [the first day of the week] were going to a village that was seven miles from Jerusalem; its name was Emmaus. 14 And they talked with each other about all the things that had happened. 15 And it happened while they were talking and questioning that Jesus himself came near and accompanied them. 16 Yet their eyes were kept from recognizing him. 17 And Jesus said to them, "What is this conversation you are having with each other while you journey?" They stood in place, sorrowful. 18 Then one of them, whose name was Cleopas, replied to him saying, "Are you the only foreigner in Jerusalem who does not know the things that have happened there these days?" 19 Jesus asked them, "What kind of things?" They replied, "About Jesus the Nazarene, who was a man, a prophet mighty in deed and word before God and all the people. 20 Also how our chief priests and leaders surrendered him to be sentenced to death and crucified him. 21 But we had hoped that he was the one to soon redeem Israel. Now besides all this, instead, it is now the third day since these things have taken place. 22 Then again, certain women of our community astounded us. They were at the tomb this morning. 23 And when they did not find the body, they came back and told us they had seen a vision of angels who said Jesus was alive. 24 Then some of those who were with us went to the tomb and found it just as the women had said, but they did not see him." 25 Then Jesus said to them, "Oh, foolish souls, and how slow of heart to believe all that the prophets have spoken! 26 Was it not necessary that the Messiah should suffer these things to enter into his glory?" 27 And starting from Moses and from all the prophets, Jesus interpreted to them the things about himself in all the scriptures.

^{28} When they came near the village to which they were going, Jesus walked ahead as if he were going on. ^{29} So they urged him strongly, saying, "Stay with us, because it is almost evening and the day is nearly over." Then he went in to stay with them. ^{30} When Jesus was at the table with them, he took bread, blessed and broke it, and gave it to them. ^{31} And their eyes were opened, and they recognized him. And he vanished from before them. ^{32} They said to each other, "Were not our hearts burning within us while he was talking to us on the way, while he was opening up the scriptures to us?" ^{33} Now that same hour they rose up and returned to Jerusalem, and found the eleven and others with them gathered together. ^{34} They were saying, "Really! The Savior has risen, and has appeared to Simon!" ^{35} Then they told what had happened on the way, and how Jesus had been made known to them in the breaking of the bread.

PROCLAMATION

Text Notes

There are regular differences in how biblical passages are broken into verses between translations. In Isaiah 25, the last line of what is verse 7 in some Christian bibles like NRSV begins verse 8 in Hebrew and in Jewish bibles and other Christian bibles, like CEB. I follow the Hebrew and JPS here. In verse 9 the tense of God's salvation can be understood as past or present. God's record of faithfulness makes her trustworthy; pushing these texts into a future time diminishes that past faithfulness.

Psalm 118 is a literary work of art in Hebrew with a lattice of repeating elements that circle from the last line to the beginning in verse 25, which yields "hosanna," an alternate pronunciation for *hoshia-na* in the psalm.

Many translations of 2 Timothy 2:11–13 add "with him" throughout for poetic balance; the object and preposition are not present. Verse 12 requires an object for the verb; I have supplied "Christ" from verse 10.

In Luke 24:25 Jesus says, "Oh foolish X..." There is no noun present; the adjective includes object information, masculine or inclusive plural. Common translations are "foolish men," "ones," or "people."

Preaching Prompts

On this Principal Feast of the Resurrection, the Church proclaims that death is not the end. This notion appears intermittently in the Hebrew Bible: Elisha raises a widow's son from death in 2 Kings 4 and Daniel 12:1–2 proclaims an unambiguous resurrection. Frequently cited Job 19:26 is ambiguous and in the well-known Ezekiel 37 the dry bones represent the resurrection of the nation of Israel, see verse 11. Against this background, Isaiah 25 proclaims that the day is coming when God will destroy death forever, swallowing it up. Belief in resurrection will become normative for most traditions of Judaism, including that of Jesus, for Christians, and for Muslims.

Psalm 118 is a festival hymn in the form of a temple liturgy. It is part of the Great *Hallel* (Praise) recited on the major festivals: Passover, Pentecost (*Shavuoth*), and Booths (*Sukkot*). Many understand the Hallel to be the "hymn" that Jesus and the disciples sang after the Last Supper, particularly when it is formed as a Passover meal (though likely not a seder). In these readings Psalm 118 echoes the theme of salvation in Isaiah 25. In verse 17 the line "I shall not die but live" likely refers to deliverance from death rather than resurrection. Together these collected readings present a God who delivers on both sides of death. While the psalm emphasizes deliverance from death, 2 Timothy offers an ancient hymn for the believer confident in resurrection after death.

It's hard to know what to make of Jesus calling the disciples foolish in verse 25. It sounds like a rebuke but may have been said in humor with a twinkle, the way a text, tweet, or email may sound harsher than intended.

The road to Emmaus stories are Easter evening stories. The travelling disciples have had all day to grapple with incomprehensible claims of resurrection from sister disciples. Notably, they don't doubt the women, rather they find the whole saga—trial crucifixion, and resurrection claims—simply astounding. This is an important reminder that the terrible images of the crucifixion and the trauma it generated don't simply vanish with proclamation of the Good News. The disciples are traumatized and are riding an emotional rollercoaster.

Jesus, the Bread of Life, confected in the womb of the Blessed Virgin, makes himself known in the breaking of bread. Jesus who is bread offers bread, and Jesus who is the Word interprets the word. When Jesus interprets the scriptures—in Luke 24:27, Torah and Prophets, and in Luke 24:44, Torah, Prophets, and Psalms—the text does not say he shows where the scriptures "predict" him. Reducing the relationship of Jesus with the Hebrew Bible to prediction and fulfillment presents a skewed view of prophecy, scripture more broadly, and Jesus. Rather, I understand him to teach the scriptures that are foundational to him, his identity, his teaching and ministry, after which he patterned himself, which scriptures Christians subsequently read through Jesus.

One of the travelers is male; the other is not described. Grammatically, they could have been a woman and man or two men. There were women, children, and men in the village where they stopped absent from the text as are their hosts. The only women's voices are the echoing proclamations that Christ is risen from the dead.

MONDAY IN EASTER WEEK

1 Peter 1:3–9; Psalm 16:8–11; John 20:19–23

Note: Easter Week services do not traditionally include a Hebrew Bible Reading. In the traditional pattern the first lesson is a New Testament lesson followed by the psalm and Gospel.

1 Peter 1:3 Blessed be the God and Father of our Redeemer Jesus Christ who in great mercy has engendered a new birth for us into a living hope, through the resurrection of Jesus Christ from the dead, ⁴ into an inheritance that is incorruptible, undefiled, and unfading, kept in the heavens for you all, ⁵ who in the power of God are kept through faith for a salvation ready to be revealed in the end time. ⁶ In this you rejoice even when necessary for you to suffer various trials, ⁷ in order that the examination of your faith, more precious than gold, which though perishable is tested by fire, may be found yielding praise and glory and honor when Jesus Christ is revealed. ⁸ You have not seen him, yet you love him. You do not see him now, yet you believe in him and rejoice with a joy glorious and beyond words. ⁹ You are receiving the completion of your faith, the salvation of your souls.

Psalm 16:8–11

⁸ I keep the FAITHFUL ONE before me always;
   because she is at my right hand, I shall not be moved.
⁹ Therefore my heart rejoices, and my inner being delights;
   even my body resides in safety.
¹⁰ For you will not abandon my soul to Sheol,
   or let your faithful one see the Pit.
¹¹ You show me the way of life.
   There is fullness of joy in your presence;
   delights fill your right hand forevermore.

John 20:19 When it was evening on that day, the first of the week, and the doors of the house where the disciples were closed for fear of the Judeans, Jesus came and stood in their midst and said to them, "Peace be with you all." ²⁰ And having said this, Jesus showed them his hands and his side, and then the disciples rejoiced when they saw the Messiah. ²¹ Jesus said to them again, "Peace be with you all, just as the God of Peace has sent me, so I send you all." ²² When Jesus had said this, he breathed on them and said to them, "Receive the Holy Spirit; ²³ if you forgive the sins of any, they are forgiven them; if you retain the sins of any, they are retained."

PROCLAMATION

Text Notes

The reading from 1 Peter has rather long, unwieldly sentences that make for challenging reading, particularly aloud.

Sheol, the abode of the dead in the Israelite world view, was variously described as a place of great gloom, deep below the surface of the (flat) earth. It is an equitable destination, for great and small, righteous and wicked. Presumed to be inescapable except by the rarest of miracles, deliverance from Sheol refers to escape from death and its clutches *before* death. The "Pit" is an occasional synonym for Sheol and the grave.

The disciples in the house are as Jewish as their fellow residents of Judea, as Jewish as Jesus. It would be centuries before there was clear separation between Jews and Christians. Scriptural language pitting Jesus, his disciples, and the early Christians against "the Jews" is one of the more challenging aspects of our faith.

Preaching Prompts

These Easter Week first lesson readings explore some of the Church's earliest reflections on resurrection. All of the psalms focus on God's deliverance from death, and its abode in the Israelite world view, Sheol. The Gospel readings center the stories from immediately after the resurrection.

The Epistle addresses believers who, like us, have not seen Jesus yet believe. The active voice in the Epistle emphasizes that the readers and hearers, and we, are being kept by God and that they and we are receiving the salvation of our souls. Rather than a fixed point at which we "were" saved, we live into our salvation in faith.

The second person addresses of the Epistle and psalm, the first to the reader, the second to God, do not include gendered language. There are, of course, women among the believers to whom the Epistle is written, and women who would have prayed, and perhaps composed, the psalmist's prayer. We are left to imagine them.

The women are necessarily absent from the Gospel, having proclaimed the good news of Jesus's resurrection to male disciples who still don't quite get it, let alone its implications for a fearless life. They, Mary Magdalene and other women suggested by the "we" in John 20:2, are arguably still telling the news. What to make of the gift of the Holy Spirit breathed onto those disciples hiding in the house? It matters that the power and authority to forgive and retain sins is connected to the receipt of the Holy Spirit, grammatically and theologically. The text appears to be organizing, if not setting up a hierarchy in the community. This early statement of the nascent community's priorities shows them continuing Jesus's radical work, declaring the forgiveness of sins.

TUESDAY IN EASTER WEEK

1 Corinthians 15:3–7; Psalm 18:1–6; Luke 24:36–43

1 Corinthians 15:3 For I handed on to you all as primary what I in turn had received, that Christ died for our sins in accordance with the scriptures. ⁴ And that he was buried, and that he was raised on the third day in accordance with the scriptures. ⁵ And that he was seen by Cephas, then the twelve. ⁶ Then he was seen by more than five hundred sisters and brothers together, many of whom remain, though some have died. ⁷ Then he was seen by James, then all the apostles.

Psalm 18

¹ I love you, MIGHTY ONE, my strength.
² The ROCK WHO GAVE US BIRTH is my rock,
   and my fortress, and my deliverer,
   my God, my rock in whom I take refuge,
   my shield, and the horn of my salvation, my stronghold.
³ I call upon the HOLY ONE, may she be praised,
   and from my enemies I shall be saved.
⁴ The snares of death encompassed me;
   the rivers of wickedness assailed me.
⁵ The snares of Sheol encircled me;
   the snares of death confronted me.
⁶ In my distress I called upon SHE WHO HEARS;
   to my God I cried for help.
   From her temple she heard my voice,
   and my cry came before her, to her ears.

Luke 24:36 While they [two of Jesus's disciples] were talking about this [his resurrection], he himself stood between them and said to them, "Peace be with you." ³⁷ Now they were frightened and became terrified, and thought they were seeing a spirit. ³⁸ Jesus said to them, "Why are you troubled, because of thoughts rising in your hearts? ³⁹ Look at my hands and my feet; that it is I. Touch me and see; for a spirit does not have flesh and bones as you see I have." ⁴⁰ And saying this, Jesus showed them his hands and his feet. ⁴¹ Yet still disbelieving and in their joy and wondering, he said to them, "Have you any food here?" ⁴² They gave him a piece of broiled fish, ⁴³ and he took it in their presence and ate.

PROCLAMATION

Text Notes

One of the ways in which the translation of the scriptures is often anti-Judaistic is the intentional changing of Jewish names in the New Testament to Gentile forms.

"James" in 1 Corinthian 15:7 is a case in point. His name is Jacob, *Iakob* in Greek; yet translators use "Jacob" for the Hebrew Bible patriarch occurring in the New Testament while treating the Hebrew names of people in the Jesus story differently. Changing *Mariam*, Miriam, to Mary is another example of what is a standard practice. These changes obscure and in some cases erase the primary Jewish identity of the family and followers of Jesus.

The occasion of Psalm 18 is David's escape from Saul; that introduction takes up the first verse in Hebrew. The psalm proper begins with "He said," often included with the introductory verse. David's "love" in what is now verse 1, as Christian translations number the psalms, is *racham*, mother-love, love that is rooted in the womb, *rechem*, and otherwise used only by God to express her love. From David we should perhaps read it as gesturing toward a reciprocal love that originates deep within.

Verse 3 of the psalm has the passive "be praised" without supporting grammar. Other translators have added "*worthy to* be praised." Some translations render verse 3 in the future, see NRSV and KJV; however the introduction makes clear David is reflecting on his past deliverance. The imperfect here is more present, i.e., because of God's faithfulness, whenever I call on God as before, I shall be saved.

The Gospel uses the same word for spirit (as in the Holy Spirit) for spirit of the dead, or what we might hear as "ghost" in Luke 24:37 and in verse 39.

Preaching Prompts

Given that the Epistles predate the Gospels, the brief telling of the good news of Jesus's resurrection triumph over the grave is one of the first recorded articulations of the gospel. It lacks all of the narrative detail and the women evangelists collectively or by name. Not only is Mary Magdalene missing, but there is no mention of Mary the mother of Jesus or the beloved disciple. It lacks the angels and reports only Peter (called Cephas) and the twelve as initial witnesses. The text does go on to position Paul as in the chain of apostles.

The mention of James receiving his own postresurrection appearance is significant. Long understood to be the brother of Jesus, the appearance has been interpreted as confirming James as leader of the emerging church. While the Epistle is invested in hierarchy (hence the lack of women) and continuity, Jesus also takes time to appear to family in the person of his beloved brother. The appearances to the more than five hundred in the plural form that can be inclusive, mixed—with only one male required, or all male—suggest Jesus going to his beloveds to comfort and assure them after his death.

Jesus's evening journey with the pair, or perhaps couple, of disciples on the road to Emmaus reads like an expansion of the note in 1 Corinthians 15 about Jesus's appearances to so many. Even with the scolding of beloved teacher and friend, the account reads as comforting and affectionate. As with the five hundred, only one of these disciples must be male grammatically; I chose to read the other as female, likely a spouse.

WEDNESDAY IN EASTER WEEK

1 Corinthians 15:12–20; Psalm 30:1–5; Luke 24:44–53

1 Corinthians 15:12 Now if Christ is preached as raised from the dead, how can some of you say there is no resurrection of the dead? [13] For if there is no resurrection of the dead, then Christ has not been raised; [14] and if Christ has not been raised, then our preaching has been in vain along with your faith. [15] Then we are even found to be false witnesses of God, because we bore witness of God that God raised Christ—whom God did not raise if the dead are not raised. [16] For if the dead are not raised, then Christ has not been raised. [17] And if Christ has not been raised, your faith is useless and you are yet in your sins. [18] And therefore those who have died in Christ have been destroyed. [19] If for this life we have only hoped in Christ, we are of all people most pitiable. [20] But now indeed Christ has been raised from the dead, the first fruits of those who have died.

Psalm 30

1   I will exalt you, ARK OF SAFETY, because you have pulled me up
      and have not let my enemies rejoice over me.
2   HEALING ONE, my God, I cried to you for help,
      and you healed me.
3   EVER-LIVING GOD, you brought my soul up from Sheol;
      you preserved my life from descent to the Pit.
4   Sing praises to the FAITHFUL GOD, you her faithful;
      give thanks remembering her holiness.
5   For her fury is a moment, her favor a lifetime.
      Weeping may pass the night, yet in the morning, joy.

Luke 24:44 Jesus said to [the two disciples], "These are my words that I spoke to you while I was still with you all, because everything must be fulfilled in the teaching of Moses, the prophets, and the psalms written about me." [45] Then he opened their minds to understand the scriptures. [46] Then he said to them, "So it is written, the Messiah is to suffer and to rise from the dead the third day, [47] and repentance and forgiveness of sins is to be preached in his name to all nations, beginning from Jerusalem. [48] You are witnesses of these things. [49] Now look! I am sending you the promise of my Abba. You all stay in the city until you have been clothed with power from on high."

^{50} Then Jesus led them out as far as Bethany, and lifting his hands, he blessed them. ^{51} While he was blessing them, Jesus retreated from them and was carried up into heaven. ^{52} And they worshiped him, and returned to Jerusalem with great joy; ^{53} and they were in the temple every day blessing God.

PROCLAMATION

Text Notes

Both of the readings from 1 Corinthians 15 and Luke 24 continue from the previous day, even though not contiguous.

Preaching Prompts

People have grappled with the Jesus story from the very beginning. Even in a world in which miracles were accepted uncritically, some of the claims about Jesus were astounding—a word that occurs often in the Gospels. As now, there were those for whom a literal resurrection was difficult to believe. Paul's rebuttal draws a straight line from the resurrection to the forgiveness of our sins and our salvation.

The wonder and incredulity of the disciples on the Emmaus road contrasts with doctrinal disputers in Corinth. The disciples are overjoyed and accept the miracle, though they do not seem to understand it. Jesus calls them back to the Jewish scriptures, somewhat fewer than would eventually be canonized: Torah, Prophets, and only psalms from the third traditional division, Writings. (In the Hebrew Bible the Prophets include Joshua, Judges, Samuel, Kings, Isaiah, Jeremiah, Ezekiel, and the Minor Prophets. The Writings include everything else not in the Torah; Daniel is not a prophet in Jewish tradition.) In other passages, the scriptures consist of the Torah (Law) and Prophets suggesting the Writings were still in formation (see Matthew 22:40; Luke 16:16; Acts 13:15, Romans 3:21).

Physical salvation is the theme of the psalm as it is all of Easter Week. Deliverance, salvation, and resurrection are available to all without regard for gender or its performance. However, the scriptures and their writers will try to make these stories make sense in the world they knew, with all of its hierarchies in place for the most part.

THURSDAY IN EASTER WEEK

1 Corinthians 15:35–44; Psalm 49:5–15; John 21:4–14

1 Corinthians 15:35 Now then, someone will ask, "How are the dead raised? In what kind of body do they come?" ^{36} Fool! What you plant is not brought to life unless it dies. ^{37} Now about what you plant, you do not plant the body that will be, but a bare seed, for example, wheat or of some other grain. [38] Yet God gives it a body as God wills, and to each kind of seed its own body. [39] Not all flesh is the same flesh, rather there is one flesh for human beings, another for animals, another for birds, and another for fish. [40] Yet there are heavenly bodies and earthly bodies, while the glory of the heavenly is one kind, and that of the earthly is another. [41] There is one glory of the sun and another glory of the moon, yet another glory of the stars; each star even differs in glory.

[42] So it is with the resurrection of the dead. What is planted is perishable; what is raised is imperishable. [43] It is planted in dishonor; it is raised in glory. It is sown in weakness; it is raised in power. [44] It is planted a physical body; it is raised a spiritual body. If there is a physical body, there is also a spiritual body.

Psalm 49:5–15

5 Why should I fear in evil days,
   when iniquity at my heels surrounds me?
6 Those who trust in their wealth
   and praise of the abundance of their riches?
7 Certainly, it cannot redeem a person,
   or can one give [it] to God as their ransom.
8 For the redemption-price of a soul is costly,
   they come to an end, forever.
9 Shall one should live eternally
   and never see the Pit?
10 For when one sees the wise, they die;
   the foolish and ignorant perish together
   and leave to others their wealth.
11 Their graves are their homes for all time,
   their dwelling places from generation to generation,
   though they put their name on lands.
12 Humanity will not recline in grandeur;
   rather they are like the animals that perish.
13 This is the way of the foolish,
   those pleased with their own words. *Selah*
14 Like sheep they are set for Sheol;
   Death shall be their shepherd.
   The upright shall rule over them until the morning,
   and their form shall waste away;
   Sheol shall be their abode.
15 But God will ransom my soul,
   for from the grasp of Sheol she will take me. *Selah*

John 21:4 Now when morning came, Jesus stood on the beach; but the disciples did not know that it was Jesus. ⁵ Jesus said to them, "Children, do you have any fish prepared?" They answered him, "No." ⁶ Then he said to them, "Cast the net to the right side of the boat, and you will find some." So, they cast it, and they were not able to drag it in because of the abundance of fish. ⁷ That disciple whom Jesus loved said to Peter, "It is the Messiah!" When Simon Peter heard that it was the Messiah, he put on some clothes, for he was naked, and threw himself into the sea. ⁸ But the other disciples came in the boat, dragging the net full of fish, for they were not far from the land, only two hundred cubits [about a hundred yards] off.

⁹ As soon as they turned back to land, they saw a fire there, with fish laid over it, and bread. ¹⁰ Jesus said to them, "Bring some of the fish that you have just caught." ¹¹ So Simon Peter went up and dragged the net to land, full of large fish—one hundred fifty-three—and with so many the net was not torn. ¹² Jesus said to them, "Come and eat." Now none of the disciples dared to ask him, "Who are you?" because they knew it was the Messiah. ¹³ Jesus came and took the bread and gave it to them, and did the same with the fish. ¹⁴ Now this was the third time that Jesus appeared to the disciples after he was raised from the dead.

PROCLAMATION

Text Notes

There are a couple of phrases in the psalm—in verses 7 and 13—that are difficult to translate. I have drawn from the translations of the Jewish Publication Society and Robert Alter (*The Hebrew Bible: A Translation with Commentary*).

Preaching Prompts

Resurrection is the foundation of the Gospel Easter story and even when proclaimed as a certainty, holds a full share of mystery. It seems unreasonable to expect folk to have no questions or to mock them, or call them names (i.e., "fool" in 1 Corinthians 15:36), for asking. The Gospel story, resurrection included, is strong enough to bear the weight of our questions, and God, unlike the apostle, is eternally patient with them.

The psalmist trusts in God for her deliverance, recognizing that wealth is of no avail and there is no price that can be placed on a human life.

John 21 offers a potential narrative response to the questioners mocked in the Epistle. What kind of body do the resurrected have? In this story, the body is one that is solid and tangible, capable of mundane tasks like cooking; one that is recognizable to those who had known the formerly dead. While not putting an end to questions about the resurrection, John 21 demonstrates that the resurrected Jesus has the same demeanor and shows the same care for his disciples that he did in his previous life.

While some forms of fishing were likely performed by women or men, the drag-net fishing indicated by the text, along with Peter's casual nudity, suggest only male disciples were present. This is in keeping with the theme that the male disciples needed to be convinced.

FRIDAY IN EASTER WEEK

Romans 6:5–11; Psalm 86:8–13; Mark 16:9–15, 19–20

Romans 6:5 For if we have been united in a death like Christ's, we will certainly be so in the resurrection. [6] This we know, that our old self was crucified with him so that the body of sin might be destroyed, and we might no longer be enslaved to sin. [7] The woman or man who has died is freed from sin. [8] But if we have died with Christ, we believe that we shall also live with him. [9] We know that Christ, being raised from the dead, will never die; death no longer has dominion over him. [10] For dying, he died once to sin, in living, he lives to God. [11] So also should you consider yourselves dead to sin and alive to God in Christ Jesus.

Psalm 86:8–13

[8] There is none like you among the gods, MOST HIGH,
and there are no works like yours.
[9] All the nations that you made shall come,
and they shall bow down before you Sovereign One,
and they shall glorify your name.
[10] For you are great and work wonders;
you are God, you alone.
[11] Teach me, HOLY ONE, your way,
that I may walk in your truth;
let my heart be undivided to revere your name.
[12] I give thanks to you, Sovereign One my God, with my whole heart,
and I shall glorify your name forever.
[13] For great is your faithful love toward me;
you have delivered my soul from the depths of Sheol.

Mark 16:9 Now after he rose early on the first day of the week, Jesus appeared first to Mary Magdalene from whom he had cast out seven demons. [10] She went out and she told the ones mourning and weeping who had been with him. [11] But when they heard that he lives and was seen by her, they did not believe. [12] After this Jesus was made known in another form to two of [the disciples] as they were walking into the countryside. [13] And they went back and told the rest, but they did not believe them. [14] Now later on, while they were sitting at the table, Jesus appeared to the eleven themselves and he rebuked their lack of faith and stubbornness, because they did not believe those [the women] who saw Jesus after he had risen. [15] Then Jesus said to them, "Go into all the world and proclaim the good news to all creation.

[19] And then Jesus the Messiah, after he had spoken to them, was taken up into heaven and sat down at the right hand of God. [20] And they went out proclaiming the good news everywhere. The Messiah worked with them and confirmed the message by the signs that followed.

PROCLAMATION

Text Notes

Mark's Gospel has a variety of endings that shock many Bible readers who think the scriptures were unchanged from inception. They are missing from the oldest most reliable manuscripts, Sinaticus and Vaticanus, and from more than a hundred Syriac, Coptic, and Armenian manuscripts; in many of the manuscripts in which they are found, they are set off with notations equivalent to an asterisk denoting lack of originality. There is near universal acceptance that verses 1–8 are original. Some scholars further subdivide the remaining verses. The Church (across denominations) treats them as authoritative to varying degrees and they do appear in an abridged form in the lectionary of the Episcopal Church.

In Mark 16:12 the description of Jesus appearing in "another form" to two disciples "walking in the countryside" closely resembles the Emmaus Road story in Luke 24. In verse 14 Jesus "reprimands" or "rebukes" the (presumably male) disciples for not believing "those" who proclaimed his resurrection. I have specified "the women" here; they were "those" who were not believed: Mary Magdalene, another Mary, and Salome in Mark 16:1.

Preaching Prompts

Whether in spite of or because of being part of the addendum to Mark, 16:14 includes a strong rebuke by Jesus for those who did not believe the gospel of his resurrection from the dead preached by women, perhaps because it was preached by women. It still speaks to those who discount the words and ministries of women. The disciples are sent to preach to all creation and Jesus won't let them be treated like the women: he will work with them, verse 20, providing signs to confirm the message. For the women and the few male disciples, his appearances were the sign. And for some, women and men, surely the women's witness was sufficient. It would have been enough for children. The signs and ascension in verse 19 point to a new reality: Jesus will not continue to appear as he had. And at some point the signs will come to an end as well. All that will remain will be the proclamation of the gospel by women and men and the faith of those who choose to believe.

SATURDAY IN EASTER WEEK

Acts 13:29–38; Psalm 116:1–9; Matthew 28:8–10, 16–20

Acts 13:29 Now when they had finished doing everything written about him, they took him down from the tree and laid him in a tomb. ³⁰ But God raised him from the dead. ³¹ He appeared for many days to those [women and men] who traveled with him from Galilee to Jerusalem, and they are now his witnesses to the people. ³² And we proclaim the good news to you that what God promised to our mothers and fathers ³³ God has fulfilled for us, their children, by raising Jesus; as also it is written in the second psalm,

"You are my Son; today I have begotten you."

³⁴ Because God raised him from the dead, never to return to corruption, God spoke thusly,

"I will give you the holy promises of David."

³⁵ Therefore David has also said in another psalm,

"You will not let your Holy One experience corruption."

³⁶ For indeed David, after he had served the purpose of God in his own generation, died, and was placed beside his mothers and fathers, and experienced corruption; ³⁷ yet the one whom God raised up saw no corruption. ³⁸ Let it be known to you, therefore, my sisters and brothers, that through this man forgiveness of sins is proclaimed to you.

Psalm 116:1–9

¹ I love the GOD WHO HEARS,
   for God has heard my voice and my supplications.
² For she opens her ear to me,
   whatever day I call.
³ The snares of death encompassed me;
   the torments of Sheol took hold of me,
   I found distress and sorrow.
⁴ Then I called on the name of the HOLY ONE OF OLD:
   "HOLY ONE, please, save my life!"
⁵ Gracious is the FOUNT OF JUSTICE, and righteous;
   our God loves [like a mother].
⁶ The FAITHFUL ONE protects the simple;
   I was brought low and she saved me.
⁷ Return, O my soul, to your rest,
   for the GRACIOUS ONE has dealt generously with you.
⁸ For you have delivered my soul from death,
   my eyes from tears,
   my feet from stumbling.

⁹ I shall walk before the AUTHOR OF LIFE
　　in the lands of the living.

Matthew 28:8 So the women left the tomb quickly with fear and great joy and ran to tell his disciples the news. ⁹ Then all of a sudden Jesus met them and said, "Shalom!" And they came to him, took hold of his feet, and bowed down worshipping him. ¹⁰ Then Jesus said to them, "Fear not; go and tell my sisters and brothers to go to Galilee; there they will see me."

¹⁶ Now the eleven disciples went to Galilee, to the mountain to which Jesus sent them. ¹⁷ And when they saw him, they bowed down worshipping him; but some doubted. ¹⁸ Then Jesus came and said to them, "All authority in heaven and on earth has been given to me. ¹⁹ Go therefore and make disciples of all nations, baptizing them in the name of the Father and of the Son and of the Holy Spirit, ²⁰ and teaching them to obey everything that I have commanded you. Now look, I am with you always, to the end of the age."

PROCLAMATION

Text Notes

In Acts 13:33–35, Paul cites Psalm 2:7 (note the psalms are known to be numbered while chapter and verse numbers would not be added for centuries), Isaiah 55:3, and Psalm 16:10 from the LXX. Paul is in synagogue addressing "Men of Israel, and others who fear God." Women were not excluded from synagogue and would have also been present. "God-fearers" was often language for Gentile worshippers. Paul's language, "men" and "brothers," excludes women and renders them invisible in this passage. Are women to understand themselves included, or is Paul specifically addressing men exclusively, figuring they'll pass the good news on to the women in their lives? I read his language as customarily androcentric and patriarchal as the bulk of scripture and make women visible as appropriate.

In Matthew 28:8, the word translated as "authority" also means "power." In verse 10 Jesus tells the women to tell his "siblings" to go to meet him in Galilee. That certainly includes the eleven male disciples but not necessarily limited to them. At some point the eleven receive other more specific instructions to go to a particular mountain indicated by verse 16.

Preaching Prompts

In Acts 13, Paul tells the gospel story adding his own proof-texting exegesis of the Hebrew Scriptures to "prove" that Jesus, who was nothing like the warrior messiah many expected and some scriptures predicted, was nevertheless the fulfillment of the scriptures. Paul is demonstrating the flexibility of the scriptures for reinterpretation in every age; rereading them in light of Jesus yields tantalizing and suggestive readings, which now with full knowledge of the Jesus story seem specifically predictive.

These are particularly Christian ways of reading the Hebrew Bible. It is important to remember that Jewish readings, even of passages considered messianic, do not always focus on a single individual. Sometimes the entire nation is the messianic figure, sometimes an individual or specific ruler, sometimes an unknown individual.

In Psalm 116:5 God's love is articulated with the word whose root is "womb," often unhelpfully translated as "merciful" or "compassion."

The Gospel reading combines the resurrection appearances to the women, Mary Magdalene and the "other" Mary, and to the eleven remaining disciples. The women believe immediately and run with joy to tell the news. They are also afraid, perhaps of what this might mean, potentially more violence. The male disciples also bowed down before Jesus, but they do not yet believe. The story of the Church will soon become their story as they proclaim the resurrection they first doubted. It might be worthwhile to imagine the evangelism of the women, how the women and men they proclaimed the Good News to also became part of the new and expanding Church.

SECOND SUNDAY OF EASTER

Acts 1:3–5, 12–14 (or Deuteronomy 5:1–10); Psalm 41:1–4, 12–13; Romans 7:1–12; John 20:19–31

The Sundays of Easter traditionally have a choice of readings from the Hebrew Bible and Acts for the first lesson. This lectionary does so for Year W and offers passages from the Deuterocanonical/Apocryphal as alternate to selections from Acts in Years A, B, and C.

Acts 1:3 Jesus presented himself to the disciples, living, after his suffering through many convincing proofs, by appearing to them forty days and speaking about the reign of God. [4] And staying with them, Jesus commanded them not to leave Jerusalem, rather to wait there for the promise of the Faithful One, "what you heard from me. [5] For John baptized with water, but you will be baptized with the Holy Spirit not many days from this one."

[12] Then they returned to Jerusalem from the mount called Olivet, which is near Jerusalem, a sabbath day's journey away. [13] And when they entered the city, they went upstairs to the room where they were staying, Peter, and John, and James, and Andrew, Philip and Thomas, Bartholomew and Matthew, James son of Alphaeus, and Simon the Zealot, and Judas son of James. [14] All these were persevering in prayer together with women, including Mary the mother of Jesus, as well as his [sisters and] brothers.

Deuteronomy 5:1 Now Moses called to all Israel, and said to them:

Hear, O Israel, the statutes and case laws that I am speaking in your ears this day: You all shall learn them and observe them faithfully. [2] The AGELESS ONE our God engraved a covenant with us at Horeb. [3] Not with our mothers and fathers did the EVER-LIVING GOD engrave this covenant, but with us, we who are here today, all of us alive. [4] Face to face did the

Holy One of Old speak with you all at the mountain from the midst of the fire. [5] I was standing between the God Whose Name is Holy and you all at that time to declare to you the words of the Holy God, for you all were afraid because of the fire and did not ascend the mountain. And God said:

[6] I am the Eternal One your God, who brought you out of the land of Egypt, out of the house of slavery. [7] You shall have no other gods before me.

[8] You shall not make for yourself a sculpted image in the form of anything that is in the heavens above, or that is on the earth beneath, or that is in the water below the earth. [9] You shall not bow down to them or worship them; for I the Creator of All, your God, am a jealous God, punishing children for the iniquity of parents, to the third and fourth generation of those who hate me, [10] but showing faithful love to the thousandth generation of those who love me and keep my commandments.

Psalm 41:1–4, 12–13

[1] Happy is the woman who has understanding of the poor;
   the Faithful One delivers her in a day bringing evil.
[2] The Sheltering God protects her and keeps her alive;
   she is called happy in the land.
   You will not hand her over to the desire of her enemies.
[3] The Compassionate God sustains her on her sickbed;
   her every bedridden infirmity, you shall heal.
[4] Now I, I said, "Merciful God, be gracious to me;
   heal my soul, for I have sinned against you."
[12] Yet even me, because of my integrity, you have upheld me,
   and set me in your presence forever.
[13] Blessed be the Fire of Sinai, the God of Israel,
   from everlasting to everlasting.
   Amen and Amen.

Romans 7:1 Look, do you not know sisters and brothers—it is to those who know the law that I speak—that the law is binding on a woman or man only while that person lives? [2] Therefore a married woman, while the husband lives, is bound by law; but if the husband dies, she is released from the law concerning the husband. [3] So then, if the husband is alive, she would be called an adulteress if she became another man's. But if the husband dies, she is free from that law, and she is not an adulteress if she becomes another man's.

[4] Just so, my friends, you have died to the law through the body of Christ, so that you all may belong to another, to the one who from the dead has been raised in order that we may bear fruit for God. [5] While we were in the flesh, our sinful passions as a result of the law were at work in our members to bear fruit for death. [6] But now we are released from the law, dead to that which held us, so that we are slaves in the newness of the Spirit, not under the old letter.

[7] What then should we say? That the law is sin? By no means! Yet, if it were not for the law, I would not have known sin. I would not have known what it is to covet if the law had not said, "You shall not covet." [8] Yet seizing an opportunity in the commandment, sin produced in me all kinds of covetousness. Apart from the law sin is dead. [9] Now, I was at one time alive apart from the law, but when the commandment came, sin revived [10] and I died. And the commandment that was to be life was found to be death to me. [11] For sin, seizing an opportunity in the commandment, deceived me and through it killed me. [12] So the law is holy, and the commandment is holy and just and good.

John 20:19 When it was evening on that day, the first of the week, and the doors of the house where the disciples were closed for fear of the Judeans, Jesus came and stood in their midst and said to them, "Peace be with you all." [20] And having said this, Jesus showed them his hands and his side, and then the disciples rejoiced when they saw the Messiah. [21] Jesus said to them again, "Peace be with you all, just as the Living God has sent me, so I send you all." [22] When Jesus had said this, he breathed on them and said to them, "Receive the Holy Spirit; [23] if you forgive the sins of any, they are forgiven them; if you retain the sins of any, they are retained."

[24] But Thomas, one of the twelve who was called Didymus (the Twin) was not with them when Jesus came. [25] So the other disciples told him, "We have seen the Messiah." But he said to them, "Unless I see the mark of the nails in his hands, and put my finger in the mark of the nails and my hand in his side, I will not believe."

[26] And within eight days his disciples were again in the house, and Thomas was with them. Jesus came, though the doors were shut, and stood among them and said, "Peace be with you all." [27] Then he said to Thomas, "Put your finger here and look at my hands. Bring your hand and put it in my side and do not doubt, rather believe." [28] Thomas answered him, saying, "My Savior and my God!" [29] Jesus said to him, "Was it because you have seen me that you believed? Blessed are those who have not seen and yet believe."

[30] Now Jesus did many other signs in the presence of his disciples, which are not written in this book. [31] But these are written that you may come to believe Jesus is the Messiah, the Son of God, and that through believing you may have life in his name.

PROCLAMATION

Text Notes

In Acts 1:12 "a sabbath's day journey" indicates the amount of walking one could do on Sabbath; across time the distance has ranged from one-third to two-thirds of a mile with variables such as whether one is pasturing animals and whether one is still in a city (determined by how far apart are the houses). It is certainly possible that the sisters of Jesus were present with his male siblings in verse 14; the grammar allows for inclusion.

In Deuteronomy 5:1 "case laws" is indebted to the CEB. The root of *mishpatim* is the root of a judge and her judgments and includes the sense of governance. The Hebrew idiom for covenant making is "to cut," reflecting the practice of carving them in stone literally or symbolically; "engrave" captures the sentiment. The chapter begins addressing the people using plural forms, "you all"; verse 6 and following address a singular grammatically masculine subject: a representative adult, male, free, enslaving, heteronormatively married, parenting Israelite. The "house of slavery" (or "enslavement") can also be translated "the house of slaves" or "enslaved persons." Verse 7 can be translated as: You shall have no other gods *in my face*. "Generation" is missing from the MT in verses 9–10 but traditionally supplied from the LXX and the Peshitta. Some translations avoid the divine jealousy in verse 9 (JPS "impassioned," Fox "zealous"); however, the biblical imagination supplied God with human characteristics, including male rage justifying violence against a female spouse. This language and its theological implications should not be glossed over. Also in verse 9, those who hate God are literally "my haters," strong language softened to "rejecting" God in NRSV and JPS.

The contemplative subject of the psalm is a singular masculine subject that might be translated, "Happy is the man . . ." or "Happy is the person . . ." Functionally, there is no reason this person cannot be a woman. While in other places I translate "woman or man" or "person," here I use "woman" because women so often work with and are numbered among the poor. The last line of verse 2 is imperative: "you will not" or "do not" (hand over) which the LXX, Targum, and Peshitta read as "he [meaning God] will not hand over." It is common for psalms to move between second and third person. The "desire" of the enemy (or "will" in NRSV, CEB, JPS, and KJV) is "soul."

The primary language of marriage for women in Greek is subordinate, *hypandros*, "under + man," see Romans 7:2. In verse 3 the married woman "becomes a man's"; the expression lacks an object noun so other translations substitute verbs "lives with," "marries," etc. That "belonging" will be repeated with reference to Christ in the following verses using the same verb. In verse 8, "covetousness" includes physical and sexual desire as well coveting possessions.

In verse 19 of the Gospel, I use "Judeans" because there is not a distinction between Jews and Christians in the setting of the text and because the language "*the* Jews"—emphasis on the indirect article—particularly on the lips of Christians has often presaged and preceded violence.

Preaching Prompts

"Christ is Risen" is still news, new news, good news, unimaginable news. In Acts and in the Gospel, Jesus visits his family and friends, comforting them, assuring them, maintaining his pastoral role through earth-and-heaven-shaking momentous events. He breathes on them the breath of God, the Holy Spirit, strength and companionship for the journey ahead. Jesus is still confirming his resurrection, appearing to his disciples, not (merely) to cement a doctrine, but to comfort their hearts.

The lesson from Deuteronomy, which will continue in next week's readings, emphasizes that the Church is just one of the ways God has gathered her people across time and that our foundation is a shared heritage. And while supercessionist readings abound, even in scripture, Paul's somewhat tortuous grammar and logic in Romans make the point that "the Law," Jewish law, the Torah and commandments, are not to be disdained or demeaned and are in fact a continuing site of God's revelation. There is no law/grace binary here.

In Acts 12:14 women and men who followed Jesus pray together, "persevering in" or "devote themselves to" prayer until Pentecost. Only Mary the mother of Jesus is named. The mention of Jesus's siblings makes it possible that his sisters are there. All that is known of his sisters is that there is more than one and they came with his Mama to get him when they heard he was in trouble, see Matthew 13:56 and Mark 6:3. Other likely candidates are the women who proclaimed his resurrection: Mary Magdalene, the "other" Mary (Matthew 28:1), Mary the mother of James (who may be the former), and Salome (Mark 16:1), Joanna and the unnamed women in Luke 24:10, and perhaps women who followed and bankrolled Jesus like Susanna (Luke 8:3). These women will be part of the Pentecost spectacle which Peter will explain in Acts 2:17 by quoting Joel 2:28 where "daughters and sons prophesy."

This translation of Psalm 41 makes a strong claim that women are not only included in masculine language, but that they can be read as primary recipients of the promises of God on their own. This claim often stands against the witness of scripture to the treatment of women in its pages and the history of the world and the Church. If it is indeed a claim worth defending, that task falls to preachers and theologians and biblical scholars. When a woman is the singular subject of the psalm, the "will" or "desire of the enemy" becomes much more provocative.

Specific resurrection appearances to women are limited to the environs of the tomb and the first chapter of Acts. Anywhere his disciples are, as throughout John 20, there are women, among the disciples and in the families and homes of the disciples; some would be in both categories. In whose home were they meeting in John 20:19? Who and where were the women of that household? Verse 30 offers space for speculation: *Now Jesus did many other signs in the presence of his disciples, which are not written in this book.* Even with four sanctioned Gospels and scores of apocryphal ones, the half has never been told of the women who followed Jesus and his time with and teaching to them.

THIRD SUNDAY OF EASTER

Acts 1:6–8 (or Deuteronomy 5:11–22); Psalm 78:1–7; Romans 13:8–10; Matthew 22:23–33

Acts 1:6 When they [the disciples] came together, they asked Jesus, "Rabbi, is this the time when you will restore sovereignty to Israel?" [7] He replied, "It is not for you to know the times or seasons that the Creator has set through divine authority. [8] But you will receive power when the Holy Spirit comes upon you, and you will be my witnesses in Jerusalem, in all Judea and Samaria, and to the end of the earth."

Deuteronomy 5:11 You shall not lift up the name of the MOST HIGH your God as though it were nothing, for the DREAD GOD will not acquit anyone who treats God's name as though it were nothing.

[12] Observe the sabbath day and keep it holy, as the HOLY ONE your God commanded you. [13] Six days you shall labor and do all your work. [14] Yet the seventh day is a sabbath to the HOLY ONE your God; you shall not do any work—you, or your daughter or your son, or your female slave or your male slave, or your ox or your donkey, or any of your livestock, or the migrant in your towns, so that your female slave and your male slave may rest as you do. [15] Remember that a slave were you in the land of Egypt, and the FAITHFUL ONE your God brought you out from there with a mighty hand and an outstretched arm; therefore, the HOLY ONE your God commanded you to keep the sabbath day.

[16] Honor your mother and your father, just as the CREATOR OF ALL, your God, commanded you, so that your days may be long and that it may go well with you in the land that the FAITHFUL ONE your God is giving you.

[17] You shall not murder. And:

[18] You shall not commit adultery. And:

[19] You shall not steal. And:

[20] You shall not bear false witness against your neighbor. And:

[21] You shall not covet your neighbor's wife. And:

You shall not desire your neighbor's house, or field, or female slave or male slave, or ox, or donkey, or anything that belongs to your neighbor.

[22] These words the FIRE OF SINAI spoke to your whole assembly at the mountain from the midst of the fire, the cloud, and the thick darkness; a great voice and added no more. God wrote them on two tablets of stone and gave them to me.

Psalm 78:1–7

[1] Give ear, my people, to my teaching;
   incline your ear to the utterances of my mouth.
[2] I will open my mouth in a proverb;
   I will utter riddles from of old.

³ Which we have heard and known,
   and which our mothers and fathers have told us.

⁴ We will not hide them from their daughters and sons;
   we will recount to generations to come
   the praiseworthy deeds of SHE WHO SPEAKS LIFE,
   and her might and the wonderful works she has done.

⁵ She gave her decrees for Rebekah's descendants
   and placed teaching among Sarah's offspring,
   which she commanded their mothers and fathers
   to make known to their daughters and sons.

⁶ In order that a coming generation, children yet to be, might know,
   and will rise up and tell their daughters and sons.

⁷ Then they will put their confidence in God,
   and not forget the works of God, but will keep her commandments.

Romans 13:8 Owe no one anything, except to love one another; for the one who loves another has fulfilled the law. ⁹ The commandments, "*You shall not commit adultery; You shall not murder; You shall not steal; You shall not covet*" and any other commandment are summed up in this word, "Love your neighbor as yourself." ¹⁰ Love does no harm to a neighbor; therefore, love is the fulfilling of the law.

Matthew 22:23 The same day [that Jesus taught about taxes] some Sadducees came to him, saying there is no resurrection; and they questioned him, saying, ²⁴ "Teacher, Moses said, 'If a man dies without having children, his brother shall marry the [widow] woman, and raise up offspring for his brother.' ²⁵ Now there were seven brothers among us; the first married, and without having offspring, leaving the woman to his brother. ²⁶ The same for the second, and the third, to the seventh. ²⁷ After everything the woman died. ²⁸ In the resurrection, then, for which of the seven will she be wife? For they all had her."

²⁹ Jesus answered them, "You all are wrong, because you know neither the scriptures nor the power of God. ³⁰ For in the resurrection they neither marry nor are given in marriage, rather they are like angels in heaven. ³¹ And about the resurrection of the dead, have you all not read what was said to you by God, ³² 'I am the God of Abraham, the God of Isaac, and the God of Jacob'? God is God not of the dead, but of the living." ³³ And when the crowd heard it, they were astounded at his teaching.

PROCLAMATION

Text Notes

Acts 1 begins by summarizing Jesus's ministry in Luke through instructions given to the apostles in verses 1–3. In the following verses the "they" and "them" seem to refer to a larger group than the disciples which becomes clear by verse 14, setting the stage for Pentecost in chapter 2.

Deuteronomy 5:11 is difficult to translate sensibly. Most literally it is an instruction not to "lift" the divine Name as a *sheva*, a vowel substitute enabling vowel-less consonants and syllables to be pronounced (in the same way as a zero is a numeric place holder). So, do not treat God's name like *that*, as though it were nothing, an "empty" thing—following Fox's "emptiness." In verse 14, the "migrant," "stranger," "sojourner," or "resident alien" is "yours" as is every other person and piece of property in the verse; they are not just in your town but part of you and your community. The "thou shalt nots," verses 17–21, begin with "and" as do the vast majority of sentences in biblical Hebrew; its omission erodes the cumulative sense of the commandments. However, beginning the sentence with "and" may read as a vocal tic. The single difference between the corpora of the Ten Commandments in Exodus and Deuteronomy is the double use of the verb "to covet" in Exodus 20:14 and the use of "covet" followed by "desire" in Deuteronomy 5:21. This "desire" is the same as the "craving" for meat in Numbers 11:4.

Romans 13:9 quotes the Decalogue in Exodus 20:13–15, 17 and Deuteronomy 5:17–19, 21 and secondarily, Leviticus 19:18. *Kakon* in verse 10 has a range that includes "evil," "bad," "harm," and "wrong."

The Sadducees cite Deuteronomy 25:5 in Matthew 22:24.

Preaching Prompts

In spite of the significant presence of women among Jesus's disciples in Luke, the companion to Acts, particularly at his crucifixion and resurrection, the minimization of women in Acts is surprising and disheartening. Are we to imagine that none of the women from Luke except the Blessed Mother continued with the disciples? The disappearance of women whose names are preserved and appear repeatedly, like Joanna and Mary the mother of James, is perplexing and the absence of Mary Magdalene, astonishing. That the women who uprooted their lives to follow and support Jesus out of their own means, and in some cases were eyewitnesses to his resurrection, would not make this last trip does not seem credible. In spite of the minimal acknowledgment of women among the disciples and new believers, I read both the disciples and crowds as inclusive even when Peter or Paul address the "men of Israel" (see Acts 2:22, 29; 3:12; 5:35; 13:16; 21:28).

Deuteronomy 5 marks the rare place where women and children saw the manifestation of God along with Moses and the men. Should the liberated have included eunuchs, there would also have been those who did not fit neatly in the binary framework gazing at God veiled in smoke and fire.

Psalm 78 offers such a transgenerational reading, through these women and men and their children and descendants, God builds families, communities, and peoples, all the family of God. In this family, as in many on a much smaller scale, there are divisions and hostilities, enmities and ruptures that also cross generational lines and lineages and trouble the relationship between God and humanity.

"Marrying and being given in marriage" in verse 30 of the Gospel is framed with women as passive if not as objects. While their voices are missing, what might the end of such marriages and those endured by their foremothers have meant to them? Might that not be good news?

As Eastertide readings, these texts invite us to consider our communities and their structures. Is the Church today a continually unfolding "new thing" with astonishing liberty, or is it a continuation of the biases and hierarchies of our ancestors?

FOURTH SUNDAY OF EASTER

Acts 2:22–24; Deuteronomy 18:15–22; Psalm 9:9–14;
2 Corinthians 4:7–12; Luke 7:18–23

Acts 2:22 [Peter said,] "Men of Israel, listen to these words: Jesus of Nazareth, a man attested by God in your midst with deeds of power, marvels, and miracles that God did through him among you, as you yourselves know: [23] This man, through the definite plan and foreknowledge of God, betrayed by the hands of the lawless, you all crucified and killed. [24] He who God raised up freed from the birth-pangs of death, because it was not possible for him to be held in its power."

Deuteronomy 18:15 A prophet from among you, from your own kin, like me, shall the Majestic One your God raise up for you; you all shall heed such a prophet. [16] This is according to everything you asked of the Mighty One your God at Horeb on the day of the assembly when you said: "Not again, to hear the voice of the Holy One of Old, my God, or this great fire see again, lest I die." [17] Then the Holy One said to me: "They have done well in what they said. [18] A prophet I shall raise up for them from among their own kin, like you, and I will put my words in the mouth of the prophet, who shall speak to them everything that I command. [19] And it shall be that anyone who does not heed the words that the prophet shall speak in my name, I shall attend to them. [20] But a prophet who presumes to speak in my name a word that I have not commanded the prophet to speak, or who speaks in the name of other gods, that prophet shall surely die." [21] Should you say within your heart, "How can we recognize a word that the Most High has not spoken?" [22] If a prophet speaks in the name of the Wisdom of the Ages but the thing does not happen or come about, it is a word that the One God has not spoken. The prophet has spoken it presumptuously; do not fear it.

Psalm 9:9–14

[9] She Who is Faithful is a stronghold for the oppressed,
a stronghold in times of trouble.

10 They trust you, they who know your name,
for you do not forsake those who seek you REDEEMING GOD.

11 Sing praises to the HOLY ONE enthroned in Zion.
Declare her deeds among the peoples.

13 Be gracious to me, GRACIOUS ONE.
See what I suffer from those who hate me.
You lift me up from the gates of death,

14 so that I may recount all your praises,
and in the gates of Daughter Zion,
rejoice in your salvation.

2 Corinthians 4:7 Now we have this treasure in earthen vessels, so that this supreme power is God's and not of us. 8 In every way are we oppressed, but not crushed; perplexed, but not in despair; 9 persecuted, but not forsaken; knocked down, but not destroyed; 10 always bearing forth in the body the death of Jesus, in order that the life of Jesus might also be revealed in our bodies. 11 Always, for as long as we live, we are being given up to death for the sake of Jesus, so that the life of Jesus may be revealed in our mortal flesh. 12 Thus death is at work in us, but life in you all.

Luke 7:18 Now, the disciples of John brought news of all these things [that Jesus raised a person from the dead] to John. And John called two in particular among his disciples. 19 He sent them to the Messiah to ask, "Are you the one who is to come, or are we to wait for another?" 20 When the disciples had come to Jesus, they said, "John the Baptizer has sent us to you to ask, 'Are you the one who is to come, or are we to wait for another?'" 21 By that time Jesus had cured many people of diseases, plagues, and evil spirits, and to many blind persons he gave sight. 22 So Jesus answered them, "Go and take this news to John, what you have seen and heard:

those who were blind receive sight,
those who were lame walk,
those who were diseased-in-skin are cleansed,
those who were deaf hear,
those who were dead are raised,
those who are poor have good news proclaimed to them.

23 And blessed is anyone who takes no offense at me."

PROCLAMATION

Text Notes

The lines of Peter's speech in Acts 2 do not fall easily into complete sentences. I have not forced them. Their form suggests an emotional passionate delivery.

My translation of Deuteronomy 18:22 is influenced by Everett Fox, expanding the Hebrew "if the word *is not or does not come*" to "does not happen or come about."

"Bearing forth" in 2 Corinthians 4:10 has the sense of carrying something around and displaying it. Also, in verses 10 and 11, "be revealed," *phanerōthē*, evokes an epiphany with its shared root.

Jesus's response to John's disciples in Luke 7:22 is a series of paired words with the occasional conjunction, lacking even direct objects:

blind receive-sight,

lame walk,

lepers clean,

and deaf hear,

dead raised,

poor good-news-proclaimed.

The translator must supply the connective tissue of grammar and syntax. These word pairs suggest a highly performative delivery like spoken word poetry, rap or the preaching tradition of the black church. "Diseased-in-skin" acknowledges the full range of skin disorders included under the ancient understanding of leprosy.

Preaching Prompts

These Eastertide texts focus not only on the raising of the dead, but also the raising of leaders, the organization of the people of God after the transformative miracles of the exodus and resurrection of Jesus. In Acts 2 Peter proclaims the raising of Jesus from the dead. In Deuteronomy 18 the people whose descendants would ask for a king against God's and Samuel's better judgment tell Moses to ask God to raise up another prophet like Moses. The psalmist is raised from the gates of death in Psalm 9. The follower of Jesus is raised from every tribulation and oppression in 2 Corinthians 4, bearing the death and resurrection of Jesus in their bodies.

Peter addresses his remarks to the men of Israel exclusively, apparently discounting the presence of the women in the public crowd and their participation in the Jesus movement. The people who ask for another Moses word their request in such a way as to seem to preclude another Miriam. I argue Deborah was Moses's successor; she and he were both prophet and judge unlike Joshua (Samuel would be the last to hold both titles). Folk are always looking for the next great man. John's disciples want to know if Jesus is that One. The cycle will continue after his resurrection. The disciples will look for another apostle who will be lost to history. Paul will assert his preeminence as an apostle; extracanonical writings will argue for Thecla and Mary Magdalene. In recent history much has been made of the futility of the search for the next Martin Luther King (but not the next Coretta Scott King or Betty Shabazz).

Resurrection represents the ultimate display of power in the world of the text and in the world that reads the text. It is important to reiterate that resurrection weaves through the scriptures as a witness to God's power, Elijah in 1 Kings 17, Elisha in 2 Kings 4, Jesus prior to his own resurrection, Peter in Acts 9, and Paul in Acts 20 all raise the dead. Life is the gift of God and not even death will thwart God's intent for humanity.

FIFTH SUNDAY OF EASTER

Acts 5:12–16 (or Deuteronomy 28:1–14); Psalm 147:12–20; 2 Corinthians 4:13–15; John 5:25–29

Acts 5:12 Now, many signs and wonders were done among the people through the apostles; they were all together in the Portico of Solomon. [13] None of the others dared to join them, but the people extolled them. [14] Yet more believers were added to Christ, a multitude of both women and men. [15] So much so that they even carried the sick into the streets, and laid them on cots and mats, so that Peter's shadow might overshadow some of them as he passed. [16] Multitudes would also gather from the towns around Jerusalem, bringing the sick and those tormented by unclean spirits, and they were all made well.

Deuteronomy 28:1 Now then, it shall be that if you truly heed the voice of the HOLY ONE your God, to be watchful and to perform all God's commandments that I am commanding you today, then the SOVEREIGN ONE your God will set you high above all the nations of the earth. [2] And all these blessings shall come upon you and overtake you, if you obey the JUST ONE your God:

[3] Blessed shall you be in the city and blessed shall you be in the field.
[4] Blessed shall be the fruit of your womb, the fruit of your ground, and the fruit of your livestock, both the calving of your cattle and the lambing of your flock.
[5] Blessed shall be your basket and your kneading bowl.
[6] Blessed shall you be when you come in and blessed shall you be when you go out.

[7] The FAITHFUL ONE will set up your enemies who stand against you to be struck before you; they shall come out against you one way and flee before you seven ways. [8] The CREATOR OF ALL will command the blessing upon you in your barns, and in all that you undertake. God will bless you in the land that the HOLY ONE your God is giving you. [9] The HOLY ONE will establish you as a people holy to God, just as God has sworn to you, if you keep the commandments of the RIGHTEOUS ONE your God and walk in God's ways. [10] All the peoples of the earth shall see that you are called by the name of the MOST HIGH, and they shall fear you.

[11] The Gracious One shall grant you excess out of goodness, in the fruit of your womb, in the fruit of your livestock, and in the fruit of your ground in the land that the Ageless One swore to your mothers and fathers to give you. [12] The Generous One will open for you the rich storehouse of God, the heavens, to give the rain of your land in its season and to bless all the work of your hands. You will lend to many nations, but you will not borrow. [13] The Sovereign will make you the head, and not the tail; you shall be only at the top, and not at the bottom, if you heed the commandments of the Worthy One your God, which I am commanding you today, to be watchful and to perform them. [14] And do not turn aside from any of the words that I am commanding you today, either to the right or to the left, to follow other gods to serve them.

Psalm 147:12–20

[12] Praise the Ever-Living God, O Jerusalem!
Praise your God, O Zion!

[13] For she strengthens the bars of your gates;
she blesses your children within you.

[14] She sets peace at your border;
she satisfies you with the finest of wheat.

[15] She sends forth her word to the earth;
her word runs swiftly.

[16] She lays down snow like wool;
she scatters frost like ashes.

[17] She hurls down hail like crumbs—
who can stand before her cold?

[18] She sends forth her word, and melts them;
she makes her wind blow, and the waters flow.

[19] She declares her word to Rebekah's line,
her statutes and ordinances to Sarah's seed.

[20] She has not dealt thus with any other nation;
they do not know her ordinances.
Praise the Wisdom of the Ages!

2 Corinthians 4:13 Now we have the same spirit of faith that is in accordance with scripture: "I believed, and so I spoke"; and we believe, and so we speak. [14] We know that the one who raised Jesus the Messiah will raise us also with Jesus and will bring us with you all into the presence of Jesus. [15] Indeed, the whole is for your sake so grace through many more may increase thanksgiving to the glory of God.

John 5:25 "Truly, truly, I tell you all, the hour is coming, and is now here, when the dead will hear the voice of the Son of God, and those who hear will live. [26] For just as the Living God has life internally, just so God has granted the Son to have life internally. [27] And God has given the Son authority to render justice, because he is the Son of Woman. [28] Do not be astonished at this; for the hour is coming when all who are in their graves will hear his voice [29] and will come out—those who have done good, to the resurrection of life, and those who have done evil, to the resurrection of judgment.

PROCLAMATION

Text Notes

In Deuteronomy 28:1 "heed" or "hear" has the force of "obey" when combined with the voice of God, hence "obey" in JPS and NRSV, "hearken" in KVJ and Fox, and "heed" here and in Alter. In the same verse I render "to observe and to do" with "to be watchful and to perform" from NETS. "Calving" and "lambing" in verse 4 are from JPS. The blessings in verses 3–6 are addressed to a singular masculine subject as are the Ten Commandments, to individual representative free male heteronorma-tive slave-holding Israelites. The remainder of the passage continues to address this subject. The final verse of the passage is treated as a continuation of the conditional clause in the preceding verse by JPS and NRSV counter to the pointing of the MT; I and CEB, Alter, and KJV preserve its independence.

Jerusalem and Zion are both feminine; all of the discourse to them in Psalm 147 is in second person feminine, as one would speak to an individual woman in bib-lical or modern Hebrew. The "wind" of verse 18 is *ruach*, meaning both wind and spirit contextually. In verse 19, "Rebekah's line" represents "Jacob" and "Sarah's seed" stands in for "Israel."

Second Corinthians 4:13 cites Psalm 116:10 (which is Psalm 115:1 in the LXX, which varies significantly in the psalter and several other books).

In John 5:27, the work of justice is more than passing sentence; rather "judging" or "execute judgment" or "rendering a verdict" are but one dimension of justice work. The traditional translation "Son of Man" rests on conflating men ("man/kind") with humanity. In the Hebrew Scriptures Jewish and Christian translations use variations of "mortal" and "human" (being/one). "Son of Woman" fits well within this semantic range and makes explicit the woman-born humanity of Jesus.

Preaching Prompts

In the first church and in our own, Eastertide teaching and preaching centers the resur-rection, the most dramatic evidence of the power and faithfulness of God. God's faith-fulness is ancient; the Torah is both witness to it and evidence of it, celebrated in the psalm. The Deuteronomy text is a formal act of witness. The miracles performed by the apostles in Acts bore witness to the power of the living Christ and to his power among those who walk in the way of Jesus. And in the Eastertide Gospel, God who is worthy of reverence and exaltation shares authority with God's child, the woman-born Jesus, to raise the dead in the final, dual resurrection, to reward and recompense.

There are women among those healed in Acts, but no mention of women disciples performing the miracles as Peter does here and Paul does elsewhere. It is worth asking if the Holy Ghost power of Pentecost poured out on "daughters and sons" and "the enslaved, women and men" restricts miraculous gifts of power to one gender or two individuals.

The promises of fecundity in Deuteronomy 28:4 and verse 11, conditional guarantees of fertility *if* you are faithful enough, can be quite painful for folk living with infertility and can promote self-blaming. Indeed, the witness of the biblical text that God grants fertility by fiat is at odds with the lived experience of many. Framing these stories with a discussion of how the genre functions—an ancient Afro-Asiatic trope signaling the import of the character thus born—may be helpful, but ultimately these texts require a great deal of sensitivity in preaching.

Between the resurrection of Jesus and the final resurrection, the Church is called to life, a life apart from all of the dead and death-dealing things that would prevent us from living fully in Christ, i.e., "those that are in their graves" in John 5:28. What might those graves be and what might be in them? The dead names and past images of trans children of God, the suffocating closets queer kin have left behind, inadequate theology, patriarchal language and constructs, past affiliations, relationships and behaviors that harm self or others. In the words of the Epistle, "we believe, and so we speak." The Church will come out of these graves one day.

SIXTH SUNDAY OF EASTER

Acts 17:1–4, 10–12 (or Deuteronomy 28:58–68);
Psalm 145:8–19; Romans 6:5–11; John 11:17–27

Acts 17:1 Paul and Silas had traveled through Amphipolis and Apollonia. They came to Thessalonica, where there was a Jewish synagogue. [2] As was his custom Paul went and on three sabbaths presented to them from the scriptures, [3] explaining and demonstrating it was necessary for the Messiah to suffer and to rise from the dead: "This is the Messiah, Jesus who I proclaim to you all." [4] Now, some of [those Jews] were persuaded and joined Paul and Silas, as did a great many of the devout Greeks and not a few of the prominent women.

[10] Then, the sisters and brothers immediately that night sent Paul and Silas away to Beroea; when they arrived, they went to the Jewish synagogue. [11] These persons were more high-born and open-minded than in Thessalonica; they received the word with great eagerness. Daily they examined the scriptures to see if these things were so. [12] Thus many of them therefore believed, including highly respected Greek women and not just a few [Jewish] men.

Deuteronomy 28:58 If you do not diligently observe all the words of this law written in this scroll, to revere this glorious and awesome Name, the HOLY ONE your God, ⁵⁹ then the DREAD GOD will extravagantly plague you and plague your lineage with plagues great and enduring and grievous and enduring terrible diseases. ⁶⁰ God will bring back upon you all the diseases of Egypt, which you feared, and they shall cling to you. ⁶¹ Indeed every disease and plague, even if not recorded in the scroll of this law, the FEARSOME GOD will inflict upon you until your destruction. ⁶² You all shall be left few in number rather than being as the stars in the heavens for multitude, because you did not obey the MOST HIGH your God. ⁶³ And it shall be just as the FAITHFUL ONE delighted over you, prospering you all and multiplying you, thus will the INSCRUTABLE GOD take delight over you to eradicate you all and destroy you; you all shall be torn up from the land that you are entering to possess. ⁶⁴ The JUST GOD will scatter you among all peoples, from one end of the earth to the other; and there you shall serve other gods, of wood and stone, which neither you nor your mothers or fathers have known. ⁶⁵ Among those nations you shall find no respite; there shall be no resting place for the sole of your foot. There the SOVEREIGN GOD will give you a trembling heart, failing eyes, and a forlorn spirit. ⁶⁶ Your life shall hang by a thread before you; night and day you shall be in terror, with no assurance of your life. ⁶⁷ In the morning you shall say, "If only it were evening!" and in the evening you shall say, "If only it were morning!" because of the terror that shall terrorize your heart and the sights your eyes shall see. ⁶⁸ The HOLY ONE OF SINAI will bring you back in ships to Egypt, by a path I told you you would never see again; and there you shall offer yourselves for sale to your enemies as slaves, female and male, but there will be no buyer.

Psalm 145:8–19

[May be read with *Blessed be the* LIVING GOD *and blessed be her name forever and ever* as an antiphon at the end of each verse following the preserved text in the Dead Sea Scrolls.]

⁸ Full of grace and a mother's love is the MOTHER OF ALL,
    slow to anger and abounding in faithful love.
⁹ The WOMB OF LIFE is good to all,
    and her mother-love is upon all she has made.
¹⁰ They shall praise you, WELLSPRING OF LIFE, all your works,
    and all your faithful shall bless you.
¹¹ Of the glory of your majestic rule shall they speak,
    and your might shall they declare,
¹² to make known to the woman-born her mighty works,
    and the glorious splendor of her majestic rule.
¹³ Your majesty is an everlasting majesty,
    and your sovereignty endures throughout all generations.
    [*Blessed be the* LIVING GOD *and blessed be her name forever and ever.*]
    Faithful is the EVER-LIVING GOD in all her words,

and gracious in all her deeds.

[*Blessed be the* LIVING GOD *and blessed be her name forever and ever.*]

¹⁴ The MERCIFUL ONE upholds all who fall,
and raises up all who are bent over.

¹⁵ The eyes of all look to you,
and you give to them their food at the right moment.

¹⁶ You open your hand,
and satisfy the desire of every living thing.

¹⁷ The FAITHFUL ONE is righteous in all her ways,
and loving in all her works.

¹⁸ The EVER-PRESENT GOD is near to all who call on her,
to all who call on her in truth.

¹⁹ The desire of all who revere her she fulfills;
and their cry she hears and delivers them.

Romans 6:5 For if we have been united in a death like Christ's, we will certainly be so in the resurrection. ⁶ This we know, that our old self was crucified with him so that the body of sin might be destroyed, and we might no longer be enslaved to sin. ⁷ The woman or man who has died is freed from sin. ⁸ But if we have died with Christ, we believe that we shall also live with him. ⁹ We know that Christ, being raised from the dead, will never die; death no longer has dominion over him. ¹⁰ For dying, he died once to sin, in living, he lives to God. ¹¹ So also should you consider yourselves dead to sin and alive to God in Christ Jesus.

John 11:17 When Jesus arrived [in Bethany], he found that for four days Lazarus had already been in the tomb. ¹⁸ Now Bethany was near Jerusalem, about two miles away. ¹⁹ So, many of the Judeans had come to Martha and Mary to console them about their brother. ²⁰ When Martha heard that Jesus was coming, she met him; however Mary remained at the house. ²¹ Martha said to Jesus, "Rabbi, if you had been here, my brother would never have died. ²² Yet even now I know that whatever you ask of God, God will give you." ²³ Jesus said to her, "Your brother will rise." ²⁴ Martha said to him, "I know that he will rise in the resurrection on the last day." ²⁵ Jesus said to her, "I am the resurrection and the life. The one who believes in me, even though they die, they will live, ²⁶ and everyone who lives and believes in me will never die. Do you believe this?" ²⁷ She said to him, "Yes, Rabbi, I believe that you are the Messiah, the Son of God, the one who comes into the world."

PROCLAMATION

Text Notes

In the world of the text, a "synagogue" is a generic gathering place; it was not yet (nearly) exclusively a place of Jewish worship, hence the need to specify "Jewish" in the text.

"To have words" in Acts 17:2 can mean anything from discussing to disputing; here it is "at" them rather than "with" them, yielding "presented to them." In verse 11 the same word means both "high-born" and the characteristic of being open-minded deriving from that status or accompanying education. While many translations present the women and men as equally high in standing, the adjective is feminine plural and thus refers only to the women; likewise, "Greek" is feminine plural. The men are neither Greek nor of high status. This text is one of very few places where women precede men in the order of their mention.

In Deuteronomy 28:59 I translate the plaguing of Israel with "extravagantly" from the root that means "wonderful" with a nod to Phyllis Trible's chapter subtitle, "An Extravagance of Violence" from her groundbreaking volume, *Text of Terror*. In verse 66, "hang" is expanded to "hang by a thread" following Everett Fox.

Psalm 145 uses the root *rchm*, which is derived from the womb, *rechem*, to articulate God's feelings for Israel in verses 8–9, accordingly, I translate the sentiment as "mother-love" rather than the traditional "compassion," which severs the link between the terms and their semantic range. In verse 10 "the woman-born" are the "children of humanity" and "majestic rule" replaces "kingdom." Psalm 145 varies significantly among manuscripts and traditions; it occurs as a responsive psalm in the Dead Sea Scrolls (DSS) with the line "Blessed be the LIVING GOD and blessed be her name forever and ever" at the end of every preserved verse; some are broken off.

In verse 13 of the psalm, the Hebrew MT has only two lines, represented in the JPS and KJV; the LXX and Peshitta have a second pair of lines about the fidelity of God represented in the NRSV and CEB, and among the Dead Sea Scrolls (DSS), the 11QPs[a] manuscript includes the fidelity lines and language of blessing before and after. I have included all of these verses in brackets that the reader might make her own choices. Following the convention of Martin Abegg, Peter Flint, and Eugene Ulrich, editors of the English-language *Dead Sea Scrolls Bible*, phrasing unique to the DSS is in italics. (Further, the fidelity lines use *kurios*, "Lord," in the LXX and its equivalent *mry'* in the Peshitta and *Elohim*, "God," in the DSS. In the blessing lines, the scribe renders the divine Name in archaic paleo-Hebrew rather than the common script of the era, a not infrequent practice emphasizing the Name.)

Preaching Prompts

These lessons speak of the power of God, to raise the dead to life in Acts, Romans, and the Gospel, the power resident in the dread and awesome Name of God in Deuteronomy 28, and in the psalm, the power to provide and preserve.

In Acts the story of Jesus is compelling and contentious. Paul's conversion and evangelism mark the beginning of what will be seen by others as a break with his Judaism, whereas in his time and for him, Judaism was as much an ethnicity as religious identity, not one that could be chosen or given up. The tensions between the followers of Jesus and their Judean kin—the root word is a geographic, ethnic, and cultural/religious marker—these tensions are internal to the Jewish community while written at a time when those who would come to call themselves Christians would see themselves as separate and distinct from their Jewish forbears. Their language on contemporary lips on the other side of centuries of Christian anti-Judaism, anti-Semitism, supercessionism, and of the Holocaust resonate differently.

The alternate first lesson from Deuteronomy is severe and threatening. It lays out the consequences of failing to follow God faithfully. It is an exemplar of a prevailing biblical theology: God blesses and rewards the good and curses and punishes the wicked. That theology pervades the canon and endures. It is useful to address it in times of crisis and before and between crises.

Romans 6 speaks of the freedom of the believer in generic terms that I have made explicit for women and men in verse 7. Hindsight makes it easy to see how past generations failed to live in to that freedom. We as individuals and collectively as the Church may have died to sin and been buried in our baptisms to be raised with Christ, yet sin endures within and among us in all of our communities, including the Church. The gender-based hierarchies of the cultural habitus of the text endure as though they were the words of life and not the rough setting of the jewel of the gospel.

Martha's statement to Jesus in John 11:21 is stronger than it has often been translated. Not "my brother would not have died," but "my brother would *never* have died." That same "never" is included by Jesus in his response, "Everyone who lives and believes in me will never die." That speaks to me of death as portal to eternal life and not a permanent estate. Secondarily, while this reading ends before Lazarus's raising, it is noteworthy that he is raised to life in the same old world. Life in Jesus happens here among the brokenness, failings, and limitations of the present world.

FEAST OF THE ASCENSION

Acts 1:1–11; Psalm 24; Revelation 3:20–22; Luke 24:46–53

Acts 1:1 In the first writing, I worked on, Theophilus, everything Jesus did and taught from the beginning [2] until the day he instructed the apostles whom he had chosen through the Holy Spirit and was taken up to heaven. [3] Jesus presented himself to them, living, after his suffering through many convincing proofs, by appearing to them forty days and speaking about the reign of God. [4] And staying with them, Jesus commanded them not to leave Jerusalem, rather to wait there for the promise of the Faithful God, "what you heard from me." [5] For John baptized with water, but you will be baptized with the Holy Spirit not many days from this one."

⁶ When they [the disciples], came together, they asked Jesus, "Rabbi, is this the time when you will restore sovereignty to Israel?" ⁷ He replied, "It is not for you to know the times or seasons that the Sovereign God has set through divine authority. ⁸ But you will receive power when the Holy Spirit comes upon you, and you will be my witnesses in Jerusalem, in all Judea and Samaria, and to the end of the earth."

⁹ And saying this, as they were watching Jesus was taken up, and a cloud took him out of their sight. ¹⁰ While they were gazing up toward heaven as Jesus was going, suddenly two in white robes stood by them. ¹¹ They said, "Galileans, why are you standing looking up into heaven? This Jesus, who has been taken up from you into heaven, will come in the way as you saw him go into heaven."

Psalm 24

¹ To the Creator of All belongs the earth and all that fills her,
the world, and those who dwell in her.
² For God upon the seas has founded her,
and on the rivers has established her.
³ Who shall ascend the hill of the Holy One?
And who shall stand in God's holy place?
⁴ The woman or man who has clean hands and pure hearts,
who does not lift up their [hands] to what is false,
and do not swear deceitfully on their souls.
⁵ [Instead] they will lift up a blessing from the Faithful God,
and what is right from the God of their salvation.
⁶ Such is the generation of those who seek God,
who seek the face of the God of Rebekah. *Selah*
⁷ Lift up your heads, you gates!
and be lifted up, you everlasting doors!
that the One of glory may come in.
⁸ Who is the One of glory?
The Fire of Sinai, strong and mighty,
the God who is Majesty, mighty in battle.
⁹ Lift up your heads, you gates!
and be lifted up, you everlasting doors!
that the One of glory may come in.
¹⁰ Who is this One of glory?
The Commander of heaven's legions,
God is the One of glory. *Selah*

Revelation 3:20 "Look! I stand at the door and knock. If you hear my voice and open the door, I will come in to you and dine with you, and you with me. ²¹ To the one who conquers I will give a place with me on my throne, just as I myself conquered and sat down with my Abba on God's throne. [22] Let anyone who has an ear listen to what the Spirit is saying to the churches."

Luke 24:46 Then Jesus said to them, "So it is written, the Messiah is to suffer and to rise from the dead the third day, [47] and repentance and forgiveness of sins is to be preached in his name to all nations, beginning from Jerusalem. [48] You are witnesses of these things. [49] Now look! I am sending you the promise of my Abba. You all stay in the city until you have been clothed with power from on high." [50] Then Jesus led them out as far as Bethany, and lifting his hands, he blessed them. [51] While he was blessing them, Jesus retreated from them and was carried up into heaven. [52] And they bowed down and worshiped him, and returned to Jerusalem with great joy; [53] and they were in the temple every day blessing God.

PROCLAMATION

Text Notes

The divine beings in Acts 1:10 are described as "men" using the human term. Curiously, there are no female divine beings, messengers, angels, etc., in the canon. It is not clear whether women are present at the Ascension, obscured by masculine grammar. If they are not present, it is worth asking why not when women have been the birthing wombs and companion witnesses, participants in and preachers of the entire Christ story. It is tempting to say the women were out in the world proclaiming the gospel while the men still needed one more sign. Yet, there were women with these very men (who are identified as the remaining apostles by name in Acts 1:13). If they were not with them at the Ascension, how did they learn of the meeting place? Since they seemed to have arrived at the same time, they could not have been very far. The texts and the cultures of the biblical world collude to minimize and erase women.

In Psalm 24:1–2 I have retained the feminine grammatical gender of the earth, since it fits well with the contemporary notion of earth as mother. In verse 6 "the God of Rebekah" replaces "the God of Jacob."

Preaching Prompts

Chronologically, the Gospel for the Feast of the Ascension goes before the first reading from Acts. It may be useful to reread the Acts account of the Ascension *after* the Gospel, perhaps at the beginning of the sermon (if tacking it on to the Gospel seems like liturgical heresy). The Gospel points to the Ascension in Acts 1, and Acts 1 points to Pentecost, coming soon in the next chapter.

In the Ascension the glory of the Resurrection ratchets up another level. The risen Christ appears to followers—addressed as "men" but possibly inclusive—and prepares the burgeoning church for the baptism of the Holy Spirit. The psalm makes clear that God is the One of glory and only the pure-hearted can stand in her presence. The multiple Ascension accounts highlight the divinity of the post-Ascension Christ. Revelation 3 reminds us that the divine, risen, and ascended Christ is not so far away that he cannot come to us. He can and will still meet us at the table; for the Church that is primarily in the Eucharist. Christ also comes to us in communion with one another. That communion, whether at the Eucharist or beyond, is communal not hierarchal, though the scriptures and their authors will continue to assert ancient hierarchies, particularly along class and gender lines.

SEVENTH SUNDAY OF EASTER

Acts 18:24–27; Deuteronomy 29:10–15; Psalm 111; 1 Peter 1:3–9; John 11:28–44

Acts 18:24 Now a certain Jewish man, Apollos by name, a native of Alexandria, an eloquent man well-versed in the scriptures, came to Ephesus. [25] This man had been instructed in the Way of the Messiah and spoke with a fiery spirit and taught accurately the things concerning Jesus, though he knew only the baptism of John. [26] He began to speak boldly in the synagogue, but when Priscilla and Aquila heard him, they took him in and explained the Way [of God] to him more accurately. [27] And when he wished to cross over into Achaia, the sisters and brothers encouraged him and wrote to the disciples to welcome him; upon his arrival he greatly helped those who had through grace come to believe.

Deuteronomy 29:10 You all are standing (here) today, all of you, in the presence of the FIRE OF SINAI your God—your leaders of your tribes, your elders, and your officials, all the men of Israel, [11] your little ones, your women, and the immigrants who are among you in your camp, from the cutter of your wood to the drawer of your water—[12] to enter into the covenant of the CREATOR OF ALL your God, which the MOST HIGH your God is making with you and by God's oath today, [13] in order that God may establish you today as the people of God, and that God would be your God, just as God told you and just as God swore to your ancestors, to [Sarah and] Abraham, to Isaac [the son of Sarah], and to Jacob [born of Rebekah]. [14] Not just with you all am I inscribing this covenant and this oath, [15] but also with those who are here standing with us today in the presence of the WISDOM OF THE AGES, our God, and (even) with those who are not here with us today.

Psalm 111

[1] Hallelujah!
  I will give thanks to the HOLY GOD with my whole heart,
    in the council of the upright, and in the congregation.
[2] Great are the works of the CREATOR OF ALL,
    sought after by all who delight in them.

³ Glorious and majestic is her work,
and her righteousness endures forever.

⁴ She has become renowned by her wonderful deeds;
gracious and loving is the MOTHER OF ALL.

⁵ Meat she grants to those who revere her;
she is ever mindful of her covenant.

⁶ The power of her works has she shown her people,
giving them the heritage of the nations.

⁷ The works of her hands are faithful and true;
all her precepts are trustworthy.

⁸ They are established forever and ever,
to be performed with faithfulness and uprightness.

⁹ Redemption has she sent to her people;
she has commanded her covenant forever.
Holy and awesome is her name.

¹⁰ The reverence of SHE WHO IS WISDOM is the beginning of wisdom;
all those who practice it have a good understanding.
Her praise endures forever.

1 Peter 1:3 Blessed be the God and Father of our Redeemer Jesus Christ who in great mercy has engendered a new birth for us into a living hope, through the resurrection of Jesus Christ from the dead, ⁴ into an inheritance that is incorruptible, undefiled, and unfading, kept in heaven for you all, ⁵ who in the power of God are kept through faith for a salvation ready to be revealed in the end time. ⁶ In this you rejoice even when necessary for you to suffer various trials, ⁷ in order that the examination of your faith, more precious than gold, which though perishable is tested by fire, may be found yielding praise and glory and honor when Jesus Christ is revealed. ⁸ You have not seen him, yet you love him. You do not see him now, yet you believe in him and rejoice with a joy glorious and beyond words. ⁹ You are receiving the completion of your faith, the salvation of your souls.

John 11:28 Now when Martha had said this ["Yes, Rabbi, I believe that you are the Messiah, the Son of God, the one who comes into the world"], she went back and called her sister Mary privately, "The Teacher is here and calling for you." ²⁹ And when Mary heard that she got up quickly and went to Jesus. ³⁰ Now Jesus had not yet come to the village, but was still in the place where Martha had met him. ³¹ Thus the Jewish community who were with her in the house and consoling her saw Mary get up quickly and go out; they followed her thinking she was going to the tomb to weep there.

³² So when Mary came where Jesus was seeing him, she knelt at his feet saying to him, "Rabbi, if you had been here, my brother would not have died." ³³ Thus when Jesus saw her weeping and the Jewish folk who came with her also weeping, his spirit was disturbed and

he was deeply moved. [34] And he said, "Where have you laid him?" They said to him, "Rabbi, come and see." [35] And Jesus wept. [36] Therefore the Jewish people (with her) said, "See how he loved him!" [37] Yet some of them said, "Could not the one who opened the eyes of the blind man have done something so that this man would not have died?"

[38] Jesus, again deeply moved within himself, came to the tomb; it was a cave, and a stone was lying against it. [39] Jesus said, "Take away the stone." Martha, the sister of the dead man, said to him, "Rabbi, already there is a stench because it has been four days." [40] Jesus said to her, "Did I not tell you that if you believed, you would see the glory of God?" [41] So they took away the stone. And Jesus lifted his eyes (upward) and said, "Abba, I thank you for having heard me. [42] I know that you always hear me, for the sake of the crowd standing here have I said this, so that they may believe that you sent me." [43] And when he had said this, with a loud voice he cried out, "Lazarus, come out!" [44] The dead man came out, bound hand and foot with strips of cloth, and his face wrapped in a cloth. Jesus said to them, "Loose him, and let him go."

PROCLAMATION

Text Notes

While Acts 18:25 makes reference to "the Way of the Lord [Messiah here]," "the Way" in verse 26 is amended to "the Way of God" in some manuscripts. It is included in brackets as it appears in the dominant Nestle-Aland Greek text (28th revision).

Due to variant numbering practices, the Deuteronomy lesson begins with verse 9 in the MT and Jewish translations such as JPS, Fox, and Alter. In 29:13 (in NRSV and other Christian editions) the patriarchal lineage is amended to name Sarah as a recipient of a divine promise herself and the mother of the subsequent patriarchs. The phrasing is careful not to specify the matriarchs as covenant partners given the frequent reiteration of the covenant as being dependent on circumcision and the regular treatment of women as "add-ons" as in verse 11. The NRSV translation of verse 14 inexplicably includes the phrase "not only with you who stand here with us today before the LORD our God," relocated from verse 15, an unnecessary modification as aptly illustrated by the JPS and Fox translations in addition to the present one and counter to MT, LXX, the Dead Sea Scrolls, and the Peshitta.

In Psalm 111:3 I replaced the nouns "honor and majesty" with the adjectives "glorious and majestic" for smoother English grammar, following JPS in part. God's *tzedakah* primarily means "righteousness" but also has the sense of "beneficence," including generosity to the poor as in JPS. In verse 4 God's love is articulated with *racham,* which has the womb, *rechem,* as its grammatical root, informing the choice of MOTHER OF ALL as the divine name. The "meat" God provides is literally "prey"; God is apparently quite the huntress. In verses 5 and 10 the verb *y-r-'* is translated "revere," well within the semantic range and preferable to "fear."

The expression "the Jews" often has a negative resonance in the scriptures and in the world in which the scriptures are read. In John 11:31, 33, and 36, "Jewish community" softens the traditional translation. The author excludes Mary and Martha from the category *Ioudaioi* because she is a follower of Jesus according to the use of the term in his time. In the world of the text, Mary and Martha are *Ioudaioi*, Judean and Jewish, as is Jesus. In place of "Lord" with its slaveholding connotations, I use "Rabbi" in verses 32, 34, and 39. In verse 33 the disturbance in Jesus's spirit can also be understood as an articulation of some sort, i.e., a rebuke, harsh language, or something spoken in anger, hence KJV's "groaning."

Preaching Prompts

As Eastertide comes to a close, the telling and teaching of the Way of Jesus becomes paramount. Orthodoxy and heterodoxy have become concerns for the Church. For some that will result in a significant narrowing of what is the gospel and who is empowered to teach and preach it. In Acts Priscilla and her husband "take in" a junior colleague (in terms of preparation) and supplement his education. They do not shame, censure, or fire him. And he does not reject their teaching or Priscilla's leadership. Their different understandings do not lead to schism.

Priscilla is a Jewish woman evicted from Rome with her husband in the Jewish expulsion ordered by Emperor Claudius in Acts 18:2 and is one of the teaching elders or leaders of the early church. (Bernadette Brooten has demonstrated conclusively that women leaders in the ancient synagogue used the title in her book of the same title; as male Christian leaders adopted the language, it is reasonable to presume Christian women did as well.) Priscilla, sometimes rendered Prisca, is listed before her husband more often than not indicating to some that she was the senior, more learned disciple (Acts 18:2, 18, 26; Romans 16:3; 1 Corinthians 16:19; 2 Timothy 4:19). Her name certainly precedes in the reeducation of Apollos. Paul describes her and her husband—in that order—as his coworkers in Romans 16:3 and she is listed first as pastor of the house church in 2 Timothy 4:19. (I say "pastor" because there is no dispute that men led the churches in their homes when listed; I reckon her as more senior pastor than copastor.)

As an alternate first lesson, Deuteronomy also makes the point that the people of God are fundamentally and radically inclusive, even in Deuteronomy, which is also fundamentally nationalistic. Adults and children of every known gender, people in every economic tier—laborers, likely enslaved, and those who benefit from their labor—along with immigrants and generations yet to come become the people of God. The psalm celebrates that covenant and God's fidelity to it across the ages. It also celebrates the colonization and occupation of Canaan, an opportunity to reflect on our own history and weaponization of theology.

This final Eastertide Gospel brings the season to a close with the discipleship of Mary and Martha, the resurrection of Lazarus foreshadowing that of Jesus, and a circle of care between Jewish followers of Jesus and their Jewish neighbors and kinfolk. Unlike many antagonistic portrayals of Jewish characters, the Jewish folk in John 11 are neighbors comforting Mary and Martha as members of their community after the death of their brother and weeping with them, suggesting strong ties.

Jesus's question about the location of Lazarus's body anticipates the questions about the disposition of his own at the end of this same Gospel in John 19:41; 20:2, 13, 15. The gesture toward Jesus's own death and his grieving for and with his friends emphasize his humanity and mortality. At the same time, he is much more than human, God-born, fathered by God who "engenders" our new birth in the Epistle. That birth is our inheritance and the source of our hope as we live in a time where we cannot see Jesus.

PENTECOST VIGIL (OR EARLY SERVICE)

Joel 2:27–32 (or Exodus 19:1–19); Psalm 139:7–14; Acts 2:1–18; John 4:7–26

Joel 2:27 You all shall know that I am in the midst of Israel,

> and that I, the HOLY ONE OF SINAI, am your God and there is no other.
> And my people shall not be put to shame ever again.
> 28 And it shall be after that,
> I will pour out my Spirit on all flesh;
> and your daughters and your sons shall prophesy,
> your elders shall dream dreams,
> and your youths shall see visions.
> 29 Even on the enslaved women and men,
> in those days, will I pour out my Spirit.

30 I will place portents in the heavens and on the earth, blood and fire and pillars of smoke. 31 The sun shall be turned to darkness, and the moon to blood, before the great and terrible day of the DREAD GOD comes. 32 Then it shall be that everyone who calls on the name of the FAITHFUL GOD shall be saved; for in Mount Zion and in Jerusalem there shall be those who escape, as the HOLY ONE OF OLD has said, and among the survivors, those whom the GOD WHO SAVES calls.

Exodus 19:1 On the third new moon after the women, children, and men of Israel had gone out of the land of Egypt, on that day, they entered the wilderness of Sinai. 2 They had journeyed from Rephidim, entered the wilderness of Sinai, and camped in the wilderness; Israel camped there in front of the mountain. 3 Then Moses went up to God and the HOLY ONE OF

OLD called to him from the mountain, saying, "Thus you shall say to the house of Jacob, and tell the women, children, and men of Israel: [4] You all have seen what I did to the Egyptians, that I raised you all up on the wings of eagles and brought you all to myself. [5] Now, if you all obey my voice and keep my covenant, you all shall be my treasure from among all peoples, for the whole earth is mine. [6] And you all shall be for me a sovereignty of priests and a holy nation. These are the words that you shall speak to the women, children, and men of Israel."

[7] So Moses came and called the elders of the people and placed before them all these words that the HOLY ONE had commanded him. [8] Then the people, women and men, all answered together: "Everything that the HOLY ONE has spoken we will do." And Moses conveyed the words of the people to the HOLY ONE OF SINAI. [9] Then the HOLY ONE said to Moses, "I will come to you in an impenetrable cloud, so that the people can hear when I speak with you and also trust you always." When Moses had told the words of the people to the HOLY ONE, [10] the HOLY GOD said to Moses:

"Go to the people and have them consecrate themselves today and tomorrow. Have them wash their clothes, [11] and be prepared for the third day, because on the third day the MOST HIGH will come down upon Mount Sinai in the sight of all the people. [12] You shall set a boundary around the people, saying, 'Take heed not to go up the mountain or to touch the edge of it yourselves; anyone who touches the mountain shall surely be put to death. [13] No hand shall touch them, rather they shall be stoned or shot with arrows; whether animal or human, they shall not live.' When the ram's horn sounds a long blast, they may go up on the mountain." [14] So Moses went down from the mountain to the people. He consecrated the people, and they washed their clothes. [15] And Moses said to the people, "Prepare for the third day; do not go near a woman."

[16] And it was on the third day as morning came there was thunder and lightning, as well as a cloud heavy upon the mountain, and a blast of a trumpet so loud that all the people who were in the camp trembled. [17] Then Moses brought the people out of the camp to meet God. They stationed themselves at the base of the mountain. [18] Now Mount Sinai was in smoke, because the HOLY ONE OF OLD had descended upon it in fire; the smoke ascended like the smoke of a kiln, while the whole mountain shook violently. [19] And it was that as the sound of the trumpet grew stronger and stronger, Moses would speak and God would answer him in thunder.

Psalm 139:7–14

[7] Where can I go from your spirit?
Or where from your presence can I flee?

[8] If I ascend to the heavens, there you are;
if I recline in Sheol, see, it is you!

[9] If I take up dawn's wings
if I settle at the farthest reaches of the sea,

[10] even there your hand shall lead me,
and your right hand shall hold me fast.

¹¹ If I say, "Surely darkness shall cover me,
and night will become light behind me,"

¹² even darkness is not dark to you;
night is as daylight,
for dark is the same as light.

¹³ For it was you who crafted my inward parts;
you wove me together in my mother's womb.

¹⁴ I praise you, for I am awesomely and marvelously made.
Wondrous are your works;
that my soul knows full well.

Acts 2:1 When the day of Pentecost had come, they were all together in the same place. ² And there came suddenly from heaven a sound like the sweeping of a mighty wind, and it filled the entire house where they were sitting. ³ Then there appeared among them divided tongues, as of fire, and one rested on each of them. ⁴ And all of them were filled with the Holy Spirit and they began to speak in other tongues just as the Spirit gave them to speak.

⁵ Now there were dwelling in Jerusalem devout Jews from every nation under heaven. ⁶ Now at this sound the crowd gathered and was confused because each heard them speaking in the native language of each. ⁷ Amazed and astounded, they asked, "Are not all these who are speaking Galileans? ⁸ And how do we hear, each in our own native language? ⁹ Parthians and Medes and Elamites, and those who live in Mesopotamia, Judea and Cappadocia, Pontus and Asia, ¹⁰ Phrygia and Pamphylia, Egypt and the parts of Libya adjacent to Cyrene, and visitors from Rome, both Jews and proselytes, ¹¹ Cretans and Arabs, we hear them speaking in our own tongues about God's deeds of power." ¹² All were amazed and questioning to one another saying, "What does this mean?" ¹³ But others mocking said, "They are filled with new wine."

¹⁴ But Peter, standing with the eleven, raised his voice and addressed them, "Judeans and all who live in Jerusalem, let this be known to you all, and attend to my speech. ¹⁵ For these persons are not drunk as you suppose, it is only the third hour [nine o'clock] in the morning. ¹⁶ No, this is what was spoken through the prophet Joel:

¹⁷ *'In the last days it will be, God declares,*
that I will pour out my Spirit upon all flesh,
and your daughters and your sons shall prophesy,
and your young men shall see visions,
and your elders shall dream dreams.

¹⁸ *Even upon my slaves, both women and men,*
in those days I will pour out my Spirit;
and they shall prophesy.'"

John 4:7 A Samaritan woman came to draw water. Jesus said to her, "Give me a drink." ⁸ Now his disciples had gone to the city to buy food. ⁹ The Samaritan woman said to him, "How are you, a Judean, asking a drink of me, a woman of Samaria?" (Judeans do not share things in common with Samaritans.) ¹⁰ Jesus answered and said to her, "If you knew the gift of God and who is the one telling to you, 'Give me a drink,' you would have asked him, and he would have given you living water." ¹¹ The woman said to him, "Sir, you have no bucket, and the well is deep. From where do you get that living water? ¹² Are you greater than our ancestor Jacob, the one who gave us the well, and with his daughters and sons and his flocks drank from it?" ¹³ Jesus answered and said to her, "Everyone who drinks of this water will thirst again. ¹⁴ But the one who drinks of the water that I will give will never thirst. The water that I will give will become in them a fount of water springing up into eternal life." ¹⁵ The woman said to him, "Sir, give me this water, that I may never thirst or keep coming here to draw water."

¹⁶ Jesus said to her, "Go, call your husband, and come [back] to this place." ¹⁷ The woman answered and said to him, "I have no husband." Jesus said to her, "You said rightly, 'I have no husband.' ¹⁸ For five husbands have you had, and now the one you have is not your husband. What you have said is true!" ¹⁹ The woman said to him, "Sir, I see that you are a prophet. ²⁰ Our mothers and fathers worshiped on this mountain, yet you say in Jerusalem is the place where people must worship." ²¹ Jesus said to her, "Believe me, woman, the hour is coming when neither on this mountain nor in Jerusalem will you worship the Sovereign God. ²² You all worship what you do not know; we worship what we know, for salvation is from the Judeans. ²³ But the hour is coming, and now is, when the true worshipers will worship the Sovereign God in spirit and truth, for these are the worshippers the Sovereign God seeks. ²⁴ God is spirit, and those who worship God must worship in spirit and truth." ²⁵ The woman said to Jesus, "I know that Messiah is coming" (the one who is called Christ). "When he comes, he will proclaim all things to us." ²⁶ Jesus said to her, "I am, the one who is speaking to you."

PROCLAMATION

Text Notes

Verse numbers in Christian Bibles diverge from those (now) in Hebrew and Jewish Bibles. What is Joel 2:28 in Christian texts is 3:1 in Jewish texts such as the JPS *Tanakh* and Hebrew Masoretic Text, as well as other ancient texts including the LXX and Peshitta. "Elders" in verse 28 is an inclusive plural that grammatically includes women; it can represent chronological age or status. The "elders of Israel" served as an administrative layer (Numbers 16:25; Deuteronomy 27:1, 31:9; Joshua 7:6, 8:10; 1 Samuel 4:3). They are only spoken of as a group so it is unclear if there were any women among them. In Joel "elders" is paired with "youth," indicating it should be read chronologically, and therefore I argue, inclusively.

In Exodus 19:10 and 14, "consecrate" or "sanctify" has a reflexive sense; one does it to oneself, primarily through water: bathing and washing one's clothing. Scholars from the rabbinic period (Rashi, Ramban, Ibn Ezra, and Nahmanides) understand Moses's sanctification of the people to be a charge to them to sanctify themselves, hence the JPS, "warn them to stay pure."

The use of the masculine pronoun "him" for both a person who transgresses the boundary of the mountain and the mountain itself means that in verse 13 the referent of "no hand shall touch him/it" is unclear.

In Psalm 139:14, "marvelous" and "wondrous" are the same word. I alternate them for alliteration to give a sense of the poetry.

The author limits the multinational Jews in Jerusalem to "devout men" in Acts 1:5 as though there were no women or none of the women were devout. The androcentric language discounts women living in the city and women who did make the journey. Yet Deuteronomy 16:11 specifies celebrating the festival with daughters and sons and women and men who are enslaved in the household (no mention of wives). Similarly, Peter addresses "men of Judea" but also "all who live in Jerusalem" in 1:14; I treat both as inclusive.

Preaching Prompts

Pentecost, the fiftieth day, marks the end of the Festival of Weeks, *Shavuoth* (from the Hebrew for "weeks"), originally named the festival of "Harvest," see Exodus 23:16; Leviticus 23:15–16. The seven weeks follow from Passover and the festivals are entwined. By the time of the New Testament, it was also understood as the anniversary of the revelation of the Torah on Mount Sinai in Exodus 19. These traditions underlie the outpouring of the Holy Spirit on that selfsame day. The Christian observance is inexorably linked to its ancestral Jewish heritage.

Because of its citation in Acts 2, the primary Pentecost narrative, Joel 2 is regarded as fulfilled in the event in Christian interpretation. In Joel, repeated in Acts, "everyone who calls upon the name of the Holy One shall be saved" (or "rescued") means two very different things in each of those contexts. In the Hebrew Bible salvation, rescue, and deliverance are normally corporate (with few exceptions) and relate to physical safety from threats of violence, war, occupation, and even natural and ecological disasters (as is the case in Joel). In the New Testament, the Church has replaced the nation as the frame of reference; to call upon the name, now of Jesus, is to profess faith in him. It is important to tell the Christian story without erasing or rewriting the story of God's faithfulness to Jewish people or their Israelite ancestors.

Exodus 19 is the story of God's covenant with Israel ratified on Sinai with God present in veiled majesty. The language is by turns inclusive and exclusive, inviting reflection on who we understand to be part of and to represent the people of God. The traditional language for Israel, "the sons" or "children of Israel," is both andro-centric and inclusive. In verse 8 the people "all" answer, meaning women and men; children would not be subject to a legal agreement like the covenant. ("Children" in the commandments refers to adult children in relation to their parents.) "People" is inclusive and yet is sometimes used as though men are the only ones who count; in verse 15 Moses tells the "people" not to approach women, presumably for sex. In this construction women are not "people." Perhaps more disturbing, Moses *adds* this line to God's instructions and receives no rebuke. (Compare God's directive in verses 10–13 with those of Moses.) The attempts of Moses and his writers notwithstanding, God appears to all the women, children, and men of Israel. Though earlier in Exodus the people see God regularly in the alternating pillars of cloud and fire, God's appearance in verse 15 is perhaps closer than the front of their vanguard and much more dramatic with the addition of thunder and lightning and the sound of God's voice.

Who experiences the touch of the Holy Spirit in Acts 2? Who are the "they"? If they are the upper room community, then they are Mary the mother of Jesus and other unnamed women along with the eleven remaining apostles (Acts 1:13–14), plus a newly elected apostle (who will immediately disappear), verses 23–26. "They" may also refer to the larger group of one hundred and twenty in the following verse. An intriguing possibility reads the two together: Mary and an undisclosed number of women together with the twelve apostles constituted the one hundred and twenty. This might explain why Peter chooses Joel to explain the phenomenon, because of its explicit inclusivity.

The *Samarians* were the inhabitants of the northern monarchy of Israel who ultimately fell to Assyria and were largely deported. The land was repopulated with other conquered peoples and their descendants became known as *Samaritans* (see 2 Kings 17:24–34). Judeans held them in low esteem because of their mixed heritage to which they attributed the differences between their worship traditions. Notably, the Samaritan Pentateuch is the entirety of their Bible; nothing else is canonical, which remains the case for Samaritan Jews in the present. (Ἰουδαίοις should be understood as "Judean" in opposition to Samaritan, as both communities are Jewish.) The dispute about the mountain in John 4:20–22 is rooted in one of the many differences between the Samaritan and Judean Torahs: Whether the mountain in Deuteronomy 27:4 on which Joshua (8:30) later built an altar is Ebal (Judeans) or Gerazim (Samaritans). As a result, the Samaritan temple was built on Mt. Gerizim, the "this mountain" of John 4:22. Palestinian Samaritan Jews continue to worship on the mountain, the temple long destroyed by the Romans in 70 CE.

In John 4:12 the woman mentions Jacob and his children (or sons) which I have made explicitly inclusive given that Jacob had an unknown number of daughters, including one named Dinah, among his thirty-three children (see Genesis 37:55, 46:15).

PENTECOST PRINCIPAL SERVICE

Acts 2:1–17 (or Isaiah 44:1–8); Psalm 104:1–4, 10–15, 27–30;
Romans 8:14–17, 22–27; John 14:8–17

Acts 2:1 When the day of Pentecost had come, they were all together in the same place. ² And there came suddenly from heaven a sound like the sweeping of a mighty wind, and it filled the entire house where they were sitting. ³ Then there appeared among them divided tongues, as of fire, and one rested on each of them. ⁴ And all of them were filled with the Holy Spirit and they began to speak in other tongues just as the Spirit gave them to speak.

⁵ Now there were dwelling in Jerusalem devout Jews from every nation under heaven. ⁶ Now at this sound the crowd gathered and was confused because each heard them speaking in the native language of each. ⁷ Amazed and astounded, they asked, "Are not all these who are speaking Galileans? ⁸ And how do we hear, each in our own native language? ⁹ Parthians and Medes and Elamites, and those who live in Mesopotamia, Judea and Cappadocia, Pontus and Asia, ¹⁰ Phrygia and Pamphylia, Egypt and the parts of Libya adjacent to Cyrene, and visitors from Rome, both Jews and proselytes, ¹¹ Cretans and Arabs, we hear them speaking in our own tongues about God's deeds of power." ¹² All were amazed and questioning to one another saying, "What does this mean?" ¹³ But others mocking said, "They are filled with new wine."

¹⁴ But Peter, standing with the eleven, raised his voice and addressed them, "Judeans and all who live in Jerusalem, let this be known to you all, and attend to my speech: ¹⁵ For these persons are not drunk as you suppose, it is only the third hour [nine o'clock] in the morning. ¹⁶ No, this is what was spoken through the prophet Joel:

¹⁷ *'In the last days it will be, God declares,*
that I will pour out my Spirit upon all flesh,
and your daughters and your sons shall prophesy,
and your young men shall see visions,
and your elders shall dream dreams.
¹⁸ *Even upon my slaves, both women and men,*
in those days I will pour out my Spirit;
and they shall prophesy.'"

Isaiah 44:1 Hear now, Jacob [Rebekah's child], my slave,
Israel whom I have chosen!

² Thus says the WELLSPRING OF LIFE who made you,
   who shaped you in the womb and will help you:
   Fear not, Jacob [Rebekah's son], my slave,
   Jeshurun whom I have chosen.
³ For I will pour water upon thirsty soil,
   and streams upon the dry ground;
   I will pour my spirit upon your descendants,
   and my blessing on your offspring.
⁴ They shall spring up in green [places],
   like willows by flowing waters.
⁵ This one will say, "I am GOD'S,"
   that one will name the name of Jacob,
   another will write on their hand, "This belongs to GOD,"
   and adopt the name of Israel.
⁶ Thus says the AGELESS GOD, the Sovereign of Israel,
   and Israel's Redeemer, the COMMANDER of heaven's legions:
   I am the first and I am the last;
   apart from me there is no god.
⁷ Who is like me? Let them proclaim it,
   let them declare it and set it out before me.
   Who like me from old has laid out things which are coming?
   Let them declare to us what will come.
⁸ Fear not and be not afraid;
   have I not from old told you and declared it?
   You all are my witnesses!
   Is there any god besides me?
   There is no rock; I know not one.

Psalm 104:1–4, 10–15, 27–30

¹ Bless the FOUNT OF LIFE, O my soul.
   MOTHER OF ALL, my God, you are very great.
   You don honor and majesty,
² Wrapped in light as a garment,
   you stretch out the heavens like a tent-curtain.
³ She who lays on the waters the beams of her upper chambers,
   she who makes the clouds her chariot,
   she is the one who rides on the wings of the wind.
⁴ She is the one who makes the winds her celestial messengers,
   fire and flame her ministers.

10 She is the one who makes springs gush forth in the torrents;
    they flow between the hills.
11 They give drink to every wild animal;
    the wild donkeys slake their thirst.
12 By the torrents the birds of the heavens dwell;
    among the branches they give voice.
13 She is the one who waters the mountains from her high chambers;
    the earth is satisfied with the fruit of your work.
14 She is the one who makes grass to grow for the cattle,
    and vegetation for human labor,
    to bring forth food from the earth,
15 and wine to make the human heart rejoice,
    with oil to make the face shine,
    and bread to sustain the human heart.
27 All of these hope in you
    to provide their food in due season.
28 You give it to them, they glean it;
    you open your hand, they are well satisfied.
29 You hide your face, they are dismayed;
    when you collect their breath, they die
    and to their dust they return.
30 You send forth your spirit, they are created;
    and you renew the face of the earth.

Romans 8:14 Now as many as are led by the Spirit of God are daughters and sons of God. ¹⁵ For you all did not receive a spirit of slavery to fall again into fear, but you have received a spirit of adoption through which we cry, "Abba! Father!" ¹⁶ It is that same Spirit who bears witness with our spirit that we are daughters and sons of God. ¹⁷ And if daughters and sons, then heirs, heirs of God and heirs with Christ, if it is true that we suffer with Christ so that we may also be glorified with Christ.

¹⁸ I consider that the sufferings of this present time are not worth comparing with the glory about to be revealed to us. ¹⁹ For the creation waits with eager longing for the revealing of the daughters and sons of God; ²⁰ for the creation was subjected to futility, not of its own will but by the will of the one who subjected it, in hope ²¹ that the creation itself will be set free from its bondage to decay and will obtain the freedom of the glory of the daughters and sons of God. ²² We know that the whole creation has been groaning in labor pains until now; ²³ and not only the creation, but we ourselves, who have the first fruits of the Spirit, groan inwardly while we wait for adoption, the redemption of our bodies. ²⁴ For in hope we were saved. Now hope that is seen is not hope. For who hopes for what is seen? ²⁵ But if we hope for what we do not see, we wait for it with patience.

26 Likewise the Spirit helps us in our weakness; for we do not know how to pray as is necessary, but that very Spirit intercedes with sighs too deep for words. 27 And God, who searches the heart, knows what is the mindset of the Spirit, because the Spirit intercedes for the saints according to the will of God.

John 14:8 Philip said to Jesus, "Rabbi, show us the Father, and we will be content." 9 Jesus said to him, "Have I been with all of you all this time, Philip, and you still do not know me? The one who has seen me has seen the Father. How can you say, 'Show us the Father'? 10 Do you not believe that I am in the Father and the Father is in me? The words that I speak to you I do not speak on my own; but the Father who dwells in me does the works of God. 11 Believe me that I am in the Father and the Father is in me; but if not, then believe because of the works themselves. 12 Very truly, I tell you all, the one who believes in me will also do the works I do and even will do greater works than these, because I am going to the Father. 13 And whatever you all ask in my name I will do, so that the Father may be glorified in the Son. 14 If you all ask me anything in my name, I will do it.

15 "If you love me, you will keep my commandments. 16 And I will ask the Father, and God will give you another Advocate, to be with you forever. 17 This is the Spirit of truth, whom the world cannot receive, because it neither sees nor knows the Spirit. You know the Spirit, because the Spirit abides with you, and the Spirit will be in you.

PROCLAMATION

Text Notes

See the discussion of the Acts 2 text in the readings for the Pentecost Vigil/Early Service.

Jeshurun, in Isaiah 44:2, is something of a pet name for Israel from Deuteronomy (see verses 32:15; 33:5, 26). In verse 4 there is a missing noun to describe the site of flourishing; I have supplied "places."

Psalm 104 switches between second and third person as is common in the genre. Verses 14–15 use the word that means both bread and food in general in both senses.

In the Hebrew Bible the Spirit of God (and more broadly) is grammatically feminine. This is not easily visible when reading in English. Translators have historically avoided grammatical constructions that would require a pronoun for the Spirit in the First Testament. Rather, they repeat "the spirit" as the perpetual subject. I have adopted that practice for the translation of John 14:17.

In Greek, in the Septuagint and Christian scriptures, the word for "spirit" is neuter, meaning that in the breadth of the scriptures the spirit is anything and everything but masculine. The deliberate choice to render the spirit in masculine terms in Latin texts such as the Vulgate reflects theological commitments apart from the grammar of the texts. If we were to hear Jesus speak John 14:17 in Aramaic, we would most likely hear:

"This is the Spirit of truth, whom the world cannot receive, because it neither sees her nor knows her. You know her, because she abides with you, and she will be in you."

Preaching Prompts

The outpouring of the Holy Spirit on Pentecost marks the dawn of the Church, but it is not the dawn of the Holy Spirit; she births creation, hovering over her newly hatched brood in Genesis, and breathes through the scriptures, celebrated in the final verse of the psalm. Here in Isaiah 44, she is God's promise for coming generations. The God of wind and flame in Psalm 104:4 is the same God, the same Spirit who is the wind and breath of the Pentecostal fire.

Isaiah 44 is significant for its strident monotheism in a largely henotheistic tradition. Henotheism is the worship of one god above others while not denying the existence of the others, i.e., "God of gods," and "choose this day whom you will serve," etc. But in Isaiah 44:8 God says she has never even heard of another god in the rhetoric of her poet-prophet. This is a bold, audacious claim, for the author is not ignorant of the world around her, nor is the God for whom she speaks. Rather, it is both creation and affirmation of a worldview, as is the Pentecost moment.

The psalm is rich with the majesty of creation. And in Romans 8:20 and 22 that same creation waits, longing for us, humanity, to live into the fullness of our glory as the children of God. That same mighty fire swirling spirit pays for us to live up to and into our full potential like the rest of creation, even when we do not know the words to pray. Indeed, language as we understand it is insufficient; the spirit intercedes, advocates, in sounds, sighs, beyond our capacity to interpret. The Gospel promises us that Advocate, Comforter, Intercessor who will be with us forever.

TRINITY SUNDAY

Hosea 11:1–4; Psalm 130:5–8; 131:1–3; 2 Peter 1:16–18; Matthew 28:16–20

Hosea 11

1 When Israel was a child, I loved them,
   and out of Egypt I called my child.
2 They, the Baals, called to them,
   they went out to the Baals;
   they sacrificed and to idols,
   they offered incense.
3 Yet it was I who walked toddling Ephraim,
   taking them by their arms;
   yet they did not know that I healed them.

4 I led them with human ties,
with bonds of love.
I was to them like those
who lift babies to their cheeks.
I bent down to them and fed them.

Psalm 130

5 I wait for the WOMB OF CREATION, my soul waits,
and in her word I hope.
6 My soul keeps watch for the Creator,
more than those who watch for the morning,
more than those who watch for the morning.
7 Israel, hope in the MOTHER OF CREATION!
For with the CREATOR OF ALL there is faithful love,
and with her is abundant redemption.
8 It is she who will redeem Israel
from all their iniquities.

Psalm 131

1 WOMB OF LIFE, my heart is not lifted up,
nor my eyes exalted;
I do not keep company with things
great and too wondrous for me.
2 Rather, I have soothed and quieted my soul,
like a weaned child with her mother;
my soul is like a weaned child within me.
3 Israel, hope in the WELLSPRING OF LIFE
from now until forever.

2 Peter 1:16 For we did not follow sophisticated mythologies when we made known to you all the power and coming of our Redeemer Jesus Christ, rather we had been eyewitnesses of his majesty. 17 For Christ from God the Sovereign received honor and glory, a voice came to him from the Majestic Glory, saying, "This is my Son, my Beloved, with whom I am well pleased." 18 And we ourselves heard this voice that came from heaven, while we were with him on the holy mountain.

Matthew 28:16 Now the eleven disciples went to Galilee, to the mountain to which Jesus sent them. 17 And when they saw him, they bowed down worshipping him; but some doubted. 18 Then Jesus came and said to them saying, "All authority in heaven and on earth has been given to me. 19 Go therefore and make disciples of all nations, baptizing them in the name of the Father and of the Son and of the Holy Spirit, 20 and teaching them to obey everything that I have commanded you. Now look, I am with you always, to the end of the age."

PROCLAMATION

Text Notes

In the first line of Hosea 11, "boy," a very ambiguous term, ranges from prepubescent to young adult and can also represent minor or junior status among adults. The passage moves between conceptions of Israel as a singular collective "boy," to a notion of individuals, "them," in the first two verses. In verse 3, "toddling" renders a verb made out of the word for foot, consistent with the child learning to walk and still being nursed, verse 4. Human "ties" in verse 4 is a pun, on ropes and cords and the bonds of human relationships.

In Psalm 130:8 Israel is a singular entity and their sin is also collective and singular here.

Preaching Prompts

The three-fold way in which God has been traditionally named is male in form (Father and Son) and function (the postbiblical construction of the Holy Spirit as male). This rubric, which seeks to articulate the essential nature and identity of God to be used in worship and prayer, liturgy and preaching, allows men and boys to hear themselves and their pronouns identified with God along with the exclusion and invisibility of women and girls and nonbinary persons. This exclusion is formative for men and boys in casting gender hierarchy from which they benefit in divine terms. For those who do not hear their pronouns invoke their creation as *imago dei* in the language of the Church, trinitarian language and the observance of Trinity remain a sanctified proclamation of male divinity. For this reason, this project offers more ways to name God, drawn from the scriptures.

While the overwhelming majority of God-language is masculine, there remains a significant collection of feminine imagery for and descriptions of God. The description of the soul as a weaned child in Psalm 131:2 invokes an image of God as the mother upon whose breast it rests.

The Epistle writer uses rare language for God, Majestic Glory, in 2 Peter 1:17. (Hebrews uses "the Majesty," on high in 1:3 and in heaven in 8:1.) The Epistle also comes with a healthy caution for those caught up in the Church's often heated, occasionally violent debates over the Trinity, its Persons, and their relationships, hierarchy, and origins. In disputes about "sophisticated" myths or mythologies—and, I add, theologies, philosophies, and church doctrines—the writer turns to their witness to the faith, what they saw and heard. In turn, they pass their testimony down to us.

Matthew 28:19 is the place where what has become the primary Trinitarian formula occurs. (Galatians 4:6 has the same elements but presented discursively: "And because you are children, God has sent the Spirit of God's Son into our hearts, crying, 'Abba! Father!'") While the traditional language will always have a place in the liturgical lexicon, Trinity Sunday offers an opportunity to craft language that draws more widely on the biblical texts and traditions.

Some of mine include:

Sovereign, Savior and Shelter;

Author, Word, and Translator;

Parent, Partner, and Friend;

Majesty, Mercy, and Mystery;

Creator, Christ, and Compassion;

Potter, Vessel, and Holy Fire;

Life, Liberation, and Love.

SEASON AFTER PENTECOST (29)

The Season after Pentecost runs nearly thirty weeks. It is a season focused on the growth of the Church historically and, contemporarily, the growth of her members. This lectionary will focus on the stories of monarchs and monarchies, providing a curriculum through which those who read and preach these texts will engage in consecutive Bible study through Ruth, Samuel, and Kings. Counter to the traditional lectionary, the Hebrew Bible lesson drives the other choices.

PROPER 1 (CLOSEST TO MAY 11)

Ruth 1:1–14; Psalm 80:1–7; 1 Thessalonians 5:12–24; Mark 12:41–44

Ruth 1:1 In the days when the judges judged, it happened that there was a famine in the land, and a man of Bethlehem in Judah went to sojourn in the country of Moab, he and his wife and their two sons. ² And the name of the man was Elimelech and the name of his wife Naomi, and the names of his two sons were Mahlon and Chilion; they were Ephrathites from Bethlehem in Judah. They went into the country of Moab and remained there. ³ Then Elimelech, the husband of Naomi, died, and she was left, she and her two sons. ⁴ They abducted Moabite women for themselves; the name of the one was Orpah and the name of the second, Ruth. And they lived there about ten years. ⁵ They also died, both of them, Mahlon and Chilion, and the woman was left without her two sons and without her husband.

⁶ Then she got up, she and her daughters-in-law and she returned from the country of Moab, for she had heard in the country of Moab that the FAITHFUL ONE had considered God's people and given them food. ⁷ So she set out from the place where she was while there, with her two daughters-in-law, and they journeyed on the road to return to the land of Judah. ⁸ Then Naomi said to her two daughters-in-law, "Go, return, each to your mother's house. May the HOLY ONE deal kindly with you, as you have done with the dead and with me. ⁹ The SAVING GOD grant that you may find security, each in the house of your own husband." Then she kissed them, and they wept aloud. ¹⁰ They said to her, "We will return with you to your people." ¹¹ Then Naomi said, "Turn back, my daughters, why will you go with me? Are there yet sons in my belly that may become your husbands? ¹² Turn back, my daughters, go your way, for I am too old to be with a man. Let me say I have hope and even was with a man tonight and give birth to sons. ¹³ Would you then wait and hope until they were grown? Would you then refrain from marrying? No, my daughters, it has been far more bitter for me than for you, because the hand of the SAVING GOD has turned against me." ¹⁴ Then they wept aloud again. Orpah kissed her mother-in-law, but Ruth clung to her.

Psalm 80:1–7

¹ Shepherd of Israel, pray, hearken,
  you who lead the line of Rebekah like a flock.
  You, enthroned upon the cherubim, pray, shine forth.
² Before Ephraim and Benjamin and Manasseh,
  stir up your might and come to save us!
³ God restore us and let your face shine,
  that we may be saved.
⁴ SOVEREIGN of heaven's vanguard,
  how long will you fume at the prayers of your people?
⁵ You have fed them tears for bread,
  and you have given them tears to drink thrice over.
⁶ You make us the scorn of our neighbors;
  our enemies laugh among themselves.
⁷ God of heaven's vanguard, restore us and let your face shine,
  that we may be saved.

1 Thessalonians 5:12 We appeal to you all, sisters and brothers, to acknowledge those who labor with you all, and lead you all in Christ, and admonish you all. ¹³ Esteem them more than before in love because of their work. Be at peace among yourselves. ¹⁴ Now we urge you, kindred, to admonish the undisciplined, encourage the discouraged, support the weak, be patient with all. ¹⁵ See that none of you repays evil for evil, rather always seek to do good to one another and to all. ¹⁶ Rejoice always. ¹⁷ Pray without ceasing. ¹⁸ In all things give thanks, for this is the will of God in Christ Jesus for you all. [19] Quench not the Spirit. [20] Do not despise the words of women or men who prophesy, [21] rather examine everything. To what is good, hold fast. [22] Avoid every appearance of evil.

[23] May the very God of peace sanctify you all wholly, and may your spirit and soul and body be kept blameless at the coming of our Redeemer Jesus Christ. [24] The one who calls you is faithful and will do this.

Mark 12:41 Now Jesus sat down opposite the treasury and watched the crowd putting money into the treasury. Many rich people put in much. [42] One poor widow came and put in two small Greek copper coins, which together are worth the smallest Roman coin. [43] Then Jesus called his disciples and said to them, "Truly I tell you all, this poor widow has put in more than all those giving to the treasury. [44] For all of them out of their abundance have given but she out of her lack has put in everything she had, her whole livelihood."

PROCLAMATION

Text Notes

The judges (Ruth 1:1) were rulers or governors in addition to resolving disputes and settling claims. They were the de facto leaders of the people. Verse 2 identifies the children as "his," Elimelech's, not "theirs," though Naomi's maternity will be established later in verse 4. As Hebrew does not have specific words for "wife" and "husband," Naomi is Elimelech's "woman" in verse 3 and he is her "man" in verse 4.

Normally "to take" a wife indicates a consensual union through the verb l-q-ch. In Ruth 1:4 the verb is n-s-', which primarily means "lift up"; it indicates abduction here and in other places such as the abduction of the Shiloh virgins in Judges 21:23. "Marriage" and "marry" reflect the Western world rather than the language of the text. There is a word that signifies marriage, b-'-l, which also means to master (the root is the same as Baal and as a noun means "lord" and "master"). It is rarely used, and not at all in Ruth.

In the psalm "the line of Rebekah" replaces "Joseph" in verse 1. The root of "thrice over" in verse 5 shares its form with the number three, see Alter's "triple measure" following the Targum and "three times over" in the CEB.

"Women and men who prophesy" expands "prophet" in 1 Thessalonians 5:20, reflecting the activity of prophets of both genders in both testaments, i.e., Miriam, Deborah, Huldah, Noadiah, Anna, the four virgin daughters of Phillip in Acts 21:9, and the Corinthian women prophets in 1 Corinthians 11:5. (For more on these and others, see my *Daughters of Miriam: Women Prophets in Ancient Israel*.)

The widow put in two *lepta*: the CEB notes observe that a *lepta* was "the smallest Greek copper coin, each worth 1/128 of a single day's pay," and that a *kodrantes* was "the smallest Roman coin, equal in value to two *lepta*."

Preaching Prompts

The theme of faithfulness binds these readings: While Naomi's family has suffered wave after wave of hardships, she has heard a report of God's faithfulness and changed the course of her life trusting in that faithfulness. Similarly, the psalmist trusts in the faithfulness of God. The Epistle and Gospel portray human faithfulness in service of the God who is faithful, those who labor and lead in the early church, and the widow who gives all she has to live on.

A close reading of Ruth reveals many surprises and challenges to the romantic readings common to many; in this way Ruth's story is a fit predecessor to David's story. Ruth and Orpah were trafficked and may not have been well received upon their return home. Interestingly, Orpah and Ruth come from matrilineal, if not matriarchal, households indicated by "mother's house" in 1:8. (Israelite households include both mother's houses and father's house.)

The vulnerability of Naomi and Ruth, and to a lesser degree of Orpah, set the stage for the monarchal epic that marks the golden age of ancient Israel. They are part of a mobile population crossing international conflict-ridden borders in search of bare sustenance, as Moab and Israel were often at war.

Psalm 80 could well be the prayer of someone trying to eke out a life in the borderlands as well as Naomi's prayer for sustenance. Food insecurity was a regular condition for the vast bulk of Israelites; part of the promise of Canaan was that it "flowed milk and honey," making it a paradise of sorts.

Part of the labor of the church in 1 Thessalonians and beyond was relief of the food insecure and otherwise impoverished, like the widow in the Gospel. The poor are yet with us as Jesus said they would be. Women and children account for the majority of those living without adequate housing and food; gay and trans teens are particularly vulnerable to sexual exploitation, violence, and suicide. Contrasting God's faithfulness, these lessons also disclose the reality (and potential for) sexual transactions as a survival mechanism. Extending God's faithfulness, these lessons also reveal the role of the Church and community in meeting the need of our most vulnerable members.

PROPER 2 (CLOSEST TO MAY 18)

Ruth 1:15–22; Psalm 44:1–4, 8, 17, 23–26; Acts 6:1–6; Luke 18:1–8

Ruth 1:15 Naomi said, "Look, your sister-in-law has gone back to her people and to her gods; go back after your sister-in-law." [16] But Ruth said,

> "Do not press me to forsake you
> or to turn back from following you.
> Where you go, I will go,

where you abide, I will abide;
your people shall be my people,
and your God my God.

17 Where you die, I will die,
there will I be buried.
May the HOLY ONE OF OLD do thus and more to me,
if even death parts me from you."

18 When Naomi saw that Ruth had strengthened herself to go with her, she ceased speaking to her. 19 So the two of them traveled until coming to Bethlehem. When they came to Bethlehem, the whole town was buzzing over them; and the women said, "Is this Naomi?" 20 Naomi said to the women,

"Call me not Naomi [Pleasant One],
call me Mara [Bitter One]
for Shaddai [the Breasted One] has greatly embittered me.

21 I went away full,
but the HOLY ONE OF SINAI brought me back empty.
Why call me Naomi?
The HOLY ONE has spoken against me,
and Shaddai [the Breasted One] has brought evil upon me."

22 So Naomi returned with Ruth the Moabite woman, her daughter-in-law, with her; she was the one who came back from the country of Moab. They came to Bethlehem at the beginning of the barley harvest.

Psalm 44:1–4, 8, 17, 23–26

1 God, with our ears have we heard,
our mothers and fathers have told us,
the deeds you did in their days,
in the days of old:

2 You with your own hand displaced nations,
and you planted them;
you afflicted peoples,
and you set free them.

3 For not by their own sword did they inherit the land,
nor did their own arm save them;
for it was your right hand, and your arm,
and the light of your countenance,
for you delighted in them.

4 You are my Sovereign and my God;
you command deliverance repeatedly for the line of Rebekah.

8 In God we glory all the day,
   and give thanks to your Name for all time. *Selah*

17 All this has come upon us,
   yet we have not forgotten you,
   or been false to your covenant.

23 Rouse yourself! Why do you sleep, my ruler?
   Awaken yourself! Do not cast us off forever!

24 Why do you hide your face,
   forgetting our affliction and our oppression?

25 For our necks lay upon the dust;
   our bellies cling to the ground.

26 Raise yourself as our help;
   redeem us for the sake of your faithful love.

Acts 6:1 Now in those days as the number of disciples was multiplying, the Hellenists grumbled against the Hebrews because their widows were being neglected in the daily food distribution ministry. [2] And the twelve called together the multitude of the disciples and said, "It is not right that we should forsake the word of God in order to minister upon tables. [3] Appoint then kindred, seven of whom there is good testimony from among yourselves, full of the Spirit and of wisdom, whom we may task to this need. [4] But we will devote ourselves to prayer and to ministering the word." [5] What they said pleased the whole multitude [of disciples], and they chose Stephen, full of faith and the Holy Spirit, together with Philip, Prochorus, Nicanor, Timon, Parmenas, and Nicolaus, a convert [to Judaism] from Antioch. [6] They had them stand before the apostles, who prayed and laid their hands on them.

Luke 18:1 Jesus told the disciples a parable about the need to pray continually and not be discouraged. [2] He said, "There was a judge in a certain city who neither feared God nor respected people. [3] There was a widow in that city and she came to him continually and saying, 'Grant me justice against my accuser.' [4] And he was not willing for some time; but later he said to himself, 'Though I do not fear God or respect anyone else, [5] yet because this widow persists in troubling me, I will grant her justice, so that she may not ultimately come to violence against me.'" [6] And the Messiah said, "Listen to what the unjust judge says. [7] And will not God grant justice to the elect of God who cry to God day and night? Will God forbear in helping them? [8] I tell you all, God will quickly grant justice to them. And yet, when the Son of Woman comes, will he find faith on the earth?"

PROCLAMATION

Text Notes

In Ruth 1:20 and 21, God is called *Shaddai*, translated as "Almighty" in most mainline translations; yet the root of the word is not "might" or "strength" but arguably "breast," *shad*. Another argument is that Shaddai is related to Akkadian "mountain," or a class of Arabian deities. Feminist scholars have remarked upon the desire of traditionally trained, primarily male, scholars to find an etymology outside of the obvious cognate, breast. What is not disputed is that Shaddai is invoked in contexts where God is promising or providing fertility, such as Genesis 28:3 and 35:11. Genesis 49:25 offers a blessing from "the God of your father, who shall help you; and by Shaddai, who shall bless you with blessings of the heavens above, blessings of the deep that lies below, blessings of breasts (*shadim*) and womb." (*Shadim* is the plural of *shad*.) There is a possibility that the Akkadian cognate "mountain" is also breast imagery with the mountains as breasts (and snow cap as nipple) that nourish the world through their lifegiving water in the desert realm. Bearing these considerations in mind, I translate Shaddai as "Breasted One."

In Psalm 44:4 "the line of Rebekah" stands for "Jacob." In the same verse, "salvation" or "deliverance" is plural, hence "repeatedly." "Ruler" in verse 23 replaces "lord," *adonai*—not the Tetragrammaton. Though *nephesh* generally means "soul" or perhaps better, "life-breath," signifying "life" broadly, it occasionally means "neck" or "throat," the passage through which the life-breath escapes. Here combined with "bellies" it indicates a prostrate person, as in Alter.

Diakonia, "service" and "ministry," includes the care of and provision for widows as a religious duty and the practical mechanics of the task (Acts 6:1–2) and likewise, the ministry of the word (as in verse 4), preaching, and evangelism. In verse 3 *adelphos*, "kindred," can refer to a gender-inclusive or all-male group. They are to select seven men, *andras*, not persons or women.

The "justice" the widow seeks in verse 4 of the Gospel, *ekdikēson*, includes the notion of vengeance; her adversary—one possible translation of *antidikou*—can also be understood as a plaintiff or accuser who has brought legal charges against her. In Luke 18:5 the corrupt judge uses a bit of dramatic hyperbole with the verb *hypōpiazō*, meaning "to blacken the eye." While most translations treat the expression as euphemistic for "wearing [him] out," the BDAG *Greek-English Lexicon of the New Testament and Other Early Christian Literature* lists as its first meaning: "to blacken an eye, give a black eye, strike in the face . . . of a woman who is driven to desperation and who the judge in the story thinks might in the end express herself physically. . . . Hyperbole is stock-in-trade of popular storytelling. Some prefer to understand [*hypōpiazō*] in this pass[age] in [this] sense." In 1 Corinthians 9:27 Paul describes "punishing" (or "pummeling") his body using the same verb.

Preaching Prompts

In the lessons from Ruth, Acts, and Luke, community members meet the needs of those in want of food, shelter, and justice. The psalmist seeks an unresponsive God.

One could imagine Naomi's lament in Ruth 1:20–21 as a response to praying something like Psalm 44, calling on God to rouse herself and meet her needs, reminding her of her previous faithfulness to her people. Ultimately, she finds the help she needs with her home-folk, her kinfolk. Widowhood in Ruth, Acts, and Luke also connects these passages.

While the passage in Acts 6 is ostensibly about a disparity in the treatment of widows in the nascent Jesus-following community based on ethnicity, it presents a perceived disparity in the value of different sorts of ministries, perhaps pitting the food pantry against the pulpit. It is also possible all of the widows are Jewish and the distinction is between Greek-speaking and therefore Hellenized Jewish widows and Aramaic-speaking widows, remembering that Hebrew and Aramaic were not generally distinguished. In his *Yale Anchor Bible* commentary on Luke, Joseph Fitzmyer highlights Paul's use of "Hebrew," *Hebraioi*, as a cultural marker for himself, though he is an apparently prolific Greek speaker. Used this way, the term seems to evoke a sense of keeping to traditional rather than colonized culture and values.

Whether serving food or serving at the eucharistic table is meant is unclear; linguistically, both are possible. In the *Women's Commentary*, Margaret Aymer notes that the "tables" may be a euphemistic reference to banking, considering the concerns of the larger narrative; "tables" were used to manage and administer funds, including the charitable work of the newly formed community, and would have evoked banking to early readers and hearers. Further, widows are more than bereaved wives in the early Christian community; they are official functionaries and yet another reading might be that the disparity was in who gave acts of charity rather than who received. See Bonnie Thurston's *The Widows: A Women's Ministry in the Early Church*.

The decision makers in Acts 6:3 are most likely men, "brothers" who are to choose among themselves, "men" to address the perceived inequity. In so doing, they enshrine another. Acts 9:36 explicitly names Tabitha a disciple; it is unreasonable to imagine she is the only woman disciple known to the author of Luke-Acts. Where are the other women disciples and what do they have to say about the treatment of their sisters? Notably the women who followed Jesus are virtually missing from Acts with the exception of "certain women" in 1:14. This is in sharp distinction to the number of women in Luke who follow, accompany, and support Jesus and serve as eyewitnesses to his death and resurrection. Their rare and precious firsthand testimony seems to have no value to the community that claims to follow Jesus.

Though the scriptures regularly present widows as vulnerable, victims, and potential victims, the widow in Luke 18 demonstrates the persistence and resourcefulness of women to, in womanist parlance, "make a way out of no way" and survive until they can thrive. For an analysis of the stereotypical use of widows and widowhood in Luke-Acts, see Febbie Dickerson's *Luke, Widows, Judges, and Stereotypes*.

PROPER 3 (CLOSEST TO MAY 25)

Ruth 2:1–16; Psalm 112; 1 Timothy 6:17–19; Luke 12:13–21

Ruth 2:1 Now Naomi had a relative through her husband, a warrior-hearted man of worth, from the family of Elimelech, and his name was Boaz. ² And Ruth the Moabite said to Naomi, "Let me go to the field and glean among the ears of grain, behind someone in whose eyes I may find favor." Naomi said to her, "Go, my daughter." ³ And she went, and came and gleaned in the field behind the reapers. As it happened, she happened upon the part of the field that belonged to Boaz, who was from Elimelech's family. ⁴ Then suddenly, Boaz came from Bethlehem. He said to the reapers, "GOD be with you." They answered, "GOD bless you." ⁵ Then Boaz said to his boy stationed over the reapers, "To whom does this girl belong?" ⁶ The boy stationed over the reapers answered, "She is the Moabite, the one who returned with Naomi from the country of Moab. ⁷ She said, 'Please, let me glean and gather among the sheaves behind the reapers.' So, she came, and she has been standing from the morning until now, only resting in the shelter a little."

⁸ Then Boaz said to Ruth, "Have you not heard my daughter? Go not to glean in another field neither leave this one, thus you will cling to my girls. ⁹ Keep your eyes on the field that is being reaped, and follow after them [the girls]. Have I not commanded the boys not to touch you? When you thirst, go to the vessels and drink from what the boys have drawn." ¹⁰ Then she fell on her face and bowed down to the ground, and said to him, "Why have I found favor in your sight, that you would distinguish me, as I am a foreigner?" ¹¹ And Boaz answered and said to her, "It has been told to me, all that you have done for your mother-in-law after the death of your husband, that you have forsaken your mother and father and your native land and came to a people that you did not know before yesterday. ¹² May the HOLY ONE OF OLD reward your works, and may you have a full recompense from the HOLY ONE, the God of Israel, under whose wings you have come for refuge." ¹³ Then Ruth said, "May I continue to find favor in your eyes, my lord, for you have comforted me and have spoken to the heart to your slave woman, and I, I am not one of your slave women."

¹⁴ Boaz said to her when it was time to eat, "Draw near, and eat from this bread, and dip your piece in the vinegar." And she sat beside the reapers, and he handed her some roasted grain; and she ate and was satisfied, and she had some left over. ¹⁵ When Ruth got up to glean, Boaz commanded his boys saying, "She may even glean between the sheaves, and do not humiliate her. ¹⁶ You must also pull out some for her from the bundles, and leave them for her to glean, and do not rebuke her."

Psalm 112

¹ Hallelujah!
  Happy is the woman or man who reveres the FAITHFUL ONE,
  in whose commandments they deeply delight.

² Mighty in the land will be their descendants;
    the generation of the upright will be blessed.
³ Wealth and riches are in their houses,
    and their righteousness endures forever.
⁴ They rise in the darkness as a light for the upright;
    gracious, loving as would a mother, and righteous.
⁵ It is well with the woman or man who is gracious and lends;
    they conduct their concerns with justice.
⁶ For the righteous will never be shaken [this is true] forever;
    they will be remembered forever.
⁷ Of evil tidings they have no fear;
    their hearts are firm, trusting in the WORTHY ONE.
⁸ Their hearts made steady; they will not fear;
    in the end they will look upon their foes.
⁹ They disperse [their resources]; they give to the poor;
    their righteousness endures forever;
    their horn is exalted in honor.
¹⁰ The wicked see and are angry;
    they gnash their teeth and melt;
    the desire of the wicked will be destroyed.

1 Timothy 6:17 Charge the rich of the present age to be not arrogant or to hope in the uncertainty of riches, but rather in God who richly provides us with everything for our enjoyment. ¹⁸ [Charge them] to do good, to be rich in good works, generous, and maintain community. ¹⁹ Thus will they store up for themselves a good foundation for the future so that they may seize the life that is truly life.

Luke 12:13 Someone in the crowd said to Jesus, "Teacher, tell my sibling to divide the inheritance with me." ¹⁴ But Jesus said to him, "Friend, who appointed me a judge or arbitrator over you?" ¹⁵ Then Jesus said to the crowd, "Beware! Be on guard against all kinds of greed; for one's life is not one's abundance of possessions." ¹⁶ Then Jesus relayed a parable to them saying: "A certain rich person produced land crops abundantly. ¹⁷ And the person pondered internally, 'What should I do, for I have no place to store my crops?' ¹⁸ Then that person said, 'This will I do: I will pull down my barns and build larger ones and I will store there all my grain and my goods. ¹⁹ And I will say to my soul, 'Soul, you have many goods laid up for many years; relax, eat, drink, be merry.' ²⁰ But God said to the rich person, 'Fool! This very night your soul will be demanded back from you. And the things you have prepared, whose will they be?' ²¹ So it is with those who store up treasures for themselves but are not rich toward God."

PROCLAMATION

Text Notes

Used for Boaz in Ruth 2:1, *gibor* indicates a man of status, often a warrior; the term is compounded with *chayil,* meaning both warrior and one who holds the values of a warrior, including wealth acquired through military exploits. Boaz will address Ruth as a woman of *chayil* in 3:11. In Proverbs 31, the Queen Mother instructs her son not to give his *chayil* to unworthy women and instructs him on the value of a woman of *chayil*; *chayil* is explicitly martial and refers to armies, e.g., Pharaoh's army throughout Exodus. "Warrior-hearted" encompasses the full range and does not dilute the meaning for women as do many translations such as "worthy woman/wife," "noble," or the infamous, "Who can find a virtuous woman."

In verse 5 and following, the text uses diminutive language, "youth/girl/boy" for Boaz's servants and for Ruth. This is the same language Jeremiah uses when he says, "I am only a boy," in response to God's call in Jeremiah 1:6. There is a pun in verse 8. Boaz tells Ruth to cling to his girls the way she clung to Naomi, using the same verb. In verse 9 Boaz tells Ruth to follow "them," which in this case is feminine plural and refers to the girls and not the boys. God's wings in Ruth 2:12 suggest a mother bird.

In the acrostic psalm 112, in verse 4 the verb *racham* expresses a feeling rooted in the womb, its grammatical root, *rechem*. Generations of male translators render it "to have compassion" or "be merciful," stripping root and referent. Its most iconic uses are for the sex-worker confronted with the possibility of her child being sawn in half surrendering him "because her mother-love burned within her" in 1 Kings 3:25 and the "can a woman forget her nursing child or show no mother-love to the child of her body" in Isaiah 49:15. Verse 6 includes "forever" on each line, though the first is often omitted; the addition of "true" permits its retention and comprehension. Verse 8 ends with model subject "look[ing] upon their foes," with no further description, frustrating translators. I have left it so following the MT, LXX, and Peshitta. Others supply a variety of solutions: NRSV, "in triumph"; JPS "the fall of"; CEB "their enemies' defeat"; Alter "defeat of their enemies." Similarly, in verse 9, what is "dispersed" or "scattered" (like grain) to the poor is unnamed; I supply the generic "resources" for clarity.

The passage from 1 Timothy is a continuous sentence, broken up for ease of reading. "Charge not" from verse 17 applies throughout and is repeated in verse 18 for clarity. The adjective *koinōnikous* in verse 18 connotes community and communication and generosity in community.

Preaching Prompts

These lessons are bound together by themes of wealth and generosity. Boaz uses his largesse to meet Ruth's material needs. In the psalm wealth is a sign of blessing, as is often but not always the case in the scriptures; the one so blessed is deeply generous as a sign of their righteousness and just deeds. Jesus's parable in Luke 12 might well be an excursus on the psalm in reverse; his wealthy exemplar is far from righteous, hoarding his resources and expending capital only in order to horde on a larger scale. The author of the Pastoral Epistle warns of the fleeting nature of material wealth and bids us put our trust in the abundant unfading riches of God.

There is a lot going on in Boaz's field in terms of gender, class, and identity. It is being worked by women and men who due to their social status relative to Boaz are called girls and boys, very much in the way some used to refer to grown men as house boys, also evoking the racist practice of black women and men being called "gal" and "boy" in (and not just) the South. In verse 9, the boys draw water, a caution against stringent notions of women's and men's work. Curiously neither the narrator nor Boaz use the language of slavery; Boaz's boy and girls may be paid workers. Ruth, who does not know their arrangements, calls herself and the women slave-women in 2:13. In 2:9, Boaz tells his boys not to touch Ruth—he says nothing about his girls. A charitable reading says his girls were already off limits, but Ruth was a foreign woman, whom the Israelites tended to view as promiscuous and enticing; she was also hungry, poor, and vulnerable. She may well have been prey without his intervention, which he knew, begging the question if there were other vulnerable women who were not off-limits.

While there are a few wealthy women in the scriptures, those who fund Jesus and the early church, there are even fewer independently wealthy women like the widow Judith. Women described as owning their homes (indicated by "her house") should be considered if not wealthy, then secure in an uncertain world. Examples would include Rahab and Delilah, the former's security achieved through sex-work, the latter unexplained. The woman whose son Elisha raises in 2 Kings 4 is married yet when she flees famine at his word it is "her household," no mention of her husband, and when the famine ends, the king restores "all that was hers, together with all the revenue of the fields from the day that she left the land until now" in 2 Kings 8:6. However, the generic wealthy person in wisdom literature and didactic texts is always male.

These readings provide the necessary if unwelcome opportunity to talk about wealth, class, and gender in our world and in the world of the text and examine our beliefs, budgets, and priorities.

PROPER 4 (CLOSEST TO JUNE 1)

Ruth 3:1–18; Psalm 68:4–11; 2 Corinthians 9:6–13; Luke 8:1–3

Ruth 3:1 Naomi, Ruth's mother-in-law, said to her, "My daughter, am I not seeking respite for you, that will be good for you? 2 Now is not Boaz our kin, with whose girls you have been? Look! He is winnowing barley on the threshing floor tonight. 3 Now bathe and anoint yourself and put on your [best] clothes and go down to the threshing floor; do not make yourself known to the man until he has finished eating and drinking. ⁴ When he lies down, note the place where he lies, and go and uncover his thighs and lie down, and he will tell you what you should do." ⁵ Ruth said to Naomi, "All that you tell me I will do."

⁶ Then Ruth went down to the threshing floor and did just as her mother-in-law commanded her. ⁷ Now Boaz had eaten and drunk and his heart was content, and he went to lie down at the end of the heap [of grain]. Then Ruth came in secret and uncovered his thighs and lay down. ⁸ At midnight the man trembled and turned and right there a woman was lying at his thighs! ⁹ Then Boaz said, "Who are you?" And she said, "I am Ruth, your slave-woman; spread your cloak over your slave-woman, for you are a kin redeemer." ¹⁰ And he said, "May you be blessed by the MOST HIGH, my daughter; your most recent act of fidelity is greater than the first; you have not gone after young men, whether poor or rich. ¹¹ And now, my daughter, fear not; all that you have spoken, I will do for you, for all the assembly of my people know you are a warrior-hearted woman. ¹² And now, it is true that I am a kin redeemer, there is a kin redeemer closer than I. ¹³ Spend the night tonight and when morning comes, if he will redeem you as kin, good; let him redeem you. If he does not want to redeem you as kin, then, as the AGELESS GOD lives, I will redeem you as kin myself. Lie down until the morning."

¹⁴ So Ruth lay at his thighs until morning, but got up before one person could recognize a neighbor for Boaz said [to himself], "Let it not be known that the woman came to the threshing floor." ¹⁵ Then he said, "Bring the cloak you are wearing and hold it out." So she held it and Boaz measured out six helpings of barley, and put it on her back; then he went into the city. ¹⁶ And Ruth came to her mother-in-law and Naomi asked, "Who are you, my daughter?" And she told her all that the man had done for her. ¹⁷ Ruth explained, "He gave these six helpings of barley to me, for he said, 'Do not go back to your mother-in-law empty-handed.'" ¹⁸ She replied, "Wait, my daughter, until you learn how the matter will shake out, for the man will not rest, but will conclude the matter today."

Psalm 68:4–11

⁴ Sing to God, sing praises to her Name;
  exalt her who rides upon the clouds;
  Holy is her Name, rejoice before her!
⁵ Mother of orphans and defender of widows,
  is God in her holy habitation!
⁶ God settles the solitary in a home, bringing prisoners into prosperity;
  while the rebellious shall live in a wasteland.
⁷ God, when you marched before your people,
  when you moved out through the wilderness,
⁸ the earth shook, even the heavens poured down,
  at the presence of God, the One of Sinai,
  at the presence of God, the God of Israel.

9 Rain in abundance, God, you showered abroad;

    when your heritage grew weary you prepared rest.

10 Your creatures found a dwelling in it;

    God, you provided in your goodness for the oppressed.

11 The AUTHOR OF LIFE gave the word;

    the women who proclaim the good news are a great army.

2 Corinthians 9:6 Now hear this: The one who sows sparingly, sparingly will also reap, and the one who sows in abundance, in abundance will also reap. 7 Each one must give as decided in your heart, not out of reluctance or under pressure, for "*God loves a cheerful giver.*" 8 And the power of God is able to grant you all every gift abundantly, so that always having enough of everything, you all may abound in every good work. 9 As it is written,

> "*God scatters generously, and gives to the poor;*
> *God's righteousness endures forever.*"

10 The one who supplies seed to the sower and bread for food will supply and multiply your seed and increase the harvest of your righteousness. 11 Enriched in every way for every kind of generosity which will yield through us thanksgiving to God, 12 for the offering of this ministry does not only supply the needs of the saints but also overflows with many thanksgivings to God. 13 Through the character of this ministry you all glorify God by your obedience to the confession of the gospel of Christ and by the generosity of your companionship with them and with all others.

Luke 8:1 Now after [a woman anointed his feet] Jesus went on through cities and villages, proclaiming and bringing the good news of the reign of God. The twelve were with him. 2 There were also some women who had been cured of evil spirits and infirmities: Mary, called Magdalene, from whom seven demons had gone out, 3 and Joanna, the wife of Herod's steward Chuza, and Susanna, and many others, who provided for them out of their resources.

PROCLAMATION

Text Notes

The text of Ruth uses questions as a narrative device throughout that are often converted to sentences in other translations; KJV tends to preserve the question form (see Judges 4:6 and Ruth 2:8–10). The same expression in Ruth 2:1 means "good for" as well as "good to" you. The word used for the lower extremities in Ruth 3:4 refers to the whole leg and particularly the thighs and genitalia as in childbirth (Deuteronomy 28:57); in Isaiah 7:20 "hair of the feet" refers to pubic hair shaved with other body hair in a ritual of humiliation. All of the slave language in Ruth is Ruth's; the narrator, Boaz, and Naomi all refer to Boaz's agricultural workers as his "girls" and "boys." Ruth refers to them and herself as enslaved (see Ruth 2:3 and 3:9), which is difficult to observe in translations that use "servant" throughout. Perhaps that communicates something about the harshness and desperation of her character's worldview.

The "kin redeemer," *go'el*, is the nearest adult male who bears responsibility for redeeming, or buying back, their hard-up kin from debt slavery and avenging their blood (Leviticus 25:25–26, 48–49; Numbers 35:12; Deuteronomy 19:6, 12). That language is also used for God redeeming Israel and applied to Jesus in the Christian Testament. Ruth's fidelity in 3:10 is what is usually described as "lovingkindness" or "faithful love" when applied to God. Boaz describes Ruth as a "warrior-hearted" woman using the same description that the narrator uses for him in 2:1 (see discussion on Proper 3). In verse 16 Naomi asked Ruth the same question Boaz asked in verse 9, "who are you?" i.e., are you betrothed? Most translations opt for the nonliteral "how is it with you" for the latter. Verses 15 and 17 lack a unit of measure and say simply "six barleys." Similarly, verse 17 lacks "handed," saying merely "empty."

The psalm portion ends with women proclaiming the good news of deliverance using the verbs that will come to mean "proclaim the Gospel" in Hebrew and Greek (the LXX uses *euaggelizo*). Unfortunately, NRSV, RSV, CEB, and KJV obscure that this "company of preachers" is exclusively female.

Second Corinthians 9:7 quotes part of the Greek text of Proverbs 22:8, which differs significantly from the Hebrew: "God blesses a cheerful and generous man." With the exception of "bless/love," it is an exact quote. Verse 9 cites Psalm 112:9, also from the LXX.

Preaching Prompts

These texts portray divine and godly human providence; necessary providence because hunger and lack were regularly the lived experience of the framers of the stories and sometimes of their preservers. God provides for Boaz, Boaz provides for Ruth and through her, Naomi; in the psalm God provides for widows, orphans, and all the creatures of earth. The Epistle calls for the very generosity that Boaz demonstrates. And in the Gospel, Mary Magdalene, Johanna, and Susanna model the generosity that the Epistle commends.

In today's Ruth reading Naomi has Ruth offer herself to Boaz, nominally under the levirate provision where a brother would marry his brother's widow to raise children in his name. Boaz is a more distant relative who will only become eligible when a nearer kinsman passes on the opportunity. One might well wonder what would happen if no relative accepted the responsibility; Ruth and Naomi would likely be indigent and perhaps turn to sex-work with no other options.

Romantic readings of Ruth often ignore Naomi's grooming of her to sexually service Boaz—make herself attractive, wait until he is drunk, uncover his thighs, and do what he tells her—as a survival strategy for them both. Note that once they determine another man has the legal right to wed her, Boaz tells her to lie back down, knowing he has no legal access to her, and tells her to sneak out in the morning when she would have been more visible. It is likely that there was sexual contact between them, which, given Ruth's vulnerable status, is problematic for contemporary readers. The story of Ruth can easily be read as a story of survival sex and draws our attention to the plight of vulnerable, hungry, desperate migrant women.

In the regendered psalm, God is the mother of orphans (fatherless children in Hebrew idiom), protector of widows, and provides homes (families) for the lonely. She is also sovereign of the skies, source of rain, and shepherd of her people. The women who functioned as town criers, proclaiming good news of victory in times of war, proclaim the good news of God's providence.

In 2 Corinthians 9, the Christian community does the work of God in sharing what they have received in abundance abundantly, following the example set by the women who followed Jesus and supported his work. Both the Epistle and the Gospel illustrate that the way of Jesus drew a diversity of followers from different class strata, and they were expected to share their resources.

A final note on the Gospel: the text says the women provided for "them." The women did not just ensure that Jesus was housed and fed and clothed; they bankrolled the entire movement, likely supporting some number of the male disciples. These lessons present women as both beneficiaries and benefactresses and from either pole, members of communities that support one another, financially when necessary. However, it should not be neglected that behind these texts and in the world that receives and reads them, there are many, many individuals and families whose needs are not met by community or kin.

PROPER 5 (CLOSEST TO JUNE 8)

Ruth 4:9–17; Psalm 107:1–9, 19–22;
1 Corinthians 12:14–26; Matthew 5:43–48

Ruth 4:9 Then Boaz said to the elders and all the people, "Today you are witnesses that I am acquiring all that belonged to Elimelech and all that belonged to Chilion and Mahlon from the hand of Naomi. ¹⁰ Also, Ruth the Moabite, the wife of Mahlon am I acquiring for myself as a wife to maintain the dead man's name on his inheritance, to reestablish the name of the deceased on his heritable property, that it may not be cut off from his kin and from the gate of his native place; today you are witnesses."

¹¹ All the women and men who were at the gate, along with the elders, said, "We are witnesses. May the FAITHFUL GOD grant that the woman who is coming into your house be like Rachel and Leah; the two of them built up the house of Israel. May you prosper in Ephrathah

and establish a lineage in Bethlehem; [12] and may your house, through the children that the FOUNT OF LIFE will give you by this young woman, be like the house of Perez, whom Tamar gave birth to for Judah." [13] So Boaz took Ruth as his own for a wife. He came to her and the SOURCE OF LIFE granted her a pregnancy, and she gave birth to a son. [14] Then the women said to Naomi, "Blessed be the FAITHFUL GOD, who has not deprived you this day of next-of-kin; and may the child's name be renowned in Israel! [15] He shall be to you a restorer of life and a provider in your latter years; for your daughter-in-law has given birth to him, she who loves you, she who is more to you than seven sons." [16] Then Naomi took the child and laid him in her bosom, and she fostered him. [17] The neighbor-women gave him a name, saying, "A son has been born to Naomi." They named him Obed; he became the father of Jesse, the father of David."

Psalm 107:1–9, 19–22

[1] Give thanks to SHE WHO IS MAJESTY, for she is good,
   and her faithful love endures forever.
[2] Let the redeemed of SHE WHO SAVES proclaim
   that she redeemed them from the hand of the foe.
[3] And she has gathered them from [all] the lands;
   from the east and from the west, from the north and from the south.
[4] They wandered in the wilderness, in the desert;
   no path to a city fit for settling did they find.
[5] They were hungry and thirsty;
   their souls fainted within them.
[6] Then they cried to SHE WHO HEARS in their trouble,
   and from their distress she delivered them.
[7] And she led them on a straight path
   to a city fit for settling.
[8] Let them give thanks to WOMB OF LIFE for her faithful love
   and her wonderful works for the woman-born.
[9] For she satisfies the thirsty soul
   and the hungry souls she fills with goodness.
[19] They cried to the MOTHER OF ALL in their trouble,
   and she delivered them from their distress.
[20] She sent forth her word and healed them
   and saved them from their pits.
[21] Let them give thanks to the WOMB OF LIFE for her faithful love
   and wonderful works for the woman-born.
[22] Let them sacrifice sacrifices of thanksgiving
   and tell of her acts with shouts of joy.

1 Corinthians 12:14 Now look, the body is not a single part but rather, many. [15] If the foot says, "Because I am not a hand, I am not part of the body," is it then, not of the body? [16] And if the ear says, "Because I am not an eye, I am not part of the body," is it then, not of the body? [17] If the whole body were an eye, where would be the hearing? If the whole body were hearing, where would be the smelling? [18] Thus it is that God has designated the parts of the body, each of them, according to the will of God. [19] If all were a single part, where would be the body? [20] Thus it is that there are many parts, yet one body. [21] The eye cannot say to the hand, "I have no use for you," nor again the head to the feet, "I have no use for you." [22] Rather, on the contrary, the parts of the body that seem to be weaker are indispensable. [23] And those parts of the body that we think dishonorable we clothe with more honor, and our unpresentable parts are treated with more decorum. [24] However our more respectable parts do not need such. Yet God has so composed the body, giving the more honor to the lesser part, [25] that there may be no division within the body, rather that the parts may have the same concern for one another. [26] And if one part suffers, all suffer together with it; if one part is honored, all rejoice together with it.

Matthew 5:43 "You all have heard that it was said, '*You shall love your neighbor* and hate your enemy.' [44] Yet I say to you all: Love your enemies and pray for those who persecute you, [45] so that you may be children of the One in heaven who begot you; for the sun—which belongs to God—rises on the evil and on the good, and God rains on the righteous and on the unrighteous woman or man. [46] For if you all love those who love you, what reward do you have? Do not even the tax collectors do the same? [47] And if you greet only your sisters and brothers, what more are you doing than others? Do not the Gentiles do the same? [48] Be perfect, therefore, as your heavenly Sovereign is perfect.

PROCLAMATION

Text Notes

In Psalm 107:8 and 2, "woman-born" renders the euphemism for humanity, "human children/children (or sons) of men." Son of Woman for the comparable Greek expression communicates the humanness called for in Matthew 8:20.

The choice of "unpresentable parts" in 1 Corinthians 12:23 for *aschēmona* excludes some of its translation options to avoid proclaiming as scripture that any parts of our bodies are "shameful" or "unworthy." The choice of "compose" in verse 24 is an English word play on the "parts" of the body, which parts can also be parts of a musical composition in Greek; the underlying verb means to "mix," "join" or, "unite." Also in verse 24, NRSV's choice of "dissension" gives the false impression that the text speaks against disagreement; "division" better captures *schisma*, schism, see CEB and KJV.

Preaching Prompts

The story of Ruth functions as an introduction to the story of David; it is also a story of community, relationship, and cultural values: God's relationship with Israel results in the provisioning of Bethlehem and is extolled in the psalm. Naomi returns to her community in her time of need. Ruth's relationship with Naomi grows closer while Orpah seeks the comfort of her community. And it is as a member of the same community that Boaz enters into a new relationship with Ruth that will see her and Naomi provided for. In the Epistle the God of creation also creates community, and the God who provides for creation expects this beloved community to provide and care for one another. As is often the case, Jesus expands our circles of care and concern beyond our own community and those we love to those we do not like and do not want to love.

Jesus quotes the common wisdom which is a combination of the command to love your neighbor (from Leviticus 19:18) and its interpretive corollary, hate your enemies, cited together as an equally authoritative text. This is a useful reminder that interpretations can be as authoritative as primary texts, often holding the weight of scripture. As is the case for Jesus in Matthew before his transforming encounter with the Canaanite mother, his language here about the Gentiles presents them as negative examples in stereotypical terms, an opportunity to discuss the ways in which human biases are present in the text. The call to love enemies is also a call to love those from whom we are separated by societal and cultural structures like race, class, and gender; "enemies" are just the most extreme example of the radical limitlessness of our love.

PROPER 6 (CLOSEST TO JUNE 15)

1 Samuel 1:1–6, 9–18; Psalm 113; Colossians 4:10–17; Matthew 15:21–28

1 Samuel 1:1 Now there was a certain man of Ramathaim, a Zuphite from the hill country of Ephraim, whose name was Elkanah son of Jeroham son of Elihu son of Tohu son of Zuph, an Ephraimite. ² He had two wives; the name of the one was Hannah, and the name of the second, Peninnah. Peninnah had children, but Hannah had no children.

³ Now this man went up year by year from his town to worship and to sacrifice to the SOVEREIGN of heaven's vanguard at Shiloh; there the two sons of Eli, Hophni and Phinehas, were priests of the HOLY ONE OF OLD. ⁴ And it was, on the day Elkanah sacrificed, he would give to his wife Peninnah and to all her daughters and her sons portions [of the sacrifice]. ⁵ But to Hannah he gave a double portion, because he loved her, though the WOMB OF LIFE had closed her womb. ⁶ Her rival used to provoke her severely, to irritate her, because the WELLSPRING OF LIFE had closed her womb.

⁹ After they had eaten and drunk at Shiloh, Hannah rose and presented herself before the HOLY ONE OF OLD. Now Eli the priest was sitting on the seat beside the doorposts of the

temple of the HOLY ONE. [10] Hannah's soul was embittered, and she prayed to the SOURCE OF LIFE, and she wept profusely. [11] And she vowed a vow and said, "HOLY ONE of heaven's legions, if only you would truly look on the affliction of your slave-woman, and remember me, and not forget your slave-woman, but will give to your slave-woman man-seed, then I will place him before you as a nazirite all the days of his life. He shall not drink wine or strong drink, and a razor shall not go upon his head."

[12] And it was as she increased praying before the FAITHFUL ONE, Eli was observing her mouth. [13] Now Hannah, she was speaking in her heart, only her lips moved; her voice was not heard. So, Eli took her for a drunkard. [14] And Eli said to her, "How long will you remain drunk? Put your wine away woman—away from you!" [15] Then Hannah responded and said, "No, my lord, I am a woman whose spirit has hardened; I have not drunk either wine or strong drink; I have been pouring out my soul before the GOD WHO HEARS. [16] Do not regard your slave as a worthless woman, for I have been speaking from my great grief and vexation all this time." [17] Then Eli answered and said, "Go in peace; the God of Israel grant the petition you have made to God." [18] And Hannah said, "May your slave-woman find favor in your eyes." Then the woman went on her way to her quarters, ate and drank with her husband, and her countenance was sad no longer.

Psalm 113

1 Hallelujah! Give praise, you slaves of the MOST HIGH;
   praise the Name of the WISDOM OF THE AGES.
2 Let the Name of the HOLY ONE OF OLD be blessed,
   from this time forth forevermore.
3 From the rising of the sun to its going down
   the Name of the AUTHOR OF LIFE is praised.
4 SHE WHO IS WISDOM is high above all nations,
   and her glory above the heavens.
5 Who is like the MOTHER OF ALL our God, who sits enthroned on high,
   yet bends down to behold the heavens and the earth?
6 She takes up the weak out of the dust
   and lifts up the poor from the ashes.
7 She sets them with the rulers,
   with the rulers of her people.
8 She makes the woman of a childless house
   to be a joyful mother of children.

Colossians 4:10 Aristarchus my fellow prisoner greets you all, so too Mark the cousin of Barnabas, about whom you have received instructions, if he comes to you, welcome him. [11] And Jesus who is called Justus [greets you]. These of the circumcised are my only coworkers for the realm of God, and they have been a comfort to me. [12] Epaphras, who is one of you, a slave of the Messiah Jesus, greets you all. He is always fighting for you all in his prayers, so that you may stand mature and fully assured in everything that is the will of God. [13] For I testify for him that he has [done] much hard labor for you all and for those in Laodicea and in Hierapolis. [14] Luke, the beloved physician, and Demas greet you. [15] Give my greetings to the sisters and brothers in Laodicea, and to Nympha and the church in her house. [16] And when this has been read among you all, make it so that it is read in the Laodicean church; and you all read the one from Laodicea. [17] And say to Archippus, "See that the ministry you have received in the Messiah, that you fulfill it."

Matthew 15:21 Jesus left the place [where he had been teaching] and went back to the regions of Tyre and Sidon. [22] Just then a Canaanite woman from that area came out and shouted, "Have mercy on me, Sir, Son of David; my daughter is badly demon-possessed." [23] But Jesus did not answer her a word. Then his disciples came and implored him, saying, "Send her away, for she keeps shouting after us." [24] Now Jesus answered, "I was not sent to any except the lost sheep of the house of Israel." [25] But she came and knelt before Jesus, saying, "Rabbi, help me." [26] Then Jesus said, "It is not good to take the children's food and throw it to the dogs." [27] But she said, "Yes, Rabbi, yet the dogs eat the crumbs that fall from their lord's table." [28] Then Jesus answered her, "Woman, great is your faith! Let it be for you as you wish." And her daughter was healed that moment.

PROCLAMATION

Text Notes

In verse 5 in Hebrew, Hannah's portion is a "nose" portion with "double" being construed from context. The alternate equally common meaning for *apayim*, "anger," is not helpful here.

The Dead Sea Scrolls (DSS) versions of 1–2 Samuel offer a significant number of corrections to the text, most of which occur in the NRSV—look for the letter Q in the translation notes at the bottom of the text, present in every NRSV Bible. (Indeed, the NRSV is the first scholarly post–DSS discovery Bible and includes some 100 corrections.) The DSS are authoritative because they are the oldest most complete manuscripts of the scriptures that have ever been found.

I follow the DSS, including "nazirite," "all the days of his life," and "he shall not drink wine or strong drink" in 1:11 from scroll 4QSam^a. In verse 11 Hannah asks for the gender-specific "seed of men," here "man-seed," elsewhere "man-child." I also include "she presented herself to the Holy One" in verse 9 and "she went to her quarters, ate and drank with her husband" from the LXX, which shares content with the DSS here.

The presence of "Nympha and the church in her house," attested in what is the oldest most authoritative manuscript that includes the passage, raised questions for early curators of the scriptures, which were not resolved by the change of her name to a male form in later manuscripts, including the *Textus Receptus* used for the KJV where she has been masculinized. The purported masculine form, *Nymphas*, does not exist in the historical or literary record, while Nympha occurs some sixty times. (See Ross Kraemer's entry in *Women in Scripture: A Dictionary of Named and Unnamed Women in the Hebrew Bible, the Apocryphal/Deuterocanonical Books, and the New Testament*.) That Colossians also calls for submissive women/wives has led to further speculation, including that Nympha was a widow (see the *Wisdom Commentary* on Colossians by Cynthia Briggs Kittredge and Claire Miller Colombo).

In Matthew 15:23, "send her away" is "loose her," i.e., "cut her loose." Early church interpreters read that to mean the disciples urged Jesus to set her free of the demon, rehabilitating the image of the disciples, though Jesus refuses their request and hers. However, the term also has the sense of "divorce" and therefore, "send away." In verse 26, Jesus infamously uses the word "dogs" (actually "little dogs") in analogy to the woman and her daughter. Many readers hear the word "bitch," female dog, on the lips of Jesus and are disturbed, if not horrified. Others work to ameliorate the comparison to an unclean animal that was used to indicate contempt in the Hebrew Scriptures, see 1 Samuel 17:43; 2 Samuel 3:8; 2 Kings 8:14; Proverbs 26:11. In verse 28, that "moment" is that "hour."

Preaching Prompts

These texts focus on women and their households; in three, children (or their lack) characterize those homes, not unexpected in the world of the Hebrew Scriptures. However, in the Epistle, the members of Nympha's household are the members of the church in her home, a church that surely she leads.

The first lesson proffers Hannah and her desperate plea for a child. The many biblical accounts of miraculous pregnancies that do not conform to the lived experience of most people can be difficult for women with unwelcome infertility. Peninnah is often demonized in the text and interpretive tradition. It's worth thinking about the hurt Penninah felt as a woman who had fulfilled society's expectation, yet was unloved and unfavored. Note: In the ancient Israelite sacrificial system most offerings (except whole burnt offerings) were split between God and the giver. Select parts could only be offered to God with designated portions for the giver and his or her family; women and men made these offerings.

Psalm 113 shares with Hannah's hymn and Mary's Magnificat the language of reversal, lifting the poor and weak/needy (Psalm 113:7–8; 1 Samuel 2:7–8; Luke 1:52–53). One of the Magnificat's reversals seems to speak more to Hannah than to Mary: a mother of many who is forlorn like Peninnah and a previously barren woman who gives birth like Hannah. The psalm affirms that God provides infertile women with children, equated to a proper "home," and some suggest that it was prayed or recited by women living with infertility. There is no broad consensus as to whether the psalm pre- or postdates Samuel. It will be important to affirm dependence on God without demeaning child-free homes and families.

Nympha was most likely Greek, due to her Greek name (young woman or bride or sister-in-law) and due to Paul—commonly agreed upon as the author—stipulating the previous group of addresses as Jewish. The congregation in her home points to her autonomy; it is her home and she is not identified as a widow. Given her support of the church which likely extends beyond providing it a home, she is undoubtably of means. Nympha is clearly the leader of that church; Paul's letter is to her among others. She is a witness to the diversity and inclusivity of the church from its birth even as some were inscribing hierarchy upon it.

Jesus sought respite by going to the shore. In a shocking scene, Jesus denies a desperate woman and her child the help and healing for which the mother begs, bearing uncomfortable witness to the humanity of Jesus in an unwelcome way. Jesus seems to display ethnocentric bias—a challenging reading for those who understand having and acting on bias to be sinful, which would be incompatible with most Christologies. Yet all of Jesus's comments about Gentiles in Matthew to this point are negative: "Do not even the Gentiles do the same?" (5:47); "do not heap up empty phrases as the Gentiles do" (6:7); "it is the Gentiles who strive for all these things" (6:32); "let such a one be to you as a Gentile and a tax collector" (18:17) and Jesus initially excludes Gentiles from receipt of the gospel: "Go nowhere among the Gentiles, and enter no town of the Samaritans" (10:5), until this conversation. Not only is her daughter healed, but Jesus will withdraw the ethnic limitations he placed on the gospel and send his disciples "into all the world."

The age of the demon-possessed daughter (or what malady her possession might represent) is unknown; it may be useful to allow for the possibilities of the daughter as both a child and an adult and see how each shapes the preaching.

PROPER 7 (CLOSEST TO JUNE 22)

1 Samuel 1:19–28; Psalm 69:10–20, 30–33; Acts 2:43–47; Matthew 15:29–39

1 Samuel 1:19 Hannah and Elkanah rose early in the morning and bowed down and worshiped before the HOLY ONE OF OLD; then they turned back and went to their house at Ramah. Elkanah knew his wife Hannah, and the HOLY ONE remembered her. [20] And it was with the turning of the days that Hannah conceived and gave birth to a son. She called his name Samuel (God hears), for she said, "From the GOD WHO HEARS have I asked him."

²¹ Now the man Elkanah went up along with his whole household to offer to the HOLY ONE the yearly sacrifice, and on account of a vow. ²² Yet Hannah did not go up, for she said to her husband, "[Not] until the child is weaned, then will I bring him, that he may be seen in the presence of the MOST HIGH and remain there perpetually. I will present him as a nazirite in perpetuity, for all the days of his life." ²³ Her husband Elkanah said to her, "Do what is best in your eyes, stay until you have weaned him. May the FAITHFUL GOD establish the words of your mouth." So, the woman remained and nursed her son until she weaned him. ²⁴ And she took him up with her after she had weaned him along with a three-year-old bull, an ephah of flour, and a jug of wine. Hannah brought him to the house of the EVER-LIVING GOD at Shiloh and the boy was just a little boy. ²⁵ Then they slaughtered the bull, and they brought the boy to Eli. ²⁶ And Hannah said, "My lord! As you live, my lord, I am the woman, the one who was standing beside you in this [place] to pray to the GOD WHO HEARS. ²⁷ For this boy I prayed; and the FAITHFUL GOD gave me my asking, what I asked from God. ²⁸ Therefore have I bequeathed him to the GRACIOUS GOD; all his days will he be a bequest to the GOD WHOSE NAME IS HOLY."

So she left him there and she bowed down and worshipped the FAITHFUL GOD.

Psalm 69:10–21, 30–33

¹⁰ Now I humbled my soul with fasting,
　　and they reviled me.
¹¹ And I wore sackcloth as my clothing,
　　and I became to them a byword.
¹² They speak against me, they who sit in the city gates,
　　while the drunkards make songs [about me].
¹³ Yet I make my prayer to you, the WISDOM OF THE AGES.
　　At a favorable time,
　　God, in the wealth of your faithful love, answer me,
　　with your certain salvation.
¹⁴ Rescue me from the mire,
　　and let me not sink;
　　let me be delivered from my enemies
　　and from the deep waters.
¹⁵ Let not the flood waters overwhelm me,
　　let not the Deep swallow me up;
　　let not the Pit close its mouth over me.
¹⁶ Answer me, GRACIOUS GOD, for your faithful love is good;
　　according to the wealth of your maternal love, turn to me.
¹⁷ Do not hide your face from your slave,
　　for I am in distress; hurry to answer me.
¹⁸ Draw near to my soul and redeem her,
　　on account of my enemies, deliver me.

¹⁹ Indeed, you know of my reviling,
and my shame and my disgrace;
all my adversaries are before you.
²⁰ Reviling has broken my heart,
and I am despair.
I looked for consolation, but there was none;
and for comforters and I found none.
³⁰ I will praise the name of God with song;
I will magnify her with thanksgiving.
³¹ This will please the CREATOR OF ALL more than an ox
or a bull with horns and hooves.
³² Let the oppressed see it and be glad;
you who seek God, let your hearts flourish.
³³ For the FAITHFUL GOD hears the needy,
and those who belong to her and are imprisoned,
she does not despise.
³⁴ Let the heavens and earth praise her,
the seas and everything that moves in them.

Acts 2:43 Awe came upon everyone, because many wonders and signs were being done by the apostles. ⁴⁴ All who believed were as one and held all things in common. ⁴⁵ They sold their possessions and property and distributed the proceeds to all, as any had need. ⁴⁶ Daily they continued with the same purpose in the temple; they broke bread at home and ate their food with gladness and simplicity of heart. ⁴⁷ They praised God and had the gratitude of all the people. And day by day the Holy One added to their number those who were being saved.

Matthew 15:29 After Jesus had left [Tyre and Sidon], he went by the Sea of Galilee, and he went up the mountain, sitting down there. ³⁰ Great crowds came to him, bringing with them disabled, blind, and mute people, and people missing body parts along with many others. Then they put them at his feet, and he healed them ³¹ so that the crowd was amazed when they saw mute people speaking, people missing body parts made whole, disabled people walking, and blind people seeing. And they praised the God of Israel.

³² Then Jesus called his disciples to him and said, "I have compassion for the crowd, because they have stayed with me for three days now and have nothing to eat, and I do not want to send them away hungry, for they might collapse on the road." ³³ The disciples said to him, "Where are we to get so much bread in the desert as to feed so great a crowd?" ³⁴ Jesus asked them, "How many loaves do you have?" They said, "Seven, and a few small fish." ³⁵ Then ordering the crowd to sit down on the ground, ³⁶ he took the seven loaves and the fish, and giving thanks he broke them and gave them to the disciples; the disciples gave them to the crowds. ³⁷ And all of them ate and were filled, and they took up the abundance

of fragments, seven baskets full. [38] Those who ate were women and children besides four thousand men. [39] Then sending away the crowds, he got into the boat and went to the region of Magadan.

PROCLAMATION

Text Notes

According to Targum Onqelos, Hannah worships on her own in 1 Samuel 1:19, without her husband. She names her child in accordance with the broader practice in ancient Israel; the episodes where God or a father name a child should be viewed as exceptions. Hannah's participation in the slaughter of her offering is signaled by the "they" in verse 25; the exact nature of that participation is unclear. I chose "GOD WHO HEARS" to render the divine name in 1 Samuel 1:20 to reiterate the etymology of Samuel's name. Some scholars argue that the etymology belongs more properly to Saul whose name stems from the verb for "to ask"; the "bequest" of verse 28 is the same spelling and pronunciation of Saul, *Shaul*. Hannah's last line in verse 22, "I will present him . . ." comes from the Qumran scroll 4QSamª and is not present elsewhere. According to the older reading supported by the LXX, in verse 23 Elkanah prays that God would establish the words of *Hannah's* mouth; the Masoretic Text has "the words of God's mouth." The same scroll corrects "three bulls" in verse 24 to "three year-old bull." The end of verse 24 is simply the word for "boy" or "youth" repeated twice; the meaning must be reconstructed and construed from context. I use "bequeath/bequest" in verse 28 to mirror the continuing verb "ask" now in a causative form that indicates fulfilling a request. The very last line occurs in two forms: "They bowed down and worshipped God there" from the MT and "she left him there and worshipped" from Qumran.

In verse 12 of the psalm, the words "about me" are lacking at the end of the verse but clearly implied. The "Deep" and the "Pit" in verse 15 are legendary sites associated with death, in some ways parallel to Sheol. In verse 16 God's maternal love is love that emanates from and shares the same root as the womb. The grammatical gender of the soul is feminine, hence my "Draw near to my soul and redeem her" in verse 18 (along with the Targum and LXX) counter to the first person in NRSV, CEB, and JPS. Hooves in verse 31 are the euphemistic "dividers."

In Matthew 15:30–31 I have changed "the mute, the blind" to "mute people, blind people," because people are not their disabilities. In verse 32 "compassion," *splagchnizomai*, emanates from the *splagchnon*, "inner organs," similar to the way mother-love comes from the womb. I have inverted the order of the diners in verse 38, removing the women and children from the ancillary position.

Preaching Prompts

God provides. God provides the child for which Hannah longs, a common biblical trope with little correlation in the scripture reading world, making this a difficult text to receive as exemplar. In the psalm that reads as though Hannah penned it herself, God provides emotional support and relief for the oppressed, including oppressive interpersonal dynamics; a reminder that not all violence and conflict is physical. In Acts 2 the community that walks the Way of Jesus provides for the needy in their midst, following the example of Jesus in today's Gospel.

The healings in today's Gospel immediately follow the healing of the Canaanite woman or girl at her mother's request. Word has gotten out. Has she become an evangelist in the space between two verses? Jesus has traveled back from the shore to an unidentified mountain near the Sea of Galilee; the sea was a bit over twenty miles away as the crow flies. While they are in Galilee, there is no telling from whence the people have come. Jesus sits as though for teaching yet is unclear whether that was his initial purpose; they were there for three days, verse 32, with no mention of teaching at all. Jesus seems to have simply made himself available for whatever needs the people had. Three days at the feet of Jesus, witnessing miracle after miracle. Was that all that happened before the multiplication miracle? Did people visit with Jesus? Did he walk among them, touching, blessing, encouraging, or even playing with the children? The treasure of those three days is made more complicated by a text that reflects the cultural values of its age, that variably abled people need to be fixed, and that wholeness and health look a particular way.

As in the previous story, the disciples fall significantly short of being pastoral. They are not yet shepherds. They do not see the need and when made aware of it, focus on their limitations and finite resources. There is no little boy and his lunch. The meager resources are either their own or they have collected them, perhaps from mothers or wives or often erased female disciples who packed a lunch.

PROPER 8 (CLOSEST TO JUNE 29)

1 Samuel 2:18–21, 26; Psalm 144:3–4, 12–15; 1 Peter 2:4–10; Mark 7:10–13

1 Samuel 2:18 Now Samuel was ministering in the presence of the HOLY ONE OF OLD, a boy dressed in a linen ephod. [19] A little robe would his mother make for him and bring up to him year by year, when she went up with her husband to offer the yearly sacrifice. [20] And Eli would bless Elkanah and his wife, and say, "May the HOLY ONE repay you (Elkanah) with seed from this woman in place of the bequest she made to the FOUNT OF LIFE"; and then they would return to their home.

²¹ And the FAITHFUL ONE attended Hannah and she conceived and gave birth to two daughters and three sons. And the boy Samuel grew up there in the presence of the LIVING GOD.

²⁶ Now the boy Samuel went on and grew in goodness with the MOST HIGH and with humanity.

Psalm 144:3–4, 12–15

³ WOMB OF LIFE, what is humanity that you even know them,
　or the woman-born that you think of them?
⁴ Humanity is like a breath;
　whose days are like a passing shadow.
¹² Our sons in their youth
　are like plants full grown,
　our daughters are like cornerstones,
　cut for the building of a palace.
¹³ Our barns are full,
　from produce of every kind;
　our sheep have increased by thousands,
　many thousands in our surroundings.
¹⁴ Our cattle are heavy,
　there is no breach in the walls, no exile,
　and no cry of distress in our surroundings.
¹⁵ Happy are the people to whom such blessings fall;
　happy are the people whose God is the WOMB OF LIFE.

1 Peter 2:4 Come to Jesus, a living stone, although rejected by humanity yet chosen and precious to God. ⁵ And are yourselves, like living stones, being built into a spiritual house to be a holy priesthood, to offer spiritual sacrifices acceptable to God through Jesus Christ. ⁶ Thus scripture contains [the following]:

"See, I am laying in Zion a stone,
a cornerstone chosen, precious;
and whoever believes in that stone will not be put to shame."

⁷ To you all who believe then, a precious honor; but for those who do not believe,

"The stone that the builders rejected
has become the chief cornerstone,"

⁸ and

"A stumbling stone,
and a rock of offence."

They stumble over the word *disobeying, disobedient* by design.

[9] Yet you all are a chosen race, a *royal priesthood, a holy nation*, God's own possession, in order that you may proclaim the mighty acts of God who called you out of shadow into God's marvelous light.

[10] Once *not a people*,
but now God's people;
once *bereft of mercy*,
but now rich in mercy.

Mark 7:10 "Now Moses said, '*Honor your mother and your father*' and '*Whoever speaks evil of mother or father must surely die*.' [11] But you all say that if anyone tells father or mother, 'A Korban—gift-offering [to God]—is whatever support you might have had from me.' [12] Then, you all release them from any obligation for mother or father. [13] Thus you all make void the word of God through your tradition that you all have handed on. And you all do many things like this."

PROCLAMATION

Text Notes

In 1 Samuel 2:19, all of the action verbs are feminine; they are Hannah's, even when her husband is with her. This is a common feature of biblical Hebrew, a singular verb (any gender) followed by a plural subject indicating that the first person led in the action and the other followed. On the other hand, the blessing of Elkanah in verse 20 is spoken to him alone: May God repay "you," masculine singular. "Repay" comes from the DSS text supported by the LXX. Without the corrections from Qumran, the MT says that Samuel "grew up with God" in verse 21.

In Psalm 144:3, "woman-born" replaces "children of man."

First Peter 2 is a mélange of texts, including a quote from Isaiah 28:16 in verse 7 that closely corresponds to the Greek LXX, but not exactly, yet is closer to the LXX than the Hebrew Masoretic Text. In the MT the stone is "tested," as in "tried and true," and "precious." In the LXX the two-fold description becomes three-fold, "expensive, chosen (or elect), and "precious." The NT text preserves "elect and precious." The root of "precious" is used in noun form applied to believers, hence "precious honor." Here, NRSV's "he is precious" is without foundation.

The latter phrase reveals more variability, in the MT it is "the one who trusts will not fear/panic" where the NT following the LXX has "the one who believes/trusts will not be put to shame." It should be noted that the practical meaning of *pistis* changes significantly between the testaments. As a result of the Jesus story, the broad sense of trust as in "trusting God" becomes "believe in Jesus as the Son of God." However, where both ancient texts fail to specify in whom or in what the trusting person trusts, the NT generates a potentially masculine subject, "the one who trusts in him," as both Jesus and the stone in Greek are both grammatically masculine. (It should be noted that in Greek this same pronoun can be neuter, masculine, and feminine.) In contrast, in Hebrew the stone is grammatically feminine; here one could translate "the one who trusts her will never be put to shame." I use "that stone" in my translation to preserve the ambiguity of the early traditions and wordplay of the epistle.

The Targum (which includes translation and interpretation intertwined) also reads Isaiah 28:16 as pertaining to a male person: "Behold I am appointing in Zion a king, a mighty king, a warrior and a terrifying one . . . and the righteous who believe in these things, when the distress comes, they will not be shaken."

First Peter 2:8 cites Isaiah 8:14 with similar alteration. In Isaiah God will become a "a stone one strikes against and a rock causing stumbling" in the MT. The LXX diverges significantly: "If you trust in God . . . you will not meet God as a stumbling caused by a stone nor as a fall [in death] caused by a rock." That "fall" is deadly; *ptōmati* means "corpse." The NT text has "rock of offense," using *skandalou* in place of rock that leads one to fall (making the "fall" into sin as explained by verse 9). In verse 8 *apeithountes* means "disobey" and "disbelieve" so I include both options.

Verse 9 draws upon the "priestly kingdom and holy nation" of Exodus 19:6. Here I render "darkness" as "shadow," avoiding the light/dark binary with its racial implication in its history of interpretation. And verse 10 quotes Hosea 2:23 where the lack of mercy is a lack of the maternal love of God, *rachum*, rooted in the womb, *rechem*, its grammatical root.

Jesus quotes the commandment to honor parents in Exodus 20:12, duplicated in Deuteronomy 5:16, and the prohibition against reviling parents in Exodus 21:17 and Leviticus 20:9 in Mark 7:10. Verse 11 has "release from doing (or working) for mother or father"; I use "obligation" for simplicity.

Preaching Prompts

The primary role of women presented in the scripture is wife-and-mother, a compound identity and role. Girls are few and far between, as are children in general with the exception of birth chronicles, genealogies, and miraculous births and pregnancies. Daughters appear more rarely. In these lessons I suggest reading them as emblematic of the fullness of the people, of Israel, of God, of the Church, regularly obscured by those who hold the center of attention.

In 1 Samuel God attends to Hannah and blesses her with daughters and sons after she gifts her son to God. "Attend" has the sense of an administrator assessing and addressing identified issues; in Exodus 4:31, God attends Israel with the Exodus as the result, and in Ruth 1:6 God attends her people in Bethlehem and provides them food in famine. In the psalm, daughters are the "cornerstone" of the community, perhaps best understood as a metaphor for perpetuating the nation. While the authors may have thought exclusively in terms of reproduction, we are not limited to that scope. In 2 Peter, that very same cornerstone imagery is used for Jesus. Daughters are not explicitly present rather, hidden in the body of the people, of the church; they too are now part of a holy and loyal priesthood. This is an extraordinary claim because women and their daughters were excluded from the Israelite priesthood. And in the Gospel, daughters as well as sons are equally capable of abandoning their parents in need and reviling them.

Together, these lessons call our intention to the vast inclusive nature of our communities, particularly those members who are often overlooked. Gender is the metric in these texts and in this reading, but there are many other ways to identify ourselves in our constituent members. The 2 Peter text also calls for the discarding of those who do not believe "by design." I suggest a wider reading in which those who do not believe are neither discarded by God nor beyond the embrace of her love.

PROPER 9 (CLOSEST TO JULY 6)

1 Samuel 2:12–17, 22–25; Psalm 49:1–2, 5–9, 16–17;
1 Timothy 6:6–16; Luke 16:10–13

1 Samuel 2:12 Now the sons of Eli were worthless; they had no knowledge of the HOLY GOD. [13] The practice of the priests toward the people was: when any woman or man sacrificed an offering, the priest's boy came while the meat was boiling, with a three-pronged fork in his hand. [14] Then he violently shoved it into the pan, or kettle, or caldron, or pot, and all that the fork brought up the priest took for himself. This is what they did to all the women and men of Israel who came there, to Shiloh. [15] Even more, before the fat was burned to smoke, the priest's boy came and said to the one who was sacrificing, "Give up some meat to roast for the priest; for he will not accept boiled meat from you, but only fresh." [16] And if the woman or man said to him, "Let them burn the fat to smoke first, and then take for yourself what you wish," he would say, "No! Now! You will give it, and if not, I will take it by force." [17] Thus the sin of [Eli's] boys was very great in the sight of the HOLY ONE OF OLD; for the men treated the offerings of the MOST HIGH with contempt.

[22] Now Eli was very old. He heard all that his sons were doing to all Israel, and how they lay the women who were stationed at the entrance to the tent of meeting. [23] He said to them, "Why do you do these things I'm hearing—evil things—from all these people? [24] No, my sons; it is not a good report that I'm hearing the people of the HOLY ONE OF SINAI passing around. [25] If a woman or man sins against another person, God can be entreated but if against the HOLY ONE someone sins, who can entreat for them?" Yet they would not listen to the voice of their father; for it was the will of the DREAD GOD to kill them.

Psalm 49:1–2, 5–9, 16–17

1 Hear this, all you peoples;
     give ear, all who dwell in the world,
2 children of earth, children of Eve,
     rich and poor together.
5 Why should I fear in evil days,
     when iniquity at my heels surrounds me?
6 Those who trust in their wealth
     and praise of the abundance of their riches?
7 Certainly, it cannot redeem a person,
     or give to God as a ransom.
8 For the redemption-price of a soul is costly,
     they come to an end, forever.
9 Shall one should live eternally
     and never see the Pit?
16 Fear not when some become rich,
     when the glory of their houses increases.
17 For in their death they will take nothing;
     their glory will not go down after them.

1 Timothy 6:6 Of course, there is great gain in godliness with contentment. 7 For nothing did we bring into the world, so we can take nothing out of it. 8 But if we have food and clothing, with these we will be content. 9 Now those who want to be rich fall into temptation and a trap. And many foolish and harmful passions plunge women and men into ruin and destruction. 10 For the root of all evil is the love of money, and some desiring [it] have wandered away from the faith and pierced themselves with many pains.

11 But as for you, child of God, shun all this; pursue righteousness, godliness, faith, love, endurance, gentleness. 12 Fight the good fight of the faith; take hold of the eternal life, to which you were called and to which you professed the good profession in the presence of many witnesses. 13 I charge you in the presence of God, who enlivens all things, and of Christ Jesus who, in his testimony before Pontius Pilate made the good profession, 14 to keep the commandment without spot or blame until the appearing of our Redeemer Jesus Christ, 15 who God will reveal in God's own time—God who is the blessed and only Sovereign, the Power beyond all powers and Majesty of majesties. 16 It is God alone who has immortality and dwells in light unapproachable, whom no human has seen or can see; to God be honor and everlasting might. Amen.

Luke 16:10 "The woman or man who is faithful with little is faithful also with much; and the woman or man who is dishonest in a very little is dishonest also in much. 11 If then you all have not been faithful with the dishonest wealth, who will trust you with [what is] true?

¹² And if you all have not been faithful with what belongs to another, who will give you what is your own? ¹³ No slave can serve two masters; for a slave will either hate the one and love the other or be devoted to the one and despise the other. You cannot serve God and wealth."

PROCLAMATION

Text Notes

Eli's sons were "sons of Belial," or "sons of worthlessness." In verse 13 the worshipper "sacrifices a sacrifice." As the Hannah story among others makes clear, women as well as men offered sacrifices. "Man" in the texts is generic and usually rendered "person" as in NRSV. The action of the boy on behalf of Eli's sons is physically violent; they "smite" the fork into the pots in verse 14. "Fresh" meat in verse 15 is "living," but of course the animal has been slaughtered, so recently living, i.e., "fresh." In verse 22 Eli's sons "lay," not "lay with" the women they abuse; the preposition is lacking in Hebrew. Often this formulation indicates a lack of consent or inappropriate coupling (see Reuben's rape of Bilhah in Genesis 35:22). The women's "stationing" is articulated with the verb that describes waging war and as a noun, *tzavaoth*, indicates a military unit, a "host" in older translations, often in regard to God's legions of heavenly warriors—grammatically feminine plural. In Exodus 38:8, the women who are in their own *tzavaoth* unit stationed at the tabernacle donate their mirrors for the sanctuary laver; I relate them to the woman described as "guarding" the temple complex gate in John 18:16–17.

The second line of Psalm 49:2 can be translated variously, including as "children of earth," "woman-born," or as here, "children of earth and Eve." The underlying text is *beney adam, beney ish*, the first pair meaning "mortal," "human/ity," "children (or sons) of humanity" using the broadest meaning of *adam*—note the lowercase; it is not a person's name here. *Adam*, person and people, shares its root with *adamah*, making humanity precisely children of earth. The second pair of words parallels the first, as is common in biblical Hebrew poetry; this is quite literally "children (or sons) of men." Pairing "Eve" and "earth" preserves the poetry of the piece and makes visible the nod to ancestral creation encoded in "*adam*." "Glory in verse 16 includes wealth and honor.

In 1 Timothy 6:10, *odynais* can be either "pains" or "sorrows." While the Epistle is purportedly written to Timothy by Paul (it is among the disputed Epistles), it was also written to the ancient church and received as speaking to us. Therefore, I have changed "man of God," specific to Timothy in verse 11, to "child of God," applicable to him and all future readers. The claim that no one can or has seen God in 1 Timothy 6:16 is at odds with numerous texts in which Hagar, Moses, Isaiah, and Ezekiel indeed saw God. The sentiment is in accord with later tradition that held persons only saw attributes of God, like her glory.

The latter portion of Luke 10:11 lacks a proper object; it ends with "who will trust you [all] with the true."

Preaching Prompts

The tangled threads of greed and wealth come together in these lessons. Eli's sons lusted for and reveled in power over the people, stealing their offerings and God's and using their power to manipulate or steal sexual access to women. The psalm warns of trusting in wealth and affirms the infinite value of a soul, of life—we are worthy of God's redemption. The Epistle urges contentment with one's resources and cautions against love for money, not money itself. The Gospel articulates how wealth can become an idol whose veneration diverts worship from God.

The story of Eli's family drama raises the question of whether Eli's wife, the mother of his children, was still in the picture and, if so, how she felt about the condemnation of her children, young men, to death. She can be read back into the story as a mother whose children are caught up in the criminal justice system, whose sons are guilty, but are still her children. God's intent to kill them prevents them from heeding their father's counsel and perhaps repenting, similar to the hardening of Pharaoh's heart, one of the more challenging biblical worldviews.

The younger priests were entitled to a portion of most sacrifices (including the breast and right thigh); that was their primary provision, see Leviticus 7:28–36 and Numbers 6:20. Leviticus 3:16 declares, "All fat is the Holy One's." Texts calling for the fat to be burned completely as a type of incense offering to God are legion: Exodus 29:13, 22; Leviticus 3:3–4, 9–10, 14–17; Numbers 18:17.

The rhetoric in Luke describes a world with which I am unfamiliar, a world in which the enslaved "love" their enslavers, even if it is just a rhetorical proposition or launching pad. I am, however, familiar with the wider world of the scriptures, a world in which slavery is normative for everyone including Jesus and its abolition unimaginable. In my experience, the Church has failed to adequately address Jesus's acceptance of slavery without critique of the institution (or at least his portrayal as such).

PROPER 10 (CLOSEST TO JULY 13)

1 Samuel 4:2, 5–11, 19–22; Psalm 77:1–12, 19–20;
Romans 5:1–5; John 14:25–31

1 Samuel 4:2 The Philistines deployed against Israel and the battle was lost and Israel was struck down by the Philistines, and they killed on the field of battle four thousand men.

⁵ Now it happened as the ark of the covenant of the Fire of Sinai came into the camp, all Israel shouted a great shout and the earth herself echoed it. ⁶ And when the Philistines heard the sound of the great shout, they said, "What is this great shout in the camp of the Hebrews?" Then they learned that the ark of the Ancient Of Days had come to the camp. ⁷ And the Philistines were afraid; for they said, "Gods have come into the camp." And they

said, "Woe to us! Never has there been such a thing. ⁸ Woe to us! Who can deliver us from the hand of these mighty gods? These are the gods who smote the Egyptians with every kind of plague in the wilderness. ⁹ Strengthen yourselves and be men, O Philistines, lest you become enslaved to the Hebrews as they were enslaved to you; be men and fight."

¹⁰ So the Philistines fought, and Israel was defeated and fled, each to their tent. Now there was a very great slaughter and there fell from Israel thirty thousand foot-soldiers. ¹¹ Then the ark of God was taken and the two sons of Eli, Hophni and Phinehas, died.

¹⁹ Now Eli's daughter-in-law, the wife of Phinehas, was pregnant, about to give birth and when she heard the news that the ark of God was taken and that her father-in-law and her husband were dead, she squatted and gave birth, for her labor pains came on and overwhelmed her. ²⁰ Then at the moment of her death, the women standing with her said to her, "Fear not, for you have given birth to a son." But she did not answer or incline her heart. ²¹ She named the child "Ai Kavod," Ichabod, meaning, "Woe [Ai]! The glory [Kavod] has departed from Israel," because the ark of God had been captured and because of her father-in-law and her husband. ²² She said, "The glory has departed from Israel, for the ark of God has been taken."

Psalm 77:1–12, 19–20

¹ With my voice to God I cry aloud,
  with my voice to God, that she may hear me.
² In the day of my trouble the Holy One I seek,
  my hand at night is stretched out without rest;
  my soul refuses to be comforted.
³ I contemplate God, and I groan;
  I meditate, and my spirit faints. *Selah*
⁴ You hold my eyelids open;
  I am distraught and cannot speak.
⁵ I consider the days of old,
  and remember the years of time past.
⁶ I contemplate my song in the night with my heart;
  I meditate and search my spirit:
⁷ "Will the Holy One reject for all time,
  and never again show favor?
⁸ Has her faithful love ceased for all time?
  Has her promise ceased to pass from generation to generation?
⁹ Has God forgotten to be gracious?
  Has she in anger closed off her mother-love?" *Selah*
¹⁰ And I say, "This is what ails me,
  that the right hand of the Most High has changed."
¹¹ I will contemplate the deeds of the AGELESS GOD;
  and I will remember your wonders of old.

¹² I will meditate on all your work,
and reflect on your deeds.
¹⁹ In the sea was your way, and your paths in the many waters,
yet your footsteps were not seen.
²⁰ You led your people like a flock,
by the hand of Miriam, Aaron, and Moses.

Romans 5:1 Now, since we are made righteousness through faithfulness, we have peace with God through our Savior Jesus Christ. ² Through Christ we have obtained access to this grace in which we stand and we rejoice in our hope of God's glory. ³ And not only that, for we also rejoice in our sufferings, knowing that suffering produces endurance, ⁴ and endurance character, and character hope, ⁵ and hope does not disappoint, because God's love has been poured into our hearts through the Holy Spirit, She, who has been given to us.

John 14:25 "These things have I said to you while I am still with you all. ²⁶ But the Advocate, the Holy Spirit, whom the Most High will send in my name, She will teach you all things and She will remind you all of all that I have said to you. ²⁷ Peace I leave with you; my peace I give to you all. Not as the world gives do I give to you. Let not your hearts be troubled, nor let them fear. ²⁸ You have heard me say to you all, 'I am going away and I am coming to you.' If you loved me, you would rejoice that I am going to the Creator, because the Almighty is greater than I. ²⁹ And now, I have told you this before it happens, so when it happens, you all might believe. ³⁰ I will no longer talk much with you, for the ruler of this world is coming and has nothing in me. ³¹ Rather, that the world may know that I love the Creator of All, just as the Sovereign God commands me, so I do. Rise now, let us leave this place.

PROCLAMATION

Text Notes

First Samuel 4:2 employs a number of idioms: the Israelites are "smote" ("smitten" in the KJV) and they are *defeated* "before" (or "in the face/presence" of) the Philistines. In verse 5, the "noise" that the earth makes is not specified; I have supplied "echo." The earth is grammatically feminine in Hebrew; "herself" emphasizes the anthropomorphism of the earth in the verse. In verses 7–8 the word *elohim* has two senses; plural in form it means "gods" in the Philistine purview, and as a majestic plural it refers to the singular Israelite "God." In verse 10 "footers" indicates "foot-soldiers" or infantry. Ichabod's name in verse 20 can also be understood as "Where is the glory" as the consonants for "woe" and "why" are the same. However, the vowel pattern corresponds to "woe."

The opening of Psalm 77 is staccato, "my voice to God," duplicated in the first and second lines of the first verse. The verb translated as "stretch out" in verse 2 most properly means "pour out," leading Robert Alter to amend "hand" to "eye." The JPS labels the verse "Hebrew uncertain." The psalm uses the verb "to remember" in the sense of "contemplate" in verses 3 and 6. The divine love in verse 9 has its origin in the womb with which it shares a grammatical root.

In both iterations, Habakkuk 2:4 and Romans 5:1, "justified by faith/fulness" is notoriously difficult to translate. "Faith" as a belief in someone or something, i.e., God, is not a Hebrew biblical concept. The word *'-m-n*, root of "amen," means "faithful," and "faithfulness," and "trust" and "trustworthy. Its Greek equivalent, *pistis*, initially had the same semantic range; however it was adapted to refer primarily to faith *in* Jesus as the Child of God, his resurrection, etc. Nevertheless, the word maintains its full semantic range. Theologically speaking, there is no small difference between the claim that a believer is made righteous by her own act of faith or belief and that God makes a believer righteous through her own divine faithfulness.

The ubiquity of masculine grammar in each passage contributes to the difficulty. Whose faith or faithfulness is being invoked? In Habakkuk, is the righteous person being justified by her own faithfulness to God or by God's faithfulness to her? Similarly, in Romans, is the righteous person justified by her faith or belief in Jesus as the Messiah or is she justified by God's faithfulness to her? The grammar and semantic ranges allow for all of these. My choice of "faithfulness" here leaves open these possibilities to be explored by the preacher while retaining fidelity to both textual traditions.

The Spirit is grammatically feminine in Hebrew and Aramaic, the primary languages of Paul's (and Jesus's) culture and scriptures. This is regularly obscured by traditional translators who omit the feminine pronoun, but only with reference to the spirit, while simultaneously employing masculine pronouns for God in the Hebrew Bible. The corresponding Greek pronoun is neuter. I offer the feminine pronoun as a contextually appropriate option for readers, preachers, and lectors in Romans 5:5 and John 14:26.

In John 14 Jesus uses "Father" as a title, "*the* Father," and not relationally, "*my* Father." Since God's engendering of Jesus is not the basis for the title here, I use a variety of divine titles in the reading to name God. The Peshitta addresses this by using "my Father" throughout. In verse 30 the nonhuman "ruler of this world," while never named (here or in John 12:31 or 16:11), is nonetheless presumed to be Satan by most interpreters. Additionally, in verse 30, NRSV's insertion of "power" is without foundation.

Preaching Prompts

These lessons offer reflections on the ways in which people experience the presence of God internally and externally across the canons of scripture. In 1 Samuel 4, the presence of God is enthroned upon and above the Ark of the Covenant. God and her Ark were in residence in the sacred city of Shiloh tended by Samuel, successor to Eli. After a military rout, it was decided to bring this earthly manifestation of God to the battlefront that she might smite the enemies of Israel. God had no such plans. She refused to allow herself to be manipulated in that way. She was present with her people but silent in their defeat and in their dying.

Using my exegetical imagination, I see the psalmist as a survivor of that battle, or perhaps a survivor's widow—irreconcilable dating notwithstanding. Her God too is present, keeping her awake in the night by "holding her eyelids open." But the presence of God is not a comfort to her either as she reflects on the past mighty acts of God and the sorrow of her current circumstances. Paul assures that God is indeed present with those who suffer like the psalmist, present in the believer in the form of the Holy Spirit. In the Gospel set before Paul's affirmation, Jesus promises the perpetual presence and companionship of the indwelling Spirit of whom Paul teaches.

Each of these texts speak of the companioning of God but not always in the way or with the results that persons may wish. While we might affirm the presence of God in all times, in all places, and with all persons, that does not preclude suffering, sorrow, or loss. That is a reality for women, men, and nonbinary persons in the text, in the world that reads the text, and across time.

PROPER 11 (CLOSEST TO JULY 20)

1 Samuel 8:1, 4–18; Psalm 72:1–4, 12–14, 18–19; Acts 17:1–7; John 6:14–20

1 Samuel 8:1 Now it was that when Samuel was old that he made his sons judges over Israel.

⁴ Then all the elders of Israel gathered themselves together and came to Samuel at Ramah. ⁵ They said to him, "Look here! You—you are old, and your sons do not walk in your ways; now then, set up for us a ruler to judge us, like all the heathen nations." ⁶ But the thing was evil in Samuel's sight when they said, "Give us a ruler to judge us." Then Samuel prayed to the HOLY ONE OF OLD.

⁷ And the HOLY ONE said to Samuel, "Hearken to the voice of the people in all that they say to you; for it is not you they have rejected, but it is me they have rejected from ruling over them. ⁸ Like everything else they have done to me, from the day I brought them up out of Egypt to this very day, forsaking me and serving other gods; they are doing the same to you. ⁹ Now then, hearken to their voice; but—you shall testify against them, and show them the judgment of the ruler who shall rule over them."

¹⁰ So Samuel relayed all the words of the HOLY ONE to the people who were asking him for a ruler. ¹¹ Samuel said, "This will be the judgment of the ruler who will rule over you all: your sons he will take and set them aside for himself in his chariots and in his cavalry, and to run before his chariots. ¹² And he will set aside for himself commanders of thousands and commanders of fifties, and some to plow his plowing and to reap his reaping, and to make his furnishings of war and the furnishings of his chariots. ¹³ Your daughters he will take to be

apothecaries and cooks and bakers. ¹⁴ He will take the best of your fields and vineyards and olive orchards; he will take and give to those who serve him. ¹⁵ One-tenth of your grain and of your vineyards he will take and give to his eunuchs and those he enslaves. ¹⁶ Your male slaves and your female slaves, and the best of your cattle and donkeys, he will take and put them to his work. ¹⁷ Your flocks he will tithe . . . and you all, you shall be his slaves. ¹⁸ And you all will cry out on that day in the face of your sovereign, whom you have chosen for yourselves; and GOD WHOSE NAME IS HOLY will not answer you all on that day."

Psalm 72:1–4, 12–14, 18–19

¹ God, give the ruler your justice,
  and your righteousness to a ruler's son.
² May the [next] ruler judge your people with righteousness,
  and your afflicted ones with justice.
³ May the mountains raise up well-being for the people,
  and the hills, righteousness.
⁴ May the ruler do justice for the poor of the people,
  grant deliverance to those born in need
  and crush the oppressor.
¹² For the ruler delivers the needy when they call,
  the oppressed and those who have no helper.
¹³ The ruler has pity on the poor and the needy,
  and saves the lives of the needy.
¹⁴ From oppression and violence the ruler redeems their life;
  and precious is their blood in the sight of their ruler.
¹⁸ Blessed be the FOUNT OF JUSTICE, the God of Israel,
  who alone does wondrous things.
¹⁹ Blessed be her glorious name forever;
  may her glory fill the whole earth.
  Amen and Amen.

Acts 17:1 Paul and Silas had traveled through Amphipolis and Apollonia. They came to Thessalonica, where there was a Jewish synagogue. ² As was his custom Paul went and on three sabbaths presented to them from the scriptures, ³ explaining and demonstrating it was necessary for the Messiah to suffer and to rise from the dead: "This is the Messiah, Jesus who I proclaim to you all." ⁴ Now, some of [those Jews] were persuaded and joined Paul and Silas, as did a great many of the devout Greeks and not a few of the prominent women.

⁵ Then the [other] Jews became jealous, and enlisting some immoral men in the marketplaces, they formed a mob and stirred up the city in an uproar and they attacked Jason's house searching for Paul and Silas to bring out to the gathering. ⁶ Now when they could not find them, they dragged Jason and some believers before the city leaders, shouting, "These are

the ones who have disrupted the [entire] world and are now here. [7] This Jason has received them as guests and they are all in opposition to the decrees of the emperor, saying that there is another sovereign named Jesus."

John 6:14 When the people saw the sign that Jesus had done [multiplying the loaves and fish], they said, "This is indeed the prophet who is to come into the world." [15] When Jesus realized that they were about to kidnap him in order to make him king, he withdrew again to the mountain by himself.

[16] And when it was evening, his disciples went down to the sea. [17] And they boarded a boat and headed across the sea to Capernaum. It was now dark and Jesus had not yet come to them. [18] The sea surged; a strong wind was blowing. [19] When they had rowed about twenty-five stadia [three or four miles], they saw Jesus walking upon the sea and coming near the boat and they were terrified. [20] But he said to them, "It is I; be not afraid."

PROCLAMATION

Text Notes

The people ask Samuel in verse 5 for the same kind of governance he provided, one based in the grammatical root for judges and judging, but they want a monarch rather than another judge. The Hebrew vocabulary for "monarchy" uses the same root word for noun and verb, i.e., "rulers rule," a common feature of the language. In addition, the word is the same for both genders, which does not work for "king," "queen," and "reign." (Think: prophets and prophetesses prophesy prophecy.) "Female and male rulers rule in a realm" may be as close as we can get to preserving both form and function.

Samuel tells the people that a monarch will take their daughters to be "mixers of ointments" in verse 13. In Sirach 38:8, the mixer is an apothecary working with a physician. In other texts the mixer makes scented ointment and incense for use in worship; in yet others the mixer makes perfume (see Exodus 30:25, 35; 37:29; Ecclesiastes 10:1; 1 Chronicles 9:30; Sirach 49:1). I chose "apothecary" to denote their skill, which could be channeled for either purpose.

Throughout Psalm 72 I use "the ruler" for the monarch and his son and the many masculine pronouns for clarity and for the broader utility of this psalm beyond male monarchs. In verses 2 and 12, the people are afflicted (or oppressed) through a poverty that is imposed on them through unjust means, hence punishment of "the oppressor" in verse 4; Hebrew's lexicon of poverty has different words for different contexts. "Those born in need" replaces "children/sons of the needy" in the same verse. Hebrew uses "soul" for both the essence of a person's life, what we in the West tend to call a "soul," and a person's life. The language of saving and redeeming in Psalm 72:13–14 refers properly to lives; a leader's economic policies are matters of life and death. In verse 15 the "essence" of the law is the "work" of the law.

"To have words" in Acts 17:2 can mean anything from discussing to disputing; here it is "at" them rather than "with" them yielding "presented to them." In verse 11 the same word means both "high-born" and the characteristic of being open-minded deriving from that status or accompanying education. While many translations present the women and men as equally high in standing, the adjective is feminine plural and thus refers only to the women; likewise, "Greek" is feminine plural. The men are neither Greek nor of high status. This text is one of very few places where women precede men in the order of their mention.

Preaching Prompts

These lessons offer disparate models of monarchy. There is the human monarch whom Samuel predicts will plunder the people and their resources; scholars understand this passage to be a critique of Solomon. Imaginatively, Psalm 72 is a response to that critique in the form of a prayer that Solomon might receive divine guidance to avoid the pitfalls of Samuel's prophecy. In the Epistle Jesus is presented as a claimant to the throne in order to portray his followers as enemies of the state. In the Gospel Jesus goes to extreme measures to avoid having an earthly crown forced upon him; he literally (or literarily) walks on water to escape his would-be subjects. Is there any better critique of monarchy? Yet we continue to perpetuate that language and imagery.

There is no small amount of irony in Samuel raising poorly behaved sons like his mentor, Eli. As is the case with Eli's wife, nothing is known of Samuel's wife or their household. Clearly both cohabitated with their wives to some degree, producing children. If the whole family lived at the sacred site, what did that portend for any religious role for the women? Did other women seek them out for counsel or company? I have suggested in *Womanist Midrash* that the daughters and wives of Levites and priests may have, to preserve modesty, checked women for skin disease that could result in quarantine.

Paul's weekly attendance at synagogue in Acts 17:2 is customary; he is Jewish and his faith in Jesus is not regarded as a conversion. It will be centuries before Judaism and Christianity are regarded as incompatible by both communities. Jason of Acts 17, possibly the same person mentioned in Romans 16:21, bears a Greek name that may indicate an underlying Hebrew name such as Joshua, suggesting a Jewish follower of Jesus.

The new believers in Acts 17:4 include women and men from the Jewish community and Greeks who worship or study with them. It is not clear if the prominent women are prominent in the synagogue and therefore Jewish, or prominent in the Greek city of Thessalonica and therefore more likely to be Greek. Prominent women in the synagogue could include women in leadership, including of the synagogue itself. Bernadette Brooten has demonstrated conclusively that women served as leader of the synagogue (through inscriptions with names and titles in *Women Leaders in the Ancient Synagogue*).

These lessons end with the solitary Jesus walking away from the power structures of the word in dramatic fashion, simultaneously demonstrating the degree to which he transcends them. That momentary glimpse of true majesty was terrifying. This is a Jesus we cannot follow on our own, yet as in the verses beyond the reading, this is a Jesus who waits for us to make our way to him.

FEAST OF MARY MAGDALENE, JULY 22

Genesis 16:10–13; Psalm 68:4–11; Romans 16:1–16; John 20:1–2, 11–18

Genesis 16:10 The messenger of the WELLSPRING OF LIFE said to Hagar, "Greatly will I multiply your seed, so they cannot be counted for multitude." [11] Then the messenger of the FOUNT OF LIFE said to her,

> "Look! You are pregnant and shall give birth to a son,
> and you shall call him Ishmael (meaning God hears),
> for the FAITHFUL ONE has heard of your abuse.
> [12] He shall be a wild ass of a man,
> with his hand against everyone,
> and everyone's hand against him;
> and he shall live in the sight of all his kin."

[13] So Hagar named the LIVING GOD who spoke to her: "You are El-ro'i"; for she said, "Have I really seen God and remained alive after seeing God?"

Psalm 68:4–11

> [4] Sing to God, sing praises to her Name;
> exalt her who rides upon the clouds;
> HOLY is her Name, rejoice before her!
> [5] Mother of orphans and defender of widows,
> is God in her holy habitation!
> [6] God settles the solitary in a home, bringing prisoners into prosperity;
> while the rebellious shall live in a wasteland.
> [7] God, when you marched before your people,
> when you moved out through the wilderness,
> [8] the earth shook, even the heavens poured down,
> at the presence of God, the One of Sinai,
> at the presence of God, the God of Israel.
> [9] Rain in abundance, God, you showered abroad;
> when your heritage grew weary you prepared rest.

10 Your creatures found a dwelling in her;
   God, you provided in your goodness for the oppressed.
11 The AUTHOR OF LIFE gave the word;
   the women who proclaim the good news are a great army.

Romans 16:1 I commend to you all our sister Phoebe, a deacon of the church in Cenchreae, ² so that you all may receive her in Christ as is worthy of the saints, and stand by her in whatever thing she may need of you, for she has been a benefactress of many, and of myself as well.

³ Greet Prisca and Aquila, my coworkers in Christ Jesus, ⁴ and who for my life risked their necks, to whom not only I give thanks, but also all the churches of the Gentiles, ⁵ and the church in their house. Greet Epaenetus my beloved, who was the first fruit in Asia for Christ. ⁶ Greet Mary, who has worked much among you all. ⁷ Greet Andronicus and Junia, my kin and my fellow prisoners; they are eminent among the apostles, and they were in Christ before I was. ⁸ Greet Ampliatus, my beloved in Christ. ⁹ Greet Urbanus, our coworker in Christ, and Stachys my beloved. ¹⁰ Greet Apelles, who is proven in Christ. Greet those who belong to Aristobulus. ¹¹ Greet Herodion, my kinsman. Greet those who belong of Narcissus in Christ. ¹² Greet Tryphaena and Tryphosa who toil in Christ. Greet the beloved Persis who has worked much in Christ. ¹³ Greet Rufus, chosen in Christ, and greet his mother who is also mine. ¹⁴ Greet Asyncritus, Phlegon, Hermes, Patrobas, Hermas, and the sisters and brothers who are with them. ¹⁵ Greet Philologus and Julia, Nereus and his sister, and Olympas, and all the saints with them. ¹⁶ Greet one another with a holy kiss. All the churches of Christ greet you.

John 20:1 Now it was the first day of the week. Mary Magdalene came, early on while it was still dark, to the tomb and saw the stone removed from the tomb. ² So she ran and went to Simon Peter and to the other disciple, the one whom Jesus loved, and said to them, "They have taken the Messiah out of the tomb, and we do not know where they have laid him."

¹¹ Now Mary stood outside, facing the tomb, weeping. As she wept, she bent down to see in the tomb. ¹² Then she saw two angels in white sitting, one at the head and the other at the feet, where the body of Jesus had been lying. ¹³ They said to her, "Woman, why do you weep?" She said to them, "Because they have taken my Savior, and I do not know where they have laid him." ¹⁴ Having said this, she turned around and saw Jesus standing, but she did not know that it was Jesus. ¹⁵ Jesus said to her, "Woman, why do you weep? For whom do you look?" Thinking that he was the gardener, she said to him, "Sir, if you have carried him away, tell me where you have laid him, and I will take him away." ¹⁶ Jesus said to her, "Mary." She turned and said to him in Aramaic, "Rabbouni!" (which means Teacher). ¹⁷ Jesus said to her, "Do not hold me, because I have not yet ascended to the Father. Rather, go to my brothers and say to them, 'I am ascending to my Abba and your Abba, to my God and your God.'" ¹⁸ Mary Magdalene went and announced to the disciples, "I have seen the Savior"; and she told them that he had said these things to her.

PROCLAMATION

Text Notes

The language of Hagar's annunciation parallels the promise to Abraham in Genesis 13:16 closely; each is promised that their "seed" (or offspring) will be numerous beyond counting. Hagar is the first woman in scripture granted an annunciation, the unnamed mother of Samson follows in Judges 13:3–7, followed in turn by Mary the mother of Jesus. Hagar and Rebekah (Genesis 24:60) are the only women in the canon credited with their own seed/offspring; the language is usually reserved for men. (Rebekah's seed is blessed by her matrilineal family; her father Bethuel ben Milcah bore his mother's name, not his father's.) Notably, God speaks to Abraham *about* Sarah in Genesis 17:15–16, as do the divine messengers in Genesis 18:9–10, even when she is within hearing; none speak to her.

Hagar's abuse or affliction, more rightly, Sarah's abuse of Hagar in verse 11, is articulated with a verb that encodes both physical and sexual violence; the verb is also used of the abuse the Israelites suffered at the hands of the Egyptians. Some translate Ishmael's fate as living "in opposition," i.e., conflict, with his kin rather than "opposite," i.e., in their sight or presence; the verb has both senses.

The "we" in John 20:2 likely refers to other women with Mary Magdalene at the tomb. Other resurrection accounts include Mary the mother of James and Salome from Mark 16:1 and Joanna (with Mary Magdalene and James's mother) in Luke 24:10. Yet other possibilities include Jesus's aunt—the unnamed sister of Mary—with Mary the wife of Clopas, present at his crucifixion in John 19:25, and Susanna who with other women supported Jesus financially from Luke 8:3.

Mary Magdalene "messages," *aggellō*, the gospel of Christ's resurrection. The verb shares the root of messenger, one who announces, *aggelos*, commonly rendered "angel," though the term is not restricted to divine beings. Both she and the divine messengers she encountered are angels. See the use of "angel" as church leader in Revelation 2:1, 8, 12, 18; 3:1.

Preaching Prompts

For this feast of the disciple Orthodox Christians call the Apostle to the Apostles, the readings focus on women's proclamations to and about God, including their work in shaping the early church that speaks for them. Hagar is the only person in the scriptures to name God. She is a matron saint for this project in which I too name God, using God's characteristics revealed in the texts and in the experiences of its readers and hearers to render the unpronounceable name.

Hagar tells God who She is in her, Hagar's, experience and perception. In Psalm 68:12 at the command of God, an army of women proclaim the good news of God's care for her people. The language for that good news, *basarah* in Hebrew, *euaggelia* in Greek, becomes "gospel" in English, the gospel of the risen Christ that Mary Magdalene proclaimed to the absent male disciples and apostles. The women church leaders acknowledged by Paul spread that good news through Asia, though their words are lost to us.

The Magdalene texts are extensive: Matthew 27:55–61; 28:1–10; Mark 15:40–41, 47; 16:1–8 [9–11]; Luke 8:1–3; 23:55–56; 24:1–10; John 19:25; 20:1–2, 11–18. The fifty-seven verses tell a story of discipleship and faith that is virtually without peer among male disciples yet is not unique to this one woman, for there were other women at the cross and tomb who followed Jesus in life, attended him in death, and proclaimed him in resurrection. Yet she is distinguished by the preservation of her name and frequency of appearance. Mary the mother of Jesus and Mary Magdalene are the only women represented in all four Gospels, even considering the difficult to separate and identify Marys, even with multiple traditions about which Mary anointed Jesus.

Peeling back the traditions accreted around her, some of which—like the red egg—may be useful, she remains a disciple, arguably an apostle, preacher, eyewitness of the Passion, conversant with angels, benefactrix, burial attendant, healed/transformed/exorcised, messenger (angel) of the gospel.

PROPER 12 (CLOSEST TO JULY 27)

1 Samuel 9:1–3, 15–18, 10:1; Psalm 22:23–31;
1 Corinthians 4:8–13; Luke 19:11–27

1 Samuel 9:1 Now there was a man of Benjamin whose name was Kish son of Abiel son of Zeror son of Becorath son of Aphiah [himself] a son of a Benjaminite, a warrior-hearted man of substance. ² He had a son whose name was Saul, a fine young man. There was not a man among the people of Israel finer than he; he stood above and beyond everyone else. ³ Now the female donkeys of Kish, Saul's father, had strayed. So, Kish said to his son Saul, "Take one of the boys with you, get up and look for the donkeys."

¹⁵ Now the HOLY ONE had uncovered the ear of Samuel the day before Saul came, saying: ¹⁶ "About this time tomorrow I will send to you a man from the land of Benjamin, and you shall anoint him to be a leader over my people Israel. He shall save my people from the hand of the Philistines, for I have seen the humiliation of my people, because their cry has come to me." ¹⁷ When Samuel saw Saul, the HOLY ONE told him, "Here is the man of whom I spoke to you. He it is who shall govern my people." ¹⁸ Then Saul approached Samuel in the center of the gate, and said, "Tell me, please, where is the house of the seer?"

¹⁰:¹ Samuel took a vial of oil and poured it on Saul's head, and kissed him, and said, "Has not the HOLY ONE OF OLD anointed you leader over God's own heritage?

23 You who revere the FOUNT OF LIFE, praise her!
all the offspring of Leah and Rachel, Bilhah and Zilpah glorify her.
Stand in awe of her all you of Rebekah's line.

24 For she did not despise or abhor
the affliction of the afflicted;
she did not hide her face from me,
and when I cried to her, she heard.

25 On your account is my praise in the great congregation;
my vows I will pay before those who revere her.

26 The poor shall eat and be satisfied;
those who seek her shall praise the MOTHER OF ALL.
May your hearts live forever!

27 All the ends of the earth shall remember
and turn to the WELLSPRING OF LIFE;
and all the families of the nations
shall worship before her.

28 For sovereignty belongs to the SHE WHO IS HOLY,
and she rules over the nations.

29 They consume and they bow down, all the fat ones of the earth before her,
they bend their knees, all who go down to the dust,
and cannot save their soul.

30 Later descendants will serve her;
future generations will be told about our God,

31 they will go and proclaim her deliverance to a people yet unborn,
saying that she has done it.

1 Corinthians 4:8 You all already have enough. You all have already become rich! With us you all have begun to rule like royals! And I wish that you all had become royal rulers, so that we might reign with you! 9 For I think that God has set us forth, we the apostles last, like those condemned to death, because we have become a spectacle to the world, angels and mortals. 10 We are fools for Christ, but you all are wise in Christ. We are weak, but you all are strong. You all are honored, but we dishonored. 11 To this very hour are we hungry and thirsty, we are unclothed and beaten and homeless. 12 And we are weary of the work of our own hands. Being reviled, we bless; persecuted, we endure. 13 Being slandered, we proclaim comfort. We have become the garbage of the world, the scum of all things, to this very moment.

Luke 19:11 As the crowd was listening to Jesus, he added a parable to relay because he was near Jerusalem, and because they thought the reign of God was about to appear, immediately.

¹² Thus Jesus said, "A highborn person went to a distant country to receive their royal authority and then returned. ¹³ This person summoned ten of their slaves and gave them ten gold mina coins and said to them, 'Tend to business until I come back.' ¹⁴ But the citizens of their country hated this person and sent an envoy following, saying, 'We do not want this person to rule over us.' ¹⁵ And it was as in returning, having received royal authority, this person ordered these slaves, to whom had been given the money, to be summoned in order to find out what profit they had made. ¹⁶ The first came forward and said, 'Highness, your gold coin has made ten more gold coins.'

¹⁷ Then this person said to that slave, 'Well done, good slave! Because in little you have been trustworthy, take over ten cities.' ¹⁸ And the second came, saying, 'Highness, your [one] gold coin has made five gold coins.' ¹⁹ Then this person said to that slave, 'And you, be over five cities.' ²⁰ Then the other came, saying, 'Highness, here is your gold coin. I wrapped and stored it in a handkerchief, ²¹ for I was afraid of you, because you are a harsh person; you take what you did not deposit, and reap what you did not sow.'

²² This person said to him, 'I will judge you by your own words, you wicked slave! You knew that I was a harsh person, taking what I did not deposit and reaping what I did not sow? ²³ Why then did you not put my money on the banker's table? So I, when I returned, could have collected it with interest.' ²⁴ And then this person said to the bystanders, 'Take the gold coin from him and give it to the one who has ten gold coins.' ²⁵ And they said to this person, 'Highness, he has ten pounds!' ²⁶ 'I tell you, to all those who have, more will be given; but from those who have nothing, even what they have will be taken away. ²⁷ But as for these enemies of mine who did not want me to reign over them—bring them here and slaughter them in my presence.'"

PROCLAMATION

Text Notes

Gibor chayil indicates a man of significance or substance in 1 Samuel 9:1, often translated as "mighty man of valor," and also includes "man of means" with the sense that wealth is ennobling. I combined them, yielding warrior-hearted (*chayil*) including the sense of "mighty (*gibor*) warrior." Saul is "fine" ("good"), which in African American vernacular means both "good" and "good-looking." The verb *galah* means "uncover" and therefore "reveal." God's revelation to Samuel in verse 15 appears to be auditory. In verse 16 God "sees" the people in the MT; in the LXX she sees the "humiliation" of her people, making the verse correspond with Exodus 3:7. Using a verb that means "restrain" for "govern" in verse 17 indicates that someone, God, the author or editor, sees Israel as in need of a very specific sort of governance. Verse 1 in 1 Samuel 10 is longer in the LXX; the second passage connects to the contents of the following verses: "You shall rule over the people of the Holy One and you will save them from the hand of their enemies all around.

Now this shall be the sign to you that the Holy One has anointed you ruler over God's own heritage."

In Psalm 22:23, "the offspring of Jacob" are identified by their mothers/ matriarchs, enslaved and free, and similarly "Rebekah's line" stands in for "the offspring of Israel." Poverty in verse 24 of the psalm is that which comes from oppression.

The first verb in 1 Corinthians 4:9 means to "exhibit," "put on display," and "appoint." The comfort proclaimed in verse 13 of the Epistle has its roots in the word that yields "Paraclete," the comforting manifestation of the Holy Spirit.

Luke 19:11 connects to the previous passage with "while they were listening to this." I have amended it slightly for clarity. In verse 12 the highborn person receives "a kingdom." However, the character does not stay and rule but rather exercises royal authority reflected in this translation. In verse 16 I replace "Lord" with "highness." Greek *soudario,* verse 20, is indeed a small cloth used for wiping perspiration among other things, a handkerchief. Verse 23 uses "table" as a euphemism for "bank."

Preaching Prompts

It seems Americans are besotted with royalty, a bloody revolution notwithstanding. The Israelite story is much the same. The account of Saul's kingship is rooted in a desire to be like other nations without any critical analysis of the ethics of monarchy and empire or the well-being of their subjects. Saul's story (and David's when it follows) also reveals the preoccupation with physical appearance and beauty standards that by design create and impose hierarchies.

The psalm provides a portrait of true majesty. The God who reigns as sovereign over heaven and earth, mortals and angels, models a monarchy that uses its power and resources to care for the oppressed and feed the hungry. Paul's bombastic rebuttal to followers who want to elevate him and other apostles to kingship that they might revel in proximity to them exposes their hunger for power and hierarchy. Jesus exposes the absolute power and authority that come with monarchy to make a point about the injustice and inequity they leave in their wake but frustratingly does not trouble or appear to be troubled by the institution of slavery. Like monarchy, enslavement is fodder for his teaching.

Together, these texts bear witness to the futility of trying to name God in human terms or trying to confine her to human systems. We need new language. Even then, all of our language is and would be inadequate. It is important, then, to consider that any language is at best suggestive and not authoritative. God's majesty transcends the human systems for which it is named.

PROPER 13 (CLOSEST TO AUGUST 3)

1 Samuel 15:1–3, 8, 10–17, 24–25; Psalm 146; Revelation 1:4–6; Mark 6:14–29

1 Samuel 15:1 Samuel said to Saul, "I was sent by the DREAD GOD to anoint you ruler over God's people, over Israel; now then, hearken to the call of the words of the INSCRUTABLE GOD: ² Thus says the SOVEREIGN of heaven's vanguard, 'I will punish Amalek for what they did to Israel, setting against them in their ascent from Egypt. ³ Now go and smite Amalek, and put to holy destruction all they have; do not spare them and put them to death from woman to man, and from infant to nursing baby, and from ox to sheep, from camel to donkey.'"

⁸ Saul seized Agag ruler of the Amalekites alive, and put to holy destruction all the people at the edge of the sword.

¹⁰ The word of the SOVEREIGN GOD to Samuel was: ¹¹ "I regret that I crowned Saul as ruler, for he has turned away from me, and my commands he has not instituted." Then Samuel was angry, and he cried out to the GOD WHO HEARS, all night. ¹² And Samuel rose early in the morning to meet Saul, and it was told to Samuel: "Saul went to Carmel, where he erected a monument for himself, then turned around and passed by going down to Gilgal." ¹³ Now, Samuel came to him and Saul said to him, "Blessed are you by the HOLY ONE OF OLD; I have instituted the command of the HOLY ONE OF SINAI." ¹⁴ Then Samuel said, "What is this sound of sheep in my ears, and the sound of cattle I am hearing?" ¹⁵ And Saul said, "They brought them from the Amalekites, for the people spared the best of the sheep and the cattle, to sacrifice to the HOLY ONE your God; but the rest we have put to holy destruction." ¹⁶ Then Samuel said to Saul, "Stop! Let me tell you what the ANCIENT ONE said to me last night." Saul replied, "Speak."¹⁷ Samuel said, "Though you are small in your own eyes, are you not the head of the tribes of Israel? The HOLY ONE anointed you ruler over Israel."

²⁴ Saul said to Samuel, "I have sinned; for I have transgressed the utterance of the DREAD GOD and your words, because I feared the people and obeyed their voice. ²⁵ Now then, I pray, pardon my sin, and return with me, so that I may worship the HOLY ONE OF OLD."

Psalm 146

¹ Hallelujah! Praise the AGELESS ONE, O my soul!
² I will praise the EVER-LIVING GOD all my life;
   I will sing praises to my God throughout my living.
³ Put not your trust in the great, nor in any child of earth,
   for there is no help in them.
⁴ When they breathe their last, they return to earth,
   and in that day their thoughts perish.
⁵ Happy are these for whom the God of Rebekah's line is their help,
   whose hope is in the CREATOR OF ALL, their God.

⁶ Maker of heavens and earth, the seas, and all that is in them;
   keeping faith forever.
⁷ Bringer of justice to the oppressed,
   bringer of bread to the hungry;
   the COMPASSIONATE GOD sets the prisoners free.
⁸ The ALL-SEEING GOD opens the eyes of the blind,
   the JUST GOD lifts up those who are bowed down;
   The RIGHTEOUS GOD loves the righteous.
⁹ The MOTHER OF ALL cares for the stranger,
   orphan and widow she bears up,
   but the way of the wicked she confounds.
¹⁰ The MAJESTIC ONE shall reign forever,
   your God, O Zion, from generation to generation. Hallelujah!

Revelation 1:4 John to the seven churches that are in Asia:

Grace to you all and peace from the One who is and who was and who is to come, and from the seven spirits who are before God's throne, [5] and from Jesus Christ, the faithful witness, the firstborn of the dead, and the ruler of those who reign on the earth.

To Jesus who loves us and freed us from our sins by his blood, [6] and made us to reign, priests serving his God and Father, to Christ be glory and power forever and ever. Amen.

Mark 6:14 Now King Herod heard of [the teaching of Jesus], for Jesus's name had become known and some were saying, "John the baptizer has been raised from the dead and that is why these powers work through him." [15] Yet others said, "It is Elijah" while others said, "It is a prophet, like one of the prophets [of old]." [16] But when Herod heard of it, he said, "John, whom I beheaded, has been raised."

[17] For Herod himself had sent men who seized John and bound him in prison because of Herodias, the wife of his brother Philip, for Herod had married her. [18] For John had told Herod, "It is not right for you to have your brother's wife." [19] Now Herodias had a grudge against him and she wanted to kill him. But she could not. [20] This was because Herod feared John, knowing that he was a righteous man and a holy man and he protected him and listened to him, though greatly perplexed; yet it pleased him to listen to him.

[21] Now an opportune time came on Herod's birthday when he gave a banquet for his courtiers and commanders and for the leaders of Galilee. [22] And Herod's daughter Herodias came in and danced, pleasing Herod and his dinner guests. The king said to the girl, "Ask me for whatever you wish, and I will give it to you." [23] And he swore to her repeatedly, "Whatever you ask me, I will give you, even half of my kingdom." [24] And she went out and said to her mother, "What should I ask?" She replied, "The head of John the baptizer." [25] Immediately she returned to the king with haste and asked, saying, "I want immediately for you to give me on a platter the head of John the baptizer." [26] The king was deeply sorry, yet because of

his oaths and the guests, he did not want to refuse her. [27] Immediately the king sent a soldier under orders to bring John's head. And he went and beheaded him in the prison. [28] And he brought his head on a platter and gave it to the girl and the girl gave it to her mother. [29] When John's disciples heard, they came and took his body, and laid it in a tomb.

PROCLAMATION

Text Notes

I choose language to render the divine name that communicates the horror of Samuel's claim that God called for annihilation "from woman to man, and from infant to nursing baby," dreadful and inscrutable. In 1 Samuel 15:1, the "call" of the words of God is the "sound" or "voice." In the prosecution of holy war called for by God, utter annihilation is sanctified as the ultimate offering to God. People, animals, and some time the land itself is "put under the ban"—banned from existence, the living beings slaughtered, the land torn up and often salted to prevent planting. The verb *haram* means "ban," "devote" (to God), and "destroy." There is no respite, rescue, or redemption from holy destruction (Leviticus 27:28–29). Failure to complete this genocidal action is punishable—they can be shown no mercy or pity (Deuteronomy 7:2). God expresses regret—not quite repentance—for enthroning Saul in the same terms that Job expresses regret for demanding an account of God in Job 42:6.

In Psalm 146:1, "throughout my living" is derived from "in my continuing," where "continue" is the adverb meaning "longer," *'od*, with the first possessive suffix, "my" attached, a very complex idiomatic saying. The "great" in verse 2 are "nobles," sometimes royal offspring, hence "princes" in other translations. In verse 4 "Rebekah's line" replaces "Jacob." The nature of God's support for widow and orphan in verse 8 is unclear; the verb there is only used there and its derivation is unclear. NRSV's "uphold" derives from the LXX and provides the basis for my "bear up." Similarly, the Peshitta has "nourish/support."

In Revelation 1:5 the original language is "ruler of kings," a grammatical plural that would include female monarchs like Israel's own last sovereign before Roman rule, Salome Alexandra, also known as Shlomzion, the Peace of Zion. (Her sons' refusal to accept her rule—her husband passed the throne to her knowing their character—resulted in them drawing Rome into the dispute, Pompey on one side, Caesar on the other, leading to the installation of the Herods.) Likewise, "kingdom" is modified in verse 6, which has been translated as "a kingdom [and] priests" in the Vulgate, Wycliffe, RSV, NRSV, and CEB, and as "kings and priests" in Tyndale, Geneva, Bishop, and KJV. And as is the rule in this lectionary, whenever Father is used to signify parentage of Jesus, it is retained. *Kratos*, "power" in verse 6, is variably translated as "might," "strength," and "dominion."

Preaching Prompts

Monarchy forms one of the overarching motives of the scriptures because it is virtually the only system of governance extant in the world of the scriptures. Even in those systems that are not strictly monarchal, absolute hierarchical authority is the norm. Monarchy represented the ultimate in power and control over life, death, and well-being. Its ascription to God was inevitable. Human governance has evolved without a concomitant reassessment of the prevailing language, imagery, and metaphors we use for God. These lessons invite us to do just that.

Beyond moving the story of Israel's monarchy along, the fall of Saul offers a challenging study on repentance and forgiveness, and Saul's unanswered plea for pardon illustrates the difficulty in teasing out the human and divine in the scriptures. The psalmist's assurance that God is a righteous judge echoes throughout the canon and contributes to the dissonance of hearing God call for the slaughter of innocents, including babies at the breast in 1 Samuel (and elsewhere), a stark contrast with the teaching that God shows no favoritism.

One of the most problematic theological claims in the Hebrew Bible is on display in this lesson on the fall of Saul that serves as a literary foil for the selection of the beloved David, the genocidal God of the "Old Testament" often set in opposition to the loving God (and Jesus) of the New Testament. Needless to say, these claims and their underlying theology require frank discussion and thoughtful engagement, not least for what they signify about God. An important caveat is that these texts are retrospective and the bulk of them are ahistoric; Joshua is particularly notorious in this regard with eighteen of nineteen Canaanite cities claimed as utterly destroyed showing no evidence of destruction or not having been occupied at all in the relevant timeframe. (See the very helpful charts and discussion in Frank Frick's chapter on Joshua and Judges in *A Journey through the Hebrew Scriptures*.) A rare moment of grace in this story is that even though it marks God's rejection of Saul, Samuel seems not to have given up on him. More significantly, he gets angry (at God?) and pours out his heart, all night long. Yet we should remain troubled by Saul's fate and the purported fate of the Amalekites and the claims made in God's name by God's prophet.

There are women missing from the telling of Saul's fall from grace; he has a primary wife, Ahinoam the daughter of Ahimaaz (1 Samuel 14:50) and two daughters, Merab and Michal (1 Samuel 14:49). He also has a low-status wife, Rizpah. His rise and fall affected them all, not least because it brought David into their orbit, leading to the engagement of both daughters, marriage (and abandonment) of one, and ultimately the death of Merab's children and those of Rizpah, at the word of David (2 Samuel 21:8–9). In the other texts, women are subsumed in the people, congregation, and believers.

In Psalm 146, God demonstrates true majesty in her caretaking of the vulnerable: women receive care from the hand of God. Not just widowed women in verse

9 but also women who are oppressed, hungry and imprisoned in verse 7, women who are blind and bowed down in verse 8, and women who are righteous, strangers, sojourners, or immigrants, as well as women who are themselves orphans in verse 9. God's majesty rests on a foundation of righteousness and justice to which no human monarch can ever fully aspire.

The cosmic Christ of the Apocalypse of John views royal power not as something to hoard but something to distribute, subverting the monarchal hierarchy. Every believer and follower, without regard to gender or class status, is elevated to the majesty of Christ. The once gender exclusive priesthood is now transformed and open to all. This divine majesty includes and elevates.

The story of Herod, Herodias, and her unnamed daughter dramatizes how far below the divine standard human royals can fall. The women in the story demonstrate the concept of kyriarchy, the absolute power of a monarch, which trumps gender peril in the same way white privilege often does. Rather than fulfill the law, the Herods, like most, if not all ancient monarchs, set themselves above the law and take whatever they want. (The marriage of Herod and Herodias is prohibited by Leviticus 18:16.) People, their lives, and bodies are disposable playthings to them. Their human monarchy is death-dealing while the majesty of God incarnate in Christ Jesus is life-giving.

PROPER 14 (CLOSEST TO AUGUST 10)

1 Samuel 17:1–7, 12–16, 24–27; Psalm 10:1–14; Romans 8:31–39; John 10:11–16

1 Samuel 17:1 Now the Philistines gathered their encampments for war; they were gathered at Socoh, which is part of Judah and they encamped between Socoh and Azekah, in Ephes-dammim. ² And Saul and the Israelites were gathered and encamped in the valley of Elah and they organized ranks to engage the Philistines. ³ Now the Philistines were standing on this hill and the men of Israel were standing on this other hill with a valley between them. ⁴ And there went out from the camp of the Philistines a man apart [a champion], Goliath was his name, of Gath; his height was six cubits and a span [over nine feet tall]. ⁵ A helmet of bronze was on his head and he was clothed in scale armor; the weight of the bronze armor was five thousand shekels [or one hundred twenty-five pounds]. ⁶ And greaves of bronze were on his legs, and a javelin of bronze between his shoulders. ⁷ The shaft of his spear was like a weaver's beam and the iron tip of his spear weighed six hundred shekels [or fifteen pounds] and his shield-bearer went before him.

¹² Now David was the son of this Ephrathite man of Bethlehem in Judah, and his name was Jesse, and he had eight sons. And the man was, by the days of Saul, old and going as

mortals do. ¹³ Now the three eldest sons of Jesse set out and followed Saul to the battle; the names of his three sons who went to the battle were Eliab the firstborn, Abinadab his second, and the third, Shammah. ¹⁴ David was the youngest; the three eldest followed Saul. ¹⁵ David would come and go back from Saul to feed his father's sheep at Bethlehem. ¹⁶ And the Philistine came forward morning and evening and took his stand for forty days.

²⁴ And all the men of Israel in seeing the man, fled from his presence and were very afraid. ²⁵ The Israelites said, "Do you all see this man who is coming forward? He is coming forward to insult Israel. What will happen is, the man who smites him, the sovereign will make rich—great riches!—and he will give him his daughter and make his family free in Israel." ²⁶ David said to the men who were standing with him, "What shall be done for the man who smites this Philistine and takes away the reproach from Israel? For who is this uncircumcised Philistine that he should defy the ranks of the living God?" ²⁷ The people answered him according to those spoken words, "Thus shall it be done for the man who smites him."

Psalm 10:1–14

¹ Why, COMPASSIONATE ONE, do you stand afar?
 Why do you hide yourself in hard times?
² In arrogance the wicked harass the poor;
 let them be caught in the schemes they have devised.
³ For the wicked praise their [every] inmost desire,
 extort gain and bless those who despise the CREATOR OF ALL.
⁴ The wicked turn up their nose and do not seek [God];
 There is no God in all their thoughts.
⁵ Their ways prosper all the time;
 your judgments are on high, beyond them;
 all their foes scoff at them.
⁶ They say in their heart, "We shall not be shaken;
 nor [see] evil down through the generations."
⁷ Cursing fills their mouths along with deceit and oppression;
 under their tongues are trouble and iniquity.
⁸ They sit in ambush in the villages;
 in hiding places they murder the innocent.
 Their eyes surveil the vulnerable.
⁹ They lie-in-wait in secret like a lion in its den;
 they lie-in-wait that they may snatch the poor;
 they snatch the poor and drag them off in their net.
¹⁰ They stoop, they crouch,
 and the vulnerable fall prey through their might.
¹¹ They say in their heart, "God has forgotten,
 she has hidden her face, she will never see it."

12 Rise up, FAITHFUL GOD; dear God, lift up your hand;
   forget not the oppressed.
13 Why do the wicked despise God,
   and say in their hearts you shall not find out?
14 You see, you regard trouble and grief,
   to take [it] into your hands.
   Upon you the vulnerable entrust themselves;
   to the orphan you have ever [only] been their helper.

Romans 8:31 What then are we to say about these things? If God is for us, who is against us? 32 God who did not spare God's very Son, but rather handed him over for all of us, will not God with the Son also give us everything else? 33 Who will bring accusation against God's elect? It is God who justifies. 34 Who is to condemn? Christ Jesus who died, moreover, who was raised, who is at the right hand of God, is indeed the one who intercedes for us. 35 Who will separate us from the love of Christ? Will trouble, or distress, or persecution, or famine, or nakedness, or peril, or sword? 36 As it is written,

> *"For your sake we are being killed all day long;*
> *we are appraised as sheep to be slaughtered."*

37 Rather, in all these things we are more than victorious through God who loves us. 38 For I am persuaded that neither death, nor life, nor angels, nor rulers, nor things present, nor things to come, nor powers, 39 nor height, nor depth, nor any other thing in all creation, will be able to separate us from the love of God in Christ Jesus our Savior.

John 10:11 "I am the good shepherd. The good shepherd lays down his life for the sheep. 12 The hired hand, who is not the shepherd to whom the sheep do not belong, sees the wolf coming and abandons the sheep and flees, and the wolf snatches them and scatters them. 13 All because a hired hand does not care for the sheep. 14 I am the good shepherd. I know my own and my own know me, 15 just as the Shepherd-Of-All knows me and I know the Shepherd-Of-All. And I lay down my life for the sheep. 16 And I have other sheep that do not belong to this fold: I must bring them as well, and they will listen to my voice, thus there will be one flock, one shepherd.

PROCLAMATION

Text Notes

Often what biblical Hebrew designates a "mountain" as in 1 Samuel 17:3 would qualify as a "hill" elsewhere. Goliath is characterized as "a man between the armies." "Champion" is an elliptical, not literal choice; the surviving solo fighter would be the de facto champion. In the LXX Goliath is just over six feet tall. The tip of his spear is a "flame" in verse 7. Verses 12–31 are missing from the LXX, which is not simply a translation, but a translation from a different Hebrew text than the text that gave rise to the MT. The discovery of the Dead Sea Scrolls (DSS) established that among the most ancient manuscripts were versions corresponding to both MT and LXX and readings unique to the DSS. "Free in Israel" in verse 25 suggests the victor will be exempt from military or civil service projects, which were generally compulsory. "Forty days" (or "forty nights and days") is idiomatic for a good long time, like "a month of Sundays," which we would never render literally as twenty-eight weeks.

There are a number of difficulties with the text in Psalm 10. Robert Alter and JPS annotate them. "Hard" times in verse one of this song refers to drought. The use of "hard" here signifies both the hardened earth and the resulting difficult economic times. An alternate reading for the last line of verse 2 is that they, the poor, have been caught in the schemes of the wicked. "Turn their nose up" in verse 4 is a nearly literal translation of the disjointed "like a height, their nose (or countenance)." "They do not seek" lacks an object; I have supplied "God," because the verb is used primarily to seek God and God is named in and the last phrase. The second phrase of verse 6 lacks a verb.

"Trouble" in Romans 8:35 includes oppression at the hands of others as well as broader hardship or tribulation. Verse 36 quotes Psalm 44:22 (which is Psalm 43:23 in the LXX, remembering that the primary way the Greek first testament varies is in the number and sequence of books.) In verse 37 I forgo the traditional "conquerors" for the more literal "be victorious" to reject the conflation of victory in Christ with the violence of conquest.

Preaching Prompts

Deliverance from enemies is one of the major hallmarks of God's fidelity in the Hebrew Scriptures, invoked by the first lesson and psalm, and that language remains powerful in a world with interpersonal and international enmity. Women and their children were often invisible in these conflicts except as markers of brutality or valiant women like Deborah, Jael, and Judith. Yet there are mothers, wives, sisters, daughters, aunts, nieces, and grandmothers connected to each undifferentiated man in the Israelite and Philistine armies and there are David's mother and sisters, Zeruiah and Abigail, who will appear later (2 Samuel 17:25 and 1 Chronicles 2:15–16). It is worth asking how women in the text and its world experienced such deliverance; salvation of their town, protection from captivity, and abuse come to mind. While no less bloody a world, the New Testament doesn't proffer pitched battles with the occupying Romans or an upstart champion to knock them down a peg. The psalmist, apostle, and evangelist each turn heavenward for their source of salvation.

The David and Goliath story has become an archetype of the unlikely victor overcoming great odds. The story exists in a variety of forms in the Hebrew Bible: 1) the familiar story in 1 Samuel 17:1–58; 2) 2 Samuel 21:19 where Elhanan son of

Jaare-oregim, also of Bethlehem kills (another?) Goliath whose spear shaft is also a weaver's beam; and 3) 1 Chronicles 20:5 where another Elhanan, this time son of Jair, killed Lahmi the brother of Goliath who possessed yet a third weaver's beam spear shaft. The first and second Goliaths are from towns spelled with the same consonants, suggesting different versions of the same story. Similarly, the fathers of the two Elhanans from the second and third stories are variations of the same name. None of these later stories are fleshed out as well as the first. The variances point to the flexibility of storytelling and scripture and the comfort of ancient readers with hearing multiple, competing versions.

Psalm 10 might be heard as having been prayed by a woman on either the Philistine or Israelite side, experiencing the horrors of war from the perspective of those left behind to bury or mourn the dead and eke out a living from the remains of confiscated or ruined crops.

In Romans 8 Christ Jesus, the love of God incarnate, is the champion of the Christian in all contexts, from accusation to want and need, to violence and the threat of violence. However, Christ does not go into battle like David or Goliath; rather Christ accompanies and strengthens the believer, enabling them to endure and more, to declare victory over circumstances that would defeat anyone else.

In the Gospel, Jesus is bound to the sheep because they, we, are his own. He is not a mercenary who will leave when he gets a better offer, or when the flock is in danger and their defense would be at the risk of his life. A shepherd-for-hire might well leave the flock to their fate at that point. But Jesus would risk and lose his life for his sheep, for Jesus's relationship with the sheep is a reflection of his relationship with the One who shepherds him. For those who would claim to know who belongs to Jesus and who does not, there is the intriguing claim that Jesus has more sheep, another flock whom we know not. While some might read this as a statement of universal embrace, encompassing all the world's peoples and religions, this may have referred to the reconciliation of differing strands of the young Christian movement.

FEAST OF THE EVER-BLESSED VIRGIN MARY, AUGUST 15

Judith 13:18–20; Canticle 15, the Magnificat, (Luke 1:46–55); Revelation 21:1–7; Luke 1:26–38

Judith 13:18 Uzziah said to Judith, "O daughter, you are blessed by the Most High God above all other women on earth, and blessed be the Holy God, who created the heavens and the earth, who has guided you to cut off the head of the leader of our enemies. [19] Praise of you will never depart from the hearts of women and men who remember the power of God.

²⁰ May God do these things for you as an eternal exaltation, and may God visit you with blessings, because you did not withhold your life when our nation was humiliated, rather you rallied against our demise, walking straight before our God." And all the people said, "Amen. Amen."

Canticle 15, the Magnificat, Luke 1:46–55

⁴⁶ "My soul magnifies the Holy One,

⁴⁷ and my spirit rejoices in God my Savior,

⁴⁸ for God has looked with favor on the lowliness of God's own womb-slave.
    Surely, from now on all generations will call me blessed;

⁴⁹ for the Mighty One has done great things for me,
    and holy is God's name.

⁵⁰ God's loving-kindness is for those who fear God
    from generation to generation.

⁵¹ God has shown the strength of God's own arm;
    God has scattered the arrogant in the intent of their hearts.

⁵² God has brought down the powerful from their thrones,
    and lifted up the lowly;

⁵³ God has filled the hungry with good things,
    and sent the rich away empty.

⁵⁴ God has helped God's own child, Israel,
    a memorial to God's mercy,

⁵⁵ just as God said to our mothers and fathers,
    to [Hagar and] and Sarah and Abraham, to their descendants forever."

Revelation 21:1 I saw a new heaven and a new earth, for the first heaven and the first earth had passed away, and the sea was no more. ² And I saw the holy city, the new Jerusalem, descending heaven from God, prepared as a bride adorned for her beloved. ³ And I heard a loud voice from the throne saying,

"Look! The home of God is among the woman-born.
God will dwell with them as their God;
they will be God's peoples,
and the selfsame God will be with them.

⁴ God will wipe every tear from their eyes.
Death will be no more;
grief and weeping and pain will be no more,
for the first things have passed away."

⁵ And the One who was seated upon the throne said, "Look! I am making all things new." The One also said, "Write, for these words are trustworthy and true." ⁶ Then the One said

to me, "It is done! I am the Alpha and the Omega, the beginning and the end. I will give to the thirsty from the spring of the water of life freely. [7] Those who overcome will inherit these things, and I will be their God and they will be my daughters and sons.

Luke 1:26 In the sixth month the angel Gabriel was sent by God to a town of Galilee, Nazareth, [27] to a virgin betrothed to a man whose name was Joseph, of the house of David. And the name of the virgin was Mary. [28] And the angel came to Mary and said, "Rejoice, favored one! The Most High God is with you." [29] Now, she was troubled by the angel's words and pondered what sort of greeting this was. [30] Then the angel said to her, "Fear not Mary, for you have found favor with God. [31] And now, you will conceive in your womb and give birth to a son, and you will name him Jesus. [32] He will be great and will be called the Son of the Most High, and the Sovereign God will give him the throne of his ancestor David. [33] He will reign over the house of Jacob forever, and of his sovereignty there will be no end." [34] Then Mary said to the angel, "How can this be, since I have not known a man intimately?" [35] The angel said to her, "The Holy Spirit, She will come upon you, and the power of the Most High will overshadow you; therefore the one born will be holy. He will be called Son of God. [36] And now, Elizabeth your kinswoman has even conceived a son in her old age, and this is the sixth month for she who was called barren. [37] For nothing will be impossible with God." [38] Then Mary said, "Here am I, the woman-slave of God; let it be with me according to your word." Then the angel left her.

PROCLAMATION

Text Notes

In Judith 13:20 Judith's actions are described awkwardly as "rallying against" the "corpse" (understood as the eminent demise) of her people, i.e., taking action to oppose that which would end in their deaths.

Revelation 21 deploys a marriage metaphor that does not require a rigid gender binary or heteronormativity to be effective, so I have translated *aner*, "man," meaning "husband" in verse 2, as "beloved." *Nike* in verse 7 means to "overcome obstacles" or "prevail." To "be victorious" and "conquer" are also within the semantic range; however, the latter two choices do not clearly indicate struggle, and "conquer" (as in NRSV) seems unnecessarily martial here.

In Mary's languages, Hebrew for prayer and religious texts and Aramaic for daily life, the Holy Spirit is feminine. The Greek scriptures use the neuter pronoun corresponding to "it." It is not until the production of the Vulgate and other Latin texts that the masculine pronoun is inserted. While the literary language is Greek, the translation choice reflects the underlying Semitic linguistic cultural context. In verse 48 of the Magnificat, Mary uses the same slave language that Hannah does, "woman-slave of God," a common expression across the canon. When used with reference to reproduction, as here, I use womb-slave; the language of slavery pervades the scriptures and forms the rhetoric of the most familiar stories, often without examination. In verse 55 of the Magnificat I have added Hagar as a witness to God's fidelity proclaimed in the verse.

Preaching Prompts

Like Judith whose name can be translated "Jewish woman," Miriam rendered "Mary" in English (along with other Hebraic names in the Second Testament to sound less Jewish) was a Jewish woman. Where Judith is an older widowed woman when she puts her body on the line to save her people, Mary, named for the prophet Miriam like all of the "Marys," was young and on the cusp of marriage. Each woman has her bona fides established in a lengthy genealogy. Judith's is the longest of any woman in the canon, stretching from the time of Nebuchadnezzar to Simeon, Leah's son by Jacob (Judith 8:1; 9:2); though some argue against her historicity. While Judith's husband is folded into *her* genealogy, "Her husband Manasseh, who belonged to her tribe and family," Mary's genealogy is *Joseph's* genealogy.

The patriarchal genealogy fails to tell the story of Mary and Jesus as descendants of Bathsheba and David, though it does so for Joseph (Matthew 1:1–17, see verses 6 and 16, and Luke 2:4), even while naming Tamar (I), Ruth, and describing Bathsheba as the wife of Uriah but without her name (Matthew 1:3, 5–6). Mary is *presumed* to be from Joseph's tribe, Judah, following the most common marital pattern and likely from a more closely related clan within the tribe. Mary is likely not Joseph's sister, though she could be his cousin; somewhere between Solomon in verse 7 and Mattan, Joseph's grandfather, in verse 15 Mary's genealogy is obscured.

Both Judith and Mary have their virtue attested—Judith's piety as a widow (Judith 8:4–6) and Mary's virginity (Luke 1:26ff)—and both will use their bodies in scandalous ways to effect salvation. Judith entices an enemy general who seeks to seduce her—but with a maid present to testify to her virtue—and beheads the man with his own sword (Judith 13:4–10). Mary agrees to the divine pregnancy, risking being ostracized and perhaps stoned for the appearance of breaking faith with Joseph. For some readers there will always be a question of the degree to which Mary was free to refuse. That she affirmatively consents is clear: "Let it be with me according to your word." But could she refuse? Before she consents, Gabriel says: "You will . . ." The timing is crucial, helping readers and hearers grapple with consent issues in the text and the gulfs between ancient and contemporary ethical standards.

Mary and Judith are also linked in the words of blessing "among" and "above other" women in Judith 13:18 and Luke 1:42. Elizabeth, Mary's relative, could have chosen the blessing by drawing from her scriptures, from Judith and from the words of Deborah's blessing on Jael in Judges 5:24: "Most blessed of women . . . of tent-dwelling women most blessed." (Judith was included in the Greek Jewish Bible and influential where not later canonical). Like her textual sisters, Jael's story is framed by scandal, assassinating an enemy general after welcoming him to hide there; a man who was so well known as a rapist his mother imagines his delay is caused by his proclivities (Judges 4:17–24; 5:24–30). His position at his death, between (not "at" per NRSV) Jael's legs, would seem confirmation.

The blessings of Jael and Judith with their histories of violence worry the innocence of the annunciation with the reminder of the violence to which Mary is at risk now and the violence she will live to see enacted on the body of her son. In the words of another holy person, "a sword will pierce her soul" (Luke 2:35).

John (1:1) says, "The Word became flesh and dwelled, *eskēnōsen*, among us." If Jesus is the heir of Bathsheba and David according to the flesh, it is through Mary's flesh, the matrix of the Incarnation, that God comes to dwell with us. That verb, *skēnoō*, "to dwell" is also used in the second reading chosen for today: "God will dwell with them as their God." The Feast of the Ever-Blessed Virgin Mary affords an opportunity to reflect on the ways in which God dwells with us and a model of hospitality.

PROPER 15 (CLOSEST TO AUGUST 17)

1 Samuel 17:55–18:9; Psalm 47:1–2, 5–9; Hebrews 1:1–9; Matthew 5:33–37

1 Samuel 17:55 When Saul saw David go out to meet the Philistine, he said to Abner, the commander of the army, "Whose son is this boy, Abner?" Abner said, "By the soul of the king, if I knew . . ." [56] Then the king said, "You ask whose son the stripling is." [57] As David returned from smiting the Philistine, Abner took him and brought him before Saul with the head of the Philistine in his hand. [58] And Saul said to him, "Whose son are you boy?" And David answered, "I am the son of your slave Jesse the Bethlehemite."

[18:1] Now it happened by the time David finished speaking to Saul, the soul of Jonathan was bound to the soul of David, and Jonathan loved him as his own soul. [2] And Saul took David that day and would not permit him to return to the house of his father. [3] Then Jonathan made a covenant with David because he loved him as his own soul. [4] So Jonathan stripped off the robe that was on him and gave it to David, and his armor and even his sword, and his bow, and also his belt. [5] David went out and in all to which Saul sent him was successful; then Saul placed him over the warriors. And it was good in the eyes of all the people, even in the eyes of the slaves of Saul.

[6] And it was as they were coming back, when David returned from smiting the Philistine, the women came out of all the towns of Israel to sing with the dances to meet King Saul with hand drums, with rejoicing, and with musical instruments. [7] And the women sang in response to each another as they reveled,

"Saul has killed his thousands,
and David his ten thousands."

⁸ And Saul raged, hot; this saying was evil in his eyes. And he said, "They gave to David ten thousands and to me they gave thousands. There is only the throne left for him!" ⁹ So it was that Saul eyed David from that day on.

Psalm 47:1–2, 5–9

¹ All you peoples, clap your hands;
  shout joyfully to God with a joyful shout.
² For GOD WHO IS MAJESTY, the Most High, is awesome,
  a great sovereign over all the earth.
⁵ God has gone up with a shout,
  the GLORIOUS ONE with the sound of a trumpet.
⁶ Sing praises to God, sing praises;
  sing praises to our sovereign, sing praises.
⁷ For God is the sovereign of all the earth;
  sing praises with a psalm.
⁸ God is sovereign over the nations;
  God sits on her holy throne.
⁹ The nobles of the peoples gather
  as the people of the God of Hagar and Sarah.
  For to God belong the shields of the earth;
  she is highly exalted.

Hebrews 1:1 Many times and in many ways God spoke to our mothers and fathers through the prophets, female and male. ² In these last days God has spoken to us by a Son, whom God appointed heir of all there is, and through whom God created the worlds. ³ The Son is the brilliance of God's glory and reproduction of God's very being, and the Son undergirds all there is by his word of power. When the Son had made purification for sins, he sat down at the right hand of the Majesty on high, ⁴ having become as much greater than the angels as the name he inherited is more excellent than theirs.

⁵ For to which of the angels did God ever say,

"*You are my Child; today I have begotten you*"?

Or this,

"*I will be their Parent, and they will be my Child*"?

⁶ Then again, when God brings the firstborn into the world, God says,

"*Let all the angels of God worship the Son.*"

[7] On the one hand of the angels God says,

> "*God makes winds into celestial messengers,*
> *and flames of fire into God's ministers.*"

[8] But of the Son God says,

> "*Your throne, O God, is forever and ever,*
> *and the righteous scepter is the scepter of your realm.*
>   [9] *You have loved righteousness and hated lawlessness;*
> *therefore God, your God, has anointed you*
> *with the oil of gladness beyond your companions.*"

Matthew 5:33 [Jesus said] "Again, you have heard that it was said to those of ancient days, *You shall not swear falsely [or break an oath], but carry out the vows you have made to the Holy One.* [34] But I say to you: Do not swear at all, either by heaven, for it is the throne of God, [35] or by the earth, for it is God's footstool, or by Jerusalem, for *it is the city of the great Sovereign.* [36] And do not swear by your head, for you are not able to make one hair white or black. [37] Let your word be 'Yes, Yes' or 'No, No'; anything more than this comes from the evil one."

PROCLAMATION

Text Notes

First Samuel 17:55 and the first five verses of chapter 18 are missing from the LXX. Verse 55 is commonly translated as some version of "By the life (or soul) of the king, I do not know." Others change it to second person, "By your life/soul . . ." Compare NRSV, CEB, and JPS. The rather common idiomatic expression is conditional introduced with "if"; further, the negative particle "no/not" is missing.

In 1 Samuel 18:1, "by the time" is "when . . ." and in verse 5, the "warriors" are "men of war." The word most often translated "timbrel" is actually a hand drum. Extensive archaeological work, particularly by Carol Meyers, has turned up no images or evidence of the metal or other noisemakers on the drum frames; the final group of instruments in verse 6 are likely sistrums, a handheld percussive instrument that is shaken, in the broad category of a rattle. Saul's rage in verse 8 is expressed with a verb for "burning" modified by "much/greatly."

The psalmist employs a noun and verb from the same root in verse 1; the duplication is intentional. In verse 9 "the God of Hagar and Sarah" replaces "the God of Abraham."

The following verses quote the earlier scriptures widely and often out of context: Verse 5 quotes Psalm 2:7, where the anonymous psalmist says God told them they were God's begotten child, probably initially heard with regard to David. The next quote is from 2 Samuel 7:14 (and its duplicate, 1 Chronicles 17:13), where the promise of God to be a parent to a future monarch is to one of David's descendants. Given the difficulty of asserting biological gender for heavenly beings, I use the neuter "child" and "parent" in verse 5. Verse 6 quotes Deuteronomy 32:43 and Psalm 97:7 from Greek where the original "gods" were replaced by "angels" to correct toward a pure monotheism. Verse 7 quotes Psalm 104:4, playing on the primary meaning of angel, messenger. Verses 8–9 quote Psalm 45:6–7, where the first verse refers to God but the second refers to the king whose wedding psalm it is (Ahab since Jezebel is the only princess of Tyre to marry into Israel).

In keeping with the aims of this work, foremothers and female prophets are made explicit in Hebrews 1:1. *Megalōsynēs*, "Majesty," in Hebrews 1:3, as a feminine noun, marks a rare use of feminine language to describe God or her attributes in the New Testament.

In Matthew 5:33, the same word means both to swear falsely with no intention of keeping one's oath and to break an oath that one may have intended to keep. Both options are available to the reader. Though not a direct quote, in the same verse, the principle of keeping an oath to and through the point of extremis is mentioned repeatedly in the Torah (Leviticus 19:12; Numbers 30:2; Deuteronomy 23:21) and is used as the justification for the slaughter of the daughter of Jephthah by her own father in Judges 11. Verse 35 includes a snippet of Psalm 48:2 identifying Jerusalem as the city of God who reigns in and over it.

Preaching Prompts

One of the most common forms of love in the Hebrew Bible is covenant love, between God and humanity and between monarchs on behalf of their nations and between individual men. Often there is unequal power between covenant partners. Women are included in covenants as members of humanity and of the people Israel, though there are some who would argue they are not because the sign of inclusion is circumcision. (Some Jewish feminists substitute "circumcise your heart" for "circumcise your flesh.")

While the specific nature of David's covenant with Jonathan is not articulated, all covenants as well include loyalty as a primary element. Jonathan dressing David in his own clothes signifies an elevation of the shepherd boy to the same status as Jonathan, a prince. The love between Jonathan and David is more than covenant love. As David, profligate and promiscuous, would declare upon the death of Jonathan, his love for him was a wonder—miraculous would not be a stretch—and greater than the love of women (2 Samuel 1:26). The passage neither discloses nor precludes a sexual relationship. In spite of contemporary near-obsession with the two verses in Leviticus that address some male-male sexual contact in some circumstances, the vast breadth of the Hebrew Scriptures is silent on the subject and redeploys the word "abomination" to categorize lying and other ethical violations in Proverbs (3:32; 6:16; 8:7; 11:1, 20; 12:22).

God's covenant with her people emerges from God's status as a sovereign monarch. The psalm reflects the grandeur of God's status and signifies her graciousness in embracing human beings as covenant partners. Hebrews recounts God's covenants with humanity and presents Jesus as the fruit of that fidelity. Though missing from the David and Jonathan story, oaths provide the infrastructure of a covenant and lay out mutual obligations. Because of the regard in which the Israelites held vows and oaths, they were not to be taken lightly. An oath was not to be invoked in matters of casual speech. Jesus reiterates that Torah teaching in the Gospel. As the anchor and guarantor of covenants, God herself, her name, her throne, her earthly home, were not to be invoked apart from the serious and formal declaration of oaths and covenants.

The Church uses the language of covenant formally for baptism and marriage. In some traditions the language of covenant is also used less formally for commitments people make to each other and to causes such as the pursuit of justice in a particular context. More than the importance of keeping one's word, commitments, and fulfilling covenant obligations, these lessons invite us to think about the full personhood of each person in a covenant or commitment. Beyond implications for marriage, an intimate partnership, where the biblical world imagines an imbalance in status as normative, we are able to imagine and shape a world where we engage people as equal across gender, culture, and ethnic lines as we covenant together to build a world that reflects the love of the gospel.

PROPER 16 (CLOSEST TO AUGUST 24)

1 Samuel 14:49–51; 18:17–21, 29; Psalm 31:1–7, 14–16, 19–24; Romans 13:8–10; Mark 12:28–34

1 Samuel 14:49 Now the sons of Saul were Jonathan, Ishvi, and Malchishua, and the names of his two daughters, the name of the firstborn was Merab, and the name of the younger, Michal. [50] The name of Saul's wife was Ahinoam daughter of Ahimaaz, and the name of the commander of his army was Abner son of Ner, Saul's uncle. [51] Kish was the father of Saul and Ner the father of Abner was the son of Abiel.

[18:17] Then Saul said to David, "Look, here is my older daughter Merab. I will give her to you as a wife; only be my valiant warrior and fight the battles of the HOLY ONE." For Saul said [to himself], "Let me not raise a hand against him, rather let the hand of the Philistines do it." [18] Then David said to Saul, "Who am I and what is my lineage, my ancestral house in Israel, that I should be son-in-law to the ruler [of Israel]?" [19] But at the time for giving Merab the daughter of Saul to David, it happened that she was given to Adriel the Meholathite as a wife.

²⁰ Now [at the same time] Saul's daughter Michal loved David. Saul was told, and the matter was all right in his eyes. ²¹ So Saul said [to himself], "Let me give Michal to David that she may be a snare for him and that the hand of the Philistines may be against him." So, Saul said to David a second time, "Through the second shall you be my son-in-law this day."

²⁹ And Saul came to fear David more and Saul became the enemy of David every day from then.

Psalm 31:1–7, 14–16, 19–24

¹ In you, WOMB OF LIFE, I take refuge;
　　let me not ever be put to shame;
　　in your righteousness rescue me.
² Incline your ear to me;
　　quickly deliver me.
　　Be for me a rock of refuge,
　　a stronghold to save me.
³ For you are my rock and my stronghold;
　　for your Name's sake lead me and guide me.
⁴ Free me from the net that is hidden for me,
　　for you are my refuge.
⁵ Into your hand I commit my spirit;
　　you have redeemed me, ARK OF SAFETY, God of truth.
⁶ I hate those who attend to worthless vanity,
　　but in the MOTHER OF ALL I place my trust.
⁷ I will exult and I will rejoice in your faithful love,
　　because you have seen my affliction;
　　you have studied my soul's sorrows.
¹⁴ Yet I, in you I trust, FAITHFUL GOD;
　　I declare, "You are my God."
¹⁵ My times are in your hand;
　　deliver me from the hand of my enemies and those who hound me.
¹⁶ Let your face shine upon your slave;
　　save me in your faithful love.
¹⁹ How great is your goodness
　　that you have secured for those who fear you,
　　and that you do for those who take refuge in you,
　　before all the woman-born.
²⁰ In the shelter of your presence you shelter them
　　from human plots;
　　you hide them safe under your shelter
　　from contentious tongues.

21 Blessed be the MOTHER OF CREATION,
who is marvelous in her faithful love to me,
a city under siege.

22 Now I, I had said in my alarm,
"I am cut off from your sight."
However, you heard my supplications
when I cried to you for help.

23 Love GOD WHOSE NAME IS HOLY, all you her godly ones.
The FAITHFUL GOD preserves the faithful,
and repays with interest the one who acts out of pride.

24 Take courage, and she shall strengthen your hearts,
all you who wait for the MOTHER OF ALL.

Romans 13:8 Owe no one anything, except to love one another; for the one who loves another has fulfilled the law. ⁹ The commandments, "*You shall not commit adultery; You shall not murder; You shall not steal; You shall not covet,*" and any other commandment, are summed up in this word, "Love your neighbor as yourself." ¹⁰ Love does no harm to a neighbor; therefore, love is the fulfilling of the law.

Mark 12:28 Now, one of the biblical scholars came near and heard them [the other biblical scholars, the chief priests, and the elders] discussing with one another, and seeing that Jesus answered them well, the scholar asked Jesus, "Which commandment is the first of all?" ²⁹ Jesus answered, "The first is: *Hear, O Israel: the Holy One our God, the Holy is one;* ³⁰ *you shall love the Holy One your God with all your heart, and with all your soul, and with all your mind, and with all your strength.* ³¹ The second is this, *You shall love your neighbor as yourself.* There is no other commandment greater than these." ³² Then the biblical scholar said to him, "You are right, Teacher; you have truly said that '*God is one, and besides God there is no other*'; ³³ and *to love God with all the heart, and with all the understanding, and with all the strength,* and *to love one's neighbor as oneself.* This is much more important than *all whole burnt offerings and sacrifices.*" ³⁴ When Jesus saw that the scholar answered wisely, he said, "You are not far from the reign of God." After that no one dared to ask Jesus any question.

PROCLAMATION

Text Notes

In 1 Samuel 14:49 Merab is Saul's firstborn, though her brothers are listed previously. "Father's family" is translated "ancestral house" in 18:18 and "my life" as "my lineage."

In verse 4 of the psalm, "free me" is the "let my people go" verb of the exodus. In verse 9 there is only one "eye" and tears are lacking; "body" is "belly/womb." Somewhat contradictorily, "to go silently to Sheol" can also be "to go weeping to Sheol."

"Godly ones" in verse 23 are often translated anachronistically as "saints," importing Christian language and theology into the Hebrew Scriptures.

Romans 13:9 quotes the Decalogue in Exodus 20:13–15, 17 and Deuteronomy 5:17–19, 21 and, secondarily, Leviticus 19:18. *Kakon* in verse 10 has a range that includes "evil," "bad," "harm," and "wrong."

The audience for this series of teachings is identified in Mark 11:27. "Biblical scholar" more aptly describes the expertise of the scribal class than "scribe," which while accurate, can be misread as "copyist." These scholars are portrayed as exclusively male. However in the rabbinic period Beruriah (2nd C), wife of Rabbi Meir, was a well-regarded Torah scholar. Characterizing the "discussion" among religious colleagues in verse 28 as a "dispute" (NRSV) adds a level of rancor that is not present in the text.

Jesus answers the scholar's question in verse 28 with two of the core confessions of Judaism: the *Shema* and the *Ahavta* in verses 29–30. The *Shema* (Hear!) is the primary theological confession of the oneness of God from Deuteronomy 6:4. The *Ahavta* (You-shall-love) consists of the following verses, 5–9, and expresses the primary obligation toward God. Both in the Markan recitation and its Matthean parallel (22:37), Jesus adds the category "mind," *dianoias*, to Deuteronomy 6:5, which makes sense given the partial assimilation into Greek culture and its philosophical traditions into Hellenized Jewish culture.

Jesus follows the traditional two-part unit with a citation from Leviticus 19:18 to love enemies as one loves oneself; this teaching is cited throughout the Christian Testament (Matthew 5:43; 19:19; 22:39; Mark 12:31; Romans 13:9; Galatians 5:14; James 2:8). The scholar's speech in verses 32–33 combines a number of biblical phrases, "there is none other" (Psalm 86:8; Isaiah 45:21, 46:9; Jeremiah 10:6) followed by a paraphrase of Deuteronomy 6:5, and concluding with the comparative value of sacrifices and offerings from Hosea 6:6 and Micah 6:6–8.

Preaching Prompts

These passages explore love, human and divine, fallible and faultless. The soap-opera-worthy monarchal saga in the first lesson demonstrates aptly that love and marriage do not always coincide. And though the royal setting can evoke romantic readings upon first blush, in these stories love is a resource to be manipulated and exploited in the pursuit and maintenance of power. In contrast, God's faithful love in the psalm is enduring. The Epistle offers a vision of human love beyond the romantic framework, one that seeks to emulate the fidelity of God's love. And in the Gospel, Jesus offers a paradigm for love of God, love of self, and love of neighbor.

In the first lesson, Saul, like monarchs across time, uses his daughters to secure allies and loyalty. In most of the contexts in which these lessons will be read, fathers do not hold absolute sway over their daughter's lives, marriages, and ultimately, sexuality. But there are multiple social, political, cultural, and religious contexts where women, nonbinary folk, trans folk, and gender-nonconforming folk are not free to make choices about their lives, bodies, and relationships.

While love and loyalty are often intertwined in covenants between monarchs in treaties and between God and humanity articulated in covenantal terms, interpersonal human love occurs with some limitations. In most cases, men love and women are loved (passively) in terms of romantic love. Michal's unrequited love for David is the sole exception. For example, Isaac loved Rebekah (Genesis 24:67); Jacob loves Rachel more than Leah (Genesis 29:18); Samson loved Delilah (Judges 16:4); Elkanah loved Hannah (1 Samuel 1:5); the king loved Esther (Esther 2:17). Two rapists express love for their victims in Genesis 34:3 and 2 Samuel 13:1. Mothers love their children—sons (Genesis 25:28)—as do fathers (Genesis 37:3), but no one loves their daughter in the text, though Nathan evokes that love in his parable about a ewe loved as a daughter in 2 Samuel 12:3. Jerusalem/Zion is God's daughter often subject to harsh discipline; God's love for her is presumed but unspoken (Isaiah 62:11; Jeremiah 6:2, 23; Lamentations 1:6).

Covenant love is expressed between God and humanity broadly, and God and Israel in particular. God also enters into covenant with individual men but not women, not even when granting theophanies and annunciations. This is likely rooted in an Iron Age understanding of legal competence and the relative lack of independent standing for most women. The death of Justice Ruth Bader Ginsburg during the preparation of this volume occasioned a reeducation of the American public on the history of the status of women and the very recent moves to legalize equality and full standing as participatory citizens and legal and moral agents.

Paul writes, "Love does no harm to a neighbor," and Jesus links love of neighbor with love of God. Yet it does not appear that Christians have historically understood women as "neighbor." If our gospel proclamations are not true for the most marginalized among us—women, nonbinary folk, trans folk, gender-nonconforming folk, and LGBTQIA folk—then our gospel is not true.

PROPER 17 (CLOSEST TO AUGUST 31)

1 Samuel 25:14–19, 23–25, 32–34, 42–43; Psalm 37:1–2, 7–11, 16, 35–40;
Galatians 5:13–21; Luke 19:1–10

1 Samuel 25:14 To Abigail, wife of Nabal, one of the boys reported: "Look! David sent messengers out of the wilderness to greet our lord; and he screamed at them. [15] Yet the men were very good to us, and we were not put to shame, and we never missed anything all the days we were with them when we were in the field. [16] They were a wall to us even by night and also every day;

we were with them, keeping the sheep. [17] Now know this and see what you can do, for evil against our master and against all his house has been resolved. He is worthless; no one can speak to him."

[18] Then Abigail hurried and she took two hundred loaves, two skins of wine, five prepared sheep, five measures of parched grain, one hundred clusters of raisins, and two hundred fig cakes and she loaded them on donkeys. [19] And Abigail said to her boys, "Go on before me; I am coming after you." And her husband Nabal she did not tell.

[23] And Abigail saw David and she hurried and got down from the donkey, fell before David on her face, bowing to the ground. [24] She fell at his feet and said, "Upon me my lord, the iniquity; please let your slave-woman speak in your ears and hear the words of your slave. [25] Please my lord, do not set your thought on this worthless man Nabal, for as his name, thus is he; Nabal [meaning Disgrace] is his name, and he is a disgrace; now I, your slave, did not see my lord's boys whom you sent."

[32] Then David said to Abigail, "Blessed be the HOLY ONE, the God of Israel, who sent you to meet me today! [33] Blessed be your discernment, and blessed be you, who have kept me today from coming for blood and saving me from my own hand. [34] Surely as the HOLY ONE the God of Israel lives, who has restrained me from hurting you, unless you had hurried and come to meet me, truly by the light of daybreak there would not have been left to Nabal anyone urinating against a wall."

[42] [Later after Nabal's death,] Abigail hurried and got up and mounted a donkey with five of her girls at her heels; she went after the messengers of David and she became his wife. [43] David also married Ahinoam of Jezreel; both of them became his wives.

Psalm 37:1–2, 7–11, 16, 35–40

1 Be not angry on account of the wicked,
  be not envious of wrongdoers;
2 for they will soon wither like the wild grass,
  and fade like the planted grass.
7 Be still before the MOST HIGH, and wait patiently for her;
  be not angry on account of those who prosper on their path,
  or the one who carries out plots.
8 Let go of anger and forsake wrath;
  be not angry; it leads only to evil.
9 For the wicked shall be cut off,
  but those who hope in the FOUNT OF JUSTICE shall inherit the land.
10 And a little more time and the wicked will be no more;
  you will reflect upon their place and they will not be there.
11 But the humble poor shall inherit the land,
  and delight themselves in abundant well-being.
16 Better is a little that the righteous person has
  than the abundance of many wicked.

35 I have seen the wicked oppressing,
and spreading themselves out like a native green tree.
36 They passed on, and suddenly! They were no more;
though I sought them, they could not be found.
37 Regard the blameless and behold the upright,
for there will be a future for the peaceable.
38 But transgressors shall be utterly destroyed together;
the future of the wicked shall be cut off.
39 The salvation of the righteous is from the EVER-PRESENT GOD;
she is their stronghold in the time of trouble.
40 The REDEEMING GOD helps them and delivers them;
she delivers them from the wicked, and saves them,
because they take refuge in her.

Galatians 5:13 Now you were called to freedom, sisters and brothers. Only let not your freedom be an opportunity for self-centeredness, but through love become slaves to one another. 14 For the whole Teaching is summed up in a single commandment, *"You shall love your neighbor as yourself."* 15 Yet, if you bite and devour one another, see to it that you are not consumed by one another.

16 I say this, walk in the Spirit and do not gratify the desires of the flesh. 17 For what the flesh desires is contrary to the Spirit, and what the Spirit desires is contrary to the flesh; for these are in opposition to each other, to prevent you from doing whatever you want. 18 But if you are led by the Spirit, you are not under [the power of] the law. 19 Now the works of the flesh are plain. They are: sexual immorality, impurity, lasciviousness, 20 idolatry, sorcery, enmities, strife, jealousy, anger, quarrels, dissensions, heretical schisms, 21 envy, drunkenness, carousing, and things like these of which you all were [warned] before: those who do such things will not inherit the majesty of God.

Luke 19:1 Now Jesus entered Jericho and was passing through it. 2 There was a person named Zacchaeus who was a chief tax collector and was rich. 3 Zacchaeus was seeking to see who Jesus was, but was not able to on account of the crowd, being short in stature. 4 So Zacchaeus ran ahead and climbed a sycamore to see Jesus, who was going to pass that way. 5 Now when Jesus came to the place, he looked up and said to him, "Zacchaeus, hurry and come down; for I must stay at your house today." 6 So Zacchaeus hurried down and welcomed Jesus, rejoicing. 7 All who saw it began to grumble and said, "To a sinner has he gone to be a guest." 8 Zacchaeus stood there and said to the Messiah, "Look, half of my possessions, Anointed One, to the poor will I give, and if have defrauded anyone, I will pay back four times as much." 9 Then Jesus said to Zacchaeus, "Today salvation has come to this house, because he too is a child of Abraham. 10 For the Son of Woman came to seek out and to save the lost."

PROCLAMATION

Text Notes

The young man in servitude to her household tells Abigail that David and his men did not "shame" or "humiliate" him or the other servants in 1 Samuel 25:15. That "shame" could include any type of humiliation, including sexual, as in 2 Samuel 10:4 where men have their garments cut off so as to display their genitals in public humiliation; both texts use the same word. In verse 16, "even by night and also every day" translates "even night and even days." My translation of this verse is indebted to Everett Fox's translation in *The Schocken Bible, Volume II, The Early Prophets*. In verse 17 Nabal's nature is summed up in the epithet *ben belial*, "the son of worthlessness." In verse 25, Abigail begs David not to "set his heart to[ward]" Nabal. His name encodes all sorts of bad behavior from impiety to sacrilege, to disorderly conduct and sexual assault. In verse 32, "blessing" is used as a greeting ritual. Other common forms of greeting include "May God bless you" (see Ruth 2:4). Some understand the "wall pisser" of verse 35 to be a euphemism for soldier like "jarhead" or "leatherneck."

The language of Psalm 37:1 is somewhat stronger than the traditional "fret not" found in KJV and NRSV. Rather, it is the verb for burning anger that often discloses divine wrath. Verse 2 uses two different words for grass, with the latter sometimes having the sense of cultivated grass. To be "still" in verse 7 is also to be "silent," as in Aaron's silence in Leviticus 10:3 (elsewhere, Jeremiah 47:6; 48:2; Ezekiel 24:17; Amos 5:13; Psalms 4:4; 30:12; 31:17). The word used for "hope" in verse 9 can also mean "wait"; some translators (KJV, NRSV) use "wait" here while others (CEB, Alter) use "hope" to distinguish it from "wait" in verse 7, a separate word (where JPS uses "look to"). The traditional translation "meek" in verse 11 obscures the impoverished estate of the referent. Further, "meekness" is a personality and behavioral characteristic, whereas the term here denotes those who have been made humble by their impoverished circumstances, often in the biblical text through the unethical actions of others. In the same verse, "well-being," *shalom*, includes but is not limited to "prosperity" as in the NRSV. The humble poor and those who wait for and hope in God in verses 9 and 11 will inherit the "land," previously translated "earth." both translations are tenable. However, the land itself is the treasure, heritage, and promise of God. The verse is not speaking of dominion over the world as it was known. The Hebrew of verse 35 is awkward but not untenable. There is no need to replace the MT with the LXX as do the NRSV and CEB.

In Galatians 5:13 "flesh" becomes "self-centeredness." In verse 14, "Teaching" represents the fullness of what is included in the Torah: instruction, legislation, and jurisprudence among other forms. *Haireseis* in verse 20, "heresies," also means "divisions" or "factions." "Heretical schisms" encapsulates both senses.

Given "Lord" includes human beings as well as the Divine, and with regard to human beings, particularly denotes slaveholders; that language is not used for God or Jesus in this lectionary. In Luke 19:8 messianic language replaces "Lord."

Preaching Prompts

While some biblical passages equate wealth with blessing uncritically, these lessons look more deeply at what one does with one's wealth as a measure of character. Nabal was stingy and mean-spirited when he could have shown hospitality. Of people like him the psalmist counsels that they and their riches will not last, but those who have been reduced to humble circumstances through the ill-gotten gain of others will inherit the earth. In the Epistle, the teaching about greed expands from material possessions to self-centered desires contrasted with the inheritance that is the majestic realm of God. In the written Gospel, Zacchaeus comes into contact with the living gospel and his disposition toward his own wealth changes; he becomes generous and acknowledges that some of his wealth may be dishonest and pledges to restore what he has defrauded in addition to providing for the poor.

The relationship between Abigail and David is often romanticized without regard for the potentially violent context in which it began. At this phase of his life, David is a thug, robbing and extorting people for cash crops and currency on the hoof. Nabal is a vile person, a nasty drunk, a difficult if not abusive husband, but that does not entitle David to his goods; he is not yet king. Nabal had a cultural obligation to provide hospitality but that should not merit a death sentence. Yet David vowed that he would have killed them all if Abigail had not brought him the goods. He and Abigail ride off into the sunset after the death of her husband and he pulls over somewhere and picks up another woman. Abigail is more than a match for David; she has lived with and survived an abusive husband. She handled David and his demands expertly. She is equipped for their journey and whatever it will bring.

The psalmist speaks to more than the anger that can arise when contemplating the way those who have wealth, and particularly those who have earned it unjustly, seem to flourish while so many struggle and sometimes fail to meet their daily needs. She refers to the burning rage and fury that is often God's in other passages and here should be considered excessive anger rather than righteous anger. She also speaks with the perspective of God looking at the expense of time, which is minute in divine perspective. For that which is unseen and that which is not yet, she bids us wait on and hope in the God who sees us, knows us, and will not abandon us. Yet, we must acknowledge these beautiful words and hope-filled promises are not food in the belly, a roof over the head, or clothing upon one's back.

The Epistle's teaching on self-indulgent desires beyond mere material greed is cast in binary terms of the spirit versus the flesh. This language has often been used to denigrate the human person, the physical body and its biological needs. This language has been used to denigrate and stigmatize natural, healthy, sexual desire and fulfillment as well, though that is not the message of the passage. In this case the author is focusing on excessive desires and self-gratifying desires rather than condemning the care and tending of one's body and health. Mutual sexual gratification would seem to be beyond rebuke. Reading this text in conversation with the David epic begs the question of how Paul would have regarded David's conduct.

While Jesus centered much of his teaching on the poor and ministered to them, he also maintained friendships with the wealthy, including those who made their wealth off of the backs of his people by taxing them over and above what was required, in order to enrich themselves. There is a mystery in this text. Why did Jesus need to go to Zacchaeus's house? Did he make the determination before he saw him in the tree or after? Zacchaeus's conversion regarding his wealth seems immediate. There is time that is unaccounted for in the passage. At some point they moved from the tree to the house, if indeed Jesus's blessing on his house took place there. What else happened there? What was their conversation? How long did he stay? The final lines are revealing: Jesus says he has come to seek out and save the lost. Riches may buffer some of the hardships of life, but one can have all the wealth in the world and still be deeply lost.

PROPER 18 (CLOSEST TO SEPTEMBER 7)

1 Samuel 27:1–3, 8–12; Psalm 94:1–15; James 2:8–13; Mark 7:14–23

1 Samuel 27:1 David said to his heart, "Now, one day I shall be swept away by the hand of Saul; there is nothing better than that I escape to the land of the Philistines, then Saul will despair of seeking me any further within the border of Israel and I shall escape out of his hand." ² So David got up and went over, he and six hundred men who were with him, to Achish son of Maoch, ruler of Gath. ³ And David stayed with Achish at Gath, he and his troops, each man with his household, and David with his two wives, Ahinoam of Jezreel, and Abigail of Carmel, wife of Nabal.

⁸ And David and his men went up and raided on the Geshurites, the Girzites, and the Amalekites, for they were the inhabitants of the land from of old on your way to Shur and on to the land of Egypt. ⁹ Then David smote the land and there was neither woman or man living; and he took sheep and cattle and donkeys and camels and clothing and would return and come back to Achish. ¹⁰ Then Achish would ask, "Against whom did you all raid today?" And David would say, "against the Negeb of Judah," or "against the Negeb of the Jerahmeelites," or, "against the Negeb of the Kenites." ¹¹ Neither woman nor man David left living to be brought back to Gath, saying, "Lest they tell about us, and say, 'Thus did David.'" Thus was his custom all the days he lived in the country of the Philistines. ¹² Now Achish trusted David saying,

"He has made himself an abhorrent stench in the nostrils of his people, in Israel; so he shall be my slave for all time."

Psalm 94:1–15

1 God of vengeance, DREAD GOD,
 God of vengeance, shine forth!

2 Rise up, Judge of the earth;
 repay recompense on the proud!

3 How long shall the wicked, JUST ONE,
 how long shall the wicked exult?

4 They gush, they speak arrogance;
 all the workers of iniquity boast.

5 Your people, they crush, FAITHFUL ONE,
 and your heritage, they abuse.

6 Widow and immigrant they slay,
 and orphans they murder.

7 And they say, "The HOLY ONE, she does not see,
 the God of Rebekah's line does not understand."

8 Understand, you ignorant among the people;
 fools, when will you become wise?

9 The one who planted the ear, does she not hear?
 The one who formed the eye, does she not see?

10 The one who disciplines the nations,
 the one who teaches knowledge to the woman-born,
 does she not chastise?

11 The ALL-KNOWING GOD knows the thoughts of the woman-born,
 that they are but breath.

12 Blessed is the one who you admonish, JUST ONE,
 whom you instruct from your teaching,

13 to grant them respite from evil days,
 until a pit is dug for the wicked.

14 For the FAITHFUL ONE will not forsake her people;
 her heritage she will not abandon.

15 For to the righteous justice will return,
 and after it go all the upright in heart.

James 2:8 You all will do well if you actually fulfill the majestic law according to the scripture, "*You shall love your neighbor as yourself.*" 9 But if you show favoritism, you commit sin and are convicted by the law as transgressors. 10 For whoever keeps the whole law but fails in one point becomes accountable for the whole. 11 For the one who said, "*You shall not commit* *adultery,"* also said, *"You shall not murder."* Now if you do not commit adultery but if you murder, you have become a transgressor of the law. [12] So speak and so act as those who are to be judged by the law of liberty. [13] For judgment will be merciless to anyone who has shown no mercy; mercy shouts victory over judgment.

Mark 7:14 Jesus called the crowd again and said to them, "Listen to me, all of you, and understand: [15] There is nothing outside a woman or man that by going into them has the power to defile, rather what comes out of a person is what defiles a person."

[17] Now when Jesus had left the crowd and entered the house, his disciples asked him about the parable. [18] He said to them, "Are you all then also without understanding? Do you all not see that whatever goes into a woman or man from outside has no power to defile? [19] For it does not enter the heart but rather the stomach, and goes out into the sewer." (Thus Jesus declared all foods clean.) [20] Jesus also said, "It is what comes out of a woman or man that defiles. [21] For it is from within, from the human heart, that evil thoughts come: sexual immorality, theft, murder, [22] adultery, greed, wickedness, deceit, licentiousness, an evil eye [or envy], slander, pride, thoughtlessness. [23] All of these evil things come from within, and they defile a person."

PROCLAMATION

Text Notes

The text continues to refer to Abigail as the "wife" of Nabal (not "widow" in spite of NRSV and CEB) as it will for Bathsheba, though in the latter case it certainly highlights David's transgression.

In verse 6 of the psalm, *anah*—"abuse"—includes "oppression," "humiliation," and physical and sexual violence; in the same verse "orphan" is a fatherless child, hence the frequent pairing of "widow" and "orphan." "Yah," a short form of the divine Name, occurs in verse 7. Though traditionally taking masculine verbs, its grammatical form is feminine, and in some feminist and egalitarian Jewish contexts is used with feminine verbs in prayer and liturgy. Also in verse 7, "the God of Rebekah's line" is "the God of Jacob." In verse 11 *chevel* can mean "breath" or "futility."

James 2 quotes Leviticus 19:18 in verse 8 and the Decalogue in verse 11 (Exodus 20:13, 15/Deuteronomy 5:17–18). In verse 13, *katakauchatai* represents more than the "triumph" of the NRSV; it is the shout of a victorious gladiator (BDAG).

Mark 7:15, 18, and 20 use *anthropou*, man or generic human; I have specified women and men as the teaching would not have applied to minors. The question mark at the end of verse 18 in translation properly belongs at the end of the first line in verse 19 in Greek; however, in English it fits better in the earlier location. The "evil eye" in verse 22 is translated as "envy" by the NRSV and CEB; both options are available for the reader. At the end of 22 *aphrosynē* can be translated as "foolishness" and thus "folly" in the NRSV; however, it is more properly the foolishness that results from thoughtlessness.

Preaching Prompts

In the world of the Hebrew Scriptures, the heart is the locus of volition, morality, and conduct. That notion endures into the Christian Testament. What one says and does reveals who one is and the nature of one's heart. Read in conversation with the Second Testament lessons, the actions of David, God's erstwhile favorite, are alarming and appalling.

David has been anointed ruler of Israel before his family, in 1 Samuel 16:13, yet Saul still reigns. It is left to David to seize the throne himself; however, he will not raise his hand against the anointed of God (see 1 Samuel 26:6–12 and 2 Samuel 1:11–16). ("Anointed" is *mashiach*, messiah; monarchy was a messianic enterprise in ancient Israel.) Saul views David's popularity as a threat and has been seeking to kill him (1 Samuel 19:1–2, 11–15). It is in this period that David becomes a mercenary marauder in the employ of the Philistine ruler. David is supposed to decimate his own people for his overlord; instead he chooses peoples and clans that are related to or coresident with Judah. He will be able to say he never touched a hair on the head of his "own" people. He did, however, conduct a series of massacres against noncombatant peoples, murdering women and men alike—murder is a strong word and reflects my ethical assessment given these peoples were not at war and had not engaged in any hostile acts. No mention is made of the children's fate. David is an Iron Age monarch-in-training and monarchy has ever been a brutal occupation.

While Jewish and Christian readers have been socialized to read from the perspective of Israel and their heroes like David, womanist, feminist, and postcolonial readers advocate for reading from the position of the most marginalized here, David's victims. The psalm might be understood as their plea for justice in the face of unjust slaughter. To the degree that David is in service to the Philistine monarch, he is an agent of the state making a Black Lives Matter reading of the first two texts possible.

The framing of Jesus as the Son of David and of God as the supreme monarch are intended to convey power, authority, and majesty, but cannot erase the uglier legacies invoked with monarchal language, making Jesus's insistence that his realm, God's realm, is of an entirely different nature than earthly monarchies. In any configuration the psalm is a cry for justice and more, vengeance. The notion of God as a God of vengeance is ancient and enduring. The psalmist cries out for vengeance while trusting in the rightness of God's actions.

In the Epistle, James builds upon the command to love one's neighbor from the Torah and teaching of Jesus in the Gospels, also preserved in the Epistles. He offers a catalog of evidence to determine whether one truly loves one's neighbor from the heart, measurable by one's conduct. He adds a caveat: transgression of one part of the law is transgression of all. In his reckoning we are all equally guilty before the law but possess the ability to choose behavior that expresses the faith in our hearts and choose to deal with each other in mercy rather than judgment, assuring mercy for ourselves at our judgment.

Jesus uses eating and the subsequent production of waste to vividly illustrate that nothing one consumes defiles one as even kosher food becomes waste. Rather, it is what is in the human heart that defiles, as illustrated by a catalog of such behavior that overlaps with the Epistle. An editorial hand adds that Jesus had declared all foods "clean." It should be noted that this conclusion is in a second voice and is somewhat at odds with the early history of the Church and disputes over Torah observance. In all of the lessons, the truth of who we are emerges from our hearts and is made visible through our actions.

PROPER 19 (CLOSEST TO SEPTEMBER 14)

1 Samuel 30:1–8, 17–19; Psalm 71:1–6; 2 Corinthians 1:8–11; Matthew 6:9–13

1 Samuel 30:1 And it was that when David and his men came to Ziklag on the third day [after being dismissed by the Philistine ruler], the Amalekites raided the Negeb and Ziklag. They smote Ziklag and burned it with fire. ² And they took captive the women who were in it, from young to old; they did not kill any, rather they led them away and went their way. ³ So when David and his men came to the city, they found it burned and their wives and daughters and sons taken captive! ⁴ Then David and the people who were with him raised their voices and wept, until there was no more strength in them to weep. ⁵ Now the two wives of David had been taken captive, Ahinoam the Jezreelite and Abigail the wife of Nabal the Carmelite. ⁶ David was in great distress; for the people said to stone him, because the souls of all the people were embittered on account of their daughters and sons and David strengthened himself in the HOLY ONE his God.

⁷ Then David said to Abiathar the priest, the son of Ahimelech, "Bring to me the ephod." So Abiathar brought the ephod to David. ⁸ And David questioned the HOLY ONE OF OLD asking, "Shall I pursue this band? Will I overtake them?" God answered him, "Pursue, for you shall surely overtake and you shall surely rescue."

¹⁷ So David smote them from twilight until the evening of the morrow. None of them escaped, except four hundred young men who mounted camels and fled. ¹⁸ And David rescued all who the Amalekites took; David rescued his two wives. ¹⁹ None was missing, whether young or old, daughters or sons, spoil or anything that they took for themselves; David brought back everything.

Psalm 71:1–6

¹ In you, ETERNAL ONE, do I take refuge;
   let me never be put to shame.
² In your righteousness deliver me and rescue me;
   incline your ear to me and save me.

3 Be to me a fortress of rock,
   where I may ever go;
   you command my salvation
   for you are my rocky stronghold.
4 My God, rescue me from the hand of the wicked,
   from the clutch of the cruel and the ruthless.
5 For you are my hope, Sovereign, WORTHY ONE,
   my trust, from my youth.
6 Upon you I have leaned from birth;
   from my mother's belly, you cut me.
   You will I praise for all time.

2 Corinthians 1:8 Now, we do not wish for you all to be unaware, sisters and brothers, of our affliction that happened in Asia; for we were utterly crushed, forced down so that we despaired of living. 9 Instead, we received the sentence of death within ourselves so that we would rely not on ourselves but on God who raises the dead. 10 The One who from so great a deadly a peril rescued us will continue to rescue us; on God we have set our hope to rescue us again. 11 Helping us also are your prayers, so that many, for the gift to us through the prayers of many, will give thanks on our behalf.

Matthew 6:9–13

9 Pray then in this way:
   Our Parent and Provider in heaven,
   holy is your Name.
10 May your majestic rule come.
   May your will be done,
   on earth as in heaven.
11 Give us this day our daily bread.
12 And forgive us our debts,
   as we also forgive our debtors.
13 And do not bring us to the time of trial,
   but rescue us from that which is evil.

PROCLAMATION

Text Notes

The seized women (and likely girls) in 1 Samuel 30:2, 19 are either "from young to old" or "from small to great." Given the explicit mentions of daughters in verse 6, I read this in terms of age with Fox, Alter, the CEB, and the Targum, rather than in terms of status, "low-born and high-born alike," as in JPS. In the LXX, men are included among the abducted. The ephod is a priestly garment worn over the regular garment. It held the divination tools, Urim and Thummim; the breastplate with stones for each tribe was attached to the front. Traditionally one asked "yes" or "no" questions as David did here. However, God seems to speak to David apart from divination and beyond "yes" and "no." While normally worn and used by a priest, Gideon made an unsanctioned ephod in Judges 8:27. David's use of the ephod here and in 2 Samuel 6:14 suggests a priestly role for David in his own eyes and those of some of his biographers, which extended to his sons in 2 Samuel 8:18 (see 2 Samuel 6:18 where David offers sacrifice and the note on verse 14 in the same chapter in the *Jewish Study Bible*).

In verse 4 of the psalm, God is named as "Lord" (corresponding to lowercase use as is common when addressing men) in combination with God's unpronounceable Name, YHWH, usually rendered as "Lord God" (capitalized for deity). In verse 6 the "God-as-midwife" theme familiar from Psalm 22:9 takes a dramatic turn with God "cutting" rather than "drawing" the baby out. The difference is *gochi* versus *gozi*, a single letter, perhaps indicating recall of the former psalm without access to the text. The cutting itself could range from a cesarean delivery—practiced in ancient Egypt—to cutting the cord as in CEB.

The "crushing" in 1 Corinthians 1:8 likely refers to a brutal form of execution in which the condemned is slowly crushed to death by a heavy stone placed upon the torso. The linkage is strengthened by the mention of a "death sentence" in the following verse.

"Bread for tomorrow" is suggested by *epiousios*. Used only in this prayer here and in Luke 11:3; the reading is supported by BDAG and the *Jewish Annotated New Testament*. Liturgical alternatives for the "Our Father" follow after the preaching commentary. In verse 12, NRSV changes the active verb "forgive" to the passive "have forgiven," implying that one must have already forgiven one's debtors in order to be forgiven. The active verb allows a person doing the active work of forgiveness, and perhaps struggling with it, to be confident in receiving forgiveness. The petition in verse 14 is to be delivered from "the evil." While "the evil" in the prayer of Jesus is regularly personified and identified as an evil one, understood by many to be Satan, it is a much broader term that includes the evil humans do as well as supernatural evil. Grammatically, "the evil one" is a possibility; the expansive reading includes all that is evil, whether personified or dispersed.

Preaching Prompts

Salvation in the Hebrew Bible is physical and material deliverance or rescue of an individual or community from enemies. That language becomes spiritualized in the Second Testament. In the first lesson, it is Abigail and Ahinoam and the families of his troops that are in need of rescue, having been retaliated against for David's actions. Psalm 71 is a petition for rescue from someone in a situation that may not be at all dissimilar from that in which Abigail and Ahinoam found themselves. In 2 Corinthians, Paul (likely) recounts having found himself in need of physical rescue and his confidence that the God who delivered him will continue to do so. And in the Gospel, the prayer Jesus teaches his disciples includes a petition to be delivered, rescued, from evil, sharing a resonance with Psalm 71:4.

In 1 Samuel 30, David, who has made a name for himself slaughtering women and men and either killing or taking their children captive (the text neglects their fate), has his family carried off into captivity along with the families of his men. Understandably they all break down and cry at their loss and at the thought of their fate—enslavement and physical and sexual abuse. The scene is vivid and their pain palpable. After turning to God for strength, David and his men mount a successful rescue. The psalm provides a suitable prayer that fits the moment. Every moment without their wives and children was a "How long, O God" moment.

The psalmist and Paul, the likely author, trust God to deliver them in their time of need because of God's steadfast faithfulness in the past. For the psalmist, God is the midwife who brought her into the world. For Paul, God is the one who rescued him from mysterious and undisclosed danger in Asia that had the potential to cost his life.

The "Our Father" is a bedrock of Christian faith. It has been retranslated and reinterpreted by many far beyond making the opening salutation inclusive. The Rev. Yolanda M. Norton offers this version in her Beyoncé Mass:

Our Mother,
who is in heaven and within us,
we call upon your names.
Your wisdom come.
Your will be done,
in all the spaces in which you dwell.
Give us each day
sustenance and perseverance.
Remind us of our limits as
we give grace to the limits of others.
Separate us from the temptation of empire,
and deliver us into community.
For you are the dwelling place within us,
the empowerment around us,
and the celebration among us,
now and forever. Amen.

The Benedictine Women of Madison from the Holy Wisdom Monastery offer this version entitled "The Prayer of Jesus":

Holy One, our only Home
blessed be your name,
may your day dawn,
your will be done,
here, as in heaven.
Feed us today, and forgive us,
as we forgive each other.
Do not forsake us at the test,
but deliver us from evil.
For the glory, the power,
and the mercy are yours
now and forever.
Amen.

PROPER 20 (CLOSEST TO SEPTEMBER 21)

2 Samuel 1:17–27; Canticle Mater Tua Leaena (Ezekiel 19:1–3, 10–14); 1 Thessalonians 4:13–18; John 16:16–22

2 Samuel 1:17 David keened this lamentation over Saul and over Jonathan his son. [18] Then he taught the Bow [Song] to the women and men of Judah; it is written in the Book of Jashar. He said:

[19] The splendor of Israel upon heights lays slain!
How the mighty have fallen!
[20] Tell it not in Gath,
proclaim it not in the streets of Ashkelon,
lest the daughters of the Philistines rejoice,
lest the daughters of the uncircumcised exult.
[21] Hills of Gilboa,
let there be neither dew nor rain upon you,
nor offering-laden fields.
For there the shield of the mighty was abhorred,
the shield of Saul, anointed with oil no more.
[22] From the blood of the slain,
from the fat of the mighty,

the bow of Jonathan did not turn back,

and neither did the sword of Saul return empty.

23 Saul and Jonathan, beloved and delightful.

In life and in death they were not parted;

they were swifter than eagles,

they were stronger than lions.

24 Daughters of Israel, weep over Saul,

who clothed you with scarlet, in luxury,

who overlaid your garments with adornments of gold.

25 How the mighty have fallen

in the midst of battle!

Jonathan upon your heights lies slain.

26 I grieve over you, my brother, Jonathan;

a great delight were you to me;

your love to me was wonderful,

more than the love of women.

27 How the mighty have fallen,

and the weapons of war destroyed!

Canticle Mater Tua Leaena *(Ezekiel 19:1–3; 10–14)*

Ezekiel 19:1 All of you, raise a keening for the royal seed of Israel, ² and say:

What a lioness was your mother among lions!

Among young lions she lay, raising her cubs.

3 She raised up one of her cubs, who became a young lion,

who learned to catch prey, who devoured the woman-born.

10 Your mother was like a vine in a vineyard planted by the waters,

fruitful and full of branches from abundant water.

11 She had mighty branches for a ruler's scepter;

she grew tall, her height among the clouds,

and was seen because of her height

and because of her many branches.

12 Then she was uprooted in a rage, she was thrown to the ground,

the east wind withered her fruit, they were stripped off;

her strongest stem was withered, then consumed by fire.

13 Now she is planted in the wilderness,

in a dry and thirsty land.

14 Now fire has gone out from her staff, and has devoured her branches, her fruit,

now there is no mighty branch within her, no scepter for ruling.

This is a keening-lament, and it is used for lamentation.

1 Thessalonians 4:13 Now we do not want you to be ignorant, sisters and brothers, about those who have fallen asleep, so that you might not grieve as those do who have no hope. [14] For since we believe that Jesus died and rose, even so they who sleep, will God by Jesus, bring with him. [15] For this we declare to you by the word of the Most High God, that we who are alive, who remain until the coming of Jesus, will not precede those who have fallen asleep. [16] For Jesus himself, with a command, in the voice of the archangel and with the trumpet of God, will descend from heaven, and the dead in Christ will rise first. [17] Then we who are alive who are left, together with them, will be caught up in the clouds to meet Jesus in the air; and so we will be with Jesus forever. [18] Therefore comfort one another with these words.

John 16:16 [Jesus said,] "A little while, and you all will not see me, and another little while, and you all will see me." [17] Then some of his disciples said to one another, "What does this mean that he is saying to us, 'A little while, and you all will no longer see me, and again a little while, and you will see me'; and 'Because I am going to the Creator'?" [18] They said, "What does he mean by this 'a little while'? We do not know what he is talking about." [19] Jesus knew that they wanted to ask him, so he said to them, "Are you all discussing among yourselves what I meant when I said, 'A little while, and you all will no longer see me, and again a little while, and you all will see me'? [20] Very truly, I tell you all that you will weep and mourn, but the world will rejoice; you all will have pain, but your pain will turn into joy. [21] When a woman is giving birth, she has pain because her time has come. But when her child is born, she no longer remembers the tribulation because of the joy of having brought a human being into the world. [22] So you all have pain now; but I will see you all again, and your hearts will rejoice, and no one will take your joy from you."

PROCLAMATION

Text Notes

The Book of Jashar, referenced in 2 Samuel 1:18, is lost to us; it also mentioned in Joshua 10:13, where another poetic composition, a war epic, is said to be preserved in it, suggesting a collection of poetic texts. The title, *yashar*, means "upright"; hence it is likely "The Book of the Upright." The verb and noun forms of "lament" or "keen" in verse 17 are homophones of keen, *q-y-n*, as are the nominal forms in Ezekiel 19:1, 14. The repetition in 2 Samuel 1:17 is more literally "David keened a keening."

Context suggest that the "Bow" which David calls to be taught to the people of Judah is his lament. The word "song" is missing, supplied by most translators. Some understand the Bow as a call to greater skill in archery in the face of their losses; the Targum and KJV translate David commanded them to learn "to draw/use the bow," common in older translations (Wycliffe, Geneva (to shoot), Bishops, and Douay). A few drop the bow, yielding "teach" an unspecified "it" (the LXX, Wycliffe, and RSV).

I have selected the phrase *Mater Tua Leaena*, "Your Mother, A Lioness," from Ezekiel 19:1 as the title for the canticle, its central figure described as a lioness and a tree in feminine language throughout (compare CEB with NRSV which shifts to "it" in verse 11ff counter to the Hebrew). It is a lament over the decline and fall of the Judean monarchy, that last vestige of a self-governing Israel. The individual cubs are the sons of Josiah, enthroned and dethroned at the whims of their conquerors, Nebuchadnezzar and Pharaoh Neco. The lioness, singular, conflates the last two queen mothers, Nehusta and Hamutal, or may represent Judah, uncommonly in feminine language (versus the more familiar "(male) lion of Judah"). Because the fall of Judah did not only affect royal sons, I use the more inclusive "royal seed" in verse 2. For the peril faced by the last princesses of Judah, see Jeremiah 41:10; 43:5–7, and my discussion of them and the queen mothers in *Womanist Midrash*. The translation "vine in a vineyard" comes from a widely accepted correction to the original text, "vine in your blood."

The Epistle uses "Lord" repeatedly in such a way that it is not clear whether the author means God or Jesus. The translation above seeks to clarify the referents; however, the reader should be aware of the likely intentional ambiguity.

In John 16:21 I have replaced "hour" with "time" for smoothness. In the same verse, I selected "tribulation" from among the semantic range options in conversation with people who had given birth; that choice reflects the majority opinion.

Preaching Prompts

Sorrow, loss, and lament characterize these readings. Lament emphasizes the import of grieving, no matter who you are, no matter what world-changing events are unfolding. In the first lesson, David's grief is personal and public, complicated by a complicated history with Saul and Jonathan. A useful reminder that death comes, leaving some conflicts unsettled, some relationships still broken, and some hurts unresolved. Yet even lingering grief can be attenuated by joy.

Saul was the major obstacle to David's enthronement, but David refused to kill him because he was the anointed of God, God's messiah (*christos* in the LXX), a point he makes repeatedly (see 1 Samuel 16:6; 24:6, 10; 26:9, 11, 16, 23; 2 Samuel 1:14, 16). Saul's death clears the way for David, who does not celebrate, but grieves, after killing the young man Saul compelled to kill him so he would not be captured and abused. David grieves and composes a lament, normally composed and performed by women in an apprenticing guild, like those of Philistine women in verse 20 and Israelite women in verse 24 (see the discussion of women's musical and funerary guilds in my *Daughters of Miriam*.) The Israelite women would be mourning while the Philistine women would be celebrating, a useful place to discuss the effects of war and foreign policy on women.

David laments Saul and Jonathan and Jonathan's love. Curiously David does not name his love for Jonathan; Jonathan is "beloved" in verse 23, passive, no subject. Missing from Saul and Jonathan's funeral are Ahinoam bat Ahimaaz, Saul's wife and Jonathan's mother, and her daughters Michal and Mered, Johathan's sisters. His brothers are also missing, as is the second women with whom Saul had children, Rizpah (see 1 Samuel 14:49–50; 2 Samuel 21:7–8).

The portion of Ezekiel used as a canticle is a lament for a royal line; its focus is the mother of monarchs, whether human or figurative, compensating for the lack of royal women in Saul and Jonathan's funeral scene and reflecting a communal sense of loss balancing the personal nature of David's grief. The Epistle acknowledges the grief that is part of every human life, no matter their faith, while teaching that our grief is tempered by hope, the promise of the resurrection.

In the Gospel Jesus prepares his disciples for the grief they will experience when he is taken from them. Yet that grief will be transformed in the resurrection. The transformation of grief into joy is part of the cycle of life which Jesus illustrates using the pain of childbirth as a metaphor for grief and the welcoming of a new life to signal joy.

PROPER 21 (CLOSEST TO SEPTEMBER 28)

2 Samuel 11:2–15; Psalm 32:1–7; 2 Peter 3:1–4, 8–9; Matthew 5:21–26

2 Samuel 11:2 And it happened near the evening that David rose from his lying-place and went walking about on the roof of the palace and he saw a woman bathing from the roof; the woman was extraordinarily beautiful in appearance. [3] David sent someone to inquire about the woman. It was reported, "Is not this Bathsheba daughter of Eliam, the wife of Uriah the Hittite?" [4] And David sent messengers and he took her, and she came to him, and he lay with her. Then she purified herself after her defilement and she returned to her house. [5] The woman conceived, and she sent and had someone tell David, "I am pregnant."

[6] So David sent word to Joab, "Send me Uriah the Hittite," and Joab sent Uriah to David. [7] When Uriah came to him, David asked after the status of Joab, and the status of the people, and the status of the war. [8] Then David said to Uriah, "Go down to your house, and wash your feet." Uriah went out of the palace, and after him a gift from David. [9] Now Uriah slept at the entrance of the palace with all the slaves of his lord and did not go down to his house. [10] And they told David, "Uriah did not go down to his house." So David said to Uriah, "Have you not come from a journey? Why did you not go down to your house?" [11] Uriah said to David, "The ark and Israel and Judah dwell in temporary shelters and my lord Joab and the slaves of my lord are at the edge of the field, camping. Should I then go to my house, to eat and to drink, and to lie with my wife? As you live, and as your soul lives, I will not do this thing." [12] Then David said to Uriah, "Stay here this day also, and tomorrow I will send you." So,

Uriah remained in Jerusalem that day and the next. ¹³ Then David called him to dine in his presence and he drank, and David got him drunk. Then in the evening he went out to lie on his couch with the slaves of his lord, yet he did not go down to his house.

¹⁴ And it was in the morning that David wrote a [message] scroll to Joab and sent it in the hand of Uriah. ¹⁵ Now in the scroll David wrote, "Set Uriah at the frontline of the most intense battle and pull back from behind him, so he will be struck down and die."

Psalm 32

¹ Happy is the woman or man whose transgression is forgiven,
  whose sin is covered.
² Happy is the woman or man to whom the HOLY ONE does not reckon iniquity,
  and in whose spirit there is no deceit.
³ While I kept silence, my bones wasted away
  in my groaning all the day.
⁴ For day and night your hand was heavy upon me,
  my strength melted away as by the heat of summer.
⁵ My sin I made known to you,
  and my iniquity I did not hide.
  I said, "I will make known my transgressions to the GRACIOUS ONE,"
  and you forgave the iniquity of my sin.
⁶ Therefore let all who are faithful
  offer prayer to you;
  who are found at such a time,
  for a rush of mighty waters
  shall not touch them.
⁷ You are a hiding place for me;
  you keep me from distress;
  you surround me with cries of deliverance.

2 Peter 3:1 Now this, beloved, the second letter I am writing to you all; in them I am trying to arouse your genuine understanding by reminding you all ² that you should remember the words spoken in the past by the holy women and men who prophesied and the commandment of the Redeemer and Savior spoken through your apostles. ³ First of all know this, that in the last days will come scoffers scoffing and chasing after their own lusts ⁴ and saying, "Where is the promise of his coming? For, ever since our ancestors died, everything continues as from the beginning of creation!"

⁸ But this one thing, do not ignore beloved, that with the Most High one day is like a thousand years, and a thousand years are like one day. ⁹ The Most High is not slow about God's promise, as some think of slowness, but is patient with you all, not wanting anyone to perish, rather all to come to repentance.

Matthew 5:21 Jesus said, "You have heard that it was said to those of old, 'You shall not murder,' and 'whoever murders shall be subject to judgment.' ²² But I say to you all that if you are angry with a sister or brother, you will be liable to judgment, and if you call a sister or brother an idiot, you will be subject to the council; and if you say, 'You fool,' you will be subject to the hell of fire. ²³ Therefore, if you are offering your gift at the altar and you remember that your sister or brother has something against you, ²⁴ leave your gift there before the altar and go; first be reconciled to your sister or brother, and then come and offer your gift. ²⁵ Come to favorable terms quickly with your accuser while you are on the way with them or your accuser may hand you over to the judge, and the judge to the court officer, and you will be thrown into prison. ²⁶ Truly I tell you, you will never get out until you have paid the last penny."

PROCLAMATION

Text notes

In 2 Samuel 11:7 *shalom* is used for the welfare check on Joab and the people in the war. Commentators understand the "gift" in verse 8 to be some largess from David's table or holdings, agricultural stuffs, livestock, etc. In verse 11 *succoth* is the plural of "booths" or "shelters"; it is also phonetically the same as the city Succoth, which is how JPS understands it. In verse 13 Uriah's drunkenness is articulated with a verb form that lays the cause at David's feet: "he (made/got) him drunk."

In 2 Peter 3:1, *eilikrine dianoian* is "genuine" in the sense of both unadulterated and unpretentious, and "understanding" in the sense of comprehension and the intention to act on that understanding. In verse 2, "holy women and men who prophesied" renders and expands "holy prophets." "Scoffers scoffing" in verse 3 is a Hebraism; Hebrew (and Aramaic) roots form nouns and verbs—and sometimes adjectives. The nominal and verbal forms occur together but in inverse order, "they will come scoffing, scoffers." They're going "after their own lusts," here rendered "chasing after."

The Aramaic word *raka* in Matthew 5:22 means "empty-headed." "Gehenna/ Hell of fire" acknowledges that the Gehenna they could all see, the Geh Hinnom Valley just south of Jerusalem was not literally hell.

Preaching Prompts

These lessons address transgression, consequence, and repentance. It is not fashionable to speak, let alone preach, about sin in some circles. In the first lesson David's most infamous acts, the rape of Bathsheba and murder of Uriah, take center stage. In the psalm, the petitioner speaks as one who could have been the perpetrator of those or similar crimes. The Epistle speaks to a world where there seems to be no consequences for transgression or, rhetorically, to the survivors or victims of someone else's transgressions. And Jesus offers a pathway to reconciliation for those who have wronged and those who have been wronged.

David's violation of Bathsheba's body is treated as a violation of her husband's rights to and over her body and as an offense against God. She is not treated as a victim or survivor. The extolling of her beauty has been weaponized—she (and other women) tempt men with their beauty by existing and conforming to some aesthetic standard. The construction of David's sin as adultery projects blame onto Bathsheba that neither the text nor Nathan assert on God's behalf. Indeed, Bathsheba is not charged with or punished for adultery; no sin is ascribed to her in the text. Rooftops often formed an extra room in Israelite households; Bathsheba's bathing there is also not critiqued in the text as it is in subsequent interpretation. The initial mention of her bathing in verse 2 did not mention "impurity," often read as menstruation, though that term is not used. She purifies herself from her impurity—"defilement"—in verse 4 *after* David rapes her; that is a second cleansing. David's decision to gift (or pay) Uriah for a harm that he may not yet know he has suffered conjures men who after a sexual assault offer their victim money or something valuable for silence or just out of guilt. (For a detailed analysis of the passage, see the chapter on Bathsheba in *Womanist Midrash*.)

Psalm 32 is traditionally attributed to David. In terms of content, it is a good fit for a man whose recorded transgressions are legion, particularly in a test that is at turns hagiographic. It should be noted that the Hebrew formula commonly translated as "of David" actually means "to/for David." This may indicate "composed on behalf of," or "dictated by." The psalm offers assurance of the forgiveness of sin with repentance signified by confession in verse 5.

Withdrawing from worship to make amends with someone with whom you have a broken relationship might be regarded in some way as physically embodying confession and repentance, which are necessary before attempted reconciliation. The Church and larger society have often gotten this wrong, particularly with regard to so-called racial reconciliation. Jesus's description of reconciliation puts the onus on the one who knows someone has something against them, the one who wronged or is accused of wrong, rather than the one who has been done wrong. This can be read as a disruption of a power curve: it is not up to a victim to demand justice, nor should it be; rather the moral imperative belongs to the one accused of wrong. Unfortunately, this is not the paradigm the church uses in responding to those whom it has injured, particularly marginalized communities: LGBTQI persons, black women and men and other persons of color, and women of all races and ethnicities.

PROPER 22 (CLOSEST TO OCTOBER 5)

2 Samuel 13:1–16, 21–22; Psalm 103:1–17;
1 Thessalonians 2:9–12; Mark 10:13–16

2 Samuel 13:1 Now it was after [the defeat of the Ammonites]. The sister of Absalom, David's son, was beautiful; her name was Tamar and Amnon son of David loved her. [2] Amnon was distressed to the point of sickness over Tamar his sister, for she was a virgin and it seemed impossible in his eyes to do anything to her. [3] Now Amnon had a friend whose name was Jonadab, the son of Shimeah David's brother, and Jonadab was an extremely astute man. [4] He said to Amnon, "Why are you so poorly royal son, morning after morning? Will you not tell me?" Amnon said to him, "Tamar, sister of Absalom my brother, I love [her.]"

[5] Jonadab said to Amnon, "Lie down on your bed and make yourself sick and your father will come to see you, then say to him, 'Please let Tamar my sister come and feed me bread and prepare the food before my eyes so I may see it and eat it from her hand.'" [6] So Amnon lay down and made himself sick and when the king came to see him, Amnon said to the king, "Please let Tamar my sister come and make heart-cakes before my eyes that I may eat from her hand."

[7] Then David sent Tamar to the palace saying, "Go to the house of your brother Amnon and prepare food for him." [8] So Tamar went to the house of Amnon her brother; he was lying down. And she took dough and kneaded it and made heart-cakes in his sight and cooked the cakes. [9] Then she took the pan and tipped them out before him, but he refused to eat. Then Amnon said, "Send everyone out [away] from me." So everyone went out [away] from him. [10] Then Amnon said to Tamar, "Bring the food into the room that I may eat from your hand." So Tamar took the heart-cakes she had made and brought them into the room to Amnon her brother. [11] And she brought them to him to eat and he seized her and said to her, "Come, lie with me, my sister." [12] She said to him, "No! Do not my brother! Do not rape me! Such a thing is not done in Israel! Do not commit this sacrilege! [13] And I, where could I go with my shame? And as for you, you would be as one of the outcasts in Israel. Now please, speak to the king; for he will not withhold me from you." [14] He did not want to listen to her voice; he overpowered her, and he raped her and lay with her.

[15] Then Amnon hated her with a very great hatred, for greater was his hatred toward her than his love of her, so Amnon said to her, "Get up! Get out!" [16] But she said to him, "No, this great evil, sending me away, is more than what you did to me." And he would not listen to her.

[21] And the king, David, heard of all these things and he became very angry, yet he would not grieve the spirit of Amnon his son, because he loved him, for he was his firstborn. [22] Now Absalom spoke not to Amnon neither ill nor well for Absalom hated Amnon, because of that deed—he raped Tamar his sister.

Psalm 103:1–17

1 Bless the Fount of Wisdom, O my soul,
   and all that is within me, bless her holy Name.
2 Bless the Fount of Wisdom, O my soul,
   and forget not all her benefits.
3 She forgives all your sins
   and heals all your infirmities;
4 She redeems your life from the grave
   and crowns you with mercy and lovingkindness;
5 She satisfies you with good things,
   and your youth is renewed like an eagle's.
6 She Who is Wisdom executes righteousness
   and judgment for all who are oppressed.
7 She made her ways known to Miriam and Moses
   and her works to the children of Israel.
8 Wisdom's womb is full of love and faithfulness,
   slow to anger and overflowing with faithful love.
9 She will not always accuse us,
   nor will she keep her anger forever.
10 She has not dealt with us according to our sins,
   nor rewarded us according to our wickedness.
11 For as the heavens are high above the earth,
   so indomitable is her faithful love upon those who revere her.
12 As far as the east is from the west,
   so far has she removed our sins from us.
13 As a mother's love for her children flows from her womb,
   so too does Wisdom's love for those who revere her flow from her womb.
14 For she herself knows whereof we are made;
   She remembers that we are but dust.
15 Our days are like the grass;
   we flourish like a flower of the field;
16 When the wind goes over it, it is gone,
   and its place shall know it no more.
17 But the faithful love of She Who is Wisdom endures forever
   on those who revere her,
   and her righteousness on children's children.

1 Thessalonians 2:9 You all remember, sisters and brothers, our labor and our toil; night and day we worked, so that we might not be a financial burden to any of you while we proclaimed to you the gospel of God. 10 You all are witnesses, with God, how holy, just, and blameless was our conduct toward you believers. [11] As you all know, we dealt with each one of you like a parent with children, [12] urging and encouraging you and pleading that you lead a life worthy of God, who calls you into God's own realm and glory.

Mark 10:13 Now people were bringing little children to Jesus in order that he might touch them, and the disciples rebuked them. [14] But when Jesus saw this, he was angry and said to them, "Let the little children come to me, do not prevent them; for it is to such as these that the realm of God belongs. [15] Truly I tell you all, whoever does not receive the reign of God as a little child will never enter it." [16] And Jesus took them up in his arms, laid his hands on them, and blessed them.

PROCLAMATION

Text Notes

The Hebrew text of the Masoretic Text is corrected against the Dead Sea Scrolls in academic translations like the NRSV and CEB as the scrolls are the oldest most complete manuscripts, resulting in some ninety corrections in the NRSV compared to the RSV. Samuel is the most heavily corrected, slightly more than 40 percent, due in part to a number of gaps, including David's rationale for his silence after his daughter's rape: "but he would not punish his son Amnon, because he loved him, for he was his firstborn."

Tamar and Absalom were the children of Maacah, daughter of the ruler of Geshur (2 Samuel 3:3), David's fourth wife. Amnon was the son of Ahinoam (1 Samuel 25:43; 2 Samuel 3:2), David's third wife. The idiom "fell in love" is modern and inappropriate to the ancient world; in 1 Samuel 13:1 Amnon "loves" Tamar using the common verb that refers to love of Jonathan and Michal for David, and between God and humanity, both directions. I keep the word "love" rather than "infatuate" (JPS) or even "lust" because he and others use "love" talk as part of their pattern of abuse. It "seemed impossible" is something like "it would take a miracle," using the verb *p-l-'*, "to be wondrous or miraculous." His "miracle" comes in the form of Jonadab, David's nephew who facilitates the rape of his own cousin. Jonadab is described as "wise," sometimes translated as "shrewd" or "crafty."

In Psalm 103, God's love is womb-love, suggesting but not articulating an accompanying abundance of breastmilk (verses 8, 13). Mother-love in Psalm 103:13 is attributed to a father: "as a father mother-loves his children" (using the verbal form of the noun "womb." The verse could be translated: "as a father loves his children with a mother's love."

I use "astute" to articulate the nature of Jonadab's "wisdom." He tells Amnon to make himself sick using a causative verb form; the notion of pretense is not expressed but within reason. Jonadab's correct assumption that David will come see about his sick child intimates David's love for his son was well-known and stands in sharp contrast to his avoidance of his raped daughter.

The word for children in the Gospel indicates young children, ranging from infants to prepubescent young teens. Infants and young children would have been brought by a parent, most likely a mother. The response of Jesus in verse 14 can be translated as either "angry" or "indignant." I preserve his anger here, an emotion that is often presented as inappropriate for a faithful Christian.

Preaching Prompts

The language of family is used often in the scriptures to describe the relationship between Christians, our relationship with Christ, and our relationship to God. Our family systems shape much of who we are for good and ill. In these lessons, family in all of these senses provide the opportunity for ethical and theological reflection. In the first, horrific violence occurs in the family home, violence that is facilitated by one family member and left unaddressed in the echoing silence of one parent and absence of the other. Unfortunately, this kind of violence is as prevalent in the world that reads the text as it is in the text. In the psalm, the parental love of the divine mother contrasts sharply with the lack of evident parental love in 2 Samuel 13. In 1 Thessalonians, Paul assumes the posture of a nurturing parent encouraging children to grow into a worthy life. In the Gospel, Jesus is that family friend or neighbor who is a virtual member of the family, a big brother or uncle providing, in some cases, tenderness and affection that is missing at home.

The incestuous rape of Tamar II (Tamar I appears in Genesis 38:6ff) is a well-studied text, the most classic treatment in Phyllis Trible's *Texts of Terror*. David's failure to attend to his brutalized daughter stands in sharp relief to his rush to his son supposedly sick in bed. Her age is not given however, inasmuch as she was unmarried, it is possible to read her as a child given the value of a king's daughter on the marriage market; it may well be that she was too young to be married. The story bears hallmarks of rape and incest narratives with which modern readers and hearers are familiar: an absent mother figure, an untrustworthy friend or relative, inadequate response from parents and authority figures, and, less frequent, a new cycle of retributive violence. A frank discussion of rape and incest in the text and in the world reading the text can bring back memories of trauma in survivors and it is advisable to have appropriately trained pastoral counselors on hand, trusted counselors in the community to whom you can refer, and resource sheets with contact information for survivor services and helplines.

In the psalm God demonstrates parental love by both doing justice for those who have been wronged and offering the possibility of forgiveness for those who have done wrong, that balance virtually impossible for the human heart to maintain.

Both the Epistle and Gospel lessons present "families of choice," deep and abiding connections between those for whom there is no biological tie. Many whose families of origin are not safe, like Tamar, form enduring sustaining kinship ties with those who open heart and home. All too often, it is the Church and Christian families that are unsafe for survivors of sexual assault in the home and in the church, and for gay and trans kids. We are called to be family to each other, safe, nurturing, holding each other accountable, and calling to repentance and forgiving and healing with the help of God, following the example of God.

PROPER 23 (CLOSEST TO OCTOBER 12)

2 Samuel 20:1–3, 14–22; Psalm 50:14–23; 1 Corinthians 6:1–6; Mark 6:1–6

2 Samuel 20:1 Now [among the people] there was by chance a worthless man named Sheba son of Bichri, a Benjaminite. He sounded the trumpet and cried out,

> "We have no portion in David!
> No share in Jesse's son!
> Every man [back] to his tent, Israel!"

² Then all the men of Israel left from behind David and went behind Sheba son of Bichri while the men of Judah clung to their king from the Jordan to Jerusalem. ³ And David came to his Jerusalem house and the king took the ten low status wives whom he had left to watch the house and put them under watch in a guardhouse and he provisioned them but did not go to them. So were they confined until the day of their death, a living widowhood.

¹⁴ Then Sheba passed through all the tribes of Israel to Abel of Beth-Maacah and all the Bichrites assembled and they went behind him. ¹⁵ They came and lay siege against him in Abel of Beth-Maacah; they threw up a siege-ramp against the city and it stood against the rampart. Joab's people were dismantling the wall to bring it down. ¹⁶ Then a wise woman called from the city, "[All of you!] Listen! Listen! Tell Joab now, 'Come here and I will speak to you.'" ¹⁷ So he drew near to her and the woman said, "Are you Joab?" He answered, "I am." Then she said to him, "Listen to the words of your slave-woman." He answered, "I am." ¹⁸ Then she said, "They used to say this saying in former times, 'Let them ask at Abel and thus would settle the matter.' ¹⁹ I am among the most peaceful and faithful in Israel and you seek to put to death a city and a mother in Israel. Why would you swallow up the heritage of the MOST HIGH GOD?" ²⁰ Joab answered, "Far be it! Far be from me it, that I should swallow up or dismantle! ²¹ The matter is not thus! Rather a man from the hills of Ephraim—Sheba son of Bichri is his name—has raised up his hand against David, against the king; give him up, just him and I will go from the city." Then the woman said to Joab, "Look, his head shall be thrown to you beyond the wall." ²² Then the woman went to all the people with her wisdom. So, they cut off the head of Sheba son of Bichri then they threw it to Joab. And he blew the

trumpet and they dispersed from the city and all went to their homes while Joab returned to Jerusalem to the king.

Psalm 50

14 "Offer to God a sacrifice of thanksgiving,
   and remit to the Most High your vows.
15 And call on me in the day of trouble;
   I will deliver you and you shall glorify me."
16 Yet to the wicked God says:
   "What is it to you to recite my statutes,
   or raise my covenant in your mouth?
17 Now you, you hate discipline,
   and you cast my words behind you.
18 When you see a thief you befriend them,
   and with adulterers you partake.
19 You set your mouth upon evil,
   and your tongue crafts deceit.
20 You sit and speak against your kin;
   against your [own] mother's child you raise slander.
21 These things you have done and I kept myself silent;
   you thought I would be like you.
   I rebuke you and lay the indictment before your eyes.
22 Understand this, you who forget God,
   lest I tear you apart, and there be no one to deliver.
23 They who brings a sacrifice of thanksgiving honor me;
   to those who set upon the right way
   will I show the salvation of God."

1 Corinthians 6:1 Dare any of you having a concern against another, go to court before the unrighteous and not before the saints? 2 Do you all not know that the saints will judge the world? And if the world is to be judged by you, are you incompetent to try trivial cases? 3 Do you not know that we are to judge angels—to say nothing of ordinary matters? 4 If you have ordinary cases, then, do you appoint as judges those who have no standing in the church? 5 I say this to your shame. Can it be that there is no one among you wise enough to decide between one believer and another, 6 but a believer goes to court against a believer—and before unbelievers at that?

Mark 6:1 Now Jesus left that place and came to his hometown, and his disciples followed him. 2 On the sabbath he began to teach in the synagogue, and many women and men who heard him were astounded, saying, "Where did this man learn this?" And "What wisdom has been given him?" And "Such deeds of power work done by his hands! 3 Is not this the carpenter, the son of Mary and brother of James and Joses and Judas and Simon, and are not his sisters here with us?" And they were offended over him. [4] Then Jesus said to them, "Prophets are not without honor, except in their hometown, and among their own kin, and in their own house." [5] And he could do no deed of power there, except on a few sick people laying hands and curing them. [6] And Jesus was amazed at their unbelief. Then, he went about among the villages teaching.

PROCLAMATION
Text Notes

Wisdom in the Hebrew Scriptures, *chokmah*, is of "heart and hand," and often synonymous with skill; it is never limited to intellectual capacity. In Greek it is more intellectual while retaining transcendent qualities. Each is feminine and often personified as a divine character or characteristic of God and identified with *torah*. Greek wisdom, *sophia*, will be conflated with *logos*, and ultimately, Christ, marking a shift in, or expansion of, its gender.

Sheba addresses the men in his community as decision-makers, set against the woman who will decide his fate. In verse 2, the men of Israel "cling" to David the way Ruth clung to Naomi (Ruth 1:14) and spouses cling to each other (a man to his woman in Genesis 2:24), all using the same verb.

Unions with primary (*isshah*, sing., *nashim*, pl.) and secondary or low-status wives (*pilegesh*, sing., *pilegeshim*, pl.). were all legal marriages producing legally recognized children; however, only the children of a primary wife—category, not sequence—were legal heirs, though nothing prevented voluntary inheritance. These particular women were abandoned by David because his son Absalom—who had his sister's rapist murdered—raped them in 2 Samuel 16:22 as part of his campaign to usurp his father in every way.

In verse 16 "all of you" identifies the plural voice. In the same verse NRSV undercuts the woman's authority by inserting "want to" where she says "I will." Her self-abasement as his "slave-woman" is at odds with the strength of her overall portrayal but reflects a common self-deprecating practice of women and men. The sage sets herself in the tradition of Deborah as "a mother in Israel" (Judges 5:7); multiple translations sever that lineage, changing the conjunction to "city *that is* a mother." In verse 20 Joab says he would never "dismantle" God's heritage while "dismantling" the city wall in verse 15.

In verse 18 of the psalm, to "partake" with adulterers is literally "to have the same portion." This indicates more than "keeping company" as in the NRSV.

I have made the presence of women in the synagogue explicit in "many" in Mark 6:1. Not only did women participate in religious life at synagogue and temple, inscriptional evidence identifies women in leading positions, including *archisynagogos*, "leader of the synagogue" (the same title as the male leaders in Matthew 9:18; Mark 5:36, 38; Luke 8:41; 13:14; see Bernadette Brooten, *Women Leaders in the Ancient Synagogue* and Kate Cooper, *Band of Angels: The Forgotten World of Early Christian Women*). Paul would go on to arrest women and men at synagogues who followed Jesus in Acts 9:2. We don't know how many sisters Jesus had; "all" is more than one and likely more than two.

In Mark 6:2 the question of the congregants is fractured and lacking a verb, "where this (one) this (knowledge/teaching)?" Sometimes imagining accompanying gestures helps with such a construction: "Where did this one [points at Jesus] learn this [waves hands around]?" "One" can also be "person" or "man" in this context. In verse 3, "carpenter" includes more than wood-working, extending to "building" and "construction" from other materials.

Preaching Prompts

Monarchy is a bloody, messy business, making it a challenging metaphor for God. Indeed, the Gospels eschew the title "King," and while not completely rejecting the concept, i.e., "the kingdom of God," they completely redefine the concept.

David's throne was established with bloodshed and brutality, and at the same time, the fruit of God's promise and anointing. David and his enforcers regularly relied on violence and the threat of violence to secure and maintain his throne. In today's lesson, we see a woman joining them in that bloody business. Reader discomfort with a woman in this role more so than for men may reveal gender biases brought to the text.

While other texts will locate wisdom with the monarch, notably Solomon, the wisdom in this text is that of a woman who uses her wits and her words to minimize the death toll of this unstable monarchy and in the process helps stabilize David's reign.

The strong language in the psalm helps set the context for the actions of the wise woman. Defamatory language against God or against God's anointed monarch were serious crimes and could result in the death penalty. That could easily set off the profligate violence that characterizes war in and out of the text. (The relative lack of that violence in the Christian Testament owes more to Israel's lack of standing as a world power than to any significant change in human behavior.)

The Epistle offers another model of conflict resolution, one rooted in the reality that the legal system is the system of an occupying power that does not have the interests of conquered peoples at heart; it is an engine of the occupation. There are parallels to the gross inequities of our own justice system which results in disparate outcomes based on the race, ethnicity, and financial standing of persons dependent upon it. Paul calls for intracommunity adjudication. Unfortunately, we have seen religious bodies of all sorts fail to adjudicate internal wrongdoing, especially violations of vulnerable persons.

The wisdom of Jesus reflects the Greek literary context of the Christian Testament and is rooted in his teaching, teaching that transcends expectations based on what his hometown neighbors know about his family of origin. Their astonishment is a bit of a knock on Jesus's family. English translations of the New Testament regularly diminish the Jewishness of Jesus, his family, and followers by anglicizing their names: Mariam (Miriam/Mary), Iakobos (Jacob/James), Ioseph (Joseph), Simon (Simeon), and Ioudas (Judah/Judes or Jude), but ancestral figures from the scriptures with the same names are not treated that way, i.e., Rebekah's son Jacob does not become "James." Names matter and how and why we change them—particularly for other people—matter tremendously beyond the anti-Jewishness of this practice.

PROPER 24 (CLOSEST TO OCTOBER 19)

2 Samuel 21:1–14; Psalm 58; Revelation 6:9–11; Luke 6:43–45

2 Samuel 21:1 Now there was a famine in the days of David for three years, year after year, and David sought the presence of the MOST HIGH. The HOLY ONE said, "There is bloodguilt on Saul and on his house, because he put the Gibeonites to death." ² So the king summoned the Gibeonites and spoke to them. Now the Gibeonites were not of the Israelites; they were the remnant of the Amorites. The Israelites had sworn to spare them, yet Saul sought to destroy them in his zeal for the Israelites and Judah. ³ David said to the Gibeonites, "What shall I do for you and how shall I atone that you all may bless the heritage of the HOLY ONE OF OLD?" ⁴ The Gibeonites said to him, "We will take no silver or gold of Saul or of his house and there is no one for us to put to death in Israel." He said, "What do you say that I should do for you all?" ⁵ They said to the king, "The man who finished us off and intended to destroy us that we would not be able to stand in all the territory of Israel, ⁶ let seven men from his sons be handed over to us and we will hang them before the DREAD GOD at Gibea of Saul on the mountain of the LIVING GOD." The king said, "I, myself, will give [them]."

⁷ But the king had pity on Meribbaal, son of Jonathan the son of Saul because of the oath of the MOST HIGH that was between them, between David and Jonathan son of Saul. ⁸ The king took the two sons of Rizpah daughter of Aiah, whom she gave birth to for Saul, Armoni and [Mephibbaal called] Mephibosheth, and the five sons of Merab daughter of Saul, whom she gave birth to for Adriel son of Barzillai the Meholathite. ⁹ David gave them into the hands of the Gibeonites and they hung them on the mountain before the CREATOR OF ALL and they fell, the seven of them, as one. Now they were put to death in the first days of harvest, at the beginning of barley harvest.

¹⁰ Then Rizpah the daughter of Aiah took sackcloth and spread it on a rock for herself, from the beginning of harvest until rain fell on them from the heavens; she did not allow

the birds of the air to come on the bodies by day or the beasts of the field by night. [11] Now it was told David what Rizpah daughter of Aiah, the low status wife of Saul, had done. [12] Then David went and took the bones of Saul and the bones of Jonathan his son from the nobles of Jabesh-gilead who had stolen them from the square of Beth-shan where the Philistines had hung them up on the day the Philistines killed Saul at Gilboa. [13] And he brought up from there the bones of Saul and the bones of his son Jonathan and they gathered the bones of those who had been hung. [14] And they buried the bones of Saul and of his son Jonathan in the land of Benjamin in Zela, in the tomb of Saul's father Kish and they did all that the king commanded. And God granted entreaty on behalf of the land after that.

Psalm 58

1 Truly, do you speak what is right, you mighty?
   Do you judge the children of earth rightly?
2 Indeed, in your heart you work iniquity;
   your hands spread violence across the land.
3 The wicked wander from the womb;
   they err from their birth, speaking lies.
4 Venom like the venom of a serpent!
   Like the deaf adder that closes its ear,
5 so that it does not hear the voice of charmers
   or the spell speaking of the wise.
6 God, smash the teeth in their mouths;
   shatter the fangs of the young lions, DREAD GOD!
7 Let them wash away like water that wanders off;
   let her arrows fly that they be cut down.
8 Like a snail that melts as it moves;
   like the stillbirth of a woman that never sees the sun.
9 Before thorns know what it is to be a bramble,
   whether green or kindled, let God sweep them away!
10 The righteous will rejoice when they see vengeance done;
   they will bathe their feet in the blood of the wicked.
11 Then shall the woman-born say, "Surely there is a reward for the righteous;
   truly there are divine judgments on earth."

Revelation 6:9 When [the Lamb] opened the fifth seal, I saw under the altar the souls of those who had been slaughtered for the word of God and for the testimony they had given. [10] They cried out with a great voice, saying, "Dread God, holy and true, how long will it be before you judge and avenge our blood on they who dwell on the earth?" [11] Then they were each given a white robe and told to rest yet a small time, until their fellow servants and their sisters and brothers, who were soon to be killed as they had been were completed.

Luke 6:43 [Jesus said,] "Indeed, no good tree bears bad fruit, nor again does a bad tree bear good fruit. [44] For each tree by its own fruit is known. Now, figs are not gathered from thorns, nor from a thornbush are grapes picked. [45] The good person out of the good treasure of the heart produces good, and the evil person out of evil treasure produces evil; for it is out of the abundance of the heart that the mouth speaks.

PROCLAMATION

Text Notes

The Hebrew of 2 Samuel 21:5 is unclear in places; the LXX forms the basis of the translation here. In verse 6 the Gibeonites specify adult sons to hang, literally "dislocate." Some read the form of execution as "impaling" (NRSV and JPS). Alter notes that something akin to crucifixion may have been intended (*The Hebrew Bible: A Translation with Commentary*). What is clear is that they were left hanging on the instruments of their deaths. Verse 8 names Michal, Saul's daughter, as the mother of the second group of Saulide hostages. However, since her sister Merab's husband is named (1 Samuel 18:19), and Michal was sequestered by David, there is widespread agreement Merab is meant. The Targums resolve the dissonance by having Michal raise Merab's children.

The names of Rizpah's son with Saul and Jonathan's son with an unknown woman are also confused in verses 7–8, where both are called Mephibosheth; however in 1 Chronicles 8:34 and 9:40, Jonathan's son is Meribbaal; the consonantal text can mean "Baal is my master (or advocate)," or as vocalized in 1 Chronicles, "one who contends with Baal," a synonym for the honorific bestowed on Gideon, Jerubbaal, in Judges 6:32. (See P. Kyle McCarter's discussion in the *Anchor Bible Commentary* on 2 Samuel.)

A second issue is the name Mephibosheth itself, "from the mouth of shame," was highly unlikely to have been chosen by parents. Rizpah's son Mephibosheth was likely actually named Mephibaal, "from the mouth of Baal." The Baal suffix would have been altered by a later editor for pious reasons. However, the original referent was not likely the Canaanite deity, but the Israelite God; both were addressed by the same title (Baal's proper name being Haddu). Indeed, Mephibaal is attested in the Old Latin (pre-Jerome) and Lucian's recension of the LXX, (see Diana Edelman's entry, "Mephibosheth" in the *Anchor Bible Dictionary*). Hosea would try to end the broader confusion by exhorting the people not to use Baal for their God (Hosea 2:16). Since the name Meribbaal is attested in the Masoretic text, I use it for Jonathan's son. And since the name Mephibaal is attested in the broader biblical manuscript tradition, I include it as an option.

As is the case with many psalms, Psalm 58 is introduced with liturgical instructions, "to the worship leader," and, in this case, a title: "Do Not Destroy." This information is contained in the first verse of the psalm. However, Christian practice has been to exercise it and use it as a superscription while Jewish practice preserves it as the first verse, often resulting in differing verse numbers for the Psalms. Lastly, the psalm is characterized as a *miktam*, a subcategory of psalms generally understood to have initially been a written composition, possibly a poem. Curiously, the state of the Hebrew does not point to someone with high literary ability. The language is tortuous, often the words as spelled do not quite fit, while homophones and small corrections such as letter reversals make more sense. This might mean that the author was new to literacy and fits well with a character like David having not been raised in a context in which he would have been literate. This translation is dependent on the JPS and Alter translations in those places where the text is unclear; there are more than can be enumerated here. In the last verse of the psalm, *elohim* takes a plural verb that normally indicates "gods," whereas the singular refers to God. "Divine judgments" preserves the sense and likely intent.

Revelation 6:10 uses *despotes*, meaning slaveowner and the basis for English "despot," as a title for God in a call for blood vengeance. I use "Dread God" here as in Hebrew biblical passages calling for a bloody divine violence.

Preaching Prompts

These lessons are studies in vengeance, retribution, and the hope of justice in this world or the next. The first lesson is part of a larger cycle of violence and as is often the case with long-lived conflicts, some of the details of who did what to whom have been lost. Survivors of Saul's violence demand retribution in blood, an eye for an eye. Troublingly, it is God who invokes bloodguilt, which can only be satisfied with more bloodshed, but not from the perpetrator, rather the lives of his sons and grandsons would be forfeit. It would be much easier to hold this text in conversation with the gospel if it were simply David's bloodthirst.

Yet concluding God called David's attention to the bloodguilt as a prerequisite for ending the famine might be hasty. God was not amenable to the people's entreaty, "able/willing to be entreated," until the remains of the murdered men were placed respectfully to rest, the answer to Rizpah's unrecorded prayer—the psalm might well be her prayer in content and tone. The Gibeonites sought vengeance. David sought to be the instrument of that vengeance. He asked the Gibeonites, not God, as does the psalmist, how to resolve the blood-debt and unsurprisingly, came up with a very human solution, one that conveniently removed potential claimants for the throne.

Rizpah, the mother of murdered—perhaps lynched—sons, is one of the most vulnerable people in the text and one of the strongest. Rizpah has been a focus of black women's preaching for as long as I can remember. She has lost everything—her spouse and with him potentially the status that kept her fed, clothed, housed, and safe. In 2 Samuel 3:7, Saul's former commanding general is accused of raping her after Saul's death. And now David has handed her children and those of his own sister-in-law over to death in what could be called an atonement ritual. There was nothing she could do to prevent their deaths and nothing she could say to David in the aftermath. But she could bear witness to her horror and prevent her people and her king from looking away. Animal predation would have resulted in the erasure of her sons' bodies in a matter of weeks. By keeping the carrion eaters away, she ensured their slower decomposition, their unburied state an affront to Israelite values encoded in Deuteronomy 21:22–23. Her actions shame David into burying her dead and the bones of Saul and his beloved Jonathan that he had also neglected.

Psalm 58 is one of a number of imprecatory or execration psalms, psalms of cursing, including portions of 17, 26, 35, 58, and the whole of 137. Other imprecations can be found in prophetic rhetoric.

Revelation 6 presents yet more innocent slaughtered souls waiting for not only God's justice but for God's vengeance. The notion of God as a God of vengeance is ancient and enduring and not relegated to the Hebrew Scriptures. This conceptualization of God makes room for the understanding that not everyone will receive justice in this world. The Revelation text speaks to ultimate and final justice.

The Gospel turns our focus to ourselves, our own actions and those of others, including those who perpetrate acts that would lead others to seek bloody vengeance against them or appeal to God for justice. Of more importance for those who profess Christian faith and identity with our words and creeds, the Gospel makes clear it is our deeds that truly reveal who we are.

PROPER 25 (CLOSEST TO OCTOBER 26)

1 Kings 1:1–5, 11–18, 29–31; Psalm 90:1–10, 12;
Colossians 2:9–14; John 7:37–44

1 Kings 1:1 Now King David was old, advancing in days, so although they covered him with clothes, he did not get warm. ² Then his servants said to him, "Let them seek for my lord the king a virgin girl and let her stand in the presence of the king and service him. Let her lie in your bosom and warm my lord the king." ³ So they searched for a beautiful girl throughout the whole territory of Israel and found Abishag the Shunammite and they brought her to the king. ⁴ Now the girl was very beautiful, and she became the king's service-woman and attended him, yet the king did not know her [sexually].

⁵ Then Adonijah son of Haggith exalted himself, saying, "I will reign." He commissioned for himself chariots and horsemen and fifty men to run ahead of him.

¹¹ Then Nathan said to Bathsheba, Solomon's mother, "Have you not heard that Adonijah son of Haggith reigns and our lord David does not know? ¹² Come now, therefore, let me

counsel you please, so that you may save your life and the life of your son Solomon. [13] Come, go to King David, and say to him, 'Did you not, my lord the king, swear to your slave-woman, saying: Your son Solomon shall reign after me and he shall sit on my throne? Why then does Adonijah reign?' [14] Look, while you are still there speaking with the king, I myself will come after you and confirm your words."

[15] So Bathsheba went to the king's room. Now the king was very old and Abishag the Shunammite was attending the king. [16] Bathsheba bowed and prostrated herself before the king, and the king said, "What do you wish?" [17] She said to him, "My lord, you swore to your slave-woman by the HOLY ONE OF OLD your God, saying: Your son Solomon shall reign after me and he shall sit on my throne. [18] Yet now, look! Adonijah reigns now and my lord the king, you know it not.

[29] The king swore and said, "As the ETERNAL ONE lives, who has ransomed my life from every trouble: [30] As I swore to you by the FAITHFUL ONE, the God of Israel, 'Your son Solomon shall reign after me and he shall sit on my throne in my place.' Therefore, thus shall I do this day." [31] Then Bathsheba bowed with her face to the ground, and prostrated herself before the king and said, "May my lord King David live forever!"

Psalm 90:1–10, 12

[1] MOTHER OF THE MOUNTAINS, you have been our refuge
   from one generation to another.
[2] Before the mountains were born,
   or you writhed the land and the earth into birth,
   from age to age you are God.
[3] You turn mortal flesh back to the dust and say,
   "Turn back, you who are woman-born."
[4] For a thousand years in your sight are like yesterday when it is past
   and like a watch in the night.
[5] You sweep them aside; they are an illusion;
   In the morning flourishing and in the evening wilting and withering.
[6] In the morning it is green and flourishes;
   in the evening it is dried up and withered.
[7] For we are consumed in your displeasure;
   we are afraid because of your wrathful indignation.
[8] Our iniquities you have set before you,
   and our hidden sins in the light of your countenance.
[9] When you are angry, all our days are gone;
   we bring our years to an end like a sigh.
[10] The span of our life is seventy years, perhaps in strength even eighty;
   yet the sum of them is but labor and sorrow,
   for they pass away quickly and we are gone.

¹² So teach us to number our days

that we may apply our hearts to Wisdom.

Colossians 2:9 Now in Christ dwells the whole fullness of divinity, bodily. ¹⁰ And you all have in Christ come to fullness, Christ Jesus who is the head of every ruler and authority. ¹¹ In Christ also were you all circumcised without human hands, by putting off the body of the flesh in the circumcision of Christ. ¹² When you were buried with Christ in baptism, you all were also raised with Christ through faith in the power of God, who raised Jesus from the dead. ¹³ And when you all were dead in trespasses and the uncircumcision of your flesh, God brought you to life, together with Christ, forgiving us all our trespasses, ¹⁴ erasing the record that stood against us with its legal demands. God set this aside, nailing it to the cross.

John 7:37 On the last, the great day, of the festival of Booths, Jesus stood and cried out, saying, "If anyone thirsts, woman or man, come to me and drink. ³⁸ The one who believes in me, as the scripture has said, 'From their belly shall flow rivers of living water.'" ³⁹ Now he said this about the Spirit, which believers in him were to receive; for as yet there was no Spirit, because Jesus was not yet glorified.

⁴⁰ When the crowd heard these words, some said, "This is truly the prophet." ⁴¹ Others said, "This is the Messiah." But some said, "Indeed, the Messiah does not come from Galilee, true? ⁴² Does not the scripture say that the Messiah comes from the line of David and comes from Bethlehem, the village where David lived?" ⁴³ So there was a division in the crowd because of him. ⁴⁴ Some wanted to arrest him, but no one laid their hands on him.

PROCLAMATION

Text Notes

The virginal girl brought to "service" David is described with a gendered adjective lacking a noun, as his "service-woman." The verbal root has the sense of "being of use." I use "service" with its contemporary sexualized meaning deliberately here. David's sexual impotence is emblematic of his political impotence; procuring the young woman is an attempt to reinvigorate David in every way.

In Psalm 90:2 God's grammatical gender is masculine, and the imagery used for God is feminine, birthing imagery (in the cisgender ancient Israelite world), yielding the name for God in verse 1. "Turn" in verse 3 means both "turn around" and "repent." Also in verse 3, "mortal flesh" renders "man," and "woman-born" renders "children/descendants of humanity/humankind" or "mortals."

John 7:2 establishes that "the festival" mentioned is the fall festival of Sukkoth, "Booths" or "Tabernacles" (see Leviticus 23:33–36, 39–43). In the *Jewish Annotated New Testament* commentary, Adele Reinhartz notes the prominent place of water in the ceremony as the backdrop to Jesus's teaching about living water; it would make a dramatic object lesson. The scriptural "citation" of verse 38 is not found in Hebrew,

Aramaic, or Greek texts and has only passing similarity to passages such as Isaiah 44:3, Jeremiah 17:13, and Zechariah 14:8. There is a similar verse in the Gospel of Thomas which may represent an attempt to resolve the discrepancy. "The prophet" of verse 40 is likely the promised "prophet like Moses" in Deuteronomy 18:15, 18. Verse 42 likely refers to Micah 5:2 which provides the basis for the "Little Town of Bethlehem" carol; curiously there is a version in the Dead Sea Scrolls (4QXII^f) in which the "ruler" to come does not come from Bethlehem. The division in verse 43 is a "schism," *schisma*.

Lectionaries often focus on David stories because of the messianic title, Son of David. The Messiah, *meshiach*, "Anointed One" from the verb *m-sh-ch*, Christ/*christos* in Greek, is a person chosen or designated by God to serve (primarily as monarch, priests were anointed as well). David (2 Samuel 22:51; Psalm 18:50) and the Persian monarch Cyrus (Isaiah 45:1) are called "God's messiah" in the First Testament; correspondingly, the word used in the LXX in each case is *christos*, making David and Cyrus God's christs. The tradition of translating *meshiach* as "anointed" in the Hebrew Scriptures but "Christ" in the Second Testament created the misunderstanding that Jesus was the only bearer of the title.

Prophetic texts spoke of a messianic monarch who would save or redeem Israel (and sometimes the world); that redemption was understood as national deliverance from occupation and oppression, hence the question when Jesus would restore the monarchy (Acts 1:6). In order for the reinstituted monarchy to be legitimate, the monarch/messiah would need impeccable lineage, thus the resort to the line of David. Early references to the Messiah as the descendant of David include Psalm 132:11, and invoking his father, "the stump of Jesse" in Isaiah 11:1–5. In the pseudepigrapha, "messiah," "monarch," and "Son of David" come together in the Psalms of Solomon 17:21; verse 32 of the same chapter calls this monarch "Lord Messiah" (see also 3 Enoch 35:5).

Preaching Prompts

Monarchy is for the world that generated and canonized the scriptures, the primary way people think about society and governance and therefore, God's relation to and organization of the world. As postmonarchal people, many Americans romanticize monarchy even as we firmly reject it for ourselves. That romance is often around royal trappings, wealth, jewels, pomp and circumstance, power, privilege, and more recently, princesses. David's decline exacerbated the struggle for his royal power and position that characterized David's early reign and reemerged after his rape of Bathsheba. As he lay dying, none of those things matter anymore, not even the pursuit of women. He is unexpectedly chaste, literarily impotent in all ways. A contemporary reading of the desperate attempt to revitalize David may note that there is no discussion of whether Abishag or her family consented to her use or whether their child was simply taken from them for the king's harem. David is not even concerned with his lack of a designated successor. He is fully occupied with dying. It is that dying, the fate of the great and small, that links these lessons.

The psalmist reflects on the fullness of human life destined for dust and dwarfed by the scope of God's infinitude. In the Epistle our mortality is transformed by both the mortality and immortality of Christ. The Gospel points to yet another transformation of our human lives: Spirit-filled lives that pour fourth living water.

The Gospel emphasizes Jesus's descent from David, linking back to a much loved and much lamented independent monarchy. Yet, Jesus taught that the reign and realm which he ushered forth was entirely different than the monarchies of this world (John 18:36), so I suggest we hear Jesus as the son and heir of David in different terms. David is not just Israel's beloved monarch of old, but he was also a broken man who broke others while wrestling to live in the light of God's love. When the Messiah is named as the Son of Bathsheba and the Son of David, the fragile fallible humanity that is also the Messiah's lineage is fully present, pregnant with incarnational possibilities.

Lastly, John's claim "that there was yet no Spirit" in verse 39 represents at one level the author's interpretation of Jesus's words and not the words of Jesus himself, an interpretation that is quite at odds with most understandings of the Trinity (albeit itself a postbiblical understanding) and the scriptures themselves.

FEAST OF ALL SAINTS, NOVEMBER 1

Isaiah 25:1, 4a, 6–10a; Psalm 67; Romans 15:7–13; Matthew 27:50–56

Isaiah 25:1 HOLY ONE OF OLD, you are my God;
  I will exalt you, I will praise your name,
  for you have worked wonders,
  ancient counsel, faithful and trustworthy.
⁴ For you are a refuge to the poor,
  a refuge to the needy in their distress,
  a shelter from the storm and a shade from the heat.
⁶ The COMMANDER of heaven's legions will make for all peoples on this mountain
  a feast of rich food, a feast of well-aged wines,
  of rich food prepared with marrow, of refined well-aged wines.
⁷ And God will destroy on this mountain
  the shroud that shrouds all peoples,
  the veil that veils all nations.

8 God will swallow up death forever.
Then the SOVEREIGN God will wipe away tears from every face,
and will sweep aside the shame of God's people from the whole earth,
for GOD WHOSE NAME IS HOLY has spoken.
9 It will be said on that day,
Look! This is our God; in whom we hope, and who saved us.
This is the CREATOR OF ALL in whom we hope;
let us be glad and rejoice in God's salvation.
10 For the hand of the ANCIENT OF DAYS shall rest on this mountain.

Psalm 67

1 May God be merciful to us and bless us,
show us the light of her countenance and come to us.
2 Let your ways be known upon earth,
your saving health among all nations.
3 Let the peoples praise you, O God;
let all the peoples praise you.
4 Let the nations be glad and sing for joy,
for you judge the peoples with equity
and guide all the nations upon earth.
5 Let the peoples praise you, O God;
let all the peoples praise you.
6 The earth has brought forth her increase;
may God, our own God, give us her blessing.
7 May God give us her blessing,
and may all the ends of the earth stand in awe of her.

Romans 15:7 Accept one another, therefore, just as Christ has accepted you, for the glory of God. 8 I tell you that the Messiah has become a servant of the circumcised for the sake of truth to confirm the promises given to the mothers and fathers, 9 and in order that the Gentiles might glorify God on account of God's mercy. As it is written,

*"Therefore, I will confess you among the Gentiles,
and sing praises to your name,"*

10 and again it says,

"Rejoice, O Gentiles, with God's people,"

11 and again,

*"Praise the Most High, all you Gentiles,
and let all the peoples praise God,"*

[12] and again Isaiah says,

"The root of Jesse shall come,
and the one who rises to rule the Gentiles,
in whom the Gentiles shall hope."

[13] May the God of hope fill you with all joy and peace in believing, so that you may abound in hope by the power of the Holy Spirit.

Matthew 27:50 Jesus cried again with a loud voice and relinquished his spirit. [51] Then, look! The curtain of the temple was torn from top to bottom in two. And the earth was shaken, and the rocks were split. [52] And the tombs were opened, and many bodies of the saints who had fallen asleep were raised. [53] Then after his resurrection they came out of the tombs and entered the holy city and appeared to many. [54] Now when the centurion and those with him, who were standing guard over Jesus, saw the earthquake and what took place, they were terrified and said, "Truly this man was God's Son!"

[55] Now there were many women there, from a distance watching; they had followed Jesus from Galilee and had ministered to him. [56] Among them were Mary the Magdalene, and Mary the mother of James and Joseph, and the mother of the sons of Zebedee.

PROCLAMATION

Text Notes

Division of verses varies among translations for Isaiah 25. I follow the Masoretic Text and Jewish Publication Society here. Similarly, the flexibility of Hebrew tenses can place God's salvific actions in the past or future. The past tense emphasizes God's past faithfulness, laying the ground for a reasonable hope in continuing faithfulness.

Since *pateron* in Romans 15:8 can be inclusive "ancestors" or "fathers" and God's promises were not and are not limited by gender, I use the most inclusive option. In verse 9, Christ takes up the same diaconal ministry with which the women who follow him are credited. Verses 9–12 quote Psalm 18:49, Deuteronomy 32:43, Psalm 117:1, and Isaiah 11:10 from the LXX. There are some variances between the Greek and Hebrew of Deuteronomy 32:43: In the Hebrew text, "the nations, God's people" are called to rejoice while in the Greek the heavens are called to rejoice *with* God's people. (For more on the divergence between the manuscript traditions on this verse, see the annotations and comparisons in *The Dead Sea Scrolls Bible*, eds. Abegg, Flint, and Ulrich.)

The women who "ministered" to Jesus, *diakoneo*, have been understood as providing for Jesus (NRSV), serving him (CEB), and ministering to him (KJV). All are viable; however breadth rather than specificity would seem to be called for.

Preaching Prompts

For the Feast of All Saints, this lectionary turns to declarations of God's faithfulness to all peoples and nations. This passage of Isaiah speaks repeatedly to "all peoples" and "all nations" in verses 6–7, all of whom will benefit from God's death-destroying salvific work. Similarly, in the psalm, God's salvation is for all nations with all peoples invited to join in the praise of God. The Epistle focuses on the acceptance of God's gift of salvation by the Gentile nations. The Gospel takes us back to that saving work in the life and death of Jesus, hinting at the resurrection to come with the resurrection of saints who preceded Jesus in death, at the moment of his death. Meanwhile, the saints who stood bearing witness would become second-class saints in the eyes of many, excluded from ministry, ordination, and leadership based on their gender. Perhaps ironically and almost certainly intentionally, reduction of their ministry to open checkbooks exploits and limits their gifts at the same time.

PROPER 26 (CLOSEST TO NOVEMBER 2)

1 Kings 2:10–24; Psalm 127; Revelation 4:2–11; Luke 22:24–30

1 Kings 2:10 And David lay with his mothers and fathers and was buried in the city of David. [11] The days that David reigned over Israel came to forty years: In Hebron he reigned seven years and in Jerusalem he reigned thirty-three years. [12] Thus Solomon sat on the throne of his father David and his rule was extremely well founded.

[13] Then Adonijah son of Haggith came to Bathsheba, Solomon's mother. She asked, "Is it in peace that you come?" He said, "Peace." [14] Then he said, "I have something to say to you." And she said, "Speak." [15] So he said, "You know that the realm was mine and all Israel set their expectation on me to reign; however, the monarchy has turned and become my brother's, for it was his from the RULER OF ALL. [16] And now I am asking one thing of you; do not turn me away." And she said to him, "Speak." [17] And he said, "Please speak to King Solomon—he will not turn you away—that he might give me Abishag the Shunammite as my wife." [18] Then Bathsheba said, "Good. I myself will speak to the king for you."

[19] So Bathsheba went to King Solomon to speak to him about Adonijah. The king rose to meet her and bowed down to her; then he sat on his throne and had a throne brought for the king's mother, and she sat on his right. [20] Then she said, "One small request I ask of you; do not turn me away." And the king said to her, "Ask, my mother, for I will not turn you away." [21] Then she said, "Let Abishag the Shunammite be given to your brother Adonijah for a wife." [22] Then King Solomon replied and said to his mother, "Now why would you ask Abishag the Shunammite for Adonijah? Ask for him the monarchy, for he is my elder brother and the priest Abiathar and Joab son of Zeruiah are for him!" [23] Then King Solomon swore by the HOLY ONE OF OLD, "Thus may God do to me and more, for against his life has Adonijah

spoken this word. ²⁴ Now therefore as the Ageless One lives, who has prepared me and placed me on the throne of my father David and who has made me a house as God promised, today Adonijah shall be put to death."

Psalm 127

¹ Unless the Architect of Heaven constructs the castle,
   those who construct it labor in vain.
   Unless the All-Seeing God guards the city,
   the guard watches in vain.
² It is in vain that you all rise up early
   and go late to rest,
   eating the bread of painful [birthing] labor;
   for God gives sleep to her beloved.
³ Look! Children are a heritage from the Author of Life,
   the fruit of the womb a reward.
⁴ Like arrows in the hand of a warrior,
   thus are the children of one's youth.
⁵ Happy is the person
   whose quiver is full of them.
   They shall not be put to shame
   when they speak with enemies in the gate.

Revelation 4:2 Suddenly I was in the spirit, and there! a throne positioned in heaven, and upon the throne there was one seated. ³ And the one seated there looks like jasper and carnelian, and there is a rainbow all around the throne that looks like an emerald. ⁴ Also, all around the throne are twenty-four thrones, and on the thrones are twenty-four elders seated, dressed in white garments, and upon their heads, golden crowns. ⁵ Coming from the throne was lightning, and roaring, and thunder, and seven flaming torches in front of the throne blazed, which are the seven spirits of God; ⁶ and in front of the throne there is a sea of glass, like crystal. Around the throne, and on each side of the throne, are four living beings, full of eyes in front and behind:

⁷ The first being was like a lion, the second being was like an ox, the third being had a face like a human being, and the fourth being was like a flying eagle. ⁸ Now the four living creatures, each of them had six wings, full of eyes all around and inside. Without ceasing day and night they say,

"*Holy, holy, holy,*
Sovereign God Almighty,
who was and is and is to come."

⁹ And when the living beings give glory and honor and thanks to the one seated on the throne, who lives forever and an eternity, ¹⁰ the twenty-four elders fall before the one who is

seated on the throne and worship the one who lives forever and ever; they cast their crowns before the throne, saying,

11 "Worthy are you, our Savior and God,
　　to receive glory and honor and power,
　　for you created all things,
　　and by your will they existed and were created."

Luke 22:24 There was also an argument among the disciples as to which one of them should be considered the greatest. 25 But Jesus said to them, "The royals of the Gentiles lord it over them, and those who have power over them are called benefactors. 26 But not so with you all, rather the greatest among you must become like the youngest, and the leader like one who serves. 27 For who is greater, the one who is at the table or the one who serves? Is it not the one at the table? Yet I am among you all as one who serves.

28 "You are the ones who have remained with me in my trials, 29 so then I covenant with you all, just as my Abba has covenanted with me, a royal inheritance, 30 so that you all may eat and drink at my table in my realm, and you all will sit on thrones governing the twelve tribes of Israel.

PROCLAMATION

Text Notes

Adonijah's "something to say" in 1 Kings 2:14 is "a word." The "face" figures prominently in idiomatic expressions in this passage. In verse 15, all Israel sets their "faces" on Adonijah, translated "expectation" here. In verse 16, Adonijah asks Bathsheba not to "turn away [his] face," and again with Bathsheba's face in verses 17, 19, and 21.

Adonijah has the support of David's senior military commander Joab and therefore the troops along with the support of the priest Abiathar who had supported David against Saul and Absalom. Joab is the son of David's sister Zeruiah. Abiathar's support of Adonijah fractured the priesthood. In the request of verse 16, the verb and its object share the same root, "asked an asking."

Psalm 127 is a dynastic psalm attributed to Solomon. The psalm celebrates *banim*, which can be translated as children or sons as the heritage of God, e.g., a dynasty. I choose the more inclusive reading, "children." Further there is alliteration between the words for "build," "children/sons," and to a lesser extent, "house," *banah, baniym*, and *beyt*. I replicate this with "construct," "children," and the somewhat anachronistic "castle." In verse 2 the painful labor is the same word used for Eve's changed condition in Genesis 3:16, hence the expansive translation option. The mention of shame at the end of verse 5 likely refers to taunting by an enemy for the lack of children, which would have been perceived as shameful. Most often in the biblical text, this shame is imputed to women; in the grammar of this passage, it is imputed to men.

In Revelation 4:2 there is no separate noun or pronoun for the "one" seated upon the throne; the subject is built into the verb. Use of "one" rather than "a person" preserves the understanding that the occupant is not a human person.

In the Hebrew Scriptures, to judge is to govern, administer, oversee, rule, and render justice. That full sense is intended in Luke 22:30, rather than passing judgment on Israel.

Preaching Prompts

The reigns of David and Solomon represent the golden age in the history of ancient Israel; the psalm speaks of the hope for its continuation. In truth, the monarchy will begin to unravel under Solomon's costly lavish rule. When the first lesson opens, Bathsheba and Nathan have successfully gotten Solomon on the throne, but Adonijah is still a threat. He seemingly grudgingly concedes but is putting a new plan into action. With a royal woman whom he can claim is carrying David's heir, he could rally his supporters. Solomon recognizes the threat. Bathsheba's "good" in verse 18 suggests she knows the outcome of the request that Adonijah should have also known. Monarchy is a bloody business and it is well worth reconsidering whether it suits as a metaphor for God, her abode, or her management style.

The significance of Solomon enthroning his mother in verse 19 and placing her at his right hand, in the place of the royal counsel, cannot be overstated. She becomes the first of a long line of Judean Queen Mothers who serve with their sons in an official capacity, some of whom serve as regent for minor sons. (For more on the Judean and Israelite royal women, see my *Womanist Midrash: A Reintroduction to the Women of the Torah and of the Throne*.)

As human monarchy represented the ultimate manifestation of power in the ancient world so too what God envisioned as a monarch. The revelation of John offers one sketch of the heavenly monarch. Human and divine monarchies reinforce each other with the divine monarch granting earthly reigns to certain chosen ones. As the ultimate chosen one, the literal son of heaven—a royal title that would come to be used in East Asian monarchies—Jesus could claim all the dignity of royalty yet did not. This perpetually confused his disciples who jockeyed for positions of power and access to the earthly son of heaven.

In the ancient Afro-Asiatic world, monarchy was primarily but not exclusively a male occupation. In the realm of the heavens, the masculine gender is used in the text for God and the creatures of all sorts that surround the throne. Where are women and the feminine in the heavens? Absent if not read in. Here it matters particularly what language and imagery we choose to use for God. Though the seraphs, elders, and seemingly animal-headed beings are grammatically male, it cannot be easily argued that they are biologically male. It may be useful to read them as beyond the gender binary with whether the language of monarchy is useful language for God, particularly in a country that rejected monarchy long ago.

PROPER 27 (CLOSEST TO NOVEMBER 9)

1 Kings 5:1–6, 13–14; Psalm 48:1–3, 9–14; Ephesians 2:14–22; John 2:14–22

1 Kings 5:1 Now Hiram king of Tyre sent his slaves to Solomon for he heard that they had anointed him king in place of his father; for Hiram had always loved David. ² Solomon sent word to Hiram, saying, ³ "You know that my father David was not able to build a house for the Name of the ETERNAL ONE his God because of the warfare with which his enemies surrounded him, until the MOST HIGH put them under the soles of his feet. ⁴ Yet now the HOLY ONE my God has granted me respite all around; there is neither adversary nor ill fortune. ⁵ So look! I propose to build a house for the Name of the HOLY ONE my God, just as the HOLY ONE OF OLD spoke to David my father, 'Your son, whom I will set in your place on your throne, he shall build the house for my Name.' ⁶ Now then, command that they cut for me cedars from the Lebanon; my slaves will be with your slaves and wages for your slaves will I give you according to whatever you say; for you know there is no one among us who knows how to cut timber like the Sidonians."

¹³ And King Solomon imposed forced labor out of all Israel and the conscripts were thirty thousand men. ¹⁴ Now he sent them to the Lebanon, ten thousand a month in turns; one month were they in the Lebanon, two months at home, and Adoniram was in charge of the forced labor.

Psalm 48:1–3, 9–14

¹ Great is the AGELESS GOD and greatly praised,
  in the city of our God is God's holy mountain.
² Beautiful in elevation, the joy of all the earth,
  Mount Zion, in the far north,
  is the city of the great Sovereign.
³ Within her citadels God
  has made herself known as a bulwark.
⁹ We contemplate your faithful love God,
  in the midst of your temple.
¹⁰ Like your Name, God, your praise,
  reaches to the ends of the earth.
  Your right hand is filled with righteousness.
¹¹ Let Mount Zion be glad,
  let the towns of Judah rejoice
  because of your judgments.

12 Go about Zion, go all around her;
   count her towers.
13 Set your hearts upon her ramparts;
   go through her citadels,
      that you may recount to the next generation:
14 For this God is our God, our God forever and ever.
   She will be our guide until we die.

Ephesians 2:14 For Christ is our peace; in his flesh he has made all into one and has broken down the dividing wall, that is, the hostility between us. 15 Jesus has abolished the law with its commandments and ordinances, that he might create in himself a single new humanity in place of [Gentile and Jewish believers], thus making peace, 16 and that he might reconcile all to God in one body through the cross, putting to death hostility through *it [*or through him]. 17 So Jesus came and proclaimed peace to you all who were far off and peace to those who were near. 18 For through Jesus all of us have access in one Spirit to the Creator of All. 19 So then you all are no longer strangers and aliens, but you all are citizens with the saints and members of the household of God, 20 built upon the foundation of the women and men who were apostles and prophets, with Christ Jesus himself as the cornerstone. 21 In Christ the whole structure is joined together and grows into a holy temple in the Messiah; 22 in whom you also are built together spiritually into a dwelling place for God.

John 2:14 In the temple Jesus found people selling cattle, sheep, and doves, and the money changers seated at their tables. 15 Making a whip of cords, he drove them out of the temple, [including] the sheep and the cattle. Jesus also poured out the coins of the money changers and threw over their tables. 16 He told those who were selling the doves, "Take these out of here! Stop making the house of my Abba a house of commerce!" 17 His disciples remembered that it was written, *"Zeal for your house will consume me."*

18 Then the other Jews said to him, "What sign can you show us for doing this?" 19 Jesus answered them, "Destroy this temple, and in three days I will raise it up." 20 They then said, "For forty-six years this temple has been under construction, and will you raise it up in three days?" 21 But Jesus was speaking of the temple of his body. 22 After he was raised from the dead, his disciples remembered that he had said this; and they believed the scripture and the word that Jesus had spoken.

PROCLAMATION

Text Notes

This portion of 1 Kings is numbered differently in Christian and Jewish texts and translations. What is 1 Kings 5:15 in the MT and JPS is 5:1 in NRSV, CEB, KJV, etc.; the LXX follows the Jewish numbering. In verse 1 (Heb. verse 15) Hiram's "love" for David should probably be understood as "loyalty," as in CEB; Everett Fox adds "in covenant." Solomon suggests that David was unable to build the temple because he was so busy fighting his enemies. He neglects to mention that God forbade David to build the temple because his hands were so bloody (1 Chronicles 22:6–8, though it should be remembered that Chronicles represents an alternative reflection on Israel's story). In verse 4 (Heb. verse 18) "adversary" is *satan*; the term is not a proper name and has no evil connotation in the Hebrew Bible, unlike the Pseudepigrapha where the character first becomes God's adversary and subsequently, the Christian Testament.

In Psalm 48 Zion's superlatives hail from other cultures identifying their God as God of all the earth using the specific vocabulary of surrounding nations: *nof* signals "elevation" but is also the Egyptian name of Memphis, the capital city (and may also mean "fair," see JPS); Zaphon is the home of the Canaanite gods and is in the farthest northern reach unlike Zion/Jerusalem. In verse 14, God will be our God "until death"; "until we die" makes clear that it is not God who will die.

The Epistle addresses Gentile believers and discusses the relationship between Jewish and Gentile Christians. Most translations refer to "both groups" in verses 14, 16, and 18; however, the adjective also means "all," used here, which both makes more sense without the earlier verses and communicates the intent of the verse beyond its original context. Ironically, Ephesians 2:15 encodes the "hostility" of verse 14 between the two cultures and conflicts with the words of Jesus in Matthew 5:17–18: "Do not think that I have come to abolish the law or the prophets; I have come not to abolish but to fulfill. For truly I tell you, until heaven and earth pass away, not one letter, not one stroke of a letter, will pass from the law until all is accomplished."

The final phrase of verse 16 can be translated as either "through it" or "through him," that is, through Jesus. In verse 18, "Creator of All" serves as the divine title in lieu of "Father." The translation of verse 20 makes clear that women and men served as both prophets (in both testaments) and as apostles.

According to Elizabeth Struthers Malbon in the *Women's Bible Commentary*, Jesus clears everyone, buyers and sellers (explicit in Matthew 21:12 and Mark 11:15), thus the traditional language of "cleansing" is hyperbolic. However, in Luke, Jesus only drives out the sellers, while in this reading from John, only the animals are specified in Greek. The dominant translations add some version of "all of them," making John align with the larger tradition; I add "including" to demonstrate the animals are in addition to the people. The language for overthrowing the tables includes physical destruction and as a metaphor, ruining someone's life (BDAG). The whip of cords is unique to John's account. Jesus quotes Jeremiah 7:11 in all of the other gospels, that they have made his Father's house a "den of robbers." However in John 2:17, Jesus quotes Psalm 69:9, "zeal for your house has consumed me," converted into the future tense in John. In verse 18, "the Jews" is modified to "the other Jews" so as to maintain

Jesus's Jewish identity; the term has a broader meaning, including geography (Mark 1:5; Luke 1:39; John 3:22), Judean heritage and Jewish identity (Romans 3:2, 29), and distinguishing Jewish followers of Jesus from Gentile believers (Galatians 2:13–14). The scripture fulfilled in verse 22 may well be Psalm 69:9:

> For zeal for your house has consumed me;
> insults of those who insult you have fallen upon me.

Preaching Prompts

It may be difficult for Christians to understand the import of the temple in Jerusalem and the aching wound of its loss. It may not be an overstatement to say that the temple represented a physical manifestation of *Immanu-El*, God with us. Psalm 48 celebrates God's habitation in the temple, in Jerusalem. For there, God, Godself, God's visible glory and God's Name representing the essence of Godself dwelled with and among her people. The sacking of the temple was seen as a ravishment, a rape of God's holy abode and potentially the humiliation and conquest of God. To demonstrate God's continuing sovereignty, Ezekiel taught that God had removed themselves from the temple before it fell (Ezekiel 10:18–19; 11:22–23). Rebuilding the temple and restoring it to national and international glory became a drive and passion. Yet the second temple failed to live up to the glories of the first (Ezra 3:10–13). For many, the loss of the Ark of the Covenant meant that God would never dwell in successive temples in the same way as in the first. Herod famously continued to enlarge and beautify the temple. This deep national cultural investment in the splendor of the temple is why Jesus scandalized many when he said that he would tear down the temple and rebuild it in three days. In the early days of the Jesus movement, Jewish believers continued to worship at the temple and Paul continued to make his required pilgrim observances. The growing separation between the new tradition and its parent would make the temple less relevant. Both Christianity and Judaism were forced to develop post-temple theologies after its fall in 70 CE.

In the first lesson, David's time is past. His lineage will endure, though his throne will fall. Solomon inherits a wealthy stable country that he expands. He also inherits the divisions between their familial Judean supporters and the other tribes. In spite of his divinely granted wisdom, he lacks the charisma and savvyness of David. His conduct, including his sexual excesses, would be his downfall, shattering the once united monarchy. Solomon's love for foreign women is often held as his primary failing, but his economic policies devastated his reign.

Solomon conscripts able-bodied men to serve one month away and return for two months at home. Consider the impact on agricultural and pastoral work, the backbones of the Israelite economy. The effect of the conscription was so ruinous that when Solomon's son later tried to reinstitute it under the same taskmaster, the people stoned the overseer in 1 Kings 12:18 (there Adoram, understood to be the same as Adoniram here). As with all economic hardships, Solomon's policies would have been most devasting on women and children. The majesty of human monarchs always comes at a cost and those who pay it are most often those who can least afford it. Samuel's warning to the people of the cost of monarchy in 1 Samuel 8:11–17, understood by many as a retrospective on Solomon, lists all that a monarch would take from their subjects, including their daughters in verse 13.

Also often overlooked is that Solomon's expenditures of human and fiscal capital were to build a series of palaces that dwarfed the temple he built for God, including some for the foreign royal women he married. (One of David's wives was also a foreign royal; Maacah bat Talmi, the mother of Tamar and Absalom, was the daughter of King Talmi of Geshur.) The temple was sixty by twenty cubits and thirty cubits high (1 Kings 6:2); it took seven years (1 Kings 6:38). In contrast he spent thirteen years building his primary residence (1 Kings 7:1); a single hall in it was one hundred by fifty cubits, also thirty cubits high (1 Kings 7:2), a second hall was fifty by thirty cubits (1 Kings 7:6) and there were two more halls (1 Kings 7:7). His proper home was "the same construction," and he made a duplicate for the Egyptian princess he married (1 Kings 7:8). Perhaps, having exhausted his treasury, Solomon paid King Hiram of Tyre with twenty cities in Galilee (1 Kings 9:11).

The joyous song is from a time before which it would have been incomprehensible that God's abode on earth could fall into foreign invading hands. Its innocent joyous proclamations serve to emphasize the temporality of temples made with human hands.

The necessity of a temple in which God may dwell with her people remains and is redeveloped in the Epistles and in the Gospels. In Ephesians it is the community of believers that are corporately the temple of God. In other passages, the bodies of individual believers are also identified as temples of the living God (1 Corinthians 6:19). In the Gospel reading Jesus makes clear that the fullness of God dwells in him every bit as much as it dwelled in their ancestral temple, the fate of the Ark notwithstanding.

The image of the temple in Ephesians requires the inclusion of every sort of human believer, including women and girls in the ancient understanding of gender and nonbinary persons and others in ours. We are all the building blocks of God. In this imagery no bodies are excluded or disqualified due to age or gender or ability or culture of origin. Indeed, all human bodies are fit and worthy vessels for the habitation of God and God's dwelling among us is incomplete with the exclusion of any human body.

PROPER 28 (CLOSEST TO NOVEMBER 16)

1 Kings 11:26–39; Psalm 89:1–8, 14; 2 Timothy 2:8–13; John 2:1–11

1 Kings 11:26 Now Jeroboam son of Nebat, an Ephraimite of Zeredah whose mother's name was Zeruah, a widow woman, was a servant of Solomon and he raised a hand against the king. ²⁷ And this was the situation in which he raised a hand against the king: Solomon built the Millo, closing the breach in the city of his father David. ²⁸ Now the man Jeroboam was a valiant warrior, and when Solomon saw that the young man was a hard worker, he appointed him over all the forced labor of the house of Joseph. ²⁹ And it was at that time, as Jeroboam left Jerusalem the prophet Ahijah the Shilonite found him on the road. Now Ahijah had clothed himself with a new garment and the two of them were in the countryside by themselves. ³⁰ And Ahijah seized of the new garment that was upon him and tore it into twelve pieces. ³¹ Then he said to Jeroboam: "Take for yourself ten pieces; for thus says the HOLY ONE, the God of Israel, 'Look! I am about to tear the realm from the hand of Solomon and I will give you ten tribes. ³² One tribe will remain his for the sake of my slave David and for the sake of Jerusalem, the city that I have chosen out of all the tribes of Israel. ³³ This is because he has forsaken me and worshiped Astarte the goddess of the Sidonians, Chemosh the god of Moab, and Milcom the god of the Ammonites, and has not walked in my ways, doing what is right in my sight—my statutes and my ordinances—as his father David did. ³⁴ Now I will not take the whole realm from his hand and will make him ruler all the days of his life, for the sake of my slave David whom I chose, who did keep my commandments and my statutes. ³⁵ Yet I will take the realm from his son and give to you the ten tribes. ³⁶ And to his son will I give one tribe so that there will always be a lamp before me for my slave David in Jerusalem, the city that I have chosen for myself, to place my Name. ³⁷ You I shall take, and you shall reign over all that your soul desires; you shall be king over Israel. ³⁸ And it shall be if you will listen to all that I command you and walk in my ways and do what is right in my sight keeping my statutes and my commandments as David my slave did, I will be with you, and I will build you an enduring house as I built for David, and I shall give you Israel. ³⁹ And I shall punish the descendants of David for this, but not for all time.'"

Psalm 89:1–8, 14

¹ I will sing of the faithful love of the FOUNT OF LIFE forever;
   with my mouth I will make known your faithfulness from across the generations.
² When I declare that your faithful love is established forever;
   your faithfulness is established in the heavens,
³ [you responded,] "I have inscribed a covenant with my chosen one;
   I have sworn an oath to the descendants of Bathsheba:

4 'I will establish your line forever,
   your throne that I will build, will be to all generations.'"

5 The heavens confess your wonders, O WOMB OF CREATION,
   and to your faithfulness in the congregation of the holy ones;

6 For who in the skies can be compared to the WOMB OF LIFE?
   who is like the MOTHER OF ALL among the children of the gods?

7 a dread God in the council of the holy ones,
   great and terrible above all who surround her.

8 WARRIOR PROTECTRIX, who is mighty like you?
   YOU WHO ARE, your faithfulness surrounds you.

14 Righteousness and justice are the foundations of your throne;
   enduring love and faithfulness go before your face.

2 Timothy 2:8 Remember Jesus Christ, raised from the dead, from the line of David [and Bathsheba]; that is my gospel, 9 for which I suffer hardship, even to chains, like a criminal. But the word of God is not chained. 10 Because of this, therefore I endure everything for the sake of the elect, in order that they may also obtain salvation in Christ Jesus with eternal glory. 11 This is a trustworthy saying:

For if we die together, we will also live together;
12 if we endure, we will also reign together;
   if we deny [Christ], he will also deny us;
13 if we are faithless, faithful he remains,
   for he cannot deny himself.

John 2:1 On the third day there was a wedding in Cana of Galilee, and the mother of Jesus was there. 2 Jesus and his disciples had also been invited to the wedding. 3 When the wine gave out, the mother of Jesus said to him, "They have no wine." 4 And Jesus said to her, "Woman, what concern is that to you and to me? My hour has not yet come." 5 His mother said to the servants, "Do whatever he tells you." 6 Now standing there were six stone water jars for the Jewish rites of purification, each holding twenty or thirty gallons. 7 Jesus said to them, "Fill the jars with water." And they filled them up to the brim. 8 He said to them, "Now draw some out, and take it to the chief steward." So they took it. 9 When the steward tasted the water that had become wine, and did not know where it came from (though the servants who had drawn the water knew), the steward called the bridegroom 10 and said to him, "Everyone serves the good wine first, and then the inferior wine after the guests have become drunk. But you have kept the good wine until now." 11 Jesus did this, the first of his signs, in Cana of Galilee, and revealed his glory; and his disciples believed in him.

PROCLAMATION

Text Notes

"Zeruah" of Ephraim, the erstwhile Queen Mother of the schismatic monarch Jeroboam in 1 Kings 11:26 was not likely named *zeru'ah*, "diseased," rather her name may have been altered to make the pun a slur to label her son as rotten from the womb. Ephraim and Manasseh were the sons of Joseph (see verse 28), traditionally named among the tribes rather than their father.

In the traditional language of Psalm 89:3 God swears an oath to "David, my servant." Note that Bathsheba indeed has her own throne, symbolically if not literally passed down to the Judean Queen Mothers, see 1 Kings 2:19. The children of the gods refer to any number of divine or semidivine beings from other gods to angels depending on the age and redaction of the text. Warrior Protectrix in verse 8 is God of "hosts" or warriors.

Many translations of 2 Timothy 2:11–13 add "with him" throughout for poetic balance; the object and preposition are not present. Verse 12 requires an object for the verb; I have supplied "Christ" from verse 10.

Preaching Prompts

The summer season of reflection on Bathsheba, David, and their descendants comes to a close this week. In the first reading the Israelite monarchy fractures, signaling its eventual end. It will never recover. Hearing the postexilic psalm in response, the community emphasizes the faithfulness of God even in the face of this unexpected catastrophe and those that will follow. Their hopes are deeply invested in the continuation of the line of Bathsheba. Though David had many children with many women, it is the line through Bathsheba and Solomon to which the people look for a Messiah, in keeping with their religious and cultural understanding, a warrior king who will redeem them physically, violently if necessary, from the hand of oppressors. Mary and Jesus of the line of Bathsheba do not look like the continuation or fulfillment of this majestic and messianic line at first glance. But in the spirit of Bathsheba, Mary lets her son know that his time has come. The Epistle invites the believer into this glorious lineage where if we die with Christ we will live with Christ, and where, if we endure, we will reign with Christ, Jesus, son of Bathsheba.

According to the prophet Ahijah, God fractured the Israelite monarchy because of Solomon's religious infidelity. Yet, God intends to preserve the royal line of David out of fidelity to him. Following the evangelists, the Church will find in Jesus the fulfilment of God's words; however, both will overlook the significant gap between the last Davidide, Zedekiah (2 Kings 24:17–18; 25:1, 7), and Jesus. This provides an opportunity to talk about the relationship between the Testaments with nuance, going beyond simplistic fulfillment formulae.

Psalm 89 celebrates the eternal faithfulness of God, in this translation, expressing that *through* Bathsheba rather than *to* David. Such a reading does not redeem her rape; it does keep her centered in the story in which she continues to play a part.

In John 2, Mary, the mother of Jesus, prompts him to reveal himself in the miracle that is understood as the formal inauguration of his public ministry, verse 3. In so doing she leaves us with profound instructions for our Christian faith in verse 5, "Do whatever he tells you."

In these lessons, women make up the ancestral connective tissue through motherhood: Zeruah, Bathsheba, Mary (Miriam), and countless unnamed others. They and their daughters are the unnoticed unspoken citizens of all of these monarchies, supporting them through their labor: reproductive labor and social, cultural, and economic labor. They are royal women and common women, enslaved women and free women, and disciples, prophets, apostles, and eventually, martyrs. The Gospel reading concludes, "His disciples believed in him." The Gospels are grudging with the title "disciple" when it comes to women, though they clearly describe women as disciples; Tabitha is named as a disciple in Acts 9. Certainly, this first miracle of Jesus in Cana drew disciples without regard to gender, whether their names would be preserved or not.

MAJESTY OF CHRIST
(CLOSEST TO NOVEMBER 23)

2 Kings 24:8, 11–17; Psalm 47; Hebrews 1:1–9; Matthew 27:11–14, 27–37

2 Kings 24:8 Jehoiachin was eighteen years old at his reign. He reigned three months in Jerusalem and the name of his mother was Nehushta daughter of Elnathan of Jerusalem.

[11] Now King Nebuchadnezzar of Babylon came to the city while his troops were besieging it. [12] Then King Jehoiachin of Judah surrendered to the king of Babylon, himself and his mother and his slaves and his officers and his officials. The king of Babylon took him [captive] in the eighth year of his reign.

[13] He brought out from there the treasures of the house of the HOLY ONE OF OLD and the treasures of the king's house; he cut up all the vessels of gold in the temple of the HOLY ONE which King Solomon of Israel had made, just as the HOLY ONE had spoken. [14] Nebuchadnezzar took into exile all Jerusalem, all the officials, all the warriors, ten thousand exiled women and men, all the artisans and the smiths; no one remained except the poorest people of the land. [15] He took Jehoiachin into exile to Babylon; the king's mother, the king's women, his officials, and the elite of the land, he took into exile from Jerusalem to Babylon. [16] The king of Babylon took into exile to Babylon all the valiant warriors, seven thousand, the artisans and the smiths,

one thousand, all of them strong and fit for war. ¹⁷ The king of Babylon made Mattaniah, Jehoiachin's uncle, king in his place and changed his name to Zedekiah.

Psalms 47

¹ All you peoples clap your hands;
shout to God with a joyful sound.
² For the SOVEREIGN GOD, the Most High, is awesome,
a great governor over all the earth.
³ She subdued peoples under us,
and nations under our feet.
⁴ She chose our heritage for us,
the pride of Rebekah's womb whom she loves.
⁵ God has gone up with a shout,
SINAI'S FIRE with the sound of a trumpet.
⁶ Sing praises to God, sing praises;
sing praises to our Sovereign, sing praises.
⁷ For God is Sovereign over all the earth;
sing praises with a psalm.
⁸ God is ruler over the nations;
God is seated on her holy throne.
⁹ The nobles of the peoples gather,
the people of the God of Hagar and Sarah;
for to God belong the shields of the earth,
she is highly exalted.

Hebrews 1:1 Many times and in many ways God spoke to our mothers and fathers through the prophets, female and male. ² In these last days God has spoken to us by a Son, whom God appointed heir of all there is, and through whom God created the worlds. ³ The Son is the brilliance of God's glory and reproduction of God's very being, and the Son undergirds all there is by his word of power. When the Son had made purification for sins, he sat down at the right hand of the Majesty on high, ⁴ having become as much greater than the angels as the name he inherited is more excellent than theirs.

⁵ *For to which of the angels did God ever say,*
"You are my Child; today I have begotten you"?

Or this,

"I will be their Parent, and they will be my Child"?

⁶ Then again, when God brings the firstborn into the world, God says,

"Let all the angels of God worship him."

[7] On the one hand of the angels God says,

> "*God makes winds into celestial messengers,*
> *and flames of fire into God's ministers.*"

[8] But of the Son God says,

> "*Your throne, O God, is forever and ever,*
> *and the righteous scepter is the scepter of your realm.*
> [9] *You have loved righteousness and hated lawlessness;*
> *therefore God, your God, has anointed you*
> *with the oil of gladness beyond your companions.*"

Matthew 27:11 Now Jesus stood before the governor and the governor questioned him saying, "Are you the King of the Jews?" Jesus said, "You say so." [12] And when he was accused by the chief priests and elders, he did not answer. [13] Then Pilate said to him, "Do you not hear how many accusations they make against you?" [14] And he did not answer him, not one word, so that the governor was greatly astonished.

[27] Then the soldiers of the governor took Jesus into the governor's command post, and they gathered the whole cohort around him. [28] They stripped him and put a scarlet robe on him. [29] And having woven a crown from thorns, they put it on his head along with a reed in his right hand and they knelt before him and mocked him, saying, "Hail, King of the Jews!" [30] And they spat on him, and took the reed and struck him on his head. [31] After mocking him, they stripped him of the robe and put his clothes [back] on him. Then they led him away to be crucified. [32] Now going out, they found a Cyrenian man named Simon; this man they conscripted to carry his cross.

[33] And coming to a place called Golgotha (which means Skull Place), [34] they offered him wine mixed with vinegar to drink; but when he tasted it, he would not drink. [35] And when they had crucified him, "*they divided his clothes*" among themselves by "*casting lots.*" [36] Then they sat down and keeping watch over him there. [37] Now they placed over his head his charge, written as, "This is Jesus, the King of the Jews."

PROCLAMATION

Text Notes

Nebuchadnezzar's troops are called "slaves" in 2 Kings 24:11. The king's surrender in verse 12 is articulated ironically with the primary verb of the exodus, *y-tz-'*. Likewise, Nebuchadnezzar "bought out" the riches of the Jerusalem temple in verse 13 just as God brought out the Israelites. The ranks of deportees include women and men. The first accounting includes the Queen Mother, second in authority to king (listed in that order in verse 12) and the entire senior administrative team, which would have likely included women in some roles (indicated by seals from royal women and female administrators before and after the fall of Jerusalem). The second reckoning in verse 14 repeats and numbers the officials and warriors at ten thousand, and craftspersons and smiths; the former would have included women, as potting and weaving were traditionally female occupations. A third reckoning in verse 15 circled back to the surrendering of the Queen Mother and added the royal women, wives, and other women, including royal daughters and likely the surviving wives of previous monarchs, then repeated the officials a third time, and adds all of the nobles. A fourth accounting in verse 16 numbers the warriors at seven thousand and one thousand war-ready artisans and smiths. These different accountings suggest chaos and confusion rather than specificity in spite of the recorded numbers. The broader sense is that everyone who was anyone was exiled except the almost overlooked "poor of the land," tucked away at the end of verse 14, not mentioned again.

In Psalm 46:4, the "pride of Rebekah's womb" is "the pride (or majesty) of Jacob." In verse 6, "the God of Hagar and Sarah" is "the God of Abraham."

In Hebrews 1:1 the explication of prophets as female and male reminds the reader/hearer of the diversity in Israel's prophetic ranks.

"Astonished" in Matthew 27:14 can also mean "impressed." Verse 31 ends "to crucify" with no object; some translations add "him" there. Verse 35 quotes the LXX language for dividing garments and casting lots in Psalm 22:18 exactly.

Preaching Prompts

The liturgical year ends with a reflection on the Majesty of Christ as the Church prepares to begin a new year remembering his first advent while preparing for his next. As the weeks reviewing the rise and fall(s) of Israel's monarchies during Ordinary Time have made abundantly clear, monarchy is as all human institutions, an enterprise that is doomed to fail. Yet monarchy and its conventions have given us language for God, imperfect but familiar as the psalm amply demonstrates. Jesus takes that language and those conventions and inverts them; the reign of God and its majesty are very different from the splendor of the world's sovereigns.

To the fallen Judean monarchy and their Babylonian colonizers and occupiers, Jesus says the poor of the land who were deemed not worth the labor to even deport are at the heart of the reign of God. The majesty of Christ is not found in treasures of temple or palace, burgled and broken apart, but in a crown of thorns beaten in by bullies and in his battered and denuded body. This human, mortal, woman-born Jesus is the glory and majesty of God; in the words of the Epistle to the Hebrews, "the brilliance of God's glory and reproduction of God's very being." That humanness, shared with every girl and woman, boy and man, nonbinary child and adult, is also the majesty of Christ and our own.

APPENDIX
GOD NAMES AND DIVINE TITLES[1]

AGELESS GOD
AGELESS ONE
ALL-KNOWING GOD
ALL-KNOWING ONE
ALL-SEEING GOD
ALMIGHTY
ANCIENT OF DAYS
ANCIENT ONE
ARK OF SAFETY
AUTHOR OF LIFE
COMMANDER of heaven's legions
COMMANDER of heaven's vanguard
COMPASSIONATE GOD
CREATOR
CREATOR OF ALL
DREAD GOD
ETERNAL
ETERNAL ONE
EVER-LIVING GOD
EXALTED
FAITHFUL GOD
FAITHFUL ONE
FIRE OF SINAI
FOUNT OF JUSTICE
FOUNT OF LIFE
FOUNT OF WISDOM
GENEROUS ONE
GLORIOUS ONE
GOD WHO HEARS
GOD WHO IS HOLY

GOD WHO IS MAJESTY
GOD WHO IS MYSTERY
GOD WHO IS SALVATION
GOD WHO REDEEMS
GOD WHO SAVES
GOD WHO SEES
GOD WHOSE NAME IS HOLY
GRACIOUS GOD
GRACIOUS ONE
HEALING ONE
HOLY GOD
HOLY ONE
HOLY ONE OF OLD
HOLY ONE OF SINAI
INSCRUTABLE GOD
JUST GOD
JUST ONE
LIVING GOD
LOVING GOD
MAJESTIC ONE
MAJESTY
MAJESTY OF THE HEAVENS
MERCIFUL GOD
MIGHTY GOD
MIGHTY ONE
MOST HIGH
MOTHER OF ALL
MOTHER OF CREATION
MOTHER OF THE MOUNTAINS
MOTHER OF WISDOM

---

1. This list was generated in advance of preparing the manuscript and includes some titles that are not used in this resource but might prove useful for those designing worship and liturgy.

One
One God
One Who Is
Redeemer
Redeeming God
Redeeming One
Righteous God
Righteous One
Rock Who Birthed Us
Rock Who Gave Us Birth
Ruler of All
Ruler of the Multitudes of Heaven
Saving God
Saving One
Sheltering God
She Who Birthed the Earth
She Who Hears
She Who is Delight
She Who is Exalted
She Who is Faithful
She Who is God
She Who Is Holy
She Who is Majesty
She Who Is Mighty
She Who Is Peace
She Who is Strength
She Who is Wisdom
She Who is Worthy
She Who Provides
She Who Saves
She Who Sees
She Who Speaks Life
Sinai's Fire
Source of Life
Sovereign
Sovereign-Commander of winged
    warriors
Sovereign God
Sovereign One
Sovereign of heaven's vanguard
Sovereign of the vanguard of heaven
The I Am
Too Holy to be Pronounced
Wisdom
Wisdom of the Ages
Warrior Protectrix
Wellspring of Life
Womb of Creation
Womb of Life
You Who Are

Jesus/Christ Names

The Anointed
God-born
Messiah
Rabbi
Redeemer
Savior
Son of Woman
Teacher
Woman-Born

BIBLIOGRAPHY

The Anchor Yale Bible Commentaries. Garden City, NY: Doubleday, 1964.

Abegg, Martin, Peter Flint, and Eugene Ulrich. *The Dead Sea Scrolls Bible: The Oldest Known Bible*. San Francisco: HarperSan Francisco: 1999.

Aland, Barbara, Kurt Aland, et al. *Novum Testamentum Graece*. Stuttgart: Deutsche Bibelgesellschaft, 2017.

Alter, Robert. *The Hebrew Bible: A Translation with Commentary*. New York: W.W. Norton and Company, 2018.

The Anchor Yale Bible Commentaries. Garden City, NY: Doubleday, 1964.

Ariel, Israel. *Carta's Illustrated Encyclopedia of the Holy Temple*. Jerusalem: Coronet Books, 2004.

Barth, Markus. *Ephesians. Introduction, Translation, and Commentary*. The Anchor Bible, vol. 34. Garden City, NY: Doubleday, 1974.

Berlin, Adele, and Marc Zvi Brettler. *The Jewish Study Bible*. 2nd ed. Oxford: Oxford University Press, 2004.

Bloch, Ariel, and Chana Bloch. *The Song of Songs: The World's First Great Love Poem*. Modern Library Classics. New York: Random House, 1995.

Briggs Kittredge, Cynthia, and Claire Miller Colombo. "Colossians." In *Philippians, Colossians, Philemon*, edited by Mary Ann Beavis. Wisdom Commentary, vol. 51. Collegeville, MN: Liturgical Press, 2017.

Brooten, Bernadette. *Women Leaders in the Ancient Synagogue*. Brown Judaic Studies 36. Chico, CA: Scholars Press, 1982.

Byron, Gay L., and Vanessa Lovelace. *Womanist Interpretations of the Bible: Expanding the Discourse*. Atlanta, GA: Society for Biblical Literature, 2016.

Clines, David J. A. *The Dictionary of Classical Hebrew*. Rev. ed. Sheffield: Sheffield Phoenix Press, 2018.

Common English Bible. Nashville, TN: Common English Bible, 2011.

Cooper, Kate. *Band of Angels: The Forgotten World of Early Christian Women*. New York: Overlook Press, 2013.

Danker, Frederick William. *A Greek-English Lexicon of the New Testament and other Early Christian Literature*. 3rd ed. Chicago: University of Chicago Press, 2000.

Edelman, Diana. "Mephibosheth." In *The Anchor Bible Dictionary, Volume 5*, edited by David Noel Freeman et al. New York: Doubleday, 1992.

Falk, Marcia. *The Song of Songs: Love Lyrics from the Bible*. Brandeis Series on Jewish Women. Waltham, MA: Brandeis University Press, 2004.

Fox, Everett. *The Early Prophets: Joshua, Judges, Samuel, and Kings: A New Translation with Introductions, Commentary, and Notes by Everett Fox*. The Schocken Bible, vol. 2. New York: Schocken Books, 2014.

———. *The Five Books of Moses: Genesis, Exodus, Leviticus, Numbers, Deuteronomy: A New Translation with Introductions, Commentary, and Notes*. The Schocken Bible, vol. 1. New York: Schocken Books, 1995.

———. *Give Us A King! Samuel, Saul, and David: A New Translation of Samuel I and II, with an Introduction and Notes by Everett Fox*. 1st ed. New York: Schocken Books, 1999.

Freedman, David Noel. *The Anchor Bible Dictionary*. New Haven, CT: Yale University Press, 1992.

Freeman, Lindsay Hardin. *Bible Women: All Their Words and Why They Matter*. Cincinnati, OH: Forward Movement, 2014.

Frick, Frank. "Israel? A People and a Land: Joshua and Judges." *A Journey Through the Hebrew Scriptures*. Belmont, CA: Wadsworth Publishing, 2002.

Gafney, Wilda. *Daughters of Miriam: Women Prophets in Ancient Israel*. Philadelphia: Fortress Press, 2008.

———. *Nahum, Habakkuk, Zephaniah*. Wisdom Commentary, vol. 38. Edited by Barbara E. Reid. Collegeville, MN: Liturgical Press, 2017.

———. *Womanist Midrash: A Reintroduction to the Women of the Torah and the Throne*. Lexington, KY: Westminster/John Knox Press, 2017.

Henderson, J. Frank, Jean Campbell, Ruth Fox, and Eileen M. Schuller. *Remembering the Women: Women's Stories from Scripture for Sundays and Festivals*. Chicago, IL: Liturgy Training Publications, 1999.

Ilan, Tal. *Mine and Yours Are Hers: Retrieving Women's History from Rabbinic Literature*. Leiden: Brill, 1997.

The Inclusive Bible: The First Egalitarian Translation. Lanham, MD: Rowman and Littlefield, 2007.

Johnson, Luke Timothy. *The Letter of James: A New Translation with Introduction and Commentary*. The Anchor Bible, vol. 37. New York: Doubleday, 1995.

Kol HaNeshamah. Elkins Park, PA: Reconstructionist Press, 2000.

Kraemer, Ross. "Nympha." In *Women in Scripture: A Dictionary of Named and Unnamed Women in the Hebrew Bible, the Apocryphal/Deuterocanonical Books, and the New Testament*, edited by Carol Meyers, Toni Craven, and Ross S. Kraemer. Boston: Houghton Mifflin, 2000.

Lamsa, George. *The Holy Bible from the Ancient Eastern Text: George M. Lamsa's Translations from the Aramaic of the Peshitta*. San Francisco, CA: Harper and Row, 1985.

Levine, Amy-Jill. *Entering the Passion of Jesus: A Beginner's Guide to Holy Week*. Nashville: United Methodist Publishing, 2018.

Levine, Amy-Jill, and Marc Brettler. *The Jewish Annotated New Testament*. New Revised Standard Version. Oxford: Oxford University Press, 2011.

Luz, Ulrich, and Helmut Koester. *Matthew*. Hermeneia series. Minneapolis, MN: Fortress Press, 1971.

Magiera, Janet. *Aramaic Peshitta New Testament Translation: Messianic Version*. San Diego, CA: LWM Publications, 2009.

Meyers, Carol L., Toni Craven, and Ross Shepard Kraemer. *Women in Scripture: A Dictionary of Named and Unnamed Women in the Hebrew Bible, the Apocryphal/Deuterocanonical Books, and the New Testament*. Boston: Houghton Mifflin, 2000.

Moore, Carey A. *Tobit: A New Translation with Introduction and Commentary*. New York: Doubleday, 1996.

Murdock, James. *Murdock's Translation of the Syriac New Testament. Translated into English from the Peshitto Version by James Murdock*. Boston: Scriptural Tract Repository, 1892.

A New English Translation of the Septuagint (and Other Greek Translations Traditionally Included Under That Title). New York: Oxford University Press, 2000.

New Revised Standard Version. Washington, DC: National Council of Churches, 1989.

Newsome, Carol, Sharon H. Ringe, and Jacqueline Lapsley. *Women's Bible Commentary*. 3rd ed: Revised and updated. Louisville, KY: Westminster John Knox Press, 2012.

Page, Hugh. *Israel's Poetry of Resistance: Africana Perspectives on Early Hebrew Verse*. Minneapolis. MN: Fortress Press, 2013.

Rashkow, Ilona. *Taboo or Not Taboo: Sexuality and Family in the Hebrew Bible*. Minneapolis, MN: Fortress Press, 2000.

Scholz, Susanne. *Introducing the Women's Hebrew Bible: Feminism, Gender Justice, and the Study of the Old Testament*. New York: Bloomsbury T & T, 2017.

Smith, Mitzi J. *I Found God in Me: A Womanist Biblical Hermeneutics Reader*. Eugene, OR: Cascade Books, 2015.

Stamm, Johann, Ludwig Köhler, and Walter Baumgarner. *The Hebrew and Aramaic Lexicon of the Old Testament*. Leiden: Brill Academic Press, 1994.

Stein, David. *The Contemporary Torah: A Gender-sensitive Adaptation of the JPS Translation*. Philadelphia: Jewish Publication Society, 2006.

Tal, Abraham. *The Samaritan Pentateuch*. Tel-Aviv: Tel-Aviv University, 1994.

Tanakh: The Holy Scriptures: The New JPS Translation According to the Hebrew Text. Philadelphia: Jewish Publication Society, 1985.

Trible, Phyllis. *God and the Rhetoric of Sexuality*. Overtures to Biblical Theology, no. 2. Philadelphia: Fortress Press, 1978.

———. *Texts of Terror: Literary-Feminist Readings of Biblical Narratives*. Overtures to Biblical Theology, no. 13. Philadelphia: Fortress Press, 1984.

Westbrook, April D. *"And He Will Take Your Daughters . . .": Woman Story and the Ethical Evaluation of Monarchy in the David Narrative*. New York, NY: Bloomsbury T & T Clark, 2015.

Wills, Lawrence M. "Mark." In *The Jewish Annotated New Testament: New Revised Standard Bible Translation*, edited by Amy-Jill Levine and Mark Zvi Brettler. Oxford: Oxford University Press, 2011.

Winter, Miriam Therese. *The Gospel According to Mary: A New Testament for Women*. New York: Crossroad, 1993.

———. *WomanWisdom: A Feminist Lectionary and Psalter: Women of the Hebrew Scriptures, Part One*. New York: Crossroad, 1991.

———. *WomanWitness: A Feminist Lectionary and Psalter: Women of the Hebrew Scriptures, Part Two*. New York: Crossroad, 1992.

———. *WomanWord: A Feminist Lectionary and Psalter: Women of the New Testament*. New York: Crossroad, 1990.

Wisdom Commentary Series. Collegeville, MN: Liturgical Press, 2015.

Witherington, Ben. *A New English Translation of the Septuagint (and Other Greek Translations Traditionally Included Under That Title)*. New York: Oxford University Press, 2000.

SCRIPTURE INDEX

Genesis

1:1–2, 26–27; 2:1–4	133–134
2:7–9, 15–17, 21–25	23–24
2:7–9, 15–25	74–75
3:1–7	78
3:8–21	81–82
16:7–13	1
16:10–13	246
17:15–22	4–5
21:2, 8–21	134–135

Exodus

14:26–29; 15:20–21	136
15:1–3, 11, 13, 17–18	136
15:11–21	116
19:1–19	192–193

Leviticus

12:1–8	45

Deuteronomy

5:1–10	167–168
5:11–22	172
18:15–22	175
28:1–14	178–179
28:58–68	181–182
29:10–15	188

Joshua

2:1–14; 6:15–17, 22–23	136–137

Judges

4:1–10, 23	138
5:1, 4–7, 12, 24, 31	138–139
11:29–40	120–121
13:2–7	7–8

Ruth

1:1–14	205–206
1:15–22	208–209
2:1–16	213
3:1–18	216–217
4:9–17	220–221

1 Samuel

1:1–6, 9–18	223–224
1:19–28	11, 227–228
2:1–10	11–12
2:12–17, 22–25	235
2:18–21, 26	231–232
4:2, 5–11, 19–22	238–239
8:1, 4–18	242–243
9:1–3, 15–18, 10:1	249
14:49–51; 18:17–21, 29	269–270
15:1–3, 8, 10–17, 24–25	253
17:1–7, 12–16, 24–27	257–258
17:55–18:9	265–266
25:14–19, 23–25, 32–34, 42–43	273–274
27:1–3, 8–12	278–279
30:1–8, 17–19	282

2 Samuel

1:17–27	286–287
11:2–15	290–291
13:1–16, 21–22	294
20:1–3, 14–22	298–299
21:1–14	302–303

1 Kings

1:1–5, 11–18, 29–31	306–307
2:10–24	313–314
5:1–6, 13–14	317
11:26–39	322
17:8–16	57–58
17:17–24	61

2 Kings

11:1–4, 10–12	139
24:8, 11–17	325–326

Job

14:1–14	128–129

Psalm

8	24
9:1–2, 7–11, 13–14	31–32, 64–65, 139–140
9:9–14	175–176
10:1–14	258–259
16:8–11	155
17:6–9, 13, 15	49
18:1–6	157
18:2–11, 16–19	41–42, 146–147
22	121–122
22:1–11	100
22:19–31	107
22:23–31	250
24	186
27:5–7, 10–14	135
30:1–5	159
31	129–131
31:1–7, 14–16, 19–24	270–271
32:1–7	291
33:1–9	21–22
33:11–22	51–52
36:5–10	38, 114
37:1–2, 7–11, 16, 35–40	274–275
41:1–4, 12–13	168
44:1–4, 8, 17, 23–26	209–210
45:6–10, 12–15	54–55
47	326
47:1–2, 5–9	266
48:1–3, 9–14	45–46, 317–318
49:1–2, 5–9, 16–17	236
49:5–15	161
50:14–23	299
58	303
67	34, 311
68:4–11	217–218, 246–247
68:4–13	15
69:10–20, 30–33	228–229
71:1–6	282–283
71:4–11	1–2
72:1–4, 12–14, 18–19	243
77:1–12, 19–20	239–240
78:1–7	5, 172–173
80:1–7	206
86:8–13	163
89:1–8, 14	28, 322–323
90:1–10, 12	71–72, 307–308
92:1–5, 12–15	78–79
94:1–15	279
95:1–7	67
96	82
103:1–17	18–19, 295
104:1–4, 10–15, 27–30	75, 199–200
107:1–9, 19–22	221
111	188–189
112	213–214
113	224
115:9–15	8
116:1–9	61–62, 165–166
118:14–26	151–152
118:19–29	97
123	111
127	314
130:5–8; 131:1–3	203
136:1–16	86–87, 116–117
139:7–14	193–194
144:3–4, 12–15	232
145:8–19	182–183
146	58, 253–254
147:12–20	179
148	90–91

Song of Songs

4:7–16	85–86
4:9–15	54

Isaiah

2:1–5	64
7:3–16	27–28
16:1–5	51
25:1, 4a, 6–10a	310–311
25:6–9	151
26:16–19	15
44:1–8	198–199
49:1–6	110–111
49:1–13	145–146
49:5–16	98–100
51:1–8	89–90
52:1–10	37–38
60:1–6, 11	33–34
62:1–7, 10–12	40–41
66:10–13	18

Jeremiah

31:8–13	106–107

Ezekiel

17:22–24	113–114
19:1–3, 10–14	287

Daniel (LXX)

3:52–60	134

Hosea

11:1–4	202–203

Joel

2:1, 12–17, 21–22	70–71
2:27–32	192–193

Micah

4:5–10, 13a	30–31

Zephaniah

3:14–20	48–49, 93–94

Zechariah

8:1–8	66–67

Judith

8:9–10, 32–34; 13:3–14, 17–18	140–141
13:18–20	261–262
16:1–6, 13	141–142

Wisdom

5:1–5; 6:6–7	137–138
9:1–6, 9–11	21

Matthew

1:1–16	25–26
1:18–25	12–13
2:1–12	35
3:1–6, 11–17	42–43
5:21–26	292
5:33–37	267
5:43–48	222
6:1–6, 16–18	72
6:9–13	283
7:15–20	79
15:21–28	225
15:29–39	229–230
21:1–11	96–97
21:12–17	111–112
22:23–33	173
23:37–39	115
26:17–56	117–119
27:11–14, 27–37	327
27:50–56	312
27:57–66	131–132
28:1–10	142, 148
28:8–10, 16–20	166
28:16–20	203–204

Mark

1:29–31	49
6:1–6	299–300
6:14–29	254–255
7:10–13	233
7:14–23	280
10:13–16	296
12:28–34	271
12:41–44	207
13:14–22	83
14:32–15:47 (or 4:32–52)	101–104
16:9–15	76
16:9–15, 19–20	163–164

Luke

1:26–38	2–3, 94–95, 263
1:39–45	6
1:46–55	94, 262
1:46–56	8–9
2:1–14 (or 2:1–20)	16
2:15–20 (or 2:1–20)	NA
2:15–21	29
2:22–38	46
2:41–51	38–39
3:21–23, 31–38	52–53
4:16–27	59
6:43–45	304
7:11–17	62
7:18–23	176
7:24–35	68
8:1–3	218
12:13–21	214
13:18–21	91
16:10–13	236–237
18:1–8	210
19:1–10	275
19:11–27	250–251
22:14–23:56	123–126

22:24–30	315
24:13–35 (or 24:13–27)	152–153
24:36–43	157
24:44–53	159–160
24:46–53	187

John

1:1–5	32, 65
1:1–14	22
2:1–11	323
2:1–12	55
2:14–22	318
3:11–17	87
4:7–26	195
5:25–29	179–180
6:14–20	244
7:37–44	308
10:11–16	259
11:17–27	183
11:28–44	189–190
12:1–7	108
14:8–17	201
14:25–31	240
16:16–22	288
20:1–2, 11–18	247
20:1–10 (11–18)	148–149
20:19–23	155
20:19–31	169
21:4–14	162

Acts

1:1–11	185–186
1:3–5, 12–14	167–168
1:6–8	172
2:1–17	198–199
2:1–18	194
2:22–24	175
2:43–47	229
5:12–16	178–179
6:1–6	210
9:36–42	62
13:29–38	165
16:13–15	142
17:1–4, 10–12	181–182
17:1–7	243–244
18:24–27	188

Romans

5:1–5	240
6:5–11	163, 183
7:1–12	168–169
8:14–17, 22–27	200–201
8:18–25	5
8:31–39	82–83, 259
11:13–24	91
13:8–10	173, 271
15:7–13	311–312
16:1–16	247

1 Corinthians

1:25–31	65
1:26–31	38
2:1–13	67–68
4:8–13	250
6:1–6	299
9:1–10	55
12:14–26	222
15:3–7	157
15:12–20	159
15:35–44	160–161
15:45–49	72

2 Corinthians

1:8–11	283
4:7–12	176

4:13–15	179
5:16–21	25
6:2–10	42
6:16b–18	94
9:6–13	218

Galatians

3:23–4:7	100–101
4:1–7	32
5:13–21	275

Ephesians

2:4–10	79
2:14–22	318
3:1–6	52

Philippians

2:1–8	131
2:5–11	2, 28–29
3:17–21	111

Colossians

1:15–20	22
2:9–14	308
3:1–11	75–76
4:10–17	224–225

1 Thessalonians

2:9–12	295–296
4:13–18	16, 288
5:12–24	206–207

1 Timothy

4:1–6, 9–10	49
6:6–16	236
6:17–19	214

2 Timothy

1:5–10	34–35
2:8–13	152, 323

Titus

3:4–7	12

Hebrews

1:1–9	108, 266–267, 326–327
11:1–2, 23–24, 28–39	147–148
11:23–28	117
12:1–4	123

James

1:22–27	58
2:8–13	279–280

1 Peter

1:3–9	155, 189
1:22–2:3	19
2:4–10	232–233

2 Peter

1:16–18	203
3:1–4, 8–9	291

1 John

2:7–14	114–115
3:1–3	8
4:7–12	87
5:1–5	46

Revelation

1:4–6	254
21:1–7	262–263
3:20–22	186–187
4:2–11	314–315
6:9–11	303